WORLD TAX REFORM

WORLD
TAX
REFORM

Case Studies of Developed and Developing Countries

Edited by
Michael J. Boskin
and Charles E. McLure, Jr.

An International Center for Economic Growth Publication

ICS PRESS
San Francisco, California

Publication signifies that the Center believes a work to be a competent treatment worthy of public consideration. The findings, interpretations, and conclusions of a work are entirely those of the author and should not be attributed to ICEG, its affiliated organizations, its board of overseers, or organizations that support ICEG.

Inquiries, book orders, and catalogue requests should be addressed to ICS Press, 243 Kearny Street, San Francisco, California, 94108. Telephone: (415) 981-5353; FAX: (415) 986-4878.

Cover design by Judy Hicks.

Distributed to the trade by National Book Network, Lanham, Maryland.

Library of Congress Cataloging-in-Publication Data

World tax reform : case studies of developed and developing countries
/ edited by Michael Boskin and Charles E. McLure, Jr.
p.   cm.
Includes bibliographical references.
   ISBN 1-55815-092-7. — ISBN 1-55815-077-3 (pbk.)
   1. Taxation—Case studies. I. Boskin, Michael J. II. McLure, Charles E.
HJ2305.W68 1990
336.2'05—dc20   89-26902
                                                              CIP

Contents

List of Tables

List of Figures

Preface

A wave of tax reforms and tax reform proposals swept the globe in the 1980s. From one country to another, these reforms have exhibited several common features: a focus on making taxation economically "neutral" (that is, ensuring that the tax system does not distort people's economic decisions), a trend toward lower marginal tax rates, a response to international tax pressures, and a consideration—particularly in many developing countries—of the value-added tax as a broad-based source of revenue.

In late 1987 and early 1988 the International Center for Economic Growth sponsored a project on world tax reform, directed by Michael Boskin, then of Stanford University and currently chairman of President George Bush's Council of Economic Advisers. That work led to a conference in October 1988, where a group of distinguished scholars presented case studies from developed and developing countries, as well as several broad issues papers. This volume brings together the results of that conference and provides convincing evidence that we have indeed learned a great deal about effective tax policy in the past several decades. In addition, *World Tax Reform* shows where current thinking has been neglected in the policy-making process.

At the end of 1988, Dr. Boskin wrote the introduction and overview that appears as the first chapter in this book. At that point, anticipating his new responsibilities in Washington, D.C., he turned the manuscripts over to Charles E. McLure, Jr., of the Hoover Institution, to complete the editing and to write a special conclusion, which also appears herein. We list them together as coeditors of the final product.

   World Tax Reform reveals the interaction among academic thinking, administrative practice, and political reality that is causing the field of taxation to evolve so rapidly around the world. We hope the book will be useful in the tax reform debates now taking place, at both an academic and a policy-making level.

Nicolás Ardito-Barletta
General Director
International Center for Economic Growth

March 1990
Panama City, Panama

Part I

Introduction and Overview

New Directions in Tax Policy

By the mid-1980s, many of the world's countries—both advanced and developing—had either enacted or were considering substantial tax reforms. This extraordinary series of tax reforms occurred in response to intellectual, historical, and political currents that appeared during the 1970s. In some cases the reforms reflected primarily domestic economic and political circumstances; in others they reflected economic circumstances common to many countries. Ideas tried in one country then spread to others. And as the economies of the world have become more closely interrelated, the tax reforms in the largest countries, such as the United States and Japan, have affected their trading partners as well. Although the world's economies have widely varying tax systems even after a decade of reform, some common themes—most notably, the attempt to lower marginal tax rates—run through most of these reforms.

Common intellectual themes included concern about the adverse incentive effects of high marginal tax rates and about distortions caused by differential tax treatment of economically similar activities, and a downplaying of vertical equity as a central objective of tax policy. Interest in incentives started to develop especially in the 1970s, a decade in which relatively high inflation artificially increased tax rates, especially for the middle class. This episode highlighted the inequities and distortions resulting from an unindexed tax system in inflationary times. There was concern about tax evasion and about the effort diverted from productive economic activity into tax shelters and unproductive investment, and perceptions of unfairness were growing. Finally, of course, the internationalization of the world economy created competitive pressures on countries to respond to tax reforms elsewhere.

In the United States, the case with which I am most familiar, tax reform took place in response to many of the same factors that encouraged reforms in other places. Between 1965 and 1980 the number of U.S. taxpayers facing high marginal tax rates quadrupled, creating a powerful political constituency for tax reform.

Some of these issues, such as high marginal tax rates, affected developed and developing countries alike. Others had special relevance primarily for one group of countries or the other. Therefore, the lessons to be learned by individual countries from others' experiences varied with circumstance to some degree.

Because the level and structure of taxation affects so many economic decisions, the rapid pace of tax reform in many countries may well have significant, lasting effects on the world economy. Although the reform process continues in a number of countries, it is worthwhile to evaluate what has happened in major countries where reform has occurred and to set forth an agenda of reforms still to be considered. That is the purpose of this volume. It brings together leading specialists on taxation and tax reform, writing about a variety of the economies that have undergone or are considering major tax reform in both the developed and the developing worlds. The volume stresses the economics and tax policy side of the reforms, with some reference to their political context. It is hoped that similarities and differences in various country experiences can be highlighted to yield lessons about the differences between good tax policy and bad tax policy and about how to implement a strategy for reform.

The volume grew out of a project the International Center for Economic Growth (ICEG) asked me to organize in 1987. I invited leading tax experts and scholars who had participated in or observed tax reform movements in various countries, and this volume is the result of their work. Several of the authors were the primary technical participants in the tax reform process, either in their own country or in other countries. Others played a key role in evaluating alternative proposals and assisting government officials in deciding among them. I attempted not only to achieve substantial coverage by including a wide number of countries that had undergone, were undergoing, or were contemplating, tax reform, but also to represent a wide range of views on tax policy questions. As a consequence, the authors represented here express very different views on some major tax issues.

Each author was asked to write on a particular topic. The authors remain solely responsible for the views expressed in their own chapters. No attempt was made either by me, while I was still participating in the project, or by Charles McLure, to change anyone's opinions or expressions of them. But in order to offer the perspective, judgment, and experience of all of the participants as a potential input into the drafting of individual chapters, ICEG sponsored a working session for the authors to discuss first drafts of their papers. The seminar, held in San Francisco in October 1988, yielded an extremely useful interchange of information and views, and new insights and perspectives emerged.

The volume begins with two general essays on tax principles: Joel Slemrod, writing on tax principles in an international economy, focuses on the need for tax policy to include considerations of international trade in goods and capital and features of tax rules that affect multinational organizations. Arnold Harberger presents an evaluation of principles of taxation applied to developing countries, which share many concerns of advanced economies, but also have some issues that are quite specific to their circumstances, including the administrative capabilities of their tax regimes. Harberger puts these together as a set of lessons about good tax policy.

The next set of essays turns to discussions and evaluations of recent tax reform, or tax reform debates, in advanced economies. This section begins with a chapter by Michael Porter and Chris Trengove discussing tax reform in Australia, which attempted to use an unusual consensus political approach to achieve reform. Faced with an erosion of the personal income tax because of tax shelters and fringe benefits, Australia reduced its top rate from 60 to 49 percent and adopted an "imputation" system to reduce the double taxation of corporate income, but rejected a broad-based sales tax (retail sales tax or value-added tax). It also added taxation of fringe benefits, which is unusual.

John Whalley, who has been especially active in the Canadian debate on the value-added tax (VAT), then considers tax policy reform in Canada. As the largest U.S. trading partner, Canada is especially interesting because of its response to international pressures, as well as its consideration of a VAT. Whalley discusses that country's reductions in marginal tax rates, its reductions in investment credits and depreciation, and its replacement of a defective manufacturer's sales tax with a VAT. He then tries to estimate the allocative and distributional effects of reform.

Eytan Sheshinski discusses the tax reform proposals made in Israel in 1988 by a tax reform commission he headed. Israel had galloping inflation; hence, questions related to indexing, the measurement of real income, and the interaction of inflation and the tax code were among the important issues in Israel. As in many other economies, there was a concern in Israel that the tax base was eroding, and tax rates were far too high.

Yukio Noguchi discusses the tax reform debates in Japan, which focused on the hard-to-tax groups. With little emphasis on vertical equity, the debates have considered the levels of corporate income taxes, the tax treatment of interest and capital gains, the financing of social security, and a proposed land tax. To reduce individual and corporate income tax rates and to increase revenue available for social security payments, the country has instituted a small value-added tax, which has turned out to be tremendously (and surprisingly) controversial.

Ingemar Hansson and Charles Stuart address tax reform in Sweden, long one of the world's most heavily taxed economies. In the 1970s government subsidies to specific regions and industries became so high that they were crippling the Swedish economy; after substantially reducing these subsidies, Sweden has turned to a serious discussion of how to lower its virtually confiscatory marginal tax rates. The Swedish tax reform movement has responded to the prevalence of tax shelters and the disincentive effects induced by high tax rates. Hansson and Stuart explore issues such as reliance on debt finance, rate reductions, consideration of a consumption-based direct tax and cash-flow tax on corporations, and planning for additional reform.

Andrew Dilnot and John Kay discuss recent experiences in tax reform in the United Kingdom, which was one of the first countries to reduce rates and eliminate investment incentives. The authors consider the evolution of tax policy in the United Kingdom, including attempts at reforming the individual, corporate, and social security taxes. They discuss changes in the income tax, VAT, social security taxes, and local finance. They also consider constraints on the VAT imposed by the European Community, the interaction between income and social security taxes, the recent emphasis on economic neutrality, and the lack of a cohesive view of tax reform or tax policy in that country.

John Shoven discusses U.S. tax reform—especially the tax reform of 1986. He takes a professor's report card to it and concludes that it offers as many problems as solutions. Although Shoven gives the reform relatively high marks for fairness, economic efficiency, and neutrality, he fails it on the issue of economic growth, because it encourages neither savings nor investment. He gives the reform a moderate grade for simplicity, but faults it for not taxing real income and for not instituting a consumption tax.

The next set of chapters turns to a discussion of tax reform in several important developing economies. Roger Gordon leads off with his discussion of reforms of explicit and implicit taxes in the People's Republic of China. In a primarily planned economy, such as China's, taxes can be implicit in a variety of ways, as well as being levied explicitly. For example, if wages are set by a central authority, setting them at a low level is quite similar to setting them at a high level and imposing a wage tax. Similarly, the collection of "profits" from firms may resemble corporate taxation. Gordon discusses how a command economy works and does not work, the incentive effects of its tax system, and how the subject of tax reform fits into the overall aspects of economic reform in China.

Charles McLure considers tax reform in a mildly inflationary environment in Colombia, which has one of the best and most studied income tax systems among all developing countries. He discusses the need for inflation adjustment, the advice by foreign missions in the 1960s against adjustment, and the history of adjustment that has occurred since 1974. Inflation adjustment was extended to all interest in 1986 and to depreciation in 1988. McLure himself cowrote a 1988 report for the Colombian government on which the 1988 reforms were based.

Malcolm Gillis looks at Indonesia, with special reference to the value-added tax. In recent years, much attention has been placed on achievement of a "clean" VAT—one that covers virtually all value added in the economy. This means dealing with concerns for low-income individuals directly (through refundable credits against tax paid, for example), rather than by exempting necessities such as food (which may represent as much as half of GNP) from the VAT and making up the lost revenue by imposing a higher VAT rate on goods that are subject to the tax. Although Indonesia's VAT covers only the manufacturing stage (and therefore does not apply to unprocessed food and some other staples of the low-income population), it allows no exemptions, making it a relatively clean tax. Gillis also discusses the country's explicit revenue goals, distributional equity, economic neturality, and tax administration and compliance.

Francisco Gil Díaz presents a historical overview of policy and tax policy goals in Mexico. He notes the lack of a clear objective in policy, as well as the enduring complexity of the system. The government considered introducing a consumption-based direct tax, but did not do so, in part because of fears it would not be creditable in the United States.

Let me end with a personal note. After assembling the group of authors, receiving first drafts of the papers, convening the conference in October 1988, and then providing detailed comments to the various authors, I found myself in early December 1988 nominated by President Bush to be chairman of the President's Council of Economic Advisers. At that point, it became clear that I would have to end my participation in the project. I would like to thank all of the authors involved for their tremendous cooperation on the project, especially Charles McLure, who did me a great favor by agreeing to take over some of the work I would have been scheduled to do had I not entered government service.

Stanford, California
December 1988

Part II

General Issues

Tax Principles in an International Economy

One of the most profound economic changes of the postwar period has been the growing internationalization of economic activity. Sparked by the rapidly declining cost of transportation and communication, the volume of international trade has mushroomed and today is fifteen times higher than it was in 1965. The volume of foreign direct and portfolio investment has grown similarly.

The internationalization of economic activities has profound implications for tax systems, both directly and because it affects the technology of tax collection. It raises new questions and changes the answers to old ones. Openness introduces at least three important new considerations into a country's choice of tax system:

1. Factors, goods, and other potential bases for taxation can flee a country in response to taxation or other regulatory restrictions, or be attracted to a country by relatively light taxation or regulation.
2. The interjurisdictional division of revenues is not a matter of indifference. Each country must therefore "compete" with other countries for revenues.
3. It is more difficult to collect revenue from tax bases located outside the country.

I am grateful to Daniel Frisch for helpful comments on an earlier draft.

This chapter discusses the implications of these three aspects of openness for the design of capital income tax policies, beginning with a reassessment of the benefits and costs of openness in a world where distortionary taxes must be raised. The next section discusses the efficiency of alternative capital income tax structures, first from a national and then from a global perspective. The following sections treat the incidence of capital income taxes in an open economy and the promise and problems of international tax harmonization. The chapter concludes by offering some warnings to the myopic domestic tax policy maker and some challenges to the guardians of rational policy making from a global perspective.

The Benefits and Costs of Openness

The classical theory of international trade argues that cross-border trade can unambiguously improve the consumption possibilities of domestic residents. With trade, a nation's pattern of consumption need not conform exactly to its pattern of production. Furthermore, specialization of production according to a nation's comparative advantage allows resources to be used more efficiently.

The same argument applies to intertemporal trade. In the absence of international borrowing and lending, national savings would have to be exactly equal to national investment. International capital movements allow, for example, a nation with relatively favorable investment prospects to import capital (borrow), thereby raising the present value of its consumption stream. Nations with relatively unfavorable investment prospects can profit by lending capital to be utilized in other countries.

These results all pertain to a case where there are no tax-induced or other distortions in the allocation of resources. But no country is devoid of such distortions, and in their presence the case for free trade is more ambiguous. It is possible that freer trade, by raising the cost of existing distortions, is welfare-reducing. By increasing the elasticity of a country's tax bases, openness may raise the minimum level of distortion that must accompany a certain revenue requirement. As an extreme example, consider a country where the only feasible tax base is domestically located capital. The autarky rate of return to capital is less than the world rate of return, so that if the economy is opened to international capital movements, capital flows abroad to earn the higher world rate of return. However, because only domestically located capital can be taxed, too much (from an efficiency perspective) capital is exported. In equilibrium, capital will be exported until $f(1 - t) = r$, where f is the marginal product of domestic capital, t is the effective tax rate on domestic capital, and r is the world rate of return. Thus, the tax system causes investors to pass up some domestic investment whose pretax return (its contribution to national income) exceeds the world rate of return in favor of foreign investment. The welfare loss from the excess foreign investment may exceed the welfare gain from taking advantage of the favorable world rate of return.

The point of this example is that openness is a mixed blessing when the taxing authority has limited ability to tax cross-border movements of factors and goods. A discussion of tax principles in an international economy must come to terms with the real world, where the implementation of certain tax systems, which may be desirable in theory, is extremely difficult.

Efficiency

National perspective. When the goal is to minimize deadweight loss, the basic principles of taxing capital movements in a small open economy are as follows. Capital exports should occur as long as the return, *excluding* tax paid to foreign governments, exceeds the opportunity cost of these exports, which is the return on domestic investment (*including* any tax paid to the domestic government). Under certain tax systems, this condition will be ensured by the return-maximizing decisions of domestic residents. If capital income of domestic residents is taxed at the same rate regardless of origin (a residence-based system) and the tax payments to foreign governments are treated as deductible expenses, this condition will be met. This is because domestic investors treat the foreign tax as a cost like any other, as it is from the domestic standpoint. A residence-based tax system will not, however, maximize national income when used in conjunction with a foreign tax credit. Because foreign tax payments are offset by a credit against domestic taxes, they are not treated as a cost by the investor, as the domestic national interest demands. Capital exports will exceed the efficient amount.

Capital imports should occur as long as their contribution to the domestic economy, the marginal product of capital, exceeds the cost to the economy. A small country must compete with investment opportunities elsewhere, so it must offer the foreign investor the going after-tax rate of return. This level of capital imports will be achieved if such imports are completely exempt from taxation by the importing nation, because in this case foreign investors will, in their own interest, invest until the domestic marginal product equals their opportunity cost, the after-tax world rate of return. Any attempt to tax capital imports will cause the country to forgo domestic investment whose contribution to national income exceeds the cost to the nation.

There are many reasons that the supply of capital to a country may not be perfectly elastic. For a large country, the very act of importing capital will drive up the rate of return in the rest of the world, thus increasing the cost of capital. Capital exports from a large country will drive down the world rate of return. Thus a large country faces an increasing supply curve for capital. A small capital-importing country may face an increasing cost of funds if there is country-specific risk. Investors will then require a risk premium that increases with the size of the total investment in the country. Investors will also require an increasing risk premium when there is a probability of expropriation of foreigners' wealth that increases as the volume of the investment (and thus the return to expropriation) increases.

Although a tax penalty on capital flows would have an adverse effect when capital supply is perfectly elastic, it can generally enhance national income when the supply curve is upward sloping. The welfare cost of an inefficient domestic capital stock can be offset by the advantageous effect of the tax on the terms of borrowing and lending. By taxing capital flows, a country can induce an increase in the rate of return on its capital exports and a reduction in the cost of borrowing. The large country accomplishes this because its capital flows are large enough to affect the rate of return that can be earned in other countries, so that, for example, a reduction in its capital exports increases the scarcity of capital abroad and drives up its rate of return. The small country can accomplish this because restricting capital imports reduces the risk premium that must be paid, either lowering the likelihood of expropriation or the cost of country-specific risk.

Optimal policies can look very different when the possibility of strategic behavior—either cooperation or retaliation—is considered. If countries can cooperate on tax policy and thereby agree on how to divide up tax revenues, then all countries—even those with market power—can profit from allowing uninhibited capital flows. In the absence of cooperative behavior, the optimal policy of any one country depends in a complicated way on its perceptions of its rivals' likely strategic reaction and on the range of policy instruments that are subject to choice (that is, nondiscriminatory tax rates, discriminatory tax rates, worldwide versus territorial system).

Another important consideration arises when foreign investors come from countries with a foreign tax credit. If the foreign-source income is taxed on an accrual basis, then raising the tax on capital imports toward the tax rate of the capital-exporting country does not reduce the after-tax return to the investor (because the tax payments are offset by credits against their own domestic tax liability), and does not deter capital imports. Because the credit is limited to domestic tax liability, a capital-importing country that reduced its tax rate on capital imports below the rate imposed by the exporting country would lose tax revenue without seeing its domestic capital stock increased. In practice a country generally imports some capital from countries with a territorial system that exempts foreign-source income from domestic taxation. The foregoing argument does not apply to this source of capital. If feasible, the capital-importing country should levy lower taxes on capital income emanating from countries with territorial tax systems. If such differentiation is impossible, then its policy should reflect a weighting of the net benefits of taxing capital imports in the two cases. The argument must also be modified if, as in most foreign-tax-credit systems, foreign-source income is taxed upon the repatriation of profits (and not on an accrual basis) or if the firm can consolidate its worldwide income in calculating the credit.

In either case, the host tax rate may affect the after-tax return to investing, even if the tax rate is below that of the investing country (Gersovitz 1987).

A country's tax policy should be evaluated both by how well it achieves the optimal (from a national perspective) allocation of factors and by how successfully it defends (or expands) its revenue base against other countries. I argued earlier that a capital-importing country should impose origin- or source-based capital income taxes if the capital exporter's treasury will refund the tax payments to the firms. To rescind these taxes merely transfers tax revenues from the home treasury to the foreign treasury.

The inherent difficulty of allocating the income of multinational firms' income among its countries of operation makes clear the distinction between the resource-allocation and revenue-defense standards of tax policy. Multi-nationals can set inter-country transfer prices, management fees, and financial transactions to reduce the worldwide tax burden of the enterprise. It is notoriously difficult to police transfer pricing, and countries have not, for the most part, even developed policies concerning intrafirm financial transactions designed to reduce worldwide taxes.

It is in a country's interest to set its tax policy to attract taxable income to its jurisdiction, holding constant real activity such as investment. A country can achieve this by imposing low *statutory* rates on its source-based taxes. It is the difference in statutory rates that provides the incentive to use transfer pricing and financial strategies to move taxable income from one jurisdiction to another. It is, however, the difference in marginal effective rates of tax that will determine the allocation of investment. The marginal effective rate of tax on new investment depends not only on the statutory rate but also on such factors as the pattern of depreciation allowed for tax purposes, the extent of investment tax credit, and the rate of inflation. Thus, consider a country that wished to retain the effective taxation of investment so as to defend its revenue against the treasuries of capital-exporting, foreign-tax-credit countries, but wished also to defend its revenue base against transfer pricing and financial manipulation. It should maintain low statutory capital income tax rates but at the same time preserve high effective tax rates by limiting the generosity of depreciation allowances and investment tax credits.

Note that the Tax Reform Act of 1986 moved the U.S. corporate income tax system exactly in this direction, lowering the statutory rate that applies to most income from 46 percent to 34 percent, but eliminating the investment tax credit and modifying depreciation allowances so that the effective marginal tax rate on investments has probably slightly increased. Because 34 percent is at the low end of the observed range of statutory rates (except for "tax-haven" countries), it turns the United States into a magnet for internationally fungible taxable income, while not substantially disturbing its attractiveness as a locus for investment and not forgoing revenues to foreign-tax-credit countries that export capital to the United States. This is a strong argument for a low-rate, low-credit corporate tax system as opposed to a high-rate, high-credit system with similar effective tax rates. It is notable that recent tax reforms enacted or proposed in several countries have followed the lead of the United States in lowering the statutory rate of corporate tax while reducing allowances.

Global efficiency. According to the standard model, a given stock of capital in the world will be located efficiently when the pattern of taxation does not affect the choice of where to locate. This neutrality result can be achieved with any one of several tax schemes. It would be achieved if each country imposed a residence-based tax system, so that each investor is subject to a uniform effective tax rate on investment income independent of its location, and there is no tax on foreign-owned domestic investment. In this case, each country could impose a different tax rate on each investor; the crucial element is that the rate not be distinguished by the location of the capital. Note, though, that residence-based taxation will not be neutral with respect to country of residence or incorporation. Differing tax rates among nations may cause the migration of high-income individuals to low-tax-rate countries and induce incorporation in low-rate "tax havens." Neither of these cause an inefficiency, however, in the global allocation of capital.

Global efficiency will also be achieved if all countries impose an origin-based tax at the same rate. If origin-based taxes are imposed at different rates, foreign-tax-credit systems with no limitation are needed to ensure that investment decisions are not distorted by the tax system.

The foregoing discussion assumes that the direct resource cost of levying all taxes is identically zero. In fact, it is probably more costly to collect revenue from activities located outside of the country. Thus a world featuring origin-based taxes of equal rates is *more* efficient than a world featuring fully enforced residence-based taxes only, because the cost of enforcement is lower for the system of origin-based taxes. A world of unequal origin-based taxes may be more efficient than a world of residence-based taxes as well, even without operative foreign tax credits in all countries. In this case the savings in the resource cost of enforcement outweigh the welfare cost of capital misallocation.

There is a critical problem with unequal origin-based taxes, though, that is not apparent in the standard model where the source of income can be costlessly observed: multinational enterprises can utilize transfer pricing and other intrafirm but cross-jurisdiction financial transactions to allocate taxable income to countries with low tax rates. For this reason most countries that can enforce it operate a residence-based tax, usually with deferral and a foreign tax credit, in addition to an origin-based tax. The residence-based tax provides a safety net that limits the incentive of multinationals to report taxable income only in low-tax foreign countries.

An important way in which contemporary tax systems differ from the standard of equal origin-based taxes is the failure of many developed countries (including the United States, the United Kingdom, and Japan) to impose withholding taxes on portfolio income of foreigners. This tax treatment is probably motivated in part by the desire to attract or retain the financial services industry within the country's borders. Combined with the inability of most developing countries to collect taxes on their residents' foreign-source income, it provides an investment option that is entirely free of tax by either host or home country. Thus the structure of international tax systems provides an incentive for capital movement from the developing countries to these developed countries. The tax-induced unwillingness of developing countries' wealth owners to invest in their own country creates investment opportunities for investors from developed countries. The result is tax-induced cross-border wealth holdings that are excessive from the point of view of global efficiency, because they are accompanied by greater monitoring and risk-bearing costs than intraborder holdings. Although incurring some such costs is consistent with global efficiency, the monitoring costs associated with present tax systems are too great.[1]

This is a case in which cooperation between the developing and developed countries can improve global efficiency. A first step would be to negotiate information-sharing agreements that would reduce the costs of enforcing a residence-based tax. A more ambitious step would be for the developed countries to impose a common withholding tax on foreign investment income, perhaps refunding it upon receiving evidence that the investor has paid an equivalent amount of tax to the country of residence. The practical barrier to implementation of either plan is that unilateral adoption by a developed country is likely to be met by transfer of funds to alternative investments that are not encumbered by either withholding taxation or information reporting. The promise and problems of tax harmonization are discussed later in this chapter.

This situation is one example of the kind of tax-arbitrage opportunity that international financial transactions make possible. These opportunities arise whenever different investors face differing relative tax rates on alternative investments. In the above example, one investment is in the developed-country capital market and another is in the developing-country capital market. The relative tax rate on these two assets is zero for the developing-country investor and one (the same tax on both investments) for the developed-country investor, assuming a residence-based tax system applies. In this case, it is impossible that all investors will be in portfolio equilibrium, such that all alternative assets offer the same after-tax, risk-adjusted rates of return. If the pretax rates of return adjust so that one group of investors is indifferent between the assets, it is unavoidable that the other group will find one asset to dominate the other in after-tax return. Investors can make tax-arbitrage profits by holding a short position (borrowing) in the asset with the lower after-tax return and holding a long position in the higher-yielding asset. If a large number of simultaneous short and long positions are taken, the pretax rate of return on the shorted asset will tend to rise as the return on the asset held long will tend to fall. When these rates change, though, other investors who were previously indifferent between assets can claim tax-arbitrage profits.[2]

The existence of international tax-arbitrage opportunities has far-reaching implications. Unchecked, it can seriously erode the revenue-raising ability of certain countries who find their own residents reporting positive taxable income only in low-tax jurisdictions and lightly taxed assets, and reporting large amounts of negative taxable income (such as interest payments) if this interest is tax deductible. To some extent, the revenue drain from some countries will be offset by the revenue gain of other countries. Total global tax collections will, however, definitely decline as wealth owners seek out the lowest tax rates.

From an efficiency point of view, tax arbitrage induces cross-border financial transactions that are undesirable except for their tax consequences. It can cause an inefficient pattern of international risk sharing, and a socially excessive amount of resources devoted to financial services. Note that these effects occur without the necessity of any cross-border movement of physical capital; the exchange of claims for capital in given locations is sufficient. The inefficient location of physical capital may also occur, however, if the costs of cross-border wealth holdings prevent capital inflows from completely offsetting the flow of wealth from countries that cannot tax foreign-held wealth.

I have focused so far on the implications of most developing countries' inability to tax their residents' foreign-source income, combined with many developed countries' unwillingness to impose withholding taxes on foreigners' investment income. The problem may become more pervasive in the future if the technology (and willingness) to evade taxes in developed countries outpaces the enforcement technology of the tax collection agencies. The existence of tax havens has already to some degree compromised the ability of the U.S. tax authorities to impose taxes on its own residents' investment income. This specter has led some observers to warn of the coming "erosion of the global fiscal commons" (Lessard and Williamson 1987).

Incidence

There are two fundamental principles of tax-incidence analysis in any economy, closed or open. The first principle is that the relatively inelastic agents tend to bear the burden of taxation, and the relatively elastic agents tend to escape the burden. Response to taxation is elastic when there are attractive alternatives to the taxed activity. The second principle of incidence is that the burden of taxation must be traced eventually to individuals—legal entities such as corporations do not pay taxes in any meaningful sense.

How openness affects the incidence of taxation depends on how it affects the alternatives to taxed activity. If an unlimited amount of offshore investment is available at a fixed rate of return, then a tax on domestically located capital income can never be borne by domestic capital owners. They need not tolerate a lower return than is available abroad. Thus the effect of a tax on domestically located investment causes a reduction in domestic capital until its after-tax return rises to be competitive with foreign investments. An inefficient capital stock results, but in the long run the burden is shifted away from domestic capital owners to suppliers of relatively immobile factors.

Thus the assumption of an infinitely elastic supply of capital in the outside world substantially simplifies what is ordinarily a complicated problem of tracing incidence. The relevance of this result depends on whether the supply of capital is in fact perfectly elastic. If it is not, the relative elasticity of the labor supply will also determine the incidence, with the more elastic factor tending to bear less of the burden. In some subregions, the long-run elasticity of labor may be substantial, implying that a tax on domestically located capital will result in the flight of both capital and labor, little long-run decline in their rate of return, and the bulk of the tax burden falling on owners of less mobile factors such as land and other natural resources.

For domestic capital owners to bear the burden of capital income taxation, the tax must apply to the capital income of domestic residents regardless of the source of the income, leaving capital no place to run. In practice, countries differ widely in their ability to enforce such a residence-based tax.

In an open economy the second principle of incidence—that the burden of taxation must be traced to individuals—has to be interpreted carefully. Two problems arise. First, a country's government may be able to shift the burden of financing its expenditures to residents of foreign countries. In general, how the tax burden is divided among countries becomes an important issue. This potential for shifting the tax burden has been used as an argument to defend the corporate income tax (and income taxes in general) against those who would replace it with a consumption tax. Because income taxes, but not consumption taxes, may be creditable against home-country tax liability, a capital-importing country that abolishes its income tax is sacrificing the opportunity to appropriate revenues from the capital-exporting country's treasury. For this reason, some proponents of consumption taxation have been investigating the conditions under which consumption taxes may become creditable (McLure and Mutti 1988).

Second, when there is cross-border labor mobility it is not clear which citizens of a nation to be concerned with. If, for example, a progressive income tax causes the emigration of some highly skilled residents, should their welfare continue to be of concern to the taxing government? This is not an issue for the export of capital, as the earnings of the capital continue to accrue to domestic residents and remain part of national income.

The Problems and Promise of Tax Harmonization

Economists are generally respectful of the beneficial consequences of competition. Under certain conditions, we know, competition among firms can ensure that resources are not allocated wastefully. It cannot, though, ensure that the command over these resources is distributed equitably among individuals.

Should we be as respectful toward tax competition among countries? I suspect not, because the conditions necessary for the beneficial consequences of competition are almost certain to be absent in this context. There are many countries large enough relative to world markets that their tax policies have significant effects on other countries' economies. When these external effects are not considered in the formulation of policy, waste of resources often results.

To see what this means for capital income tax policies, assume that the world stock of capital is fixed, but that its location in any one country is highly elastic with respect to the rate of tax. In this case each country has the incentive to keep tax rates low to attract capital. But this policy ignores the negative externality imposed on the residents of the country from which the capital has been attracted, and tax rates in such a competitive environment will be too low compared to a cooperative solution, which in this case would impose high taxes on capital, assumed to be in fixed supply.

Of course, in the long run capital is not in fixed supply, and the rate of its accumulation may be reduced by capital income taxes. At any given time, though, governments strapped for funds have the incentive to tax away the capital already in place. This temptation can cause the persistence of capital income taxes in excess of their level if such temptation could be sworn away, an act which would certainly improve long-run welfare. From this perspective, tax competition among countries may serve as a disciplining device that can force capital income tax rates closer to where they ought to be. Whether tax cooperation would in the abstract be an improvement over tax competition is a difficult question that we are far from resolving, especially because competition and cooperation can evolve in so many different ways. Tax cooperation in today's world is limited to a fairly extensive network of bilateral tax treaties whose twin goals are generally to prevent unwanted double taxation and to ensure, through statute and exchange of information, that the appropriate tax is paid to either the source or the resident country. This treaty network has proven to be inadequate in several respects (discussed below), and the prospect of multilateral tax agreements has been recently raised. The problems and promise of a "GATT for taxes" is the subject of the next section.

A GATT for taxes? The General Agreement on Tariffs and Trade (GATT) has, by most accounts, succeeded in lowering the tariff barriers to the international flow of goods (although this success has been mitigated to some extent by the apparent growth in nontariff barriers to trade). There is no analogous multilateral agreement for taxes. Why is there no GATT for taxes?[3]

The most important reason is almost certainly that ceding tax-policy-making authority to an international agreement would compromise national sovereignty too greatly. In the case of tariffs, there exists a clear benchmark goal of zero tariffs, a goal which does not severely compromise the revenue needs of most countries. In the case of tax policy, countries differ enormously in their revenue requirements, capacity to raise taxes, and their predisposition toward alternative tax systems, including the perceived need to use tax policy to affect economic activity. For this reason I see no prospect for a comprehensive international agreement that sets severe limits on tax policy.

Are more modest goals worth pursuing? I believe so, and therefore as food for thought I offer the following skeleton of a multilateral agreement of the future:

1. *Harmonization of statutory corporate tax rates.* I believe that tax authorities will always be unable to adequately monitor the ability of multinational companies to allocate income among jurisdictions via transfer pricing and other financial transactions. The differences among countries' statutory corporate tax rates provide the incentive to shift income in this way. An agreement to keep statutory rates within a small band would minimize this problem. Note that such an agreement would not compromise the ability of countries to set the marginal effective rate of tax on new investment at any level they desired through the appropriate setting of tax depreciation schedules and investment tax credits.

2. *Harmonization of withholding taxes on passive income.* A multilateral agreement to impose a harmonized rate of withholding tax on interests, dividends, and royalties would reduce the detrimental effects of the asymmetrical ability of countries to impose residence-based taxes. It would also reduce the incentives created by the current patchwork of bilateral tax treaties for tax-treaty "shopping" by those searching for the minimum-tax way to arrange a financial transaction. (Bilateral tariff agreements would similarly lead to tariff shopping and tariff havens, and existing bilateral trade quotas have certainly encouraged quota shopping.) Many countries set themselves up as tax havens, and offer tax "sales" to tax-minimizing shoppers. A common rate of withholding would reduce the rewards to tax-haven transactions. This withholding tax would probably work best if it were made refundable to the payer upon notification that tax has been paid in the country of residence, if that country has signed the multilateral tax agreement.

3. *Policy toward nonsigners.* Countries that choose not to sign the multilateral treaty (presumably because they wish to levy rates *below* what the treaty designates) will be designated tax-haven countries. Income

earned in these countries will be taxed as accrued at the rate of the home country. In this way, the advantages of deferral or complete exemption are sacrificed. Residents of countries that do not sign the agreement are also not eligible for refund of the withholding tax levied by the treaty countries.

I am under no illusions about the possibility that a multilateral agreement like this will ever occur. The lukewarm reception given the recent proposal for multilateral information sharing is not a good sign.[4] As a nonlawyer I am blissfully ignorant of the complications such an agreement will engender, though I naively suggest that they will be no worse than the complications that arise under current practice. My modest goal is to outline the minimal structure of a multilateral agreement that will preserve a large measure of national sovereignty over capital income taxation but at the same time deal with some of the important problems caused by the current structure of national tax systems and bilateral tax treaties. In particular, an agreement of this kind would reduce the extent of inefficient cross-border capital flows caused by the inability of some countries to tax their residents' foreign-source income, and would reduce the cost of monitoring transfer pricing and other policies designed to shift reported income to low-tax jurisdictions.

Conclusions

Myopic tax policy making in an increasingly internationalized world economy has several pitfalls. A tax policy maker who mistakenly believed his (or her) country was closed would

1. Overestimate the ability to place the burden of taxation on capital owners. Where capital ownership is highly concentrated among the wealthy, the progressivity of capital taxation may exist in name only. It may ultimately be borne by owners of relatively fixed factors such as labor and land. In that case, taxes levied directly on land and labor have about the same incidence as capital taxes but do not distort the locational efficiency of capital.
2. Forgo opportunities to take advantage of foreign investors and governments. Large countries can exploit their market power, but all countries can take advantage of the arrangements that their trading partners use to alleviate double taxation.
3. See key sectors and tax revenues dwindle as other countries set their tax systems to attract capital and the tax revenues from capital income. The guardian of global welfare must be aware that each country's pursuit of its national interest with regard to tax policy will not ensure a rational allocation of resources, as each country ignores

the repercussions of its actions on the others. The likelihood of multilateral action is severely limited, though, by the unwillingness of nations to cede their sovereignty over tax policy. Nevertheless, an agreement to harmonize statutory corporate tax rates and withholding rates and to maintain a common policy toward tax havens has the potential to reduce the incentives for costly tax-base competition and cross-border investments motivated solely by tax considerations.

Principles of Taxation
Applied to Developing Countries:
What Have We Learned?

When one is asked the question "What have we learned?" one's first response is likely to be "Since when?" Each developing country has a history marked by different surrounding circumstances, different internal and external environments. As a country passes from one set of circumstances to another, the pattern of its public finances typically changes. Today we find ourselves in what seems to be a new era, different from any in the past. Without a doubt the policies applied today by the most thoughtful and enlightened governments of the developing world are distinct from those of earlier periods. I believe that the principal differences are in one way or another the product of lessons that have been learned—partly from experience and partly from new developments in economic analysis.

In this essay I shall try to juxtapose the "old" and the "new" in a number of different areas of tax policy. Quite clearly, the relevant time frame in each comparison will differ—some representing lessons learned as early as, say, the 1950s, others representing much more recent advances in our understanding.

The first section deals with the value-added tax, a fiscal innovation that has swept over half the world in the course of a mere three decades or so. Today the VAT stands as the premier indirect tax, from a technical point of view. Even though it is never a truly general tax, as its most ardent apologists would sometimes like to pretend, it is a robust and good tax, which can be designed to raise substantial revenues at small economic cost. This chapter looks at why the VAT has been so successful and examines several methods of administration and levels of coverage for this tax.

In the second section we consider uniform import tariffs. Such tariffs are clearly not the best alternatives for any country, but they have great merit in allowing a developing country to respond in an organized and rational way to protectionist pressures, by providing uniform effective protection of all import-competing activities.

The third section deals with the taxation of income from capital. Such taxation tends inevitably to reduce the size of a country's capital stock and hence to lower its level of real wages. In general, the welfare of any developing country, and of labor within that country, is best served by reducing the rate of capital income taxation. The main objection is that such rate reduction can end up simply transferring certain revenues to the treasuries of the developed countries where most multinational corporations are based. This occurs because such companies are typically liable for tax in their home countries, subject to the tax credits for the amounts paid to the countries where their foreign income is earned. If one such country fails to tax that income, the home-base country typically will tax it anyway. Thus the company receives no stimulus, but the developing country that reduced or eliminated its tax rate simply loses revenue. This section then describes a package of policies that manages to get the best of both worlds for a developing country.

The next section of this chapter deals with tax incentives designed to stimulate particular types of investment. Such incentives have been widely used in developing countries. Unfortunately, the specific policy devices employed—mainly tax credits, tax holidays, and accelerated depreciation schemes—have serious flaws. It is very easy for such devices to end up stimulating one investment with a low overall social rate of return, while simultaneously leading to the rejection of similarly situated investments (i.e., in the same region, industry, or other category being favored by the stimulus) with much higher overall rates of return. This section shows how this anomaly can be corrected through the use of better-designed tax incentives.

The final section treats the indexation (for inflation) of business enterprises' taxable income. It is noted that in addition to the familiar understatement of depreciation with an unindexed system in the presence of inflation, there are gains to debtors and losses to creditors on instruments of debt that are denominated in nominal terms. The chapter then sets forth an extremely simple system of indexing income for inflation.

Domestic Commodity Taxation: The Value-Added Tax

No public finance development of the last half century can rival the emergence and spread of the value-added tax. It is difficult for contemporary economists to believe that, barely fifty years ago, there was no such thing as a value-added tax. The French were the first to institute such a tax, in the early 1950s. What is astounding is the degree to which the idea thus planted has in subsequent decades proliferated around the world—in both developed and developing countries.

The conquest of so much territory by the value-added tax is testimony to the power of rational analysis. I, at least, know of no single country where value-added taxation reflected the victory of one interest group over another. Typically the VAT came into being as a result of people's simply becoming convinced that it was a better tax than the existing alternative. This existing alternative was typically either or both of two things: (1) a sales tax of the turnover or cascade type, where tax was imposed each time a sale took place, or (2) a melange of "little" taxes, each striking some small subset of commodities, with no coherency among their various tax bases and their tax rates.

The superiority of the value-added tax over the turnover tax is quickly seen by following a commodity through the productive chain. Under turnover taxation, tax is paid by the farmer when he sells his wheat to the miller, by the miller when he sells his flour to the baker, by the baker when he sells his bread to the retailer, and by the retailer when he makes a final sale to the consumer. In this chain the contribution of the farmer is taxed four times, that of the miller three times, and that of the baker twice. Only the value added by the retailer (that is, his retail markup) is taxed just once.

Now no one, in all of economics, has been able to come up with a reason why in this case it makes sense to tax the farmer's contribution more heavily than the miller's, the miller's more heavily than the baker's, and so on. Indeed, it is quite obvious that this cascade type of taxation gives an artificial incentive to vertical integration—that is, for a retail chain to raise its own wheat and make its own flour and bread, so that the only taxable event takes place when the bread is sold to the final consumer.

Thus, where the value-added tax was adopted mainly to replace an existing sales tax of the cascade type, the victory was won on the basis of rational arguments.

It is less easy to distill in a simple way how the VAT succeeded in replacing a whole mare's nest of "little" taxes—mainly because the mare's nest was different in each country, being the product of the country's own historical experience.[1] But the diagnosis was basically the same in all cases: there were too many "little" taxes; most of them were far too small to be sensible sources of revenue; and the bases of some of them overlapped those of others, leading to multiple taxation of the same item or activity. The fact that one simply could make no sense out of the existing melange of taxes contrasted sharply with the clear and sensible rationale underlying the value-added tax.

The initial rationalization of the value-added tax tended to view it as a fully general tax, striking all types of economic activity equally. At this stage the discussion surrounded the definition of the tax base—in particular, how investment should be treated. Should a firm's investment expenditures be first capitalized and then depreciated, as under an income tax? This would give rise to a VAT of the income type. Or should investment expenditures, like wage and salary costs, simply not be deductible from the base of the VAT? This would result in a VAT of the product type. Or finally, should investment outlays be treated in the same way as purchases of raw materials and intermediate products, being directly deducted in the computation of value added? This would yield a VAT of the consumption type.

On the choice of a base there is no serious debate. To my knowledge, every country imposing a value-added tax has opted for the consumption type. This choice has the virtue of being neutral with respect to the decision between consumption and saving—a virtue highly appreciated by the modern generation of public finance economists. But administrative considerations also tilted the choice toward the consumption type. For the product type of value-added tax, one must determine whether an item purchased by a firm was a current input or a capital item. For a VAT of the income type, one must not only make this distinction, but also set (and presumably enforce) regulations governing the pattern and speed with which capital assets may be depreciated. A consumption type of VAT is free from both of these burdens. Since both capital goods and current inputs are deductible in calculating the taxable base of a consumption-type VAT, one need not worry about distinguishing one from the other. In addition, since capital outlays are directly deductible, there is no need to consider issues related to depreciation.

The popularity of the consumption type of VAT is also related to the ease with which it lends itself to administration via the credit method. Under the credit method, each firm pays value-added tax on the full value of its sales. Offset against this are tax credits, arising out of the taxes that were paid at earlier stages on its inputs. If the earlier stage (for example, agriculture) failed to pay tax, say because it was not a part of the value-added tax network, firms at the later stage (for example, food processing) would in effect pay the tax on their own value added plus that of the earlier stage. In this case food processors would pay tax on both stages simply because they would have no "receipt" for tax paid at the agricultural stage and therefore could not claim a credit against the tax they paid on their entire sales.[2]

It is, in fact, quite possible that the total revenue yield of a value-added tax will be higher when firms at an early stage of production are left out. If all the output of farmers were sold to other entities (such as food processors and distributors) within the VAT system, these later stages would end up paying the full tax on the farmers' value added, just as the farmers themselves would if they were members of the VAT network. But when the farmers are *in* the network, they receive credit for the tax previously paid on the inputs (such as tractors, fertilizer, and gasoline) that they buy. When they are *out of* the network, no such credit is received. In practice, leaving agriculture out of the system can work either way. On the one hand, as indicated above, the credit for tax on agriculture's inputs is irrevocably lost when agriculture is out of the system. On the other hand, farmers do not typically sell all their output to entities that are in the system. Some farm products are sold directly to consumers, and in many countries small retailers (peddlers, hawkers, etc.) are also out of the network. Through these channels some fraction of farm output reaches final consumers with no VAT having been paid. The effect on revenue of leaving the farmers out thus depends on whether the VAT lost via direct sales to consumers exceeds or falls short of the VAT gained through the absence of a tax credit on farmers' inputs.

Yet another attribute of the credit method is the ease with which it can be adapted to multiple rates of tax. If a government wishes to tax one final product at 30 percent and another at 10 percent, it simply institutes these rates of tax for the sales of the respective products. Producers of these goods receive credit for taxes paid, at whatever rate, on their inputs. The rates on these earlier taxes are in effect "washed out" in the act of crediting them, leaving embodied in the product only the rate applied at the last stage. Thus firms using as inputs the products taxed at 30 percent are not penalized, nor are firms using inputs taxed at 10 percent benefited, for in both cases the credit method eliminates as a component of cost the exact amount of the tax previously paid.

This attribute of the credit method gives countries a great deal of flexibility in applying the value-added tax. A number of countries have taken advantage of this flexibility, instituting preferentially low rates for some items, together with higher rates for certain luxury or sumptuary goods. In the process a sort of tax curiosity has been invented—a value-added tax at a zero rate. "Zero rating" of a product or an activity is different from simply leaving it out of the system. For example, if agriculture were zero rated, farmers would be able to receive credit for taxes paid at earlier stages on their inputs, whereas they cannot get such credit when they are left out of the system.

Multiple-rate value-added tax systems are quite common in practice, but on the whole they are not the choice of administrators or tax experts. (Indeed, some tax experts have pronounced themselves in favor of the otherwise distinctly inferior subtraction method, simply because it is much more difficult to introduce multiple rates under that system of VAT administration.) The preference for uniformity in the rate of value-added taxation is based more on elements of political judgment and of administrative efficiency than on a straightforward application of economic principles. It was early in the story that the principles ruled. At that point, most expositions tended to treat the VAT as a truly general tax, striking the entire productive structure of the economy. Several decades of experience have taught us that such a level of generality is never approached in practice. For example, if one takes as the potential revenue of a fully general value-added tax the total consumption of a country (obtained from its national income accounts) times the tax rate (here assumed to be uniform), one finds that actual revenues are rarely more than half of this potential amount. Of course, outright evasion accounts for a portion of the shortfall, but the major part stems from items that are simply left out—imputed rent on owner-occupied dwellings is never included, and actual rent on rented dwellings only rarely. The entire medical and educational industries are typically left out, as are a great many individual service activities, such as the work of household servants and many kinds of repair services. Financial services are usually not included because of the difficulty of defining their "sales," which are clearly *not* total interest receipts for a bank or total premium receipts for an insurance company. Small farmers and small retailers are also often left out, especially so in the less-developed countries. Although in some cases leaving an activity out of the system can actually increase revenue, the total of excluded activities is great enough, and their level of sales to final consumers is important enough, that in practice the shortfall (from the potential revenue of a hypothetical fully general tax) is always large.

The reasoning above implies that those who defend uniformity in a value-added tax cannot place great weight on arguments deriving from its supposed full generality of coverage. In my view, the best argument for uniformity is based on the idea of a sort of long-term compact between the government on the one hand and economic agents on the other. Where many rates prevail, their differences typically reflect political judgments and pressures of many different types. Such pressures can and do change over time, so that uncertainty about the nature of future tax treatment will likely be greater with differentiated rates than with a uniform one. A change in a uniform rate is also likely to be motivated mainly by revenue considerations, so agents can reasonably expect that future rate changes (if any) will be moderate.[3]

A related argument justifies rate uniformity within the sector to be taxed on the grounds that the government should not modify its tax policy simply because of shifts in demand or supply among the constituent segments of the taxed sector.[4] A uniform tax can be regarded simply as a tax on the demand for the output of the taxed sector or on the use of resources within that sector, with the government basically entering into a compact not to discriminatorily exploit situations of inelastic demand or supply of particular goods. A corollary is that the government is neutral (that is, does not itself care) with respect to shifts of demand or supply within the taxed sector or within the untaxed sector.

Where the concept of a single rate of value-added tax has been accepted, there still remains the issue of drawing a line that defines the sectors to be covered. Here a simple principle of applied welfare economics can be brought into play. On the whole, an activity should be shifted from the uncovered to the covered sector if, when the tax is placed on it (and its activity level therefore declines), the resultant expansion of other activities takes place more in the covered than in the uncovered sector.[5]

This condition is more likely to be met in the case of a particular commodity, for example (1) if the commodity has good substitutes in the covered sector and only poor ones in the uncovered sector and (2) if the covered sector is already relatively large. It would be inadvisable to shift the commodity to the covered sector, however, if most of its good substitutes would be left behind in the uncovered sector. This qualification also suggests that under such circumstances an effort might be made to shift a whole package of goods, consisting of not just one commodity but also its principal substitutes, simultaneously from the uncovered to the covered sector.

The application of these rules (and some close corollaries of them) will typically lead to a large covered sector. Left out will be activities that are difficult to tax either on administrative grounds (domestic services) or for political reasons (housing, education, medical services). Once these basic decisions have been made, the rules would dictate making sure that wherever possible, close substitutes to already-taxed activities were shifted to the taxed category. At the same time the authorities should be alert *not* to shift to the taxed category items that are particularly close substitutes for others that, for one or the other of the above reasons, are predestined to remain untaxed.

The Taxation of Imports: The Uniform Tariff

The taxation of imports was historically one of the first levies to arise. The relative ease of collection at customs offices located at the border, plus the common (though false) impression that it was somehow foreigners who were being taxed, plus the natural support of any domestic producer interests that were lucky enough to be protected by the tariff—these alone are perhaps sufficient reason to explain the early emergence of tariffs as important revenue sources.

In most countries, however, the stage of revenue tariffs is long since past, and has been followed by another in which protection rather than revenue is the main motivation for tariffs. This is evident in the pattern of protection that has characterized most countries in the period since World War II, and many countries since a much earlier date. Producer interests are notoriously more compact and easy to organize than consumer interests, so it is no surprise that their pressures should have typically turned out to be the dominant ones. Moreover, producer pressures are clearly and overwhelmingly responsible not just for the high protection of their products but also for the typical pattern of import duties that we find, especially in developing countries. This pattern exhibits higher tariffs and other barriers (indeed, often outright import prohibitions) on items directly competitive with local manufacturing production, together with low or zero tariffs on the raw materials, component parts, and capital goods needed for the domestic production of these items.

In some cases producer protection came in through the "back door." Governments would impose high tariffs on luxury items not then being produced in the country. These tariffs were not thought of as being protective, or as particularly significant sources of revenue. They were instead motivated by the idea that luxury items were a low-priority use of foreign exchange, and that if these items were imported, the user should be forced to pay a heavy price. But once the tariffs were in place they functioned just as if they had been set up for protective reasons. Behind the high barriers of "luxury tariffs" there arose in many developing countries a set of small-scale, inefficient "hothouse" industries, producing at home the very luxury items that the tariffs were meant to keep out, and often using as much (or nearly as much) foreign exchange for materials, capital goods, and parts as would have been used, in the absence of the tariffs, for direct importation of the luxuries in question. Without a doubt this scenario, leading from luxury tariffs to grossly inefficient hothouse industries, is extremely costly to the countries concerned. Fortunately, there is a simple remedy, if only it is applied in time: the imposition of excise taxes rather than tariffs on luxury goods. For goods not produced at home, the luxury tax functions just like a tariff, being collected on the items as they are imported into the country. But the luxury tax has the advantage of treating foreign and home production equally. Inefficient domestic production is not stimulated, but neither is there any barrier to efficient domestic production that would be capable of meeting competition from the world market.

The severe economic costs imposed by differential tariffs on outputs and inputs were not widely recognized until the 1960s, when the modern analysis of "effective protection" was developed. The problem is that when imported inputs enter at lower tariff rates than the corresponding final products, a magnified level of protection is accorded to the use of domestic resources to make the final products in question. If a good is produced entirely at home, a 30 percent tariff invites the use of up to thirteen pesos of domestic resources in order to save a dollar of foreign exchange (assuming the market exchange rate to be ten pesos per dollar). But if the same product is produced using fifty cents of imported inputs (per dollar's worth of output), and if these inputs enter duty-free, then only fifty cents of foreign exchange is saved (per dollar of final product imports displaced), and fully eight pesos worth of domestic resources can be used to perform the necessary domestic operations. Spending eight pesos to save fifty cents is equivalent to sixteen pesos to save a dollar of foreign exchange. With a market exchange rate of ten pesos per dollar, this implies effective protection of 60, not 30 percent.

It is obvious from the above example that significant changes in effective protection can be brought about even by a moderate change in the usage of imported (or importable) inputs, or in the world price of those inputs relative to that of the final product. For example, if the duty-free usage of imported inputs amounted to sixty rather than fifty cents per dollar's worth of product, the rate of effective protection (provided by a 30 percent rate of tariff on the final product) would jump from 60 to 75 percent.

To eliminate extremes of effective protection, and to keep that rate constant regardless of changes in the relative prices of inputs and outputs, there is really only one solution, short of free trade. That solution is to have a single uniform rate of tariff, striking inputs, outputs, and capital goods alike. If the product enjoys protection at a 30 percent rate, and all imported inputs pay tariff at that same rate, it is a matter of simple arithmetic to see that domestic value added (which is the difference between value of output and value of imported inputs) also receives protection at a 30 percent rate.[6]

As a result of improved understanding of the phenomenon of effective protection, serious reform efforts in the 1970s and 1980s were aimed at bringing tariff structures closer to uniformity. These efforts have met with some resistance, both at the real-world political level and at the analytical level. I will not discuss in detail the political pressures that resist uniform tariffs. Predictably, such pressures come from those who were previously protected by high tariffs and who imported their inputs cheaply over zero or very low tariffs. These are exactly the groups that enjoyed the highest effective protection to begin with, and it is no surprise at all that they should resist its being reduced.

More interesting is the academic resistance to the idea of uniform tariffs. Perhaps the best way to start a discussion of this resistance is to recognize that no plausible case can be made for uniform tariffs as a theoretical ideal. For many countries they are a wise and prudent norm—a way of bending to protectionist pressures without breaking, a way of sending signals to the productive sector that exaggerated rates of effective protection are out of the question, a sensible rule on the basis of which authorities can resist the pressures that impinge upon them daily. But none of these virtues makes uniform tariffs a model from a strictly theoretical point of view.

In the first place, a theorist would ask, why have any tariffs at all? The only truly valid argument for tariffs entails their use by a nation to exploit whatever monopoly or monopsony power it as a nation might have in world markets. But the natural device to exploit such power would never be a uniform tariff. A large country like the United States or a large amalgam like the European Economic Community might have some monopsony power over certain of their imports, but no developing country commands any monopsony position whatsoever. Some few developing countries may have market power in particular export products (Brazil or Colombia in coffee, Chile or Zaire in copper, Argentina in wheat and meat, Bolivia in tin, Malaysia in natural rubber). But in these cases the exploitation of whatever monopoly power the country possesses would most appropriately be carried out via a tax (or other restriction) on *exports* of the commodity in question. A uniform import tariff would be a grossly inferior and indirect way of attempting to exploit such a monopoly position.

So in practice when a country opts for a uniform tariff, or when advisers (or international agencies) suggest such a goal, some concession to protectionist pressures is already involved. Those who support uniform tariffs cannot say that they are the best option, only that they are a more reasonable and more defensible way of responding to protectionist pressures than what typically now exists. The uniformity of effective protection gives the authorities a rhetorical base from which to combat the pressures of special interest groups. Implicitly they tell such a group, "We are willing to provide the stimuli for you to get 30 percent more for *saving* a dollar (by import substitution) than we are giving to those who *produce* dollars via the export route. But we do this for *all* who follow the import-substitution route. Why should *you*, in particular, get more than the others? Why should *you* end up using seventeen pesos of resources to save a dollar when other import substituters can save the same dollar for thirteen pesos?" This sort of rhetoric provides a defense the authorities can use against a whole gamut of protectionist pressures. It provides a principle that heads of state and cabinet members can communicate to their subordinates, and that the latter can understand and effectively argue for and implement.

What, then, divides those who argue for and those who argue against uniform tariffs? In the first place, the opponents of uniform tariffs sometimes assert that uniform tariffs operate as a disincentive to exports, when imported inputs are used in their production. The accepted answer to this assertion is that the rules established by the General Agreement on Tariffs and Trade (GATT) are unequivocal in permitting an exporting country to rebate to the exporter of an item any tariffs or other indirect taxes (like the VAT) that may be embodied in its cost structure. To this, it is sometimes retorted that developing countries (particularly the smaller and more backward among them) often lack the administrative capacity to carry out such a rebate scheme. To which the final rejoinder, on the part of advocates of uniform tariffs, is that the GATT has been notoriously lenient, particularly in the cases of small and backward countries, in accepting practices (like rebating a fixed percentage of cost on all exports of, say, textile products) that aim at roughly approximating the tariff-cum-indirect-tax content of the costs of exports in a given category. These crude procedures often result in exporters' being more than fully compensated for the tariff-cum-tax content of costs. Implementing these procedures, moreover, imposes only minimal administrative burdens on the authorities.

Opponents of uniform tariffs also note, quite correctly, a potential flaw in the argument that uniform tariffs always provide uniform protection to all import-substituting activities. They ask us to consider cases in which products that are exported by a country are also used as inputs in the production of some import substitutes. In these cases, the rate of effective protection exceeds the uniform rate of tariff.[7] The formula itself provides the way out of the problem. To guarantee a uniform rate of effective protection, one would have to impose a special tax (a quasi-tariff) on the use of exportable goods as inputs in the production of import substitutes. To my knowledge, no country has ever done this, nor is there much likelihood that any country will. My judgment is that this problem is only a blemish on the real-world face of uniform tariffs. Few policies provide, in their real-world implementation, the same degree of symmetry as they show on the drawing board. This is true of uniform-rate value-added taxes and also of uniform-rate tariffs. But on the whole, especially in developing countries, there is relatively limited usage of export items as inputs into the production of import substitutes. The failure to impose special taxes in such instances is not likely to cause gross deviations from the norm of uniform effective protection. In the rare case of a country where the phenomenon is of such importance as to call into question the gain that a country might make by moving toward a moderate but uniform tariff, the advocates of uniformity should graciously concede the point. I personally know of no such cases and feel confident that if they exist they are anomalies.

The Taxation of Income from Capital: Traps for the Unwary

Whenever one prepares to think seriously about the corporation income tax, it is well to spend some time at the outset contemplating the puzzling nature of this levy. It is not a tax on the income from capital in general, or even a tax on the income from the capital assets of corporations. Rather, it is a tax on just the income from corporate equity capital. This is not the place to elaborate on the merits of these three potential tax bases. Let me simply state that many economists are troubled by the distortions involved in a simple income tax, which by its nature discriminates against saving and favors current consumption. Additional distortions, above and beyond those of a simple income tax, would be introduced by any levy that struck the income from capital a second time—on top of what is paid out of such income under a general personal income tax. The distortion becomes worse if the base of this extra tax is reduced to cover only income from corporate assets rather than the income from all capital. And it becomes still worse if the base is further cut so that it covers only the income from corporate equity capital.

The first lesson we should learn with respect to capital income taxation stems from the simple intellectual exercise just described. How did we find our way, not just in one but in many countries, into something that looks so anomalous (not to say crazy) when viewed in economic terms? The answer, it seems to me, is not hard to determine. At the time the corporation income tax was first imposed, its provisions were examined more by lawyers than by economists. The income tax was a tax on the income of persons. Corporation income was taxable because it accrued to legal persons. Indeed, in the Latin world one often finds the same income tax law covering both the personal and the corporation income tax—with one part of the law dealing with "natural persons" and another with "juridical persons" (that is, corporations). It is easy to see, in these terms, how the corporation income tax came into being and proliferated so widely. What is difficult to rationalize, even to understand, in economic terms makes perfect sense in legal terms. The lesson is that we should strive to design our economic legislation in such a way that it makes eminent sense *both* from an economic *and* from a legal point of view.

The second lesson stems from the experience of countries (both developing and developed) in the period since World War II. This period is important because it encompasses a large fraction of the cases where nations have tried to keep capital from moving out. The lesson here is that it is extremely difficult to prevent capital flight when conditions are such that capital wants to flee. In other words, it is extremely easy for a country to adopt a set of tax policies that are unfavorable to investors from abroad and that cause those who already have capital invested in the country (nationals and foreigners alike) to try hard to get it out. And once such policies are in place it is extremely difficult to change course and bring the capital back again. Capital controls and other measures have not really worked as a way of keeping capital *in* a country, but that does not mean that a country cannot with considerable ease (and even without explicit intent) manage to keep capital out.

The third lesson is that in the present-day world, the taxation of income from capital in any developing country ends up reducing the size of the capital stock in that country. And since a smaller capital stock implies a lower equilibrium level of real wages and salaries, in the final analysis the workers end up bearing the brunt of any special tax on capital income. The mechanism by which the capital stock in a country is reduced by taxation is simply the search (on the part of individual holders of wealth) for the best possible rate of return. No matter what the capital stock within a country would be in the absence of special taxes on the income from capital, that stock will surely be less, often significantly less, in the presence of such a tax.

The fourth lesson deals with an exception—sometimes quite important—to the above statement. It concerns the case of multinational companies and the tax treatment their home countries accord to the income earned on their investments around the world. Frequently this treatment simply allows a foreign tax credit for any taxes paid in the host country, up to the amount that would have to be paid on the same income under the tax laws of the base country (say the United States). In such a case, a developing country has a special incentive to tax the income of a multinational as much as, say, the United States would do in any event. For if the country fails to impose a tax, the company has to pay the tax anyway—but to the U.S. Treasury instead of the developing country's own treasury.

The fifth lesson concerns how to eliminate a corporation income tax without really doing so. The key word in this lesson is *integration*. By integrating its corporation income tax with its personal income tax, a country can virtually eliminate the former tax for its own citizens. The process of integration works in the same way as tax withholding on wages and salaries. If the corporation income tax rate is 35 percent, then this fraction of the company's profits is remitted to the government. The amount of profits per share is calculated, as well as the amount of tax. Shareholders paying personal tax within the country are informed of the income accruing to them on the basis of the shares they own, plus the amount of tax that has been paid. Both figures then undergo procedures identical to those used under wage and salary withholding. The individual shareholders are required to include as part of their own income their proportionate share of the profits of the company. In turn, the tax paid by the company on these profits is credited against the tax that the individual owes. In the end, only individual tax is paid on each resident shareholder's portion of the company's earnings. No extra tax is involved. The corporation income tax, as far these shareholders are concerned, has ceased to exist.

The sixth lesson concerns a bit of public-finance sleight of hand—a mechanism whereby the corporation income tax can be effectively abolished for resident shareholders, yet maintained for nonresident shareholders (including multinational corporations that own local subsidiaries). The trick is to follow the line of integration just discussed, but to provide no mechanism by which nonresident shareholders can recover (from the country in question) the tax that was "withheld." The companies (which are the nonresident shareholders in this case) may recover via tax credits granted by their own governments (as is the case in the United States), but they will not get the money back from the treasury of the host country. This piece of magic may be the best of all possible worlds for a developing country. It eliminates the corporation income tax as a reason for local residents to hold less capital in the form of local investments, and at the same time does not gratuitously transfer tax revenue to foreign treasuries.

A variant of the preceding lesson is provided by partial integration of the corporation and individual income taxes. The most frequently encountered version of partial integration is based on dividends. All corporation profits are subject to corporation income taxes, and when the tax payment is made, the taxes are "assigned," pro rata, to dividends on the one hand and to corporate retentions on the other. The part assigned to dividends is treated as withholding. Individual resident shareholders are then required to report their dividends (grossed up so as to include taxes on the dividends but not corporate retentions nor the taxes upon them) as part of their personal income subject to tax. The tax due from the individual is then computed, and the corporation tax paid on the basis of dividends is credited against the individual's tax liability.

Obviously, partial integration does not have the same degree of merit in eliminating distortions as does full integration. Nonetheless it is a useful measure, compared with zero integration, and it has some administrative advantages vis-a-vis full integration. Our seventh lesson would be to consider partial integration a good step, moving away from a system with no integration at all, but to see it as a solution that is inferior to full integration on technical economic grounds.

Apart from the above, a very important lesson derives from an early tendency, when corporation income taxation was first implemented in a number of developing countries, to make the rates of tax progressive in a fashion similar to the progression of the individual income tax. Authorities apparently thought that corporations with more income were somehow "richer" than the rest, and possessed a greater "ability to pay" in relation to their income. Nothing, of course, could be farther from the truth. In many countries, the largest corporations have the most widely distributed shareholdings. In the United States, for example, telephone companies and other utilities have been favorite investments for small individual shareholders.

If the idea of progression has any meaning it is at the individual, not the corporate, level. The result of progressivity at the corporate level is to induce companies to "fractionate" rather than maintain an economic size. Although sometimes justified as a favor to small firms to "help them grow," a progressive rate structure in the corporation income tax is really a special tax on the growth of smaller firms. I argued above that special taxes on the income from capital are counterproductive (because they reduce the size of the capital stock in a country); I here would add that to the extent that such taxes will exist anyway it is far better for them to be uniform than to follow a progressive rate structure.

There are other lessons on the setting of rates as well. Where integration between the corporation and the individual income taxes exists (or is planned), there is great merit in setting the corporation income tax rate equal to the top-bracket individual rate. Where consideration is given to the fact that multinational companies would anyway pay tax to their home treasuries, it makes sense for developing countries to set their corporation income tax rates at levels similar to those prevailing in the principal industrial countries that serve as bases for the multinational corporations.

The above two recommendations could easily be quite contradictory. The highest rate of personal income tax might be 60 or 70 percent, while the corporation tax rate in developed countries might average around 30 or 40 percent. Fortunately, recent trends have reduced the likelihood of such a contradiction. Almost everywhere in the world, the maximum rates of personal income tax have dropped dramatically. Whereas such rates once hovered between 70 and 90 percent in a number of countries, the tendency in recent years has been to reduce them to below 50 percent. The "center of gravity" of maximum personal tax rates is today probably between 30 and 40 percent in both developing and developed countries. Fortuitously, a simultaneous tendency toward rate reduction has led to corporation income tax rates in industrial countries to be concentrated in the range of 30 to 40 percent. Hence today a typical developing country can integrate its corporation and personal income taxes, and at the same time deal with the problem of multinational companies, by adopting rate structures in the indicated range.

Tax Incentives: The Need for Rationalization

In some parts of the world (Latin America comes immediately to mind) there appears to be a propensity to introduce tax incentives in response to almost any new or promising investment idea. Help for a backward region, stimulus to a new industry, assistance for a slumping industry, provision of desired services like housing for the poor and not-so-poor—all of these have been and are the objectives of investment tax incentives in many countries.

It is easy to understand how these incentives came into being. Legislators and administrators are aware that taxing the income of enterprises acts to some degree as a deterrent to their activities. They tax these enterprises not as a caprice but because they need revenue. But new activities should not be deterred from starting up, especially not when the activities are considered desirable. So in the euphoria of contemplating new wellsprings of growth and prosperity, ministers and congressmen join to grant investment tax credits, tax holidays, accelerated depreciation schemes, and the like.

The pity is that many, probably most, of the schemes that have been implemented are ill designed. Indeed, it is likely that many of these incentives end up doing more harm than good. This is particularly unfortunate because several policy devices are available that meet the design criteria that most existing incentive schemes do not. One of the important lessons of the last fifteen years has been the "discovery" of why so many existing incentives are seriously flawed, and of exactly which incentive schemes meet rational design criteria.

The clearest case of flawed design is the investment tax credit, as it has usually been implemented in industrialized and developing countries. Such tax credits are typically calculated as a specified percentage of the costs of investment goods in the affected categories. It sounds so reasonable—if the desire is to stimulate investments of a given type, why not subsidize outlays on such investments? The problem is that the economic function of investment is to produce net income for investors, and at bottom for society. An appropriate incentive would be geared to the present value of the expected income stream rather than to the cost of the investment goods involved.

It is essential to recognize that the price paid for an investment good is (in equilibrium) the present value of all the future flows of benefit that it will generate. These flows include the recovery of the initial capital, plus the net return. The problem with the typical investment tax credit is that it subsidizes capital recovery as well as net return.

Consider an analogy with government bonds. If a government were to give something like an investment tax credit to the purchasers of its financial obligations, it would offer, say, a seven-cent credit against personal income tax for each dollar that a taxpayer spent on such obligations. Presumably, the credit would be conditioned on the individual holding the obligations to their maturity. What would individuals try to do in such circumstances? Clearly, they would flock to purchase one-year notes rather than five-year or ten-year bonds. Even better, if the tax-credit scheme allowed it they would concentrate their purchases on three-month bills. In that way, they could receive four credits each year for every $1,000 they had available for the operation. Obviously it is better to get four credits (of, say, $70 each) per year than just one credit per year. And one credit every year is better than one credit every five years (as it would be if the purchaser chose five-year bonds). The problem here is that the purchase price paid for a bond is not (except in the case of a perpetuity) the present value of its net income stream, but rather the present value of the stream of income plus amortization payments. As the term of the bond gets shorter and shorter, the fraction of its price constituted by the present value of amortization payments gets higher and higher. For an obligation that pays periodic interest and is amortized just by one final payment, the present value of amortization is simply $P/(1 + r)^N$, where P is its initial price, r the interest rate (assumed here to both the coupon rate and the relevant market discount rate), and N the term to maturity. Thus with a one-year bond, its issue price of $1,000 would represent, at a 6 percent discount rate, about 943.4 ($= 1,000/1.06$) of present value of amortization and 56.6 ($= 60/1.06$) of present value of net income.

Just as the price of a bond represents the present value of interest and amortization payments, so the cost of a machine or other physical asset tends to represent, in equilibrium, the present value of its expected stream of net income plus depreciation. The problem with the typical investment tax credit is that, in effect, it subsidizes depreciation, thus artificially biasing investors in the direction of choosing short-lived assets. The most exaggerated investment tax credit of which I am aware was one of 30 percent, which applied in Bolivia in the mid-1970s. My favorite example related to this case is an investment that costs 1,000 and "pays out" in three equal annual installments of 300 each. Obviously this investment has an overall negative economic rate of return. Yet in the presence of a 30 percent tax credit, the cost to the investor would be 700, not 1,000. The three annual flows of receipts would represent a rate of return, on this "cost," in excess of 10 percent. Here the investment tax credit would "artifically" turn a socially wasteful investment into a privately profitable one.[8]

To eliminate the bias described above, one must calibrate the incentive to the net income generated (or expected to be generated) by the assets covered. This can be done in a variety of ways. The simplest, of course, is just to reduce the rate of income tax to be paid by the enterprise in question. If the general income tax rate is 50 percent, it takes an expected yield of 20 percent to produce an after-tax return of 10 percent per annum. To stimulate a special category of investments, one could simply reduce the tax rate applying to that income to, say, 40 percent or 30 percent. This would lead enterprises to be willing to invest in assets expected to yield 16 ⅔ percent (in order to produce a 10 percent return after a 40 percent rate), or 14.3 percent (in order to produce a 10 percent return after a 30 percent rate). There is no way under this scheme to replicate the "scandal" reported above for the investment tax credit, whereby investments with socially negative yields are made privately profitable.

Reducing the rate of applicable income tax is only one of a number of devices, all of which have the attribute of giving "rational" investment incentives.[9] A second such incentive is a tax credit on net investment in the covered areas. Here the tax-paying firm receives as a credit only a specified fraction of the amount by which the cost of new investments exceeds the concurrent amount of depreciation on old investments of the covered type. This scheme can be understood as giving a full credit on the cost of each investment asset, and later imposing an "anticredit" on the depreciation allowances accruing over the life of the asset. If the purchase price of the asset is thought of as being composed of the present value of future revenue (PVY) plus present value of future depreciation allowances (PVD), then one can say that on each given asset the net investment credit subsidizes PVY and PVD at a given rate (say γ), and then takes back the subsidy on depreciation allowances (D) as they accrue. The net result, in present-value terms, is a subsidy to PVY, which obviously is similar in nature to a reduction of the regular tax rate applying to Y.

An extreme version of a rational incentive scheme is the full expensing of covered investments. The investing firms receive a credit equal to the tax rate τ times the price of the asset ($= PVD + PVY$). But once the asset has been expensed, the firm is required to pay tax at the full applicable rate on each annual flow of $Y + D$. The net result in this case is no tax at all. As Richard Musgrave long ago pointed out, full expensing effectively eliminates the enterprise income tax *qua* tax. Instead, the government becomes a τ percent partner in each investment, paying τ percent of the investment cost via the expensing route, then taking τ percent of the full benefit stream ($Y + D$) over the life of the asset.

A less extreme version of this scheme is partial expensing, whereby the investing firm expenses a fraction α of the cost of a covered investment and then is required to depreciate the remaining fraction $(1 - \alpha)$ of that cost, using the normal pattern of depreciation over the economic life of the asset.[10]

There are yet other devices that meet the condition for a rational investment incentive. All are the same in the undisturbed long run that economists are prone to contemplate. They differ in the way the flows of tax and subsidy payments are distributed over time. For example, the full expensing scheme is virtually inflation-proof, since it gives credit at the full tax rate at the time an investment is made and collects tax at the full tax rate on the annual flows of $(Y + D)$ as they occur. The net investment credit, on the other hand, is vulnerable to inflation. An investor receives full credit when the asset is bought; in later periods, however, when the depreciation of the asset is offset against later investment purchases, the depreciation is understated by the amount of accumulated inflation. The partial expensing scheme is likewise vulnerable to inflationary distortions, but a variant of it is not. This variant would simply divide the price paid for an asset into two components, *PVY* and *PVD*, the shares reflecting the pattern of benefit flows combined with the normal profile of true economic depreciation of the asset. The firm would then be allowed to take $PVD + \alpha PVY$ as an expense in the year the investment was made, subject to its later paying tax at the rate τ on the full annual flows $(Y + D)$. The net result, in present-value terms, is a tax equal to $\tau(PVY + PVD)$ minus $\tau(\alpha PVY + PVD)$ for a net tax of $\tau(1 - \alpha) PVY$.

The above family of rational incentive devices is much preferable to most of the schemes commonly found in practice. Once one realizes that the objective of rationality is met only when the incentive is somehow calibrated to Y (or *PVY*), and not to D (or *PVD*), it becomes clear why many widely used schemes fall short. Accelerated depreciation schemes tend to work capriciously among assets of different economic lives and types. It is almost impossible for an incentive scheme that operates solely on the depreciation side to end up being perfectly (or nearly perfectly) calibrated to net income Y. Similarly, tax holidays grant exemptions for a period of years. They are welcomed by investors whose projects yield much or most of their taxable income during the tax holiday years, but they mean little for projects whose main income flows will accrue after the holiday is over. Thus it is not possible for a tax holiday scheme to affect all covered investments equally, in relation to their respective present values of net income (*PVY*).

The lesson with respect to tax incentives to investment is simple. To the extent that such incentives are used for any purpose not calibrated to a specific externality, they should be chosen from a by-now ample shelf of rational investment incentives. Such a choice will provide a true incentive for covered investments while at the same time guarding against gross and avoidable inefficiencies.

Indexing the Income Taxation of Business Firms

The indexing of tax systems for inflation is a subject about which we had little organized knowledge, and virtually no experience, until the past few decades. Now a number of countries use a system of full or partial indexing. Moreover, the analytical base for dealing with the subject is now well developed. The task that remains is to disseminate the knowledge and experience we have, and perhaps to try to ensure that a wide segment of people come to appreciate the simplicity and ease of administration that characterize a well-designed indexing system.

The story can be told very simply. Historically, business firms have been among the first (and the loudest) to complain about the way inflation affects their taxes. They point out, quite rightly, that depreciation allowances based on historical cost are grossly unrealistic when substantial inflation has intervened. On this basis they argue in favor of being permitted to write up the book value of each asset so as to reflect inflation as it occurs, and then to calculate depreciation for tax purposes on the basis of this written-up value.

The problem with the above solution (partial indexation on the basis of fixed assets) is that it only does part of the job—precisely that part in which the inflationary adjustment favors the business firm. The other key part of a system of indexing concerns debt. Inflation, quite obviously, erodes the value of any debt that is expressed in nominal terms, creating a large inflationary benefit for any firm that has a significant portion of its capital in the form of debt. This inflationary *benefit* is hardly ever mentioned by those who complain so vociferously about the understatement of depreciation in an inflationary environment.

A proper indexing procedure would correct for both of these broad types of distortion that inflation introduces into the measurement of the true economic income of business enterprises. One possible procedure would be to deal specifically with each asset on one side and with each instrument of debt on the other. Such a procedure is cumbersome and tends to neglect the fact that nominal assets and liabilities run through a whole continuum—from cash on hand to accounts receivable and payable to all sorts of instruments of long-term and short-term debt.

Fortunately, there is a simpler yet completely general procedure that accomplishes the task of indexing without dealing explicitly with each and every nominal asset and liability. This procedure is based on the simple accounting equation that assets equal liabilities plus net worth (capital and surplus). It deals with real assets and liabilities in one category, nominal assets and liabilities in a second category, and net worth as the third category. Three rules govern the entire system:

1. All real or indexed assets are to be written up by the inflation factor for the period (for example, year) for which taxable income is being calculated. The aggregate amount of such write-ups for all real or indexed assets should then be added as a profit item on the income statement for the period.
2. All real or indexed liabilities, together with the capital and surplus of the firm, are to be written up by the inflation factor for the period (for example, year) for which taxable income is being calculated. The aggregate amount of such write-ups should then be added as a loss item on the income statement for the period.
3. For real depreciable assets, depreciation for the period should be calculated on the basis of the written-up value of the assets.

The interesting thing about these rules is that they make no mention of nominal assets and liabilities—that is, there is no explicit adjustment for debt items. But consider that the adjustment we would like to make with respect to these items is to attribute to the firm a profit equal to the inflation rate times nominal liabilities minus nominal assets. The accounting equation says that this is equal to (*a*), the inflation rate times real assets minus real liabilities, minus (*b*), the inflation rate times net worth capital and surplus. Note that rules 1 and 2 bring in item *a* by assigning as a profit item the aggregate adjustment on real assets and as a loss the aggregate adjustment on real liabilities. In another part of rule 2 item *b* is brought in by adding as a loss item the aggregate write-up of capital and surplus. The end result is that rules 1 and 2 effectively bring about the appropriate adjustment for nominal assets and liabilities without ever explicitly mentioning them, or the interest which they may or may not carry.[11]

The system permits all interest payments to be treated as expenses, just as they are in nonindexed accounting systems. If there is a 20 percent inflation and a firm pays an interest rate of, say, 30 percent, the system gives the firm an implicit profit of 20 percent on the loan through the adjustments indicated above, and then allows the firm to write off the 30 percent explicit interest payment as an expense. The net result is that the firm pays only 10 percentage points of real interest, and exactly that amount is the net interest deduction which the system in effect permits.

The system treats firms that are net creditors in a fashion exactly symmetrical to that accorded to net debtors. If the above debt were owed to another enterprise in the same national economy, that firm would declare as income the full 30 percent rate of interest received, but the profit and loss increments implied by rules 1 and 2 would offset 20 points of that, leaving only 10 percentage points of net taxable interest income.

It should be noted, too, that firms that hold cash are implicitly attributed a loss due to the loss of real purchasing power of that cash. Similarly, firms owing non-interest-bearing payables are attributed a gain, and those awaiting payment on non-interest-bearing receivables are attributed a loss by this system. The gain and loss in this case are precisely the inflationary change in real value of the liability or asset in question.

Two simple examples may help readers see how the system works. Consider a fixed asset that was bought at a price of 1,000 by a newly formed company with capital and surplus of 1,000. Inflation of 20 percent in the first year of use would cause the machine to be written up to 1,200 (rule 1); at the same time, by rule 2, the firm's capital and surplus would be written up to 1,200. The revaluation of the machine would cause 200 to be added as a profit item in the profit and loss statement. The revaluation of capital and surplus would cause 200 to be added as a loss item. These two adjustments cancel one another, leaving no direct impact on profits. However, by rule 3, depreciation is taken on the basis of the written-up value of 1,200; hence the widely recognized inflationary distortion of depreciation is avoided.

The second example deals with a fixed asset financed by debt. In this case, the fixed asset would be written up to 1,200, and depreciation taken on that sum just as in the previous example. Similarly, a profit item of 200 would be generated by the write-up. But in this case, the operation itself entailed no modification of capital and surplus. So the firm must pay tax on an additional income of 200. However, the firm gets to deduct the interest paid on its debt. If this interest reflects the inflation rate plus a real interest factor, the 200 of additional income is automatically canceled by the inflation factor in the interest rate, and what is left is a net deduction of the real interest actually paid. To the extent that the stipulated interest payment fails to reflect the inflation, the firm is enjoying an overall net gain on the investment of debt during the period in question. Rules 1 through 3 would in this case require that the firm pay tax on this net gain.

Conclusions

In this chapter we have explored several important advances in our understanding of tax issues and in the design and implementation of tax policies. These advances were chosen because of their relevance for responsible and efficient policy making in developing countries.

By far the most important advance, in terms of its fiscal contribution, is the value-added tax. Introduced first in France in the early 1950s, it has spread to half or more of the countries in the world, including many developing countries. Originally it was considered a very general tax, but experience has revealed that it rarely covers more than 50 to 60 percent of the tax base that a fully general tax would reach. Nonetheless, it is a robust and reliable tax, which has a low economic cost per dollar of revenue raised. Our review of the VAT focused on criteria for drawing the boundary lines of its coverage—a point that has been substantially neglected in previous treatments, and one that becomes quite important once it is recognized that full generality is beyond plausible aspiration.

A second important advance has been the recognition of the special merits of uniform tariffs. This recognition arose out of the development of effective-protection analysis in the 1960s. Few if any would argue that uniform tariffs are better than free trade. Rather, such tariffs emerge as a sound policy for a country where protectionist sentiment is too strong to be fully defeated. A moderate uniform tariff provides equal effective protection to all import-substituting activities and avoids the exaggerated economic costs that characterize the tariff structures of most developing countries today.

A third set of policies treated in this essay concerns the taxation of income from capital. Recent decades have increased our awareness of the strength of international capital movements, particularly of the virtual impossibility of any small country's forcing its own nationals to keep their savings at home. As a consequence, policies that tax the income from capital at home give rise to capital outflows. This capital flight continues until an equilibrium relationship is restored between the rates of return that can be earned at home and in the world capital market. Greater taxation of income from capital at home thus leads to less domestic capital to cooperate with the local labor force. The result is a lower level of real wages.

For capital owned by domestic residents, the best tax treatment is the integration of the corporation income tax with the personal income tax. This solution in effect converts the corporation income tax into a simple withholding device for domestic shareholders.

For foreign shareholders (particularly multinational companies) the problem is complicated by the fact that their income will likely be taxed in their home country, to the extent it is not taxed in the place where it is invested. In this case the developing country should continue to tax such income, while simultaneously integrating personal and corporation income taxes for domestic shareholders. Under this solution, foreign shareholders must turn to their own treasuries to obtain tax credits for corporation tax paid in the developing country.

The result of the recommended treatment is that the developing country's own residents are in effect exempt from corporation income tax, while nonresident shareholders (including multinational corporations) continue to pay it.

Tax incentives to particular types of investment represent a fourth set of issues dealt with in this chapter. Developing countries have not only made excessive use of such incentives, but on the whole have selected schemes that are badly designed, inducing investments in low-return operations at the expense of much better and higher-return investments. This chapter presented a number of incentive devices that are proof against this type of defect, including reducing the corporation income tax rate on favored investment categories, granting tax credits on net rather than gross investment, and full or partial expensing of investments in the affected categories. These, then, are the indicated instruments for future investment incentives in developing countries.

The last topic treated was the indexing for inflation of the income of business firms. Here a simple system was presented, which corrects not only for the understatement of depreciation that inflation typically causes, but also for the complex distortions arising from the effects of inflation on the debt of business firms and on the interest payments on that debt. This system, consisting of only three basic rules, is relatively easy to administer. Adoption of such an indexing scheme is advisable for any country suffering from chronic inflation, as well as for any that runs a significant risk of substantial spurts of inflation in the future.

These are some of the areas in which important new insights and improvements in the theory and design of tax policy have been generated during the past few decades. Together with other innovations not covered here, they have brought about significant improvements in the "tax package of choice" that serious professional observers would recommend to almost any developing country.

Part III

Tax Reform and Developed Countries

Tax Reform in Australia

Tax issues and reform proposals dominated political debate in Australia during the 1980s, but actual tax reforms were a mixed bag. Failure to index tax brackets adequately, highly distortive divergences in the tax rates on savings and investment, and frequent revisions to the tax treatment of superannuation, for example, have left Australia with something other than a "level playing field." In 1984 taxation was the subject of a national summit, chaired by the prime minister, which led to seemingly endless suggestions and countersuggestions for tax reforms, usually from lobby groups. In contrast to New Zealand, where decisive action by Finance Minister Roger Douglas led to rapid implementation of a value-added tax and other broad-based reforms, Australia demonstrated the pitfalls of a consensus-oriented framework for tax reform.

To appreciate the nature and scope of tax reform in Australia one must know something of the structure of tax collections. Australia is a federation of individual states, but, as Figure 4.1 shows, all levels of government are financed predominantly by revenue collected by the central government. State governments collect only 16 percent of total taxation revenue, sufficient to finance around half of their expenditure needs (the remainder being funded by grants from the federal government). Local governments' own collections of revenue amount to a measly 3.7 percent of the national total.

The Australian tax system is thus dominated by the way in which the federal government raises its revenue, and this in turn is dominated by

---

FIGURE 4.1   Composition of Federal and State Tax Receipts in Australia, 1986/87
                (percentage)

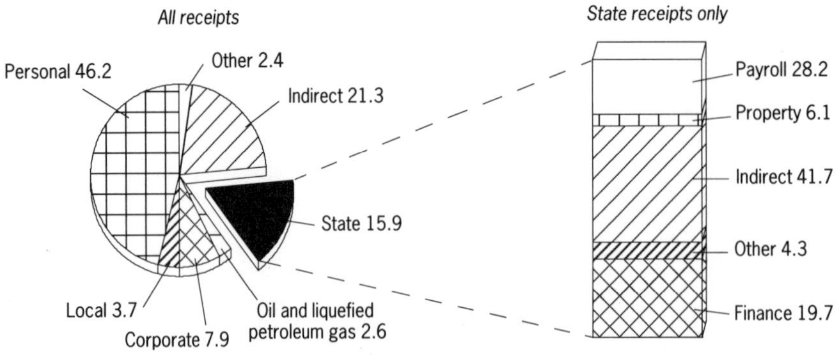

All receipts

Personal 46.2
Other 2.4
Indirect 21.3
State 15.9
Local 3.7
Corporate 7.9
Oil and liquefied petroleum gas 2.6

State receipts only

Payroll 28.2
Property 6.1
Indirect 41.7
Other 4.3
Finance 19.7

SOURCE: Australian Bureau of Statistics, *Taxation Revenue Australia (5506.0)* (Canberra, 1986/87).

---

personal and corporate income tax, as Table 4.1 illustrates. Together these instruments raise almost two-thirds of federal government receipts, and constitute over half of total national taxation.

At the outset it is worth noting that the tax reform debate in Australia has *not* been about which level of government should raise revenue, and whether it might not be desirable to have state governments more responsible for raising the revenue that they ultimately spend. Nor has the debate been greatly concerned with the structure and deficiencies of the revenue collections that state governments currently do make. Both of these issues are acknowledged as problem areas, but for the present they have been pushed well to the side.

The recent tax reform debate in Australia has almost exclusively concerned itself with the twin issues of restructuring the system of direct income tax and shifting the emphasis of tax collections from income tax to indirect tax (presumably collected at the federal level). Both issues stem from the perception that the direct tax base, which has narrowed over time, has become more and more distorting, both because of its narrowness and because of the ever-higher marginal tax rates at which revenue is collected.

The first part of the chapter discusses this background. In the second part we briefly describe the manner in which tax reform has been undertaken. In terms of outcome, all the efforts made so far to tilt the revenue emphasis away from direct, toward indirect, taxation have met with total failure. As for the restructuring of the direct tax itself, considerable progress has been made, in terms of both base broadening and rate reduction, similar to the initiatives undertaken in other countries.

The third part of the chapter notes some of the major features of the tax structure as it has emerged from the most recent policy initiatives. Of particular interest is the radical change made to the corporate tax, with the

TABLE 4.1   Federal Government Tax Receipts in Australia, 1954/55 to 1988/89

Year	Indirect taxes		Income taxes						Other taxes and receipts		Total
			Corporate		Personal						
					PAYE		Other				
	$Am	%	$Am	%	$Am	%	$Am	%	$Am	%	($Am)
1954/55[a]	789	38.7	343	16.8	720	35.3	n.a.	n.a.	187	9.2	2,039
1959/60	1,132	40.0	458	16.2	546	19.3	338	12.0	353	12.5	2,827
1964/65	1,460	33.6	725	16.7	991	22.8	580	13.3	594	13.7	4,350
1969/70	2,213	30.9	1,197	16.7	2,084	29.1	774	10.8	889	12.4	7,157
1974/75	3,724	24.4	2,447	16.0	6,071	39.7	1,643	10.7	1,406	9.2	15,291
1979/80	6,189	21.0	3,547	12.0	12,160	41.3	2,880	9.8	4,680	15.9	29,456
1980/81	6,712	19.2	4,856	13.9	14,121	40.4	3,423	9.8	5,803	16.6	34,915
1981/82	7,841	19.3	5,258	12.9	17,417	42.9	3,807	9.4	6,308	15.5	40,631
1982/83	8,942	20.2	5,107	11.5	18,840	42.5	4,126	9.3	7,328	16.5	44,343
1983/84	10,826	22.3	4,940	10.2	19,620	40.5	5,090	10.5	8,024	16.5	48,500
1984/85	12,494	21.9	6,034	10.6	22,331	39.2	6,969	12.2	9,167	16.1	56,995
1985/86	14,197	22.1	6,702	10.4	25,189	39.2	7,545	11.8	10,559	16.4	64,192
1986/87	17,121	23.5	7,888	10.8	28,136	38.6	9,937	13.6	9,764	13.4	72,846
1987/88	19,170	23.7	10,349	12.8	30,957	38.3	10,929	13.5	9,400	11.6	80,805
1988/89[b]	19,849	22.7	11,900	13.6	35,240	40.3	12,340	14.1	8,152	9.3	87,481

NOTES: n.a. = not available.
Amounts are given in millions of Australian dollars.
a. PAYE tax for 1954/55 includes other income tax on persons.
b. Estimated receipts from Budget Paper No. 1.
SOURCE: W. E. Norton and P. J. Kennedy, *Australian Economic Statistics 1949–50 to 1984–85*, Reserve Bank of Australia Occasional Paper no. 8A (Sydney, 1985); *1988/89 Budget Paper No. 1* (Canberra: Australian Government Publishing Service, 1988).

introduction of a system of full imputation. Finally, the chapter concludes with a discussion of future prospects for the tax system.

Background to Tax Reform

The backdrop to tax reform in Australia is, of course, the tax system itself and the way it has evolved over recent decades. In this section of the chapter we emphasize both those characteristics of this background that seem peculiar to Australia and those that are common to the experience of other industrialized nations.

Increasing emphasis on personal income tax. If it is possible to distinguish the single most important concern that has motivated tax reform in Australia, that concern would have to be the perception of an increasingly narrow direct tax base, accompanied by its necessary corollary, increasingly high *marginal* tax rates.

Of overwhelming importance in this regard has been the emphasis on the personal income tax as the primary vehicle of the government's revenue-raising efforts. Certainly it has been the personal income tax that has funded most of the increase in government revenues over recent decades. As Table 4.1 shows, the share of personal tax in federal government revenues has risen from around 32 percent in 1960 to its current level of well over 50 percent. The increase in the number of wage and salary earners exposed to higher and higher marginal tax rates has also created obvious incentives to arrange one's affairs in ways that lessen the impact of these rates. Evidence of this trend is provided by the plight of the pay-as-you-earn (PAYE) taxpayer,[1] as shown in Table 4.1. Over time an increasing proportion of revenues has been collected from this "captive" source.

The increased emphasis on the personal income tax is closely related to the inadequate indexation of the tax scales combined with their progressivity. Of course, many other countries have experienced a similar phenomenon, but, as demonstrated in Table 4.2, Australia has been particularly prone to this trend. Australia does not at present have an earmarked "social security" contribution scheme, unlike many other countries. Such taxes are often far less progressive than the income tax itself. While state governments do collect payroll tax at varying but basically proportional rates, the amount of these collections leaves Australia well behind in the rankings shown in the table.

The evolution of the personal income tax in Australia over the thirty years leading up to the recent tax reform exercise is summarized in Table 4.3. One change has been the amalgamation of an increasingly varied set of "concessional expenditure" deductions into a tax scale with a somewhat larger, universal tranche of tax-free income. Deductions for dependents have been a feature throughout, but have now been converted into tax rebates. A tax scale with a large number of rate bands was gradually condensed into one of only a few. And over the whole period the top rate of personal tax

TABLE 4.2   OECD and Australian Tax Shares by Source

	Personal income	Social security and payroll	Goods and services, general[a]	Goods and services, selective[b]
OECD average (%)	32.32	25.29	13.61	14.45
Australia (%)	43.94	5.83	7.41	20.84
Australia (rank in OECD)	5	20	22	5

a. General taxes on goods and services are those, like the value-added taxes adopted in Europe, that are levied across a broad range of commodities. The Australian wholesale sales tax is included in this category.
b. Selective taxes include levies on narrow groupings of commodities, such as alcohol and tobacco.
SOURCE: Organization for Economic Cooperation and Development, *Revenue Statistics*, 1984.

TABLE 4.3 Evolution of the Personal Income Tax Scale in Australia, 1954/55, 1974/75, and 1984/85

Feature	1954/55	1974/75	1984/85
Number of rates	29	14	5
Tax-free threshold	$A1,306 (11.7% of AWE)	$A2,569 (13.5% of AWE)	$A4,595 (22.5% of AWE)
Highest marginal rate	66.7% at $A199,000 (18.0 times AWE)	67% at $A102,000 (5.17 times AWE)	60% at $A35,000 (1.72 times AWE)
Treatment of dependents	Deduction worth (at AWE) $A256 (2.3% of AWE)	Deduction worth (at AWE) $A353 (1.8% of AWE)	Rebate of tax worth $A830 (4.1% of AWE)
Treatment of the aged	Not taxable until $A4,664 (42% of AWE)	Not taxable until $A6,022 (30.5% of AWE)	Not taxable until $A5,533 (27.1% of AWE)
Other concessions	Deductions from taxable income available for medical expenses, dental expenses, funeral expenses, medical insurance, life insurance and superannuation premiums, rates and land taxes, education expenses, zone allowances.	Deductions from taxable income available for medical expenses, dental expenses, funeral expenses, medical insurance, life insurance and superannuation premiums, education expenses, self-education expenses, adoption expenses, subscriptions to afforestation companies, zone allowances.	Rebate of tax for zone allowance. Rebate of tax for expenditures, totaling in excess of $A2,000, on medical expenses, funeral expenses, life insurance and superannuation premiums, education expenses, self-education expenses, adoption expenses, rates and land taxes, subscriptions to afforestation companies.

AWE = average weekly earnings.
SOURCE: *Budget Papers* (Canberra: Australian Government Publishing Service, various years); Australian Bureau of Statistics, *Average Weekly Earnings Australia (6302.0)* (Canberra).

remained roughly constant, at 66.7 percent, but fell to 60 percent by 1980/81.

One very marked change is the level of income at which taxpayers reach higher marginal tax rates. Whether measured in terms of constant prices or average weekly earnings, the level at which these rates are paid has fallen dramatically. This phenomenon is further illustrated in Figure 4.2. Here we compare the average tax rates implied by the tax scales of 1954/55, 1974/75, and 1984/85 (that is, directly preceding the tax reforms of the Hawke Labor government). The earlier two scales are shown indexed (relative to a base year of 1984/85) in two ways—using the implicit deflator for private final consumption expenditure on the one hand and the movement in average weekly earnings on the other.

The top panel of the figure suggests that there has been significant under-indexation of the scale for changes in the price level. Naturally there have been many ups and downs along the road, with (often, pre-election) "tax cuts" offsetting periods of inflation-induced effective tax increases. Another type of change is illustrated by the S-shape introduced into the 1974/75 curve, which was the result of a clear attempt by the Whitlam Labor government to increase the progressivity of the personal tax system as it then stood.

Of course, over this thirty-year period there has been substantial growth in real incomes, and the second panel of Figure 4.2 shows an even more marked increase in average tax rates, once one accounts for movements in

FIGURE 4.2   Movement in Average Tax Rates in Australia, 1954/55 to 1984/85

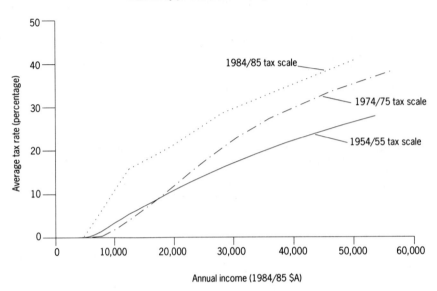

Indexed by private final consumption deflator

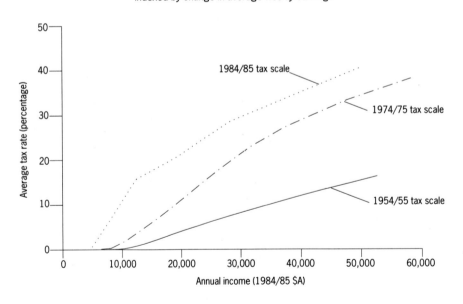

Indexed by change in average weekly earnings

SOURCE: *Budget Papers* (Canberra: Australian Government Publishing Service, various years); Australian Bureau of Statistics, *Average Weekly Earnings Australia (6302.0)* (Canberra).

those real incomes. This phenomenon has greatly facilitated the growth in revenue, and in the size of government itself, relative to the rest of the economy, as well as subjecting more and more taxpayers to higher marginal rates of tax. In terms of average weekly earnings (AWE), the top rate of 60 percent, which was reached by a person on 1.72 times AWE in 1984/85, would have required an income of 9.29 times AWE in 1954/55. And for those on average weekly earnings in 1984/85, the marginal rate of tax was 46 percent, compared with about 16 percent thirty years earlier.

In Table 4.4 we see that this trend has continued throughout the period of tax "reform." The highest rate of tax, although reduced to 49 percent, is now reached by taxpayers earning only 1.3 times the average.

Widespread avoidance and evasion. The large increase in the number of taxpayers facing high marginal tax rates has created in Australia, as in many other countries, high demand for means of avoiding and evading tax. This problem has been compounded by the growing number of tax shelters available.

One form of escape from the bite of higher marginal tax rates was the ever-widening array of employer-provided fringe benefits. Although the benefits were notionally taxable under the existing Income Tax Assessment

TABLE 4.4	Average Earnings and the Top Rate of Tax in Australia, 1954/55 to 1988/89			
Year	Average yearly earnings[a] ($A)	Highest tax bracket ($A)	Highest tax rate (%)[b]	Ratio of tax rate to average earnings (%)
1954/55	1,682	32,001	66.7	19.0
1959/60	2,149	32,001	66.7	14.9
1964/65	2,697	32,001	66.7	11.9
1969/70	3,707	32,001	66.7	8.6
1974/75	7,203	40,001	66.7	5.6
1979/80	12,042	33,217	61.1	2.8
1980/81	13,667	34,479	60.0	2.5
1981/82	15,824	35,789	60.0	2.3
1982/83	17,621	35,789	60.0	2.0
1983/84	19,111	35,789	60.0	1.9
1984/85	20,408	35,789	60.0	1.8
1985/86	21,706	35,001	60.0	1.6
1986/87	23,209	35,001	57.1	1.5
1987/88	24,605	35,001	49.0	1.4
1988/89[c]	25,958	35,001	49.0	1.3

a. Yearly figures derived from average weekly earnings of employed adult males.
b. These rates do not include the Medicare levy.
c. Growth in incomes of 5.5% is assumed for 1988/89.
SOURCE: Australian Bureau of Statistics, *Average Weekly Earnings Australia (6302.0)* (Canberra).

Act,[2] the failure of the authorities to apply the spirit of those provisions led to fringe benefits' forming an important part of many executive (and non-executive) remuneration packages. Benefits offered ranged from the ubiquitous company car to more exotic perquisites like company yachts, payment of children's school fees, and "hostess" allowances for wives of employees.

As with other countries, Australia's system of income taxation had, over time, become populated with a number of clearly identified tax shelters, that is, classes of investment specifically favored by the legislation for some reason or other. With the rising number of high marginal rate taxpayers, the attractiveness of investing in such shelters grew markedly. Some notable examples of Australian shelters are the following:

- *Gold mining.* Income from gold mining was exempt from company tax.
- *Film industry.* The local film industry was allowed a 133 percent deduction of capital invested in Australian films, together with tax exemption for 33 percent of any profits.
- *Superannuation.* Until the changes made in May of 1988 (discussed below), the income of superannuation funds was exempt from tax, contributions to funds made by employers were fully tax deductible, and lump sums (as distinct from annuities) paid out upon retirement were taxed at concessionary rates.
- *Research and development.* Investment in research and development and in high technology projects was favored by a number of initiatives, such as a 150 percent write-off of that investment.
- *Primary production.* Many types of investment (on soil conservation, fencing, storage improvements) associated with primary production have been allowed accelerated or immediate write-off. As well as constituting a form of tax shelter in itself, the tax losses available through primary production have been utilized to minimize tax payable on other sources of income. Additionally, as an industry experiencing fluctuating fortunes, primary production is "favored" with special averaging provisions in order to ameliorate the otherwise excessive taxation of primary income that would occur with the progressive tax rate scale. Both classes of special treatment have raised difficult problems as to the extent to which farm losses should be allowed against other taxable income.
- *Oil exploration.* Oil and other mineral exploration has generally been favored by allowing immediate write-off of exploration expenses. Investment in oil exploration companies also attracted a tax rebate.

Another notable form of escape from high marginal tax rates is, of course, the underground economy. Australia has had its fair share of speculation as to the size and scope of the black economy. Although estimates are no firmer than they are in other countries, the anecdotal evidence indicates that this area of activity is alive and well in those sectors of the economy to which it is particularly suited.

Avoidance and evasion activity has been of particular political importance in the movement toward tax reform. Politicians (and many others) often view this sort of activity purely in distributional terms, as a problem of making everyone pay their "fair share." Tax reform is represented as a task of pulling the avoiders into line, so that tax cuts will be possible for all those who obey the rules. The real problem with tax shelters, however, is inefficient resource allocation—they cause the market to work to align *post-tax* rather than pre-tax rates of return, resulting in economic inefficiencies. While the result in terms of base broadening may be the same, much of the blame—at least in the political arena—has typically been focused on the morality of the tax avoiders, rather than on the design defects of the tax base itself.

Narrow indirect tax base. As Table 4.2 notes, Australia ranked twenty-second, in 1983, among countries of the Organization for Economic Cooperation and Development (OECD) in terms of the revenue collected from general indirect taxes on goods and services. Many commentators on the tax system felt—and still feel—that this constitutes a major deficiency. Moreover, the adoption of a much more broad-based indirect tax (usually confusingly labeled a "consumption" tax) is seen by many as the only effective way of lowering the personal income tax burden.

What is certainly true is that existing indirect tax instruments are easily criticized. The most broad-based indirect tax is the federal government's wholesale sales tax (WST). This instrument suffers from the well-known defects of such taxes (including the exclusion of value added at the retail level, the exclusion of services, and the difficulty of defining the wholesale level) and is levied at a variety of rates on a fairly narrow range of items. Even more narrowly based, but nevertheless quite significant in revenue terms, are the excises levied on alcohol, tobacco, and petroleum products. Finally, there is a panoply of state government taxes and charges. Some of these are levied on services, but many (for example, alcohol and tobacco "franchises") are plainly levied on the sale of goods, even though state governments face a constitutional prohibition on the taxation of such transactions.[3]

Inadequate administration. While somewhat peripheral to the more familiar tax design issues, the problem of administering the tax system has emerged over recent years as an important element of the entire reform process.

The last few years have been traumatic for the Australian Taxation Office. The ATO has only a minor role in determining the direction of tax policy, but it is naturally regarded as a primary source of information on the present tax system and on the administrative feasibility and desirability of various changes. Concurrent with the debate on taxation, however, the ATO has been the subject of intense scrutiny over the adequacy of its own performance in administering the system. This scrutiny stemmed in large part from a series of "efficiency" audits performed by the commonwealth government's auditor-general.[4]

The major impressions given by these investigations were of a poorly computerized and excessively labor-intensive operation; of an administration unable to bring to tax significant components of the base (like interest income) because of the inadequacy of information returns and the inability to process effectively those information returns that were furnished; of an administration unable to provide proper information on the extent of evasion of one form and another; and of a body preoccupied with headline-grabbing "paper" avoidance schemes to the neglect of more routine and mundane collection activities.

Many of these defects have now been specifically addressed (see the discussion below), and there has been some evidence that the effect on revenue is considerable. Despite the natural focus of the reform debate on major areas of tax design, it may well prove that some of the most significant developments are those relating to simple issues of administration.

Achievement of Tax Reform

The progress on tax reform made in Australia since 1985 was the outcome of a steadily growing interest in such matters extending back over a decade. This attention was in no small measure due to the increasingly manifest weaknesses of the tax system. As a consequence, there has been bipartisan recognition that reform was long overdue—though there has not necessarily been agreement as to how that reform should occur.

Initial steps. The initial phase of the tax reform process can be traced back to the period prior to the election of the Hawke Labor government in 1983.

Contemporary interest in the tax system dates back to 1975, when two specialist committees of inquiry, the Asprey Taxation Review Committee and the Mathews Committee of Inquiry into Inflation and Taxation, reported in detail on taxation matters. Both reports were critical of the systems in existence and canvassed such major reforms as indexation of the tax system for inflation, integration of corporate and personal tax, and the adoption of a value-added tax. Like a number of full-fledged investigations conducted in other countries, however, they failed to lead to any marked change of direction. One key contributing factor to this (lack of) outcome would appear to be the attitude of the federal treasury,[5] which at the time showed little interest in a major restructuring of taxation.

More recently, the 1981 report of the Committee of Inquiry into the Australian Financial System (the Campbell Report) also tackled a number of taxation issues, including the tax treatment of businesses, superannuation funds, and other intermediaries. The report argued strongly in favor of taxation of economic income with its logical consequences of a reduction in the generosity of the tax treatment accorded to superannuation and life insurance, the closing down of other tax shelters, indexation of the tax base, and full integration of corporate and personal taxes.

Little of substance emerged, however, during the lifetime of the Fraser Liberal–National party government.[6] Treasurer John Howard's efforts to broaden the tax base met with less than total success. An attempt to apply the intent of the Income Tax Assessment Act by including in taxable income payments-in-kind—through declaring as taxable the "value" of subsidized accommodation in remote mining settlements—succeeded only in precipitating widespread industrial action and was abandoned. On the indirect tax front, efforts were made to extend the coverage of the wholesale sales tax, but they foundered on opposition from affected interest groups and failed to win legislative approval.

A longer-lasting initiative instituted by the government of Malcolm Fraser was the installation of a system of prescribed payments. Under this system, payments made to contractors in certain prescribed industries—chiefly those involving the building and allied industries, where tax evasion was long felt to be rife—are subjected to withholding of tax at source.

The consensus approach. The entry of Prime Minister Bob Hawke's Labor government into the tax reform game was clothed, like a number of other key policies, in the rhetoric of consensus.

The tax reform ball was set rolling when Hawke, seeking reelection for a second term, offered up as an election promise the notion of a "taxation summit" while being interviewed on radio. At the time this may have seemed a good idea—somewhat reminiscent of the National Economic Summit that was placed before the electorate before the 1983 elections. But whereas the economic summit proved to be a fairly innocent forum for platitudes and tokenism, the idea of applying the consensus approach to the area of taxation reform was more problematic.

The difficulties raised by the consensus approach are demonstrated by the criteria the prime minister enumerated in his formal announcement of a National Taxation Summit. Among the nine guiding principles were included requirements that there be no overall increase in the tax burden, that there be cuts to personal income tax, that tax avoidance and evasion should be "smashed," that the tax system should be simplified, that it should be fairer, that it should reduce or remove "poverty traps," and that it should attract widespread community support. Inevitably, of course, the period leading up to the summit was dominated by discussion of who would pay more and who would pay less, rather than by the principles of efficient tax design.

The agenda for the National Taxation Summit came from the government's 1985 Draft White Paper on the Reform of the Australian Tax System

(DWP), an official discussion paper documenting the deficiencies of current taxation arrangements and canvassing some options for reform.

First of all, the DWP outlined a number of potential base-broadening measures in the context of the direct income tax. Principally, these amounted to the removal of the major tax shelters in the treatment of business income, the replacement of the preexisting capital gains tax with a far more comprehensive version, the taxation of fringe benefits through the institution of an explicit fringe benefits tax, and the possibility of adopting some form of national identification or other unique numbering system as a means of combating evasion, social security fraud, and the like.

The DWP also mounted a case for indirect tax reform. This case was based first on the manifest deficiencies of the existing wholesale sales tax, but even more importantly—and somewhat curiously—on the suggestion that a partial switching from direct to indirect taxation would, of itself, improve incentives by lowering marginal tax rates. Significantly, one of the economist's main criteria for judging the desirability of such a tax switch—the removal, or lessening, of the intertemporal distortion between present and future consumption—played almost no part in the argument.

The DWP also presented three packages for reform, labeled Options A, B, and C. Option A consisted principally of the base-broadening measures alone. Given the restricted amount of revenue expected from such measures, the "tax cuts" to be delivered under Option A were fairly limited. The most adventurous option was C, which proposed the replacement of existing indirect taxes by a comprehensive broad-based consumption tax at a rate of 12.5 percent. This tax was essentially a form of retail sales tax, and offered the prospect of generating sufficient revenue to allow a significant reduction in the direct tax burden. It also offered the greatest difficulties in terms of compensation for low-income earners and welfare recipients, but even so, it was clearly the preferred path of reform for the DWP's authors.

Outcome. In terms of this preferred outcome, the tax summit was a failure. After several days of public and behind-the-scenes lobbying, the idea of implementing a new indirect tax was jettisoned by the prime minister, resulting in considerable embarrassment for the treasurer. Given that the summit was essentially a stage-managed attempt to win sufficient support for Option C, it would appear to have achieved little, once it became clear that that option lacked support. Little else emerged from the summit itself since the positions of most of the participants were widely known.

Perhaps the tax summit's most lasting legacy was in "softening up" the electorate for the tax reforms that ultimately did eventuate. In September 1985, Treasurer Paul Keating announced the government's preferred framework, basically consisting of a series of base-broadening measures combined with cuts to personal taxation and introduction of full imputation for corporate tax. Most of these measures was subsequently implemented, although some reversals were experienced, the introduction of a national identification card being the most notable example.[7]

A further set of reforms, principally in the area of business taxation and the treatment of superannuation, was announced in May of 1988. The major features of all of these measures are set out in Table 4.5 and are discussed in the next section. However, as a final commentary on the consensus approach to tax reform, it should be noted that several elements of the package have been the subject of considerable community opposition. In particular, the new fringe benefits tax and capital gains tax have been vehemently opposed by sections of the business community, although their future within the tax system now appears fairly secure.

The Current Position

In this section we assess the course that tax reform has taken thus far by reviewing the salient features of the present regime.

Personal income tax. Perhaps the most notable characteristic of Australia's personal income tax is that it remains the bulwark of the government's revenue collection. Of course, this is to be expected given the failure to introduce a new indirect tax. But the dominance of personal taxation is also the result of administrative changes to the way tax is assessed and collected and of the failure to index the tax brackets for inflation.

Since 1986 there have been some subtle yet major adjustments in the way the income tax is administered, which appear to have yielded benefits, at least in terms of revenue generation. The fiscal year 1986/87 saw the abandonment of the labor-intensive system of manual assessment, under which about one-third of the staff of the Australian Taxation Office (ATO) were engaged in the routine scrutiny of taxpayers' yearly returns. This essentially check-and-tick procedure has been replaced by a self-assessment system similar to that operated in the United States, whereby individual returns are accepted at face value, and a system of computer checks, audits, and information matching is used to achieve compliance. This change has meant the redeployment of a large number of ATO staff, but the basic assessment mechanism now seems better balanced and more cost-effective.

In combination with the move to self-assessment, the administrative treatment of deductible expenses—which had been something of a gray area—has been rationalized through the introduction of a system of substantiation. Under this system taxpayers are permitted to claim deductions below a certain threshold figure (presently $A300) even though they have little or no supporting documentation. While these deductions must be enumerated, and are supposed to be genuine, the understanding is that receipts and other supporting evidence will only be required (in the event, say, of a taxpayer

TABLE 4.5   The Progress of Australian Tax Reform

Proposals	Details	1985 decisions	Later developments
Personal taxation			
Tax scales	Size of reductions in tax rates to depend on extent of switch to indirect taxation	Limited personal tax cuts, paid for by base-broadening measures; top rate to be reduced from 60% to 49%	
National identification system	Tentative suggestion only, aimed principally at taxation	Full Australia Card proposal	Proposal abandoned in October 1987; alternative proposal based on upgraded tax file number put forward in May 1988
Concessional expenditure rebate	Abolition; replacement with rebate for unreimbursed medical expenses over $A1000	Implemented as proposed	
Indirect taxation			
Base broadening	Support for replacement of WST with a 12.5% broad-based consumption tax	Proposal abandoned; some rationalization of WST structure	Petroleum product excises increased
Business taxation			
Capital gains tax	Realization basis, on gains accruing from date of announcement; real gains and nominal losses included; exemption of principal residence	Implemented as proposed, but applying only to assets acquired from date of announcement	
Fringe benefits tax	Levied on employers at the corporate rate; abolition of deductions for entertainment	Implemented as proposed	Certain exemptions and modifications made
Negative gearing of rental property investments	Interest deductible only against rental income; depreciation allowed for new residential properties	Implemented as proposed	Decision reversed in 1987 budget

continued on following page

TABLE 4.5 (continued)

Proposals	Details	1985 decisions	Later developments
Quarantining of farm losses	Farm losses deductible only against farm income and a limited amount of nonfarm income	Implemented with less severe limit on amount of nonfarm income	
Taxation of gold mining		Not implemented	May 1988 announcement of the intention to tax income from gold mining from 1990
Capital subscribed to petroleum and afforestation companies	Abolition of rebates and deductions for this purpose; excess petroleum and mining expenses transferable between common ownership companies	Implemented as proposed	
Film industry concessions	133% deductibility and 33% exemption of earnings to be abolished	Deduction and exemption levels reduced to 120% and 20% respectively	May 1988, no exemption of income, deduction limited to 100% of investment
Accelerated depreciation	Adoption of indexed effective-life depreciation the preferred path; in the absence of indexation accelerated depreciation to be retained	No change to provisions	May 1988, introduction of effective-life depreciation
Integration of company and personal tax	Tentative support for partial or full imputation, on a revenue neutral basis	Full imputation, with a net cost to revenue	
Other			
Superannuation	No specific proposals in DWP	No major changes	May 1988, taxation of lump sums replaced by taxation of fund income as accrued and denial of deductibility for employer contributions to funds
Foreign tax credit system	Replacement of double taxation relief with a general foreign tax credit system	Implemented as proposed	May 1988 decision to tax income earned in "designated" countries on an accruals basis

Source: Budget Papers (Canberra: Australian Government Publishing Service, various years); Australia, Reform of the Australian Tax System: Draft White Paper (Canberra: Australian Government Publishing Service, 1985).

audit) from those taxpayers claiming deductions in excess of the threshold. Moreover, in this latter circumstance, receipts must potentially be furnished in support of *all* expenses claimed. Thus far, the system of substantiation appears to have been an unequivocal success for the ATO, and is credited as one of the factors leading to the better-than-expected budgetary outcomes in 1986/87 and 1987/88. The extent to which this success continues will depend on how taxpayers react as they become more familiar with the system.

The major change to the shape of the tax scale itself is the removal of the preexisting top marginal tax rate of 60 percent. The top rate has been lowered to 49 percent (actually 50.25 percent once one includes the compulsory Medicare levy[8]), and while there has been much discussion of the possibility of further reductions in this rate, particularly in view of the adoption of a 39 percent figure for corporate tax, the extent of any reductions below 49 percent is uncertain for the time being.

It is of no small significance that a Labor government has been responsible for lowering the top rate of tax. Although there is and has been disagreement as to what the top rate ought to be—the federal opposition arguing for a rate of 38 percent, combined with drastic cuts to government expenditure, at the last election—the days of rates well in excess of 50 percent seem to be past. There would appear to be a bipartisan recognition that particularly high marginal rates of tax have little more than symbolic value in terms of tax progressivity and are in fact more trouble than they are worth because of their stimulation of avoidance and evasion activity.

Like that of many other countries, Australia's personal tax scale is not formally indexed for inflation. Lack of indexation extends not only to the tax brackets themselves, but to the amounts and withdrawal thresholds of important tax rebates, such as the rebate for taxpayers with dependent spouses. We noted above how the lack of indexation has contributed to the structure (and some of the problems) of the tax regime. In the context of the present tax reform exercise, failure to index tax scales automatically has meant that the personal "tax cuts" have done little more—and at times somewhat less—than compensate taxpayers for the effects of bracket creep.[9]

Indirect taxation. As mentioned earlier, one of the major themes of taxation reform, the desire to introduce some new form of indirect taxation, was totally abandoned in the face of seemingly insurmountable political obstacles. Currently, all the major political parties are committed to platforms that specifically exclude the introduction of such a new tax, at least within the short to medium term.

Thus there has been almost no progress on the indirect tax front, not only as far as changing the mix of direct and indirect taxes is concerned, but also in restructuring the major current indirect taxes. Some modifications have been made to the wholesale sales tax, but these amount to little more than the continual tinkering that is always to be expected in the administration of such a tax. As for excises, a system of automatic semi-annual indexation for inflation has been introduced (as opposed to ad hoc budgetary announcements of increases in excises)—a step that seems somewhat hypocritical given the failure to index other parts of the tax system (most notably, the personal tax scale) where the ad hoc announcements bring political benefits rather than the bad publicity that surrounds excise increases.

One further significant step on the indirect tax front has been the conversion, in the face of falling world oil prices in 1985/86, of a substantial portion of the crude oil levy (a tax on domestic producers of crude oil that captures some of the margin between local production costs and the world price) into increased excise on petroleum products. While this step maintained government revenues even with the declining world price, and at least involved no *increase* in consumer prices, it has nevertheless exacerbated the distortive tendencies of the system of indirect taxation, since the crude oil levy, unlike the excise, does not distort consumption decisions.

Corporate taxation. It is likely that the most momentous changes to the Australian tax system have occurred in the area of corporations and the treatment of business income generally. These have moved the system firmly in the direction of taxing economic income by, on the one hand, broadening the base itself, and on the other, abandoning the classical system of corporate taxation in favor of one of full imputation of corporate tax.

The chief base-broadening measures, which were mentioned earlier, fall into the following categories:

- *Removal of shelters*. Action has been taken on most of the tax shelters that previously characterized the taxation of business income. One of the last to fall was the exemption of income from gold mining from corporate tax; the removal of this particular shelter was foreshadowed in the treasurer's 1988 May Economic Statement.
- *Entertainment deductions and fringe benefits*. Another major element of base broadening has been the explicit taxation of fringe benefits. (A precursor to the introduction of full fringe benefits taxation was the abolition, from September 1985, of any allowable deductions for entertainment expenses.) The fringe benefits tax, as introduced, is all-encompassing, purporting to cover all payments-in-kind, though with some specific and/or concessionary treatment of individual types of benefits (for example, motor vehicles). The tax is levied on employers at the rate of 49 percent, equal to the top rate of both the personal tax and, until its recent lowering, the corporate tax.
- *Capital gains*. The Australian capital gains tax (CGT) is probably closer to what economists regard as desirable than are the capital gains taxes of many other regimes. The tax is levied on real capital gains, when realized, and at the taxpayer's full marginal rate of tax (although there are some averaging provisions to prevent realized

gains from leading to excessive taxation when combined with the progressive tax scale). The major remaining defects, from the point of view of taxing true economic income, are that (1) only *nominal* capital losses are allowable for the purposes of calculating CGT, (2) the tax leads to the usual "lock-in" effect by allowing taxpayers to benefit by deferring the realization of accruing tax liabilities, and (3) the principal residence of the taxpayer is excluded from the scope of the tax. This last feature, together with the lack of taxation of the imputed income from owner-occupied housing, results in a major departure from the principles of income taxation in the case of one very prominent form of investment.

- *Changes to depreciation.* The changes to corporate taxation announced in May of 1988 included the abandonment of the previous system of accelerated depreciation (full write-off of investments in either three or five years) and its replacement with one of "true" economic depreciation (though with a loading of 20 percent on top of actual rates of depreciation). This change has largely been represented as a trade-off—somewhat along the lines of U.S. tax reforms—in return for a lower corporate tax rate. While there is undoubtedly some truth to this in terms of revenue, as far as measurement of the base is concerned, the accelerated rates of depreciation can be viewed as a political response to the distortions brought about by inflation. A relevant trade-off, therefore, would be to move to economic depreciation at the same time as the introduction of indexation of the tax base, but as yet this path remains to be pursued.

Introduction of capital gains taxation, as well as other base-broadening measures, would have threatened to convert the classical system of corporate taxation into one of true "double" taxation of corporate income. This eventuality was avoided, however, by the adoption of a major innovation—full imputation of corporate tax paid to the personal level.

The imputation system works by establishing a set of qualifying dividends that, when paid out to individual shareholders, carry with them credits for the corporate tax already paid. Based on the amount of tax actually paid in any one year, corporations are permitted to "frank" an amount of dividends equal to the residue of their taxable income—that is, dividends paid out of income in excess of taxable income (out of sheltered income) cannot be franked. When distributed to shareholders, these franked dividends serve to increase the taxable income of the individual shareholder by an amount equal to the corporate income out of which the dividend was paid, and also to extend a tax credit, in respect of that taxable income, equal to the corporate tax paid. The end result is to tax corporate income that is paid out as dividends once only, and at the marginal tax rate of the shareholder.

Moreover, it may be the case that this system of imputation approximates full integration even for corporate income that is not distributed. While it is true that if profits are retained, they will bear both corporate tax and, when realized, capital gains tax, companies also have the option of making "captive" distributions of profits that have the potential of escaping this additional liability to CGT. Just as was the case under the classical system, dividends paid in the form of, say, bonus shares are accorded the same treatment as dividends paid in cash. Whereas previously such a step was a highly undesirable means of retaining earnings within the company (since it subjected such earnings to the extra tax on dividends prior to their "reinvestment"), with imputation, payment of bonus shares offers a means of extending integration to retained earnings as well as distributions. Even though there is no formal means—of the type usually envisaged under systems of full integration—of imputing credits for tax paid on retained earnings to individual shareholders, the practical effect is very much the same, since the dilution of share values involved in the issue of bonus shares ought to serve to eliminate any future real capital gains liability.

Another important constraint facing designers of new corporate taxes is the need to meet the demands of taxation agreements with other countries, while at the same time not being overgenerous in the treatment of foreign investment in local corporations. Under imputation this constraint has been met by the cunning device of allowing imputation credits only against Australian tax liability.[10] Credits attaching to franked dividends that are paid to foreign shareholders are therefore not usable, so that such income bears the full rate of corporate tax. While the old system of withholding tax no longer applies for the payment of franked dividends, the expectation presumably is that distributions will be somewhat larger than was the case under the classical system. (For unfranked dividends, the withholding tax is still payable.)

In May of 1988, the treasurer announced, as part of a range of measures affecting companies, the lowering of the corporate tax rate from 49 percent to 39 percent. In large part this step has been viewed as one forced on the authorities in the light of lowered tax rates in other regimes (notably, New Zealand), while at the same time it compensates companies, in terms of revenue, for the elimination of the accelerated depreciation provisions.

Other aspects.

Interaction with the social welfare system. Over recent years there has been growing recognition that the tax-transfer system needs to be considered in its entirety; that is, that the various components of the social welfare system should be considered alongside the instruments of direct taxation.

This is necessary for two reasons. First, some aspects of the income tax clearly serve purposes related to social welfare. Examples in the Australian context are the tax rebates afforded to pensioners and beneficiaries and available to those supporting dependents, and of course the tax-free threshold itself. Second, there is considerable overlap between the two halves of

---

FIGURE 4.3   Effective Marginal Rates of Tax for Families in Australia, 1988

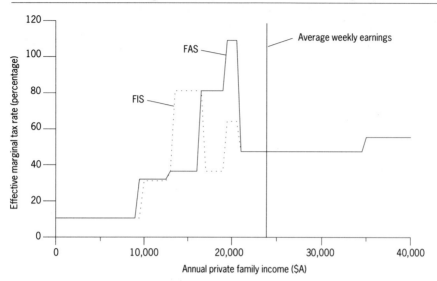

NOTE: The effective marginal tax rate (EMTR) includes net direct taxes, and the withdrawal of benefits. Calculations have been performed using the tax/transfer system as it would have applied in February 1988 to a single-income family with two children. See footnote 11 for details of the main features of the Family Income Support (FIS) and the Family Allowance Supplement (FAS).
SOURCE: Authors' estimates based on tax schedules, rebates, allowances, and deductions.

---

the tax-transfer system since, over time, both have extended their reach to lower (in the case of taxation) and higher (in the case of social welfare) income ranges.

A good example of this second phenomenon is the Family Allowance Supplement (FAS) introduced by the Labor government as part of an election commitment made in 1987. This scheme is somewhat similar to the Family Income Supplement that operates in the United Kingdom and pays means-tested benefits to families with children. The level at which benefits begin to be withdrawn is at around three-quarters of median income. The size of benefits and the rate of withdrawal is such that there is considerable overlap, for many beneficiaries, with the higher marginal rates levied under the income tax, since a rate of 40 percent applies at around median income. The situation is illustrated in Figure 4.3, which shows the "effective" (that is, including the contribution from benefit withdrawal) marginal rates of tax under the FAS scheme, and the FIS scheme that it replaced.[11]

Superannuation. Saving in the form of private pensions, or superannuation as it is termed in Australia, has long been heavily favored by the tax system. Before 1983, employer contributions to superannuation funds were tax deductible, the income of those funds was free of tax, and if the amounts owing were paid in a lump sum upon retirement, they were subjected to a minimal (5 percent of the lump sum) degree of taxation at that time. If paid in the form of an annuity, however, the private pension would be taxable at full income tax rates.

These arrangements gave to superannuation treatment that was effectively *more* generous than consumption tax treatment, and thus tended to contribute to both labor-leisure *and* consumption-savings distortions. In addition, the arrangements tended to encourage the conversion of the lump sums into other assets (a holiday house) or one-time acts of consumption (a round-the-world trip), enabling the recipient to retain eligibility for the state pension.

The Labor government's first attack on these problems involved the institution of a somewhat larger tax on the lump-sum component of superannuation benefits (15 percent or 30 percent, depending on the amount), and the introduction of an assets test to determine eligibility for the state pension. Both measures were vigorously opposed, but both survived.

Then, in the Economic Statement of May 1988, Treasurer Keating announced a thorough overhaul of the superannuation arrangements. The new provisions stipulate that employer contributions to private pension plans are no longer tax deductible and that the income of superannuation funds is to be taxable (though at a fairly low rate of 15 percent). In exchange, the tax on the lump sums when paid is reduced and in some cases removed altogether.

These changes are intended to achieve two basic objectives. The first is to lessen, to a degree, the tax advantage afforded to superannuation, while still retaining its status as a preferred form of saving. The second is to more effectively integrate superannuation funds into the new system of corporate taxation. When the income from funds was exempt from tax, fund managers had little interest in investing in companies that paid franked dividends under the imputation system. This situation has now been reversed. Indeed it was claimed at the time of the May statement that the imputation credits attaching to dividends paid to superannuation funds would be sufficient to fully extinguish their newly acquired tax liability.

Foreign-source income. At the time of publication of the Draft White Paper, Australia's treatment of income derived by residents in foreign jurisdictions was regarded by the government as seriously deficient. This treatment involved, in the absence of double taxation agreements that substituted specific arrangements, exempting income that had been taxed in another country—at whatever rate—from Australian tax.

The Draft White Paper suggested instead that a foreign-tax-credit system (FTCS) be introduced, and the government ultimately decided in the September 1985 reform package to proceed along these lines. The FTCS, which has operated since 1987/88, subjects foreign-source income to full rates of Australian tax and allows a tax credit (up to the amount of Australian tax liability) for any foreign tax paid.

The system has been further changed, however, by arrangements announced in the 1988 May statement, whereby a list of designated countries has been introduced. It is the government's intention to tax income derived in these designated countries (mostly tax havens) on an *accruals* basis, since even under the FTCS, the foreign profits of the subsidiaries of Australian companies could only be taxed when remitted in the form of dividends. In addition, where the tax system of a country is judged to be broadly similar to that of Australia, the government has also decided to modify the FTCS by exempting from corporate tax any foreign-source income. This move is a by-product of the lowering of the Australian corporate tax rate to levels similar to those of major trading partners, and is justified on the grounds of reducing compliance costs.

Future Prospects

As we noted at the outset of this chapter, much of the driving force behind tax reform in Australia stemmed from the perception that too large a share of the overall tax burden was accounted for by personal income tax, and in particular, by ordinary wage and salary earners from whom tax is collected on a pay-as-you-earn basis. Yet while tax reform has changed many features of the system, one thing it has not altered is this overwhelming emphasis on personal taxation as the primary revenue instrument. Throughout the entire reform period personal income tax has continued to account for around 53 percent of federal government revenues, while PAYE collections have remained at about 41 percent. The main reason for this continuing state of affairs is the total failure to expand, or significantly restructure, the instruments of indirect taxation. At present, this particular objective seems no closer than it did several years ago.

The result, in terms of the community's acceptance of tax reform, is consequently very much in the balance. On the one hand, base-broadening measures have led to a direct tax system that is perceived as fairer and less open to avoidance and evasion than was the case previously. But this very feature, combined with the lack of any shift in the emphasis away from direct taxation, has continued to foster calls for further progress on tax rate reduction. Abolition of the 60 percent rate has certainly helped limit some of the "higher-profile" forms of tax avoidance, but bracket creep has simultaneously driven the bulk of wage and salary earners into 40 percent and 49 percent tax brackets. This is illustrated in Table 4.6, which shows the average and marginal tax rates for persons on average earnings. The table also shows the decline in disposable incomes brought about by the failure to insulate taxpayers from bracket creep.

It seems impossible to discuss the future of the tax system without reference to questions of the size of government and broader macroeconomic considerations. At the time of the National Taxation Summit, the govern-

TABLE 4.6   Disposable Incomes and Tax Rates in Australia, 1954/55 to 1988/89

Year	Average earnings[a] ($A)	Disposable income[b] ($A)	Change in disposable income (%)	Average tax rate (%)	Marginal tax rate (%)
1954/55	14,500	13,176	n.a.	9	18
1959/60	15,801	14,095	7.0	11	21
1964/65	17,456	15,049	6.8	14	25
1969/70	20,038	16,390	8.9	18	33
1974/75	24,458	18,662	13.9	24	40
1979/80	24,084	18,694	0.2	22	33
1980/81	24,940	19,319	3.3	23	32
1981/82	26,417	20,205	4.6	24	32
1982/83	26,578	20,190	−0.1	24	35
1983/84	26,879	20,619	2.1	23	31
1984/85	27,120	20,701	0.4	24	47
1985/86	26,699	20,170	−2.6	24	47
1986/87	26,195	19,624	−2.7	25	45
1987/88	25,955	19,467	−0.8	25	41
1988/89[c]	25,958	19,249	−1.1	26	41

n.a. = not available.
a. Average yearly earnings derived from average weekly earnings of employed adult males.
b. Real disposable incomes are calculated using the implicit price deflator for private final consumption expenditure.
c. Growth in incomes and prices of 5.5% is assumed for the 1988/89 year.
SOURCE: Australian Bureau of Statistics, *Average Weekly Earnings Australia (6302.0)*, and *Australian National Accounts (5204.0)* (Canberra).

ment was at pains to emphasize that the debate on tax reform should be conducted under the assumption of revenue neutrality. This decision was a response to political opponents who were attempting to convert the issue of tax reform into one of reducing the size of the public sector and lowering the overall level of taxation. Yet despite the fact that the assumption of revenue neutrality is necessary from the theoretical perspective, the practical politics of the situation has meant that revenue neutrality has been honored more in the breach than in the observance.

Since the task of tax reform commenced, the revenue side of the federal government's budget has blossomed. This has resulted in part from the base-broadening measures, and in part from the quite cynical use of bracket creep to maintain and even increase personal taxation, despite the "tax cuts" included as part of the reform package. The major consequence has been the transformation of the usual budget deficit into a substantial surplus. By 1988/89, the public sector borrowing requirement for *all* levels of government, including public authorities, had been reduced to around zero (although a substantial stock of debt remains).

Significantly, this task—an important one in the context of Australia's fragile external balance—has been aided by reductions in the spending side of the budget. While it is apparent that in the long term inflation-induced personal tax increases have funded an ever-expanding public sector, the years since 1985 have witnessed some progress in curtailing the growth of government. Provided this resolve is maintained, there is clearly scope to honor some of the rhetoric of the tax reform campaign by permanently lowering rates of personal tax. Just how and to what extent this occurs remains for the future.

Recent Tax Reform in Canada: Policy Responses to Global and Domestic Pressures

On June 18, 1987, the Canadian federal government announced its long-awaited tax reform package (Canada. Department of Finance 1987a). The aim of reform was to reduce corporate and personal tax rates, consolidate personal rate brackets, replace deductions and exemptions at the personal level by credits, sharply reduce investment incentives in the corporate tax, and initiate major change in the sales tax area. This chapter documents these proposals, attempts to explain the objectives behind them, and evaluates some of their effects. In the process, these changes are also placed in the context of tax changes occurring in other countries at the same time, and the pressures these brought to bear in the Canadian case.

In part, the Canadian reforms reflect the influence of international factors on the national tax policies of middle-sized or small countries. They are less the outcome of a conscious strategy for improving the Canadian tax system than they are a response to pressures generated by falling corporate and personal tax rates around the world and the perception that the Canadian tax system has undermined the country's international competitiveness. This is not to say that international factors are the only ones underlying reform, but they are certainly important.

I am grateful to Michael Boskin and A. Lawrence Chickering for comments, and to Leigh MacDonald for help in preparing Table 5.1.

Canada has a federal structure, with ten provinces responsible for the majority of public sector expenditures (particularly in education and health care). These coexist with a federal government in Ottawa. Under this political structure, there is a multilevel tax system with individual, corporate, and sales taxes levied by both the provincial and federal governments and property taxes levied by municipalities. After the reform the tax system will feature federal individual income taxes ranging from 17 to 29 percent on

TABLE 5.1   Main Features of Canada's Tax System

Tax	Main features	Share of federal tax revenues in 1986/87 (%)[a]
Income tax[b]	• Annual tax on worldwide incomes of individuals	47.4
	• Indexation of rate brackets and allowances	
	• Lifetime capital gains exemption of Can$100,000; inclusion rate of ⅔ (1988) and ¾ (1989)	
	• Dividend tax credit (13⅓% of "grossed up" dividend from Canadian sources)	
	• Provincial taxes set at a fraction of federal taxes	
	• Credits for disability, pension income, Canada Pension Plan and unemployment insurance contributions, tuition fees and education, net medical expenses, charitable donations	
	• Deduction for business expenses relating to home, offices, automobiles, meals, and entertainment	
Corporate tax	• Annual federal and provincial tax on worldwide profits of corporations	12.4
	• Lower tax rate on manufacturing and processing activity	
	• Lower tax rate on small business income	
	• Tax credits to encourage R&D and investments in lower-income provinces	
	• Declining-balance capital cost allowance on manufacturing and processing equipment, extraction equipment, new mine assets, offshore drilling vessels at 25% rate (to be phased in by 1991)	
	• Investment tax credit now effectively eliminated	
	• Insurance companies and financial institutions taxed differently	
Sales and excise taxes	• Federal manufacturer's sales tax (12%); tax on value of manufactures produced or imported into Canada for domestic sale; complex definition of tax base, and limited product coverage (around 30% of consumption)	25.4
	• Provincial retail sales taxes: tax rates on retail sales value by province are Alberta, 0%; Ontario, 8%; Newfoundland, 12%; Quebec, 9%; Prince Edward Island and Nova Scotia, 10%; New Brunswick, 11%; British Columbia, 6%; Saskatchewan and Manitoba, 7%	
	• Federal and provincial excise taxes: federal taxes on tobacco and alcoholic products, 18%; gasoline, 12% (imposed on an ad valorem basis); miscellaneous taxes on automobiles and automobile air conditioners, clocks, watches and jewelry, smokers' accessories, coin-operated amusement games, playing cards, airline fares	

continued on following page

income net of deductions (with a province surcharge varying from 43 to 60 percent of federal tax),[1] federal corporate tax rates ranging from 12 to 28 percent (with additional provincial taxes varying from 10 percent to 17 percent),[2] and a federal manufacturer's sales tax system with a rate of 12 percent. This system collects federal, provincial, and local taxes amounting to about 33.5 percent of gross national product (GNP).[3] The principal elements of Canada's tax system appear in Table 5.1.

Recent changes to this system have not proved to be sweeping and do not embody the comprehensive approach of earlier reform proposals, such as that by the Carter Commission in the mid-1960s (see Royal [Carter] Commission on Taxation 1966). Rather, the recent round of tax reform in Canada has been driven by a strongly felt need in government circles to modify rather than fundamentally restructure three major components of the tax system: personal, corporate, and sales taxes.

The most significant reforms are those planned but not yet enacted for the federal sales tax. These involve replacing the existing manufacturer's

TABLE 5.1 (continued)

Tax	Main features	Share of federal tax revenues in 1986/87 (%)[a]
Property taxes (municipal)	• Annual municipal tax on assessed value of property (land and buildings)	
	• Different rates for residential and nonresidential property	
	• Business tax on one of a number of bases (rental value, real property assessment, stock in trade, square footage, plus fixed annual fees)	
Social security contribution	• Mainly Canada Pension Plan (and Quebec Pension Plan) and unemployment insurance	12.0
Resource taxes	• Federal government royalties levied on oil, natural gas, and mineral production from federally owned Crown lands including the Yukon, Northwest Territories, Beaufort Sea, Arctic Islands, Hudson Bay, and the east and west coast offshore areas	0.6[c]
	• Provincial mining tax: ad valorem tax on mining profits	
	• Provincial logging tax: charge for use of timber rights on Crown lands	
	• Federal government royalties imposed on mineral production in the Yukon and Northwest Territories	
	• Export charge on softwood lumber (federal)	
Other miscellaneous taxes	• Air transportation tax; amusement tax (provincial); meal and lodging tax (provincial); motor vehicle registration and permits (provincial); hospitalization and medical insurance premiums (provincial); land transfer tax (provincial); fur tax (provincial); insurance premium tax (provincial); racetrack tax (provincial); nonresident tax	2.2
Total		100.0

a. Total federal tax revenues in 1986/87 were Can$79.9 billion.
b. All credits are nonrefundable.
c. Does not include royalties paid for use of Crown lands.
SOURCE: Various Canadian government documents.

sales tax with a broadly based alternative sales tax, probably some form of value-added tax. For the personal and corporate taxes, despite the rate reductions and other changes, many of the central elements of the existing structure remain.

Government tax reform documents have generally not provided a rationale for change based on an analysis of where the tax system should be headed, but have largely concentrated on proposing tax changes thought to be needed in light of various pressures operating on the tax system both internationally and domestically. This chapter emphasizes how these pressures have shaped what has emerged from this reform process.

The Direction of Recent Canadian Tax Reform

Before discussing further the objectives underlying recent Canadian reform, it may help to describe the changes in more detail, including both an initial round of changes to the corporate income tax (announced in February 1986), which preceded the June 1987 package, and the plans to subsequently change the sales tax.[4]

Corporate income tax changes. The changes to the corporate income tax announced in June 1987 represent a continuation of the approach taken in a May 1985 Canadian government discussion paper *The Corporate Income Tax System: A Direction for Change*. This paper argued that the extensive use of the corporate tax as an instrument for achieving nontax policy goals in the past had led to a maze of special provisions for particular industries. In combination, these resulted in substantial variations, even if often intended, in tax treatment across sectors.

The corporate tax also favored investment in certain types of assets over others. For example, investment in equipment and machinery had generally received more favorable tax treatment than investment in buildings. Also, because of incentives for the use of tax-oriented activities to minimize taxes, many firms had accumulated substantial tax losses, making the corporate tax potentially an unstable revenue source. The 1987 reform document notes, for instance, that unused deductions were on the order of Can$13.8 billion in 1981, compared with total corporate tax collections in 1981 of Can$8.0 billion.

The idea behind reform, then, was to move the system closer to neutrality by weakening investment incentives and, as far as possible, removing differential tax treatment across investment vehicles. The theme of the 1985 discussion paper was that a system with fewer and more generally available incentives would be both simpler and more effective. Two sets of corporate tax changes resulted: Phase I in the February 1986 budget and Phase II as part of the June 1987 reform package. Phase I of the corporate changes reduced the general corporate tax rate from 36 percent to 33 percent. Phase II cut rates further to 28 percent.

In addition to rate reductions, other changes were also made. Before 1986, an investment tax credit was available on investments in agriculture, fishing, forestry, manufacturing, processing, and resource industries, and on certain construction and transportation equipment. The rate varied from 7 to 20 percent depending on the region of the country in which the investment was made. Phase I of the corporate tax changes abolished the general investment tax credit along with transportation and construction credits. Phase II reduces a special Atlantic Canada investment tax credit from 20 to 15 percent and research and development investment tax credits from 30 to 15 percent, and eliminates the research and development credit on buildings.

Changes have also been made in depreciation or capital cost allowances (CCAs). Over the years, acceleration of tax allowances for various assets has produced an uneven pattern across assets. The reform package attempts to reduce this variance in treatment by reducing CCA rates for a number of assets to 25 percent on a declining-balance basis. These include manufacturing and processing equipment, extraction equipment, new mine assets, and offshore drilling vessels.[5]

These corporate tax changes also affect the treatment of insurance companies and banks. For insurance companies the most significant changes concern the computation of Canadian investment income: the elimination of policy dividend reserves, a reduction in allowable policy reserves, and changes in the unpaid claim reserve. The 1987 changes also saw the introduction of a revised version of the 15 percent tax on investment income of life insurance companies (a similar tax had earlier operated between 1969 and 1978).

Before the reform, special rules had also applied to banks for computing loan loss reserves. They were allowed to deduct prescribed aggregate reserves (PAR) and transfer and average their loan losses over five years. The reform ends these arrangements and places deductions for bad and doubtful debt for banks on a par with those for other financial institutions.

Other corporate tax changes in the 1987 package include the elimination both of a 3 percent inventory allowance and of earned depletion allowances. Pre-start-up interest costs for real estate operators and developers now have to be capitalized. Furthermore, allowable entertainment expenses have been reduced, and the inclusion rate for capital gains has been increased first to 66.6 percent and subsequently to 75 percent.

Sales tax changes. The June 18, 1987, reform package also announced plans to change the existing federal sales tax in Canada—the manufacturer's sales tax. This will be accomplished in two stages. Stage I, announced as part of the June 18 changes, involves a series of small modifications to the existing system. Stage II, which aims for more fundamental reform, will follow, although no explicit timetable was set.

Stage I changes are largely designed to generate additional revenue to help finance personal tax cuts elsewhere in the reform package. The point of taxation for several commodities has been moved to the wholesale level (such as sporting goods and records), and the tax will now apply to the sales of marketing companies related to a manufacturer. The sales tax on cable and pay-television services has been increased by 8 to 10 percent, and a new 10 percent tax on telecommunication services has been introduced. To offset the increased sales tax burden, the refundable sales tax credit in the income tax has been increased by Can$20 per adult and Can$10 per child.

Stage II of the proposal will abolish the tax and replace it with a broadly based multistage sales tax. The aim is to deal with a long list of problems with the existing sales tax, since repeated previous attempts at piecemeal reform have been tried and found inadequate. There is a sense now that fundamental reform is necessary (see Gillis 1985).

These problems are as follows. First, there is the narrowness of the tax base. The present federal manufacturer's sales tax is collected on a base that corresponds to only about one-third of consumption, and among taxed items there are differences in tax rates. The tax also applies not only to manufactures destined for sale to consumers, but to certain capital goods and material inputs (such as fuels), resulting in pyramiding of the tax. Current estimates are that nearly one-half of the present sales tax revenue is collected on items purchased for business use (see Kuo et al. 1985). This also results in a bias against exports since the tax component of input costs is carried through to become, in effect, a tax on exports.[6] Biases also operate against the production of investment goods, both directly through taxes on capital goods and indirectly through taxes on inputs used in their production. Furthermore, since the tax is primarily collected from manufacturers, costs beyond the manufacturing stage, such as transportation costs, wholesale margins, and retail margins, are largely excluded from the tax base. This type of coverage causes tax variables to influence location and vertical integration decisions and leads to a wide variation in effective tax rates (the ratio of tax to final selling price).

There is also a bias in favor of imports, because the tax is assessed using the duty-paid value on entry to Canada. This method of valuation may exclude warranty and advertising costs and transportation costs to the border before importation into Canada, even though these costs are typically included in the tax base for domestic manufacturers. Recent estimates suggest that taxes on imports are on average 30 percent lower than those on comparable domestic products (see Canada. Department of Finance 1987c).

The diverse channels that a good may follow between the manufacturer and the consumer have also resulted in substantial use of notional, or administered, values in the calculation of taxes owed by firms. These introduce further differences across firms in effective sales tax rates and create an administratively complex system.

The June 18, 1987, tax package (also called the White Paper) suggests that a new tax could take one of three forms: a federal-only value-added tax (VAT) administered using the credit-invoice method; a federal-only goods and services tax (GST), which would be similar to a VAT except that it would be administered using a subtraction method; and a joint federal-provincial credit-invoice VAT that would also replace existing provincial retail sales taxes. The difference between the two federal-only options is largely administrative; their economic effects should be identical. A new sales tax would apply to most goods and services in the economy, including the financial sector, although the latter would be taxed in a somewhat modified form.

An integral part of any sales tax change seems certain to be an increase in the present refundable sales tax credit. This measure would be motivated by the possible inclusion of "essential" items such as food, clothing, and shelter in the new sales tax base. The magnitude of such a credit will presumably follow from the number and type of goods exempted.

Personal income tax changes. Changes to the personal income tax as part of the reform package include a reduction in statutory rates along with the conversion of many of the present exemptions and deductions into credits, concentrating the benefits of tax reductions on lower-income families.

The net effect of all these changes is to reduce the top federal marginal tax rate from 34 to 29 percent and the number of tax brackets from ten to three. The pre- and postreform rate schedules are presented in Table 5.2. The

TABLE 5.2   Federal Personal Income Tax Rates in Canada, before and after Reform, 1988

Taxable income (Can$)[a]	Statutory rates (%)	
	Before reform	After reform
0–1,334	6	17
1,334–2,668	16	17
2,668–5,336	17	17
5,336–8,004	18	17
8,004–13,340	19	17
13,340–18,676	20	17
18,676–24,012	23	17
24,012–27,500	25	17
27,500–37,352	25	26
37,352–55,000	30	26
55,000–64,032	30	29
64,032+	34	29

a. Note that the definition of taxable income is different after the reform. Postreform taxable income is closer to gross income because of the elimination of exemptions.
SOURCE: Canada, Department of Finance, *Tax Reform 1987: The White Paper* (Ottawa, June 18, 1987).

TABLE 5.3   Conversion of Exemptions to Credits under Proposed Income Tax Changes in Canada, 1987

Exemption	Existing exemption (Can$/year)	Value of credit (Can$/year)
Basic personal	4,270	1,020
Married	3,740	850
Elderly (over age 65)	2,670	550
Child (age 18 or younger)	470	65

Source: Canada, Department of Finance, *Tax Reform 1987: The White Paper* (Ottawa, June 18, 1987).

cost of these rate reductions is to be financed in part by a number of base-broadening measures described below.

Under the changes, existing exemptions will be converted to income tax credits in order to provide increased benefits to low-income individuals and households. Table 5.3 details these changes for the tax year 1988. The present exemption for children over seventeen years of age is to be eliminated.

Most other existing deductions will also be converted into credits. The disability deduction (Can$2,920 in 1988) will be converted to a credit of Can$550. Deductions for pension income, Canada Pension Plan contributions, unemployment insurance contributions, tuition fees and education, and net medical expenses (in excess of 3 percent of net income) will be converted to credits at the lower tax rate (17 percent). Charitable donations will be creditable at 17 percent for contributions up to Can$250 and at 29 percent for contributions over Can$250.

A number of deductions, including a Can$1,000 investment income deduction and an employment expense deduction, will also be eliminated. The deduction for CCA on multiple-unit residential buildings will no longer be allowed to produce a rental loss. Forward income averaging will also be gradually eliminated.

Some deductions will be retained, but only in a restricted form. These include deductions for business expenses relating to home offices, automobiles, meals, and entertainment. The CCA rate for films, which is currently 100 percent, will only apply against film income.[7]

The 1987 reforms also freeze the lifetime capital gains exemption at Can$100,000 rather than the earlier planned limit of Can$500,000, except for farmers and those with shares in small businesses. The inclusion rate of capital gains beyond the exemption will be increased from one-half to two-thirds in 1988 and 1989, and will be three-quarters thereafter.

Planned increases in contribution limits for private pensions from their current level of Can$7,000 to Can$15,500 by the year 1991 are to be phased in more slowly, so that the Can$15,500 limit will take effect in 1996.

Finally, because of the changes in corporate tax rates, the credit given to dividend income to compensate for taxes paid at the corporate level has been reduced from 33⅓ percent of cash dividends to 25 percent. This implies reducing the gross up rate from 33⅓ percent to 25 percent and reducing the credit rate on grossed-up dividends from 16⅔ percent to 13⅓ percent.

Factors Influencing the June 1987 Tax Reform Package

International factors played a role in all three tax areas covered by the proposals of Canada's June 1987 tax reform package. At the corporate level, the proposals to further lower statutory rates, eliminate the investment tax credit, and substantially reduce the acceleration of depreciation allowances reflect the direction that changes in corporate taxes have been taking in other countries. Such reforms have occurred in the United Kingdom, with its 1984 budget, and in the United States, with the 1986 Tax Reform Act, and more recent reforms (or attempted reforms) have taken place in Japan, New Zealand, and Australia (see Japan, Ministry of Finance 1988; Due 1988; Morgan 1986).

In all of these countries, including Canada, it has been argued that widespread use of investment incentives has resulted in highly variable, although on average low, effective tax rates on investments across different assets and across different industries. This variability is seen as a major source of nonneutrality in the tax system, which economic efficiency dictates should be removed. To both raise and harmonize these effective rates, investment incentives are to be phased out. And because the reform is to be revenue-neutral, the statutory rate will be lowered. Curiously, these changes in effect lower statutory rates to raise effective rates.

The international pressures operating in the Canadian case are reflected in the acceptance in Canada of the view that it is necessary to follow reductions in tax rates abroad. Reduced tax rates in the United States, it is argued, will lead to large amounts of new debt financing by Canadian affiliates of foreign parents. Around 50 percent of the Canadian manufacturing sector is foreign-owned, and since the consolidated parent-subsidiary entities span national borders, debt financing gravitates to where tax rates are higher. The situation, left uncorrected, would lead to a substantial erosion of the tax base in Canada, and therefore Canadian statutory rates must be reduced. Furthermore, many in tax policy circles in Canada believe that Canadian taxes must not become binding on foreign investment, for with lowered corporate tax rates in the United States, the foreign tax credit may no longer be large enough to offset Canadian taxes on Canadian-source foreign income repatriated to the United States.

At the personal level, the proposed changes include a consolidation of the existing ten rate brackets into three, reductions in statutory rates, the conversion of many existing exemptions into tax credits, and changes in the tax treatment of capital gains. The perceived need for some of these changes again, in part, reflects the influence of tax changes abroad. One argument is that unless Canada follows United States rate reductions at the personal level there will be increased outward migration from Canada. Another, and one that seems currently to have strong support in other countries, is that rate reductions are required to keep disincentive effects of taxes under control.

The rationale for the other changes at the personal level is less obvious. The idea of converting exemptions into credits has existed for a long time, and many arguments have been made on both sides (see Thirsk 1980). Tax design purists usually argue in favor of exemptions rather than credits, on the grounds that one first identifies the base and then applies a rate structure to it. The rationale offered for credits is that they are fairer for the poor, since all taxpayers receive equal dollar credits.

The changes in capital gains treatment seem not to be clearly motivated by well-articulated tax design objectives. There is indeed the possibility that this package of changes may have been simply a convenient way to partially limit the preferential treatment given to capital gains through a Can$500,000 lifetime exemption introduced in the first (1985) budget of the Mulroney government.

International factors are least prominent in the third component of the proposed changes, involving the federal sales tax. Here, it is the dissatisfaction with the existing sales tax that seems to be the driving force behind reform. These changes are to be implemented in two stages. The first involves a series of relatively minor modifications to the existing federal manufacturer's sales tax, which include moving the tax point to the wholesale level for several items and changing the tax treatment of marketing companies. The second stage is much more wide-ranging and involves fundamental reform of the sales tax; the proposal is to abolish the existing sales tax and replace it with some form of broadly based multistage tax.

Three options are presented in the June 18 document: a federal-only value-added tax (VAT) administered on a credit-invoice basis similar to that used in Europe, a federal-only goods and services tax (effectively a subtraction-method VAT), and a joint federal-provincial credit-invoice VAT to replace the provincial retail sales taxes as well as the federal sales tax. A credit-invoice VAT applies taxes at each stage of processing (including retailing) to the total value of sales and allows a tax credit for taxes paid on inputs. Imports are taxed on entry to the country; exports leave tax-free. A GST (or subtraction-method VAT) taxes the difference between the value of sales and material costs at each stage of processing. Its effect is the same as a credit-invoice VAT, except that no crediting mechanism is used.

By general agreement this component of the package is potentially the most significant in the whole tax reform exercise, because the change is the most extensive. It is also the most difficult to evaluate, since, at the time of writing, the details of the Stage II changes have yet to be announced.

The choice of a replacement for the existing manufacturer's sales tax has long been debated in public finance circles in Canada (see Gillis 1985). The discussion begins from the null hypothesis that a federal retail sales tax would be infeasible because it would be viewed by provincial governments as an intrusion on their taxing powers. This, in part, explains the focus on the value-added tax as an alternative broadly based tax.

Among value-added tax systems, the credit-invoice and subtraction methods are the two choices most discussed. Introducing a subtraction-method tax would be an innovative step, because it has never been used by any country. There are, however, good reasons for the lack of use. The border tax adjustments are difficult to execute if the tax is anything other than a tax on a comprehensive base at a single rate. This is because rebating taxes on exports at the border would involve calculating taxes paid earlier in the production chain, and if different rates apply to different transactions the effective tax rate is hard to calculate. Equally, calculating what tax rate to charge on imports is difficult. In addition, any multirate system is complicated to administer. The objective is to have multiple tax rates on commodities, but because transactions are taxed at different stages of production, the effective rates on a commodity basis are hard to calculate, even if the tax is fully passed forward.

A credit-invoice VAT is widely viewed as a more attractive replacement to the current sales tax, but this alternative has also been criticized. The tax could create additional compliance costs for small business, as a result of both extra record keeping and frequent filing requirements. Concerns over the treatment of small business were prominent in some of the early debates in Canada on a possible sales tax replacement, and they were one of the main reasons why other options, including the subtraction method, have also been considered as part of the reform exercise.

Because of the border tax adjustments and multiple-rate problems, it is widely believed that any joint federal-provincial subtraction-method VAT would be infeasible, and, as a result, in the federal government tax reform document the only reference is to a possible joint federal-provincial credit-invoice VAT. Such a tax would involve a uniform-rate federal tax with different rates by province to replace existing provincial taxes. Provincial surcharges would thus be applied to a uniform national base. Even this option, however, raises many questions. How will interprovincial trade and associated border tax adjustments between provinces be treated? What happens if some provinces come into the system and some stay out? Must all provinces use the common federal tax base or can provinces have some autonomy over what base their provincial surtax is applied to?

The formal rebating of taxes on interprovincial exports as they leave a province, and corresponding taxes imposed on imports entering a province, cannot be done in the same way as they are at the national border for international transactions, because there are no interprovincial border controls. A centralized agency in Ottawa that debits the account of the exporting province and credits the account of the importing province, with each transaction showing up on the federal tax return, seems to be the only way to proceed. The information-processing requirements for such a system become an issue. A system with some provinces participating and others not (with the latter maintaining their retail sales taxes) seems no less feasible than a complete joint federal-provincial plan, but strikes many as both inelegant and probably inefficient. And finally, provinces could in principle each have different tax bases, but only by further complicating the administration of an already cumbersome joint federal-provincial system.

In summary, then, there are really two distinct segments to recent Canadian tax reform. One consists of changes to corporate and personal taxes that roughly parallel those in other countries: rate reductions at the personal level and rate reductions and virtual elimination of investment incentives at the corporate level. International factors produced concern over erosion of the corporate tax base from increased debt financing and the effects on inward foreign investment and outward labor mobility. The second segment is reform of the sales tax, driven largely by dissatisfaction with the present antiquated Canadian manufacturer's sales tax. International factors, while present, are less important here, and if the proposals are implemented, the change will be deeper and more fundamental.

Economywide Effects of Canadian Tax Reform

The major aims of the Canadian tax reform are to address special problems created by lowered tax rates abroad and, more generally, to improve the efficiency of the economy, thereby enhancing international competitiveness.[8] Tax-induced inefficiencies arise from many sources. Because sectors, products, and assets are treated in different ways under the tax system, lightly taxed sectors tend to attract more resources than they would under a neutral tax system, and heavily taxed sectors, less. From an economy-wide point of view, this results in an inefficient allocation of resources (see Harberger 1974 for a discussion of the efficiency effects of taxes). Inefficiencies also arise from distortions of factor-supply decisions (including the supply of effort), distortions of intercommodity effects in consumption and intermediate use due to uneven tax treatment across products and sectors, and inter-asset distortions within sectors due to differing tax treatment among assets.

One of the more prominent objectives of the reform package for efficiency was to increase the supply of effort (labor supply) by lowering marginal tax rates. Since the largest rate reductions have been concentrated on those in higher tax brackets, it follows that the most pronounced labor-supply effects will occur there. Lowered taxes on labor income have, however, come partially at the expense of increased taxation of capital income (such as capital gains), and this reduces the level of savings. In addition, the composition of savings will change, for the relative tax treatment among savings vehicles has changed. Thus, the efficiency gains in labor supply are somewhat offset by these increased intertemporal distortions resulting from the heavier taxation of capital income.

On the investment side, prereform corporate taxes distort both the level and the composition of investment. In assessing the efficiency effects of the reform package, however, it is important to distinguish carefully between changes in statutory and effective tax rates in the corporate area. Effective tax rates not only capture reductions in statutory rates, they also indicate changes in investment incentives, because they reflect the total tax effect on investment decisions by firms (see King and Fullerton 1984). The 1986 and 1987 reforms reduce statutory tax rates but raise effective tax rates slightly, suggesting that the level of investment may fall.

Changes in the tax treatment of various types of investments will also produce interasset effects. For example, under prereform tax treatment, investment in equipment is tax-preferred relative to investment in structures, and the reform reduces the variance in tax treatment among different assets. Intersectoral effects of the corporate tax changes will occur either directly, via changes in the relative importance of sector-specific incentives, such as the manufacturing and processing incentive, or indirectly, through the removal of preferential treatment for assets heavily used by various sectors. Reduced intersectoral and interasset distortions should therefore lead to efficiency gains, which will partially offset the effects on investment of the overall increase in effective tax rates. Planned sales tax reforms are also expected to have effects on savings and investment. The reduced tax burden on capital goods should reduce the cost of capital and thus increase investment, although the magnitude of the effect is uncertain.

What one believes all these tax changes do to investment and savings depends in large part on one's assumptions. It is common, for instance, to characterize Canada as a small open economy that faces an exogenous rate of return on capital determined on world markets. It is also typical to assume that the marginal investors in Canada are foreigners. Under this scenario, changes in domestic savings have no effect on aggregate investment, and merely change the level of foreign investment. Also, changes in corporate taxes are either very important or largely irrelevant for the overall level of investment, depending upon foreign-tax-credit arrangements in source countries.

The greatest effects on the composition of consumption and production seem likely to follow from the planned sales tax changes in Stage II of the reform. The existing sales tax strikes manufacturers, creating problems of a narrow tax base and pyramiding; favors imports over domestic goods; and encourages the use of margin industries (retail and wholesale trade, transportation). Under the new broadly based tax, consumption of manufactured goods should increase, consumption of imports should decrease, and the incentive to use margin industries should be reduced.

The major distributional effects of the reforms arise from the changes in personal taxes and potential future changes in the refundable sales tax credit. Regressive measures include reductions in top marginal tax rates, reduced spreads between top and bottom marginal tax rates, and, in the long run, possibly reduced personal taxes in favor of increased sales taxes. Progressive measures include increased taxation of capital income, the conversion of exemptions and deductions to credits, enhanced federal sales tax credits, and reduced personal taxes in favor of increased corporate taxes.

On the sales tax side, regressive distributional effects follow from the inclusion in the tax base of previously nontaxed items, including food, which is more heavily purchased by low-income households, and clothing. These changes will be offset by including in the tax base all food (not just staples) and services and entertainment, which are bought in greater proportion by the rich.

Overall, the impact is difficult to gauge, especially since in the longer term an enhanced sales tax credit could prove to be the dominant factor at the low-income end. Also, there are important differences between lifetime and annual distributional impacts of taxes that need to be factored in, especially for sales tax changes (see Browning 1978; Davies, St-Hilaire, and Whalley 1985).

Some of the major efficiency and distributional effects of these changes have been evaluated in a recent paper by Hamilton and Whalley (1989a). In their paper they outline two closely related general equilibrium models based on 1980 data, which they use to evaluate each of the components of the tax reform package. One is a commodity-detailed static model, used to evaluate sales and personal tax changes. The other is a less-detailed dynamic model used to look at investment and savings effects of corporate and personal tax changes.

Taken together, results from these two models generally suggest that the 1987 package of tax reforms will improve the efficiency of the economy by removing nonneutralities in the tax system and lowering rates (see Table 5.4). According to the static model, replacing the federal sales tax (FST) with a broader-based sales tax would result in an efficiency gain equal to 0.31 percent of gross domestic product (GDP) or Can$849 million in 1980 dollars (the base year for data in their model).[9] Under the dynamic model, corporate tax changes lead to a small drop in the level of investment, but since investments are made more efficiently, the economy achieves a small efficiency gain of 0.01 percent of GDP. Personal tax changes result in an efficiency gain due to increased work incentives in the static model, increasing labor supply by 0.2 percent and producing a welfare gain equal to about 0.16 percent of GDP.

Not surprisingly, however, these estimates are sensitive to the assumed parameter values used in either model. For instance, the key parameter that determines efficiency effects of the personal tax changes is labor-supply elasticity. If this elasticity is increased, then reducing the distortions of labor supply will yield a larger efficiency gain. On the other hand, if this elasticity is lowered, the removal of distortions will have little effect on efficiency.

Also, the exact nature of the sales tax change can alter the aggregate gain estimate. Hamilton and Whalley assume a substantial increase in the sales tax credit, but if this increase is larger (or smaller), the efficiency gain will fall

TABLE 5.4   Aggregate Efficiency Effects of Canadian Tax Reforms

	National welfare gain	
	Millions of 1980 Can$	% of GDP
Sales tax reform		
Replace federal sales tax with broad-based tax	849	0.31
As above, but also remove income surtaxes and enhance sales tax credit	945	0.34
Personal tax reform	428	0.16
Combined personal and sales tax reforms	1,300	0.46
Corporate tax reforms[a]		
Combined Phases I and II	n.a.	0.01
Phase II only	n.a.	0.00

n.a. = not available.
NOTE: Both models use 1980 base period data for their assessments of tax effects.
a. These welfare measures are not annual estimates. They are the discounted present value of equivalent variations as a percentage of the discounted present value of income over a number of years generated by a dynamic equilibrium model.
SOURCE: R. W. Hamilton and J. Whalley, "Efficiency and Distributional Effects of the Tax Reform Package," in *The Economic Impacts of Tax Reform*, edited by J. Mintz and J. Whalley, Canadian Tax Paper No. 84 (Toronto: Canadian Tax Foundation, 1989), 373–98.

(or rise) correspondingly. In addition, possible exemptions from the new sales tax would also act to lower the efficiency gain. Furthermore, there could be increases in excise taxes on alcohol, tobacco, and fuel if the level of taxation on these commodities is to remain constant. This would further reduce the efficiency gain.

The Hamilton-Whalley models do not capture the intertemporal gain from removing the sales tax on capital goods or the effects of intertemporal distortions from increased taxation of capital income under the personal tax reforms.

Hamilton and Whalley calculate the marginal excess burden (MEB)—the additional welfare or misallocation cost of raising taxes—of various Canadian tax sources with their model, producing some interesting results relevant to an evaluation of the reforms (see Ballard, Shoven, and Whalley 1985). The present sales tax has the highest MEB, at Can$0.35 per dollar of tax revenue; a broadly based sales tax, at Can$0.073, is a more efficient revenue-raising tax. They do not present the MEB for the corporate tax, which is more difficult to compute in a dynamic model. In the static model, however, the personal tax is shown to be a more efficient revenue raiser than a broadly based sales tax.

The key factors explaining their last result are the effect of tax reforms on the general price level and the degree of indexation of government transfer payments. If the sales tax increase is passed on fully as an increase in consumer prices (note that this also implies an accommodating change in monetary policy) and government transfers are fully indexed, then sales tax increases will be more costly than increases in personal tax rates, which are typically assumed not to affect consumer prices (and therefore indexation).

The distributional effects of the 1987 tax changes are shown to be only mildly regressive by the Hamilton-Whalley calculations, with the largest percentage gains in real income occurring in the top income ranges. Personal tax changes reduce the overall tax on labor income and increase taxes on capital income. Average tax rates, however, are reduced for all households, and as a result the real income of every household increases. The regressivity of the rate cuts is also partially offset by the conversion of exemptions into credits and increased taxes on capital income (through changed capital gains treatment). Regressivity effects are sufficiently mild, however, that the majority of income groups experience a real income gain of around 0.5 to 1.0 percent (see column 1 of Table 5.5).

This last result is misleading, however, because the personal tax measures result in reduced government revenues in the model. Imposing a broadly based sales tax that restores government revenues to their prereform level reduces the gain to all households by about 0.3 percentage points (see

TABLE 5.5   Distributional Effects of Canadian Tax Reforms (welfare gain as a % of total income)

1986 household income range (thousands of Can$)	Effects of personal tax changes[a]		Effects of sales tax reform		Combined personal & sales tax reform (2) + (4)
	No equal yield (1)	Equal yield (2)	No change to sales tax credit (3)	With increased sales tax credit (4)	
0–5	0.1	–0.1	–0.3	12.6	12.5
5–10	0.1	–0.1	–0.1	2.9	2.7
10–15	0.4	0.1	0.1	1.4	1.5
15–20	0.5	0.2	0.2	0.5	0.7
20–25	0.4	0.1	0.2	0.0	0.1
25–30	0.4	0.0	0.3	–0.1	0.1
30–40	0.3	0.0	0.3	0.0	0.0
40–50	0.1	–0.3	0.4	0.0	–0.2
50–60	0.2	–0.1	0.4	0.1	–0.1
60–70	0.3	0.0	0.4	0.1	0.1
70–80	0.7	0.4	0.5	0.1	0.5
80–90	1.0	0.8	0.4	0.1	0.8
90–100	1.1	0.8	0.4	0.1	0.9
100+	1.5	1.2	0.3	–0.1	1.1

a. The personal tax cuts alone reduce government revenues. The equal yield simulation recoups these revenues by imposing a broad-based sales tax.
SOURCE: R. W. Hamilton and J. Whalley, "Efficiency and Distributional Effects of the Tax Reform Package," in *The Economic Impacts of Tax Reform*, J. Mintz and J. Whalley, Canadian Tax Paper No. 84 (Toronto: Canadian Tax Foundation, 1989), 373–98.

column 2 of Table 5.5) and causes several households to lose as a result of the reform.

The redistributive effects of replacing the existing sales tax by a broadly based alternative take several forms. "Essential" items, such as food, are taxed, increasing the sales tax burden on low-income groups relative to high-income groups. On the other hand, services and entertainment are brought into the tax base, tending to offset these regressive effects. The net effect of a revenue-neutral sales tax reform is a mildly regressive tax change, with only the lowest income groups worse off than before reform (see column 3 of Table 5.5).

Use of an enhanced sales tax credit, however, as the government proposes, alters the redistributive picture sharply. An increase in the credit shifts some of the real income gain from upper- and middle-income to lower-income households. In fact, since transfers are assumed to be fully indexed for price level changes in the Hamilton-Whalley model, the enhanced credit causes lower-income households to be the largest gainers from the change. Table 5.5 shows that the combined effects of the personal and sales tax reforms leave middle-income groups worse off, the lowest-income groups much better off, and upper-income groups somewhat better off.

Hamilton and Whalley also explore different approaches to offset the regressive effects of the sales tax changes, including the most commonly suggested tactic of exempting certain commodities from the tax base. Table 5. 6 reports their results.

If food is excluded from the tax base, regressivity changes a little at either end of the income distribution, but the effects are small. There is also a slight drop in the aggregate efficiency gain. Even removing food and clothing does not make a big difference.[10] It seems that including these commodities in the sales tax base does not impose a significantly increased burden on low-income households. Since higher-income households also buy these excluded items (and in larger absolute amounts), relief is granted to all. Thus, not only are commodity exemptions ineffective, they are also welfare-reducing for the economy as a whole.

Income tax credits, on the other hand, target relief at low-income households. Indeed, Hamilton and Whalley's results clearly suggest that increasing the sales tax credit dramatically changes the incidence pattern. They also require that the rate of tax be increased in order to finance the credit, creating efficiency costs.

The effects of tax credits are displayed in the final two columns of Table 5.6. The Hamilton-Whalley simulations assume two credit schemes (the credit values are deflated to 1980 values for use in their model). These credits shift gains from upper- and middle-income households to lower-income households. High-income households gain somewhat due to personal surtax reductions, but middle-income households are relatively worse off because they receive relatively few benefits from the personal surtax reductions. As a result, lower-income households are the largest gainers from tax reform

TABLE 5.6   Distributional Effects of Various Methods to Reduce Regressivity of Canadian Sales Tax Reform (welfare gain as a % of total income)

1986 household income range (thousands of Can$)	Sales tax reform (including surtax removal)				
	Comprehensive base for new tax	Exclude food from new tax	Exclude food and clothing from new tax	Income tax credit as part of change	
				Scheme 1[a]	Scheme 2[b]
0–5	–0.27	–0.15	–0.26	6.20	12.60
5–10	–0.09	0.04	–0.01	1.40	2.89
10–15	0.12	0.18	0.16	0.78	1.42
15–20	0.20	0.23	0.21	0.34	0.48
20–25	0.23	0.25	0.24	0.11	0.00
25–30	0.28	0.29	0.29	0.09	–0.10
30–40	0.34	0.33	0.34	0.15	–0.04
40–50	0.39	0.35	0.36	0.21	0.02
50–60	0.42	0.39	0.39	0.25	0.08
60–70	0.43	0.37	0.37	0.26	0.09
70–80	0.45	0.38	0.39	0.28	0.12
80–90	0.43	0.36	0.36	0.27	0.10
90–100	0.42	0.38	0.40	0.24	0.07
100+	0.25	0.14	0.11	0.09	–0.07
Aggregate efficiency gain (millions of 1980 Can$)	1,011	991	967	979	945
Gain as a % of GDP	0.36	0.36	0.35	0.35	0.34

a. Can$100 per adult and Can$25 per child for households whose net income is less than Can$23,000.
b. Can$200 per adult and Can$50 per child for households whose net income is less than Can$23,000.
SOURCE: R. W. Hamilton and J. Whalley, "Efficiency and Distributional Effects of the Tax Reform Package," in *The Economic Impacts of Tax Reform*, edited by J. Mintz and J. Whalley, Canadian Tax Paper No. 84 (Toronto: Canadian Tax Foundation, 1989).

under either of the credit options. In addition, with the large credit increase under Scheme 2, these effects are strong enough that middle-income households are actually worse off after the reform.

In practice, the distributional effects of a sales tax reform in Canada will be sensitive to the nature and magnitude of the credit as well as to the degree to which government transfer payments are indexed. It is clear from the Hamilton-Whalley results, however, that income tax credits are more effective than exemptions in addressing any regressivity effects from the planned sales tax change. Effects of the reform may thus be small in aggregate, but for subgroups and sectors, the results are more pronounced.

Conclusion

Canada's tax reform experience has had two striking features. First, there was apparently no grand design as to where the tax system as a whole should head and what the objectives of tax policy should be, making this a series of piecemeal changes grouped together under the heading of tax reform rather than a genuine system-wide reform. Second, international pressures operated strongly on the corporate components of the tax reform, although they were weaker in the personal area and only a subsidiary issue in the sales tax area.

Income tax changes appear to have relatively mild effects on resource allocation and income distribution, in part because of other changes made at the same time, which tend to offset the consequences of rate reductions. Overall, effects are positive for labor supply and for investment, despite elimination of investment incentives due to rate reductions and moves toward neutrality of tax treatment among assets. The largest effects, though, may well come from sales tax reform, which is yet to be enacted.

The 1988 Tax Reform Proposal in Israel

In the 1980s Israelis expressed great dissatisfaction with their country's personal income tax system. They believe that the existing tax system is complicated and unfair, that it distorts economic decisions, and that it does not encourage individuals to work, save, or invest to a desirable extent.

The Israeli tax system has been subject to a number of problems. It offers myriad tax benefits and exemptions that deplete revenue and have a regressive effect on income distribution. The tax burden is extremely high relative to gross national product, reaching more than 47 percent in 1987. Tax evasion and avoidance are rampant. Last, Israel has had periods of very high inflation that have eroded the tax base.

In 1988 a committee of experts offered a proposal for reform of Israel's personal income tax system. The proposal shares two features with reforms that have taken place (or are taking place) in other industrialized countries since the 1986 U.S. tax reform. First, it recommends reducing the marginal tax rates on personal income, particularly the top brackets, and broadening the tax base by eliminating tax expenditures (that is, favorable rates and exemptions on earnings). Second, the proposal suggests reducing differential tax incentives for investment. There seems to be a persistent difference between the comprehensive approach to income of the U.S. reform, in which all sources of income including interest and capital gains are taxable as ordinary income, and the approach in several other countries, which tax income from capital at much lower rates than earnings. The reform proposal in Israel uses the latter approach and adopts a low, uniform rate to tax income from capital, which offers the advantage of deductibility at the source.

This chapter begins by reviewing the problems of the tax system and the background to the 1988 reform proposal. It then describes the features of the proposal itself, starting with recommendations for adjusting the personal income tax schedule and for broadening the tax base. Finally, it discusses the proposals made for the taxation of income from capital.

Background of the Tax Reform Proposal

Four major problems have plagued the Israeli tax system. First, the proliferation of relief, benefits, and tax exemptions (tax expenditures) awarded to various individuals, groups, and corporations are a major source of inefficiency in Israel's tax system. Experts estimate that Israel's tax expenditures amount to *20 percent* of its tax revenues. Tax expenditures also have distributional implications. As seen in Figure 6.1, the high-income deciles reap most of the benefits, with the top decile alone having nearly 40 percent of the total (Center for Social Policy Studies in Israel 1985). Clearly, a reduction or elimination of these tax concessions has, in itself, a progressive aspect.[1]

The second major problem is the high burden of the level of taxes relative to gross national product (GNP). Real tax revenues in Israel have increased in the past twenty years at an average of 8 percent annually, significantly exceeding the growth rate of GNP (about 4 percent annually). In particular,

---

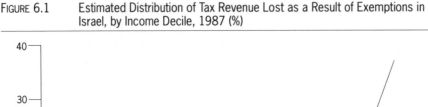

FIGURE 6.1   Estimated Distribution of Tax Revenue Lost as a Result of Exemptions in Israel, by Income Decile, 1987 (%)

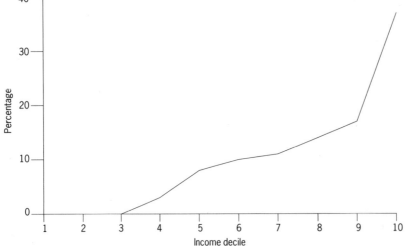

SOURCE: Ministry of Finance, *Personal Income Tax Reform: Report of the Committee of Experts* (Jerusalem, 1988).

FIGURE 6.2   Share of Taxes in Israel's GNP, 1978–1988 (percentage)

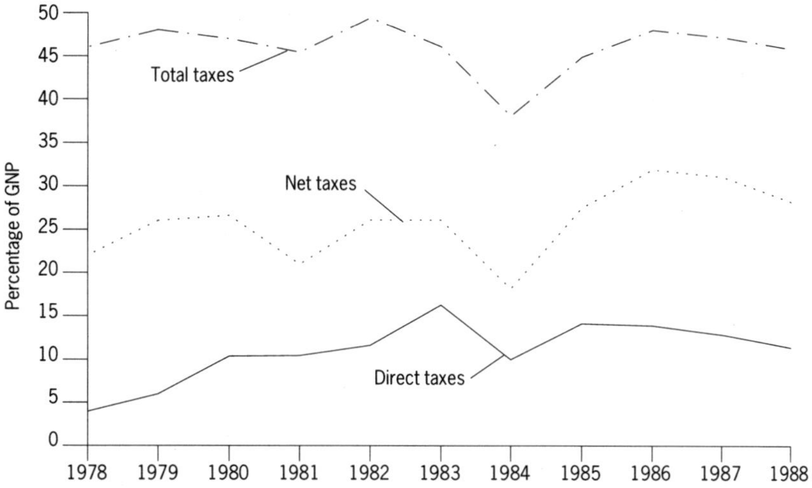

SOURCE: Israel, Central Bureau of Statistics.

the slowdown of growth in GNP following the oil crisis of the early 1970s has increased the tax burden from less than 30 percent of GNP in 1970 to more than 47 percent in 1987 (see Figure 6.2). This rate may be compared to 50 percent in Sweden, 38 percent in the United Kingdom, 29 percent in the United States, and 28 percent in Japan. The growth of tax revenues mainly reflects the increase in social security contributions and in revenues from the income tax and the value-added tax, currently at 15 percent on all goods and services excluding agricultural products and exports. The burden of taxes on earnings widened the gap between gross labor costs (to employers) and net wages, thereby increasing inflationary pressures and undermining the economy's international competitiveness.

Accompanying the growth of tax revenues has been an increase in transfer payments (such as welfare payments and subsidies), which were about 27 percent of GNP in 1987. In fact, net taxes (taxes less transfer payments) have hardly changed in relation to GNP since 1970. The inefficiency of the tax system, therefore, is related to the level of gross taxes and transfers, since both the collection of taxes and the disbursement of transfers create economic distortions.

Third, the system faces pervasive tax evasion and avoidance, encouraged by the failure to enforce the requirement to file tax returns. Obviously, there are no official estimates of the secondary economy and tax evasion, but some studies put unreported income at 15 to 20 percent of GNP (Kondor 1987). In addition to preventing a high level of tax revenues from being collected, tax evasion also presents distributional problems. Tax collection from the self-employed, for example, has been shown to lag significantly behind collection from salaried employees.

The fourth problem affecting the tax system is inflation. Inflation increased from 20 to 30 percent in the mid-1970s, to 130 percent in the early 1980s, and to over 400 percent in 1985. At that time, the government embarked on a stabilization program that drastically reduced inflation to 20 percent and then to 16 percent in 1987. Inflation has affected both the tax base and the administration of tax collection and real penalties for delays. Taxation of corporate profits has been adjusted twice, under the Law for Taxation under Inflationary Conditions in 1982 and its amendments in 1985 (these changes were recommended by the Steinberg Committee), so as to protect, to a large extent, real corporate taxes from inflation.[2] Personal income tax brackets have been partially indexed to the consumer price index (CPI) since 1976 (according to the recommendations of Ben-Shahar Committee). While this partial indexation, providing 0.7 percent for every percentage point increase in the CPI, was reasonable at the moderate inflation rates of the 1970s, it has not prevented a serious erosion in the tax structure as inflation accelerated. Furthermore, the lag in the automatic bracket adjustments every three months has increased the relative tax burden on salaried workers whose taxes are deducted at the source.

Following the U.S. tax reform in 1986, the minister of finance and the Israeli cabinet adopted major tax reform as a goal. Faced with labor union opposition to the elimination of numerous tax concessions to employees, the government announced in 1987 that the top tax bracket was reduced from 60 to 48 percent. This reduction, unaccompanied by any base broadening, has cost the treasury about NIS 1,200 million. In the wake of the inflation stabilization program in 1985 and the subsequent increase in tax revenues, the government expected the expansion of economic activity and the complementary expenditure cuts to warrant the reduction in tax revenues. On a tactical level, it expected that the tax relief provided to high-income groups would create pressure to extend the reduction in marginal tax rates to medium- and low-income levels. It was with this background that the government appointed a tax reform committee in June 1987.

The Income Tax Schedule Recommended by the Committee of Experts

In June 1987, the minister of finance named a five-member committee of experts (three economists, a lawyer, and an accountant) to reform the personal income tax. The committee was instructed to "broaden the tax base,... examining the various components of income ... for the purpose of increasing the disposable income of taxpayers in or below the 45 percent tax bracket." Regarding the resources devoted to the reform, the committee was to assume "that the [government's] budget will not be augmented for this purpose." In other words, the reform should be "fiscally neutral."

As already noted, in 1987 the minister of finance had decreed a unilateral reduction in the maximum marginal tax rate from 60 to 48 percent. The parliament (Knesset) then imposed a one-year surtax equivalent to 10 percent of the income tax paid by individuals earning more than NIS 7,400 per month. Thus, the highest effective marginal tax rate in 1987 was 54.3 percent.[3]

In the wake of this reduction, the committee of experts recommended further reductions in all marginal, and thus average, tax rates. The income tax schedule proposed by the committee is presented in Table 6.1. The maximum tax rate of 48 percent is certainly in line with postreform rates in other major countries (Table 6.2). Although it is not as low as the 33 percent in the United States,[4] it is lower than the rates of all European countries.

TABLE 6.1   Current and Proposed Tax Rates in Israel

Current		Proposed	
Monthly income ceiling (NIS)	Marginal tax rate (%)	Monthly income ceiling[a] (NIS)	Marginal tax rate (%)
1,040	20	1,040	20
1,710	30	1,400	25
2,450	35	2,000	30
3,800	45	2,700	35
3,800+	48	3,600	40
		4,500	45
		4,500+	48

NOTE: Each credit point was worth NIS 47 per month in December 1987.
a. Income ceilings and credit points should be adjusted for changes in the CPI of each month. The tax thresholds described in Table 6.1 are derived from these tax rates and credit points.
SOURCE: Ministry of Finance, *Personal Income Tax Reform: Report of the Committee of Experts* (Jerusalem, 1988).

TABLE 6.2   Top Individual Income Tax Rates in Selected Countries, 1984–1990 (percentage)

Country	1984	1988	1990
Australia	60	49	49
Canada	51	45	45
Denmark	73	68	68
France	65	57	57
Italy	65	60	60
Japan	88	76	76
Netherlands	72	70	70
Sweden	82	75	75
United Kingdom	60	60	60
United States	55	33	33
West Germany	56	56	53

SOURCE: J. Pechman, *World Tax Reform* (Washington, D.C.: Brookings Institution, 1988).

The effective tax rate in the proposed reform in Israel can be calculated from Table 6.1 and from Table 6.3, which provides the credit points allowed to each individual. For example, a married man with a nonworking wife is allowed, according to the proposal, 4¼ credit points. Each point was worth NIS 47 in December 1987. Dividing the total value of these points by the lowest marginal tax rate yields the tax threshold. As seen from Table 6.3, the proposed reform raises the threshold from NIS 764 to NIS 1,000 per month. (Similar increases in the threshold were provided to other demographic groups.) This increase, in itself, would eliminate tax obligations for about 140,000 of the low-income workers (out of a labor force of 1.7 million).

Table 6.1 also indicates that the marginal tax rates for all incomes under NIS 4,500 per month would fall substantially, from 30 to 25 percent on incomes between NIS 1,040 and 1,400, from 45 to 35 percent between NIS 2,450 and 2,700, and so on. The reduction in marginal tax rates and the increase in credit points would raise disposable income at all income levels. The increase in net income for a married man with a nonworking wife and two children is presented in Figure 6.3 and in Table 6.4.

The proposed reform includes increases of 7–8 percent in net income to those in the NIS 1,500–5,000 per month range. The method used to concentrate most of the benefits at the middle-income range (since the high-income group exclusively benefited from the reduction of the highest marginal rate from 60 to 48 percent in the previous phase of the reform) was similar to that adopted in the 1986 U.S. reform. Specifically, credit points are gradually eliminated for taxpayers with income of NIS 5,000 to 9,000 per month, effectively increasing the marginal tax rate in this range by 5 percentage points (that is, to 53 percent).

The effects of the proposed reform together with the previous reduction in the maximum tax rate are presented in Table 6.5. The combined effect is somewhat regressive, but this should be evaluated against the fact that about 70 percent of tax revenues are paid by the upper decile (with income above NIS 3,800 per month) and that the elimination of tax exemptions affected mainly the upper two income deciles (see Figure 6.1).

TABLE 6.3   Current and Proposed Credit Points and Tax Thresholds in Israel

	Credit points		Tax threshold (NIS per month)	
	Current	Proposed	Current	Proposed
Married man with nonworking wife	3¼	4¼	764	1,000
Married man with working wife	2¼	3¼	529	764
Unmarried	2¼	3¼	529	764
Married woman (filing separately)	2¼	3¼	529	764

SOURCE: Ministry of Finance, *Personal Income Tax Reform: Report of the Committee of Experts* (Jerusalem, 1988).

FIGURE 6.3   Increase in Net Monthly Income with Proposed Tax Reforms in Israel

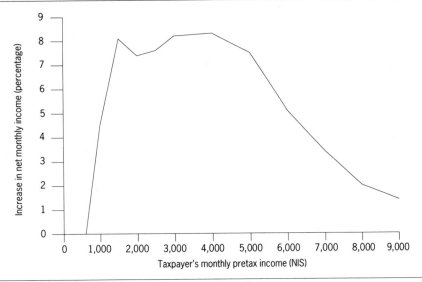

NOTE: Data are for a married man with two children and a nonworking wife.
SOURCE: Ministry of Finance, *Personal Income Tax Reform: Report of the Committee of Experts* (Jerusalem, 1988).

TABLE 6.4   Effect of the Proposed Reform on Net Income in Israel

Monthly pretax income (NIS)	Net monthly income (NIS)		Increase in net monthly income		Average tax rate (%)	
	Before reform	After reform	NIS	%[a]	Before reform	After reform
600	694	694	0	0.0	−15.7	−15.7
800	887	894	7	0.1	−10.9	−11.8
1,000	1,047	1,094	47	4.5	−4.7	−9.4
1,500	1,356	1,466	110	8.1	9.6	2.3
2,000	1,691	1,816	125	7.4	15.4	9.2
2,500	1,990	2,141	151	7.6	20.4	14.4
3,000	2,265	2,451	186	8.2	24.5	18.3
4,000	2,808	3,041	233	8.3	29.8	24.0
5,000	3,328	3,576	248	7.5	33.4	28.5
6,000	3,848	4,046	198	5.1	35.9	32.6
7,000	4,368	4,516	148	3.4	37.6	35.5
8,000	4,888	4,986	98	2.0	38.9	37.7
9,000	5,383	5,456	73	1.4	40.2	39.4
10,000	5,903	5,976	73	1.2	41.0	40.2

NOTE: This table gives data for a married man with two children and a nonworking wife. The figures in the table include child allowances and gradual elimination of credit points, or a 5 percent increase in tax in the NIS 5,000–9,000 monthly income range.
a. The increase in percent is relative to prereform net income.
SOURCE: Ministry of Finance, *Personal Income Tax Reform: Report of the Committee of Experts* (Jerusalem, 1988).

TABLE 6.5   Effect of the April 1987 Tax Cut and Proposed Reform on Net Income in Israel (NIS, December 1987 prices)

Monthly pretax income	Increase in net income		
	With April 1987 tax cut	With proposed reform	Total
600	0	0	0
800	0	7	7
1,000	20	47	67
1,500	24	110	134
2,000	32	125	157
2,500	61	151	212
3,000	71	186	257
4,000	130	233	363
5,000	250	248	498
6,000	370	198	568
7,000	490	148	638
8,000	610	98	708
9,000	730	73	803
10,000	850	73	923

NOTE: This table gives data for a married man with two children and a nonworking wife.
SOURCE: Ministry of Finance, *Personal Income Tax Reform: Report of the Committee of Experts* (Jerusalem, 1988).

Proposals for Broadening the Tax Base

The proposed reductions in marginal tax rates would be financed by a broadening of the income tax base. That is, income previously exempt from taxes (such as capital gains) or subject to favorable rates would be regarded on equal terms with earnings. Table 6.6 provides a breakdown of the proposed changes. Based on the income tax model of the treasury (which uses data from all tax returns on file), the added revenue after the first year of reform is NIS 746 million.

Tax benefits. As in other countries, the tax system in Israel has become distorted and lost much of its efficiency because of excessive use of the tax benefits and exemptions that have been introduced over time. In each case, there has been a specific activity or goal that seemed to the legislature worthy of support. However, annual budget discussions in the Knesset do not include the loss of revenues stemming from tax benefits. Consequently, there is a tendency to perpetuate benefits and exemptions whose objectives have become obsolete or that have been shown to be ineffective or misused. Vested interests that resist any change become entrenched. In most cases, the com-

TABLE 6.6   Effect of Tax Base Expansion on Israel's Tax Revenues (millions of NIS, December 1987 values)

| Factor | Added revenue after implementation of reform | | |
	First year	Second year	Long term
Capital gains from securities traded on the exchange	190	190	190
Other capital-derived revenues	58	115	230
Social benefit outlays	0	15	344
Advanced training funds[a]	88	88	88
Development areas[a]	50	50	50
Company cars	15	15	15
Employers' discounts (interest, gifts, meals)	67	67	67
Shift work	39	39	39
Medical expenses	25	25	25
Half credit point for children of working mothers	57	57	57
National insurance allowances	37	37	37
Demobilized soldiers	13	13	13
New immigrants	23	23	23
Defense ministry allowances (excluding mobility allowances)	16	16	16
Charitable donations	5	5	5
Students	16	16	16
Filmmaking, oil exploration, R&D	10	10	10
Subtotal	709	781	1,225
Transfer from second to first year	37	−41	
Total after transfer	746	740	1,225

a. Sums for this factor are half the expected gain in revenue, because half of the revenue will be returned in the form of expenditures.
SOURCE: Ministry of Finance, *Personal Income Tax Reform: Report of the Committee of Experts* (Jerusalem, 1988).

mittee has supported the elimination of these tax preferences with no direct compensation through budget expenditures.

The committee recommended abolishing tax preferences for overtime work, research and development, oil exploration, movie production, and income obtained in some geographic areas ("development towns"); income of veterans, students, and new immigrants; and a host of other benefits based on social criteria or economic activity. In all of these cases, the committee believed that direct budgetary subsidies, if desirable, are a preferred and more flexible instrument for encouraging these activities.

As Table 6.6 shows, advanced training funds are a major tax expenditure. These are funds to which employers and employees contribute similar amounts, up to a ceiling, and can be used by the employees, after a minimum period of six years, for any purpose. The employer's contributions to these funds, as well as withdrawals, are tax-exempt. With 40 percent of all workers participating in such funds, the elimination of this tax preference was a sensitive issue for Israel's trade union. Thus, while the unambiguous recommendation was to abolish this tax benefit, it was also recommended that the public sector (presumably followed by private employers) compensate workers for the lost benefit.

Transfer payments. Transfer payments include benefits paid by the social security system, such as unemployment insurance, maternity benefits, benefits to victims of work accidents, defense ministry payments to war widows and disabled veterans, and child allowances.

Except for child allowances, these transfers have all been exempt from income taxation. The committee has accepted that these payments express norms as to the "appropriate" standard of living of the respective recipients. Thus, it recommended that while these transfers should not be taxed, they should be added to any other income obtained by their recipients when calculating marginal taxes. That is, all sources of income should be brought into the taxable income base. When transfers, however, are meant as substitutes for wages or compensation for wage loss (such as during army reserve duty, for example), they should be taxed as regular income.

In 1976 deductions from taxable income for children were replaced by a tax credit per child, paid by the social security system. In a sense, this method provided a "negative income tax" for families with children whose income was below or around the threshold of the income tax. In July 1985, child allowances were eroded by the government (the first-child allowance was eliminated and the second- and third-child allowances were taxed). The committee strongly recommended reestablishing these allowances as an integral part of the income tax system, and as the main vehicle providing horizontal equity.

Benefits and exemptions for long-term savings. Many countries, including Israel, grant tax benefits and exemptions for long-term savings, especially those meant to provide for retirement (pension plans) or a "rainy day" (severance pay). There are two justifications for a special attitude toward savings. First, consumption is arguably the factor that represents one's standard of living. Taxpayers should therefore be allowed to deduct savings from taxable income so it is consumption that is ultimately taxed. This approach suggests a transition from income to consumption as the basis for personal taxation. The value-added tax, as practiced in Israel, is this kind of tax, for it permits the deduction of investments as expenses. As yet, no country has fully shifted to a consumption tax. Most, like Israel, exempt long-term savings (particularly in pension funds).

Second, with a progressive income tax, the length of the period (the calendar year, for example) used for tax computation affects an individual's liability over time. Thus, taxpayers with the same present value of income but different degrees of variation over time incur different tax liability. Through exemption, savings income can be transferred from one year to another, thereby averaging income across years. The result approaches taxation on the basis of lifetime rather than annual income.

Although one can justify favorable treatment of long-term savings, in Israel these savings enjoy a *double* exemption. Contributions to pension plans are deducted, up to a ceiling, from taxable income and withdrawals are also tax-exempt. The committee therefore recommended that contributions be deductible, but that withdrawals be taxed at the personal rate. Clearly, deducting contributions amounts to an exemption of the cumulated interest.

Since these changes, like the others suggested, should not apply retro-actively, this recommendation implied the opening of new accounts with pension funds, such that withdrawals from "old" accounts will be tax-exempt, while deposits after tax reform will be made only into the "new" funds, withdrawals from which will be taxable.

Recommendations for the Taxation of Capital Income

Israel's capital market is characterized by a stunning proliferation of tax rates, beginning with the Law for the Encouragement of Capital Investments, continuing with credit subsidies, and ending with tax exemptions on various types of capital income. There are several levels of differential rates based on the type of investor (companies or individuals), economic sector (manufac-turing, services, or finance), type of income (interest, dividend, or capital gain), location of investment (development area), and domicile of investor (foreign or Israeli residents). These distinctions result in an inefficient allo-cation of resources among sectors and parts of the country. Furthermore, in order to exploit possible advantages within this labyrinth of laws, a sizable economic sector meant solely for the purpose of tax avoidance (as opposed to tax evasion) has taken shape.

The committee's recommendations were aimed at reducing, to the extent possible, these distortions in resource allocation. Since its mandate did not include an examination of corporate taxation, it made no specific recommen-dations regarding the existing law (with one exception, concerning capital gains taxation, which is discussed below).

To arrive at an efficient allocation of resources, capital income of all kinds (interest, dividends, and capital gains) and from all sources must be taxable. In addition, the tax rate should be uniform so as to avoid creating artificial disparities in the profitability of different kinds of investment (that is, there should be tax neutrality among investments). The tax should apply to net capital income, that is, capital income less capital expenses (such as interest on loans for the purchase of assets). Furthermore, the tax base should comprise real income only (nominal income less inflationary depreciation in values); otherwise, inflation will produce profit rates other than the investments' true yield. Finally, all capital income should be added to the individual's other income (such as earned and business income), with the total subject to the progressive rates of income tax.

It seems infeasible, however, to apply the aforementioned principles and to define comprehensive income in the foreseeable future, for two reasons. First, it is difficult to unify receipts and payments transacted at different times when the price level is not static (although the inflation rate has been drastically reduced in recent years, at 16 percent annually, it still cannot be disregarded). Earned income is currently calculated in nominal values, whereas we wish to compute capital gains, for example, on a real basis. Thus it would be necessary to compute earned income based on real values as well.

Second, certain types of capital income are not actually received. The imputed income from ownership of housing is one example. Failure to include these in the definition of income for tax purposes would require that capital expenses attributable to the production of these incomes (for example, interest on mortgages) not be recognized.

These are the major reasons why the comprehensive income principle was not adopted in the reform proposal. Instead, the committee recommended a separate and equal treatment of several kinds of capital income that are now totally tax-exempt or subject to limited tax rates. These incomes would be liable to a uniform tax of 25–35 percent, a rate considerably lower than the current highest marginal rate of 48 percent. This relatively low rate is designed to compensate taxpayers for expenses toward the generation of capital income, which are not officially recognized for tax purposes. Certain other capital income, however, such as inflationary profits from various capital assets, is currently subject to extraordinarily high tax.

A major component of the reform proposal was the recommendation to tax real capital gains from securities traded on the stock exchange at a *flat rate* and, for most taxpayers, on an *accrual* basis. According to the proposal, every taxpayer's gain would be computed as:

the value of the securities portfolio at the end of the tax year
plus
sales of securities during the year by a monthly breakdown
minus
the portfolio's value at the beginning of the tax year
minus
acquisitions during the year by a monthly breakdown.

All these values should be adjusted to end-of-tax-year prices based on the consumer price index (CPI).

The simplest way to implement this recommendation is as follows: agents licensed to trade on the stock exchange (banks and private brokers) will compute the gains achieved in every client's account at the end of the tax year and will present clients with a report. Clients will file returns with information on all gains and losses in all such accounts, keeping these capital gains returns separate from and independent of the personal returns they file on other income. Because capital gains will be taxed on an accrual basis, which is slightly tougher on the taxpayer (who does not yet have the income in hand), a relatively low tax rate of 25 percent was recommended. Because this tax rate is the same for all taxpayers, banks (or brokers) can even compute the tax liability in every account and present this information to their clients.

It will be possible to offset capital losses in one tax year against capital gains during the next or the preceding year with no time limitation. Transfers from year to year (as well as tax refunds) would be fully indexed to the CPI. Permitting taxpayers to offset present losses against past gains is essential under the proposed accrual method. In this context the transfer of an account from one bank or broker to another would be considered a sale-purchase transaction.

An exception to the rule of taxation on an accrual basis would be shares held by taxpayers with controlling interest in companies. For this purpose, such a taxpayer would be defined as anyone holding at least 5 percent of a company's equity. With respect to these shares, taxpayers would be given the option of paying tax when the profit is realized, that is, when the income is actually received. In such a case, the tax would be set at the ordinary 35 percent rate recommended for other capital income, with offsetting of losses against gains allowed in subsequent but not preceding years. Furthermore, the offsetting of losses or gains in these shares against capital gains or capital losses on securities taxed by the accrual method would not be permitted.

The proposals for capital gains taxation deserve elaboration. Experts disagree on the advantages and disadvantages of accrual versus realization as the basis for taxing capital gains. The major advantage of the accrual method is that it makes computation simple, obviating the need to note the date of every purchase and sale of assets. Admittedly, because the proposal calls for taxing only real income, this method, like the realization method, requires adjustment of portfolio values at the beginning of the tax year and adjustment of the value of sales and purchases during the year to end-of-tax-year prices. But this adjustment is confined to one tax year only, while under the realization method, information must be provided on the date of purchase and on the associated index adjustments, which may extend over many years. The committee believed that there was no reasonable way for the agencies licensed to trade on the exchange to provide account holders with this information; neither is it likely that the account holders themselves could be required to perform these computations (and provide appropriate support for them). There is no doubt, however, that these bodies could easily provide the information required by the recommended accrual method. As noted above, an annual statement summarizing all transactions in a given account, adjusted to end-of-year prices, can be implemented without much difficulty.

Taxation by the accrual method would compel taxpayers to provide financial resources for the payment of tax on income that has not yet been realized. Therefore, this method might force taxpayers to realize some of their assets only for the sake of paying taxes. A considerable portion of the shares traded on the exchange are held by those with controlling interests in companies, who cannot realize their shares for the purpose of paying taxes because by so doing they would lose control of their companies. Hence it was recommended that persons with a controlling interest be taxed by the realization method.

For negotiable securities, considering the limited tax rate on these profits, the advantages of the accrual method far outweigh its disadvantages relative to the realization method. Moreover, the accrual method is conventionally used in computing ordinary income in the business sector, and there is no particular reason to insist on using a cash (realization) basis for capital gains from liquid assets such as securities traded on the exchange.

Profits from investment in mutual funds should be subject to tax under the method recommended for negotiable securities. To prevent double taxation, the committee suggested exempting income from the funds themselves or from any other investment source, excluding interest on indexed bonds, from capital gains tax. This interest should be liable to a tax of 13 percent withheld at the source. Thus, persons investing in indexed bonds through mutual funds would be taxed at the same rate (35 percent) as those who invest in indexed bonds directly. The rate $x = 13$ percent was arrived at from the equation $35 = .25 (100 - x) + x$.

In the mid-1980s, corporations in Israel increasingly gave their employees options to purchase company shares within time limitations and predetermined conditions. The intent is to allow employees to be partners in ownership and to give them a stake in the company's future success. The incidence of the tax provisions for employees' option programs is not clear. On the one hand, any benefit given to an employee at a price under market value is taxable. On the other hand, another section of the law explicitly relates to options and taxes the difference between the market value of the asset awarded under the option (the share) and the price paid for it by the employee. This raises several questions. First, when should taxation of option programs be applied—at the time the option is awarded, when it is realized (when it is converted into a share), when it is registered for trade on the exchange, or when the employee actually sells? Second, what tax should apply—the income tax (at the ordinary rate) or the capital gains tax? Third, to what extent should the award of options be recognized as an expense of the employer for tax purposes?

The answers to these questions, as given by the committee, depend on whether the option is negotiable and whether the share awarded under the option is negotiable at the point of realization. An option that can be sold on the market is indubitably tantamount to full-fledged income and is therefore liable to ordinary income tax immediately upon acquisition. A similar rule should apply, of course, to tradable shares in a company awarded to employees. In these cases, the original purpose of creating long-term identification between employees and their company surely does not exist.

There is no practical way to tax options that are not negotiable when acquired by employees, because their value is a matter of doubt. Even if the object of the option is a negotiable share, the employee's inability to trade the option makes its value to that employee uncertain. If the option is converted into a negotiable share, tax should be applied at point of conversion. Likewise, if the option is converted into a nonnegotiable share, the employee should be taxed only when the share becomes negotiable.

Because the option framework comprises a mix—income for the employee and conversion of one capital asset into another—the tax reform committee recommended that the following rule apply: the real capital gain should be computed (the value of the share less the employer's revalued payment for the option). On a yield of 8 percent for every year that the employee holds the option, the employee should pay tax at the capital gains rate (25 percent) and the regular income tax rate on any remaining value. As an example, let us consider an employee who receives at no charge a nonnegotiable share (or option) of his company, which becomes negotiable after the employee has held it for three years. The market price at the time it becomes a negotiable share is NIS 100. The real capital gain in this case would be NIS $100 - 100/1.08^3$, or NIS 20.5. The employee should pay tax at a rate of 25 percent on this sum. The remainder, NIS 79.5, should be considered ordinary income for tax purposes.

Finally, there is no reason to recognize employee options as an expense of the employer's for tax purposes. The award of options (or shares) constitutes a transfer of profits from present shareholders to the employees, not an expense for the corporation.

Concluding Comments

The report of the committee of experts on personal income tax reform (Israel. Ministry of Finance 1988), focusing on reductions in marginal tax rates and elimination of loopholes and favorable rates, was greeted favorably by economists. Although Histadruth, Israel's trade union, supported the proposed reductions in marginal tax rates, particularly in the medium- and low-income range, it opposed many of the recommendations to eliminate tax-exempt earnings (especially the advanced training funds). The minister of finance and some in the business community raised objections to the proposal to introduce a tax on capital gains. They based their arguments on the negative incentive on investments (although the combined effects of reductions in taxes on earnings and the imposition of a low tax rate on capital gains is far from certain), and also presumably on the awareness that some stock market investments are channeled profits from tax evasion. Required reporting on stock transactions, some argued, would be "disastrous" for the stock market. It is extremely difficult to evaluate these arguments quantitatively. In any case, the change in government, which occurred shortly after the committee's report was published, put tax reform on hold. It was not until in December 1989 that the government announced plans to implement some of the recommendations concerning reduction in marginal rates and elimination of tax expenditures on earnings.

The proposed uniform tax on real capital gains deserves further study. Capital gains are taxed in a number of countries, but only Australia has followed the United States in taxing them as ordinary income. Other countries, such as Canada, Sweden, and the United Kingdom, tax capital gains realized from the sale of real estate but not capital gains realized from the sale of securities (except for gains of professional traders). "This attitude reflects the long standing European view that capital gains are not income" (Pechman 1988). Fear of capital flight is also a factor. As was found in Israel, however, failure to tax capital gains makes it politically difficult to further reduce the top bracket rates.

Denmark recently introduced a reform similar to the one proposed in Israel. Individual income tax applies to labor income (earnings), and is subject to a tax schedule with three rates ranging from 50 to 68 percent. Capital income is taxed separately at a flat 50 percent rate. Interest is deductible in full against capital income, but not against labor income. A similar proposal to tax capital income at a flat 20 percent rate is currently under discussion in Japan.

There is no compelling argument in favor of taxing comprehensive income, which implies equal tax rates on earnings and on capital income. On the contrary, in general one should expect different optimal rates depending on labor and savings elasticities as well as distributional considerations. It would be interesting to determine the conditions under which capital income (interest, dividends, and capital gains) ought to be taxed at significantly lower rates than labor earnings, possibly at a uniform low rate (as proposed in Israel).

Most countries adjusted their personal exemptions and tax brackets for inflation during the 1970s. But as inflation receded, indexation was eliminated or deferred. The only countries that, like Israel, automatically index their exemptions and tax brackets are France and the United States. Sweden and the United Kingdom adjust the purchase price of assets for inflation in calculating taxable capital gains.

Finally, it is worth commenting on the issue of "fiscal neutrality." Tax reform, particularly when it affects the treatment of income from capital, generally induces changes in tax revenues that vary over time. Thus, changes in the tax treatment of interest income, which are applicable only to the interest generated by savings after the reform, but not to interest on the capital stock at the time of the reform (reflecting past savings), will generate variations in tax revenues as the ratio of "new" to "old" savings increases.

The natural interpretation of fiscal neutrality is therefore in terms of the present value of future tax revenues (allowing for uncertainty). If tax revenues are, for example, expected to increase over time, this implies a policy of increasing government debt for an interim period. Politicians resist this approach. Their usual interpretation of fiscal neutrality is a cash-flow concept, whereby outlays and revenues balance annually. Such an interpretation may significantly limit the options available for tax reform. In the case of Israel, these opposing approaches to the dynamics of tax reform have been a major reason for deferring the proposed reform, at least for now. An important research task for the future, therefore, would be to measure the economic costs imposed by such constraints on the government's debt policy.

Tax Reform Debates in Japan

In December 1988, after several years of intense public debate, a tax reform bill introducing fundamental changes to Japan's tax system passed the Japanese Diet. Although some revisions in the Japanese tax system have been made almost every year, its basic structure had remained unchanged since the Shoup Reform of 1949 in two respects: first, it relied heavily on direct taxes, especially at the national level; second, it had no broad-based consumption tax such as the value-added tax (VAT) in European countries or the sales tax in the United States. The reform has both introduced a new broadly based indirect tax modeled on the VAT and reduced the burden of the individual and the corporate income taxes. During the years leading up to the passage of the reform bill, tax reform had been one of the most important policy issues in Japan. This chapter will review the tax reform debates, analyze their origins, and evaluate their outcome.

In Japan, the tax system is administered by the national government and local governments (see Table 7.1). The latter consist of prefectures (*ken*), cities (*shi*), towns (*cho*), and villages (*son*). Direct national taxes are the personal income tax, the corporate income tax, and the inheritance tax. All other national taxes are indirect taxes, of which the liquor tax, the gasoline tax, and the commodity tax are the most important. The major local taxes are the local income tax (*jumin zei*), the property tax, and the business tax (*jigyo zei*). Social security contributions (*shakai hokenryo*) are not regarded as taxes in the Japanese system since they are collected through channels entirely separate

TABLE 7.1   Trends in Government Revenues in Japan, FY 1970–1988 (percentage of national income)

Fiscal year	National taxes (1)	Local taxes (2)	National and local taxes (1)+(2)	Social security contribution (3)	Total (1)+(2)+(3)
1970	12.7	6.1	18.9	5.4	24.3
1971	12.8	6.4	19.2	5.9	25.1
1972	13.3	6.4	19.8	5.9	25.7
1973	14.7	6.8	21.4	5.9	27.3
1974	14.0	7.3	21.3	7.0	28.3
1975	11.7	6.6	18.3	7.5	25.8
1976	12.0	6.8	18.8	7.8	26.6
1977	11.8	7.1	18.9	8.3	27.2
1978	13.5	7.1	20.6	8.5	29.1
1979	13.7	7.7	21.4	8.8	30.2
1980	14.2	8.0	22.2	9.1	31.3
1981	14.6	8.3	23.0	9.8	32.8
1982	14.8	8.6	23.3	10.1	33.4
1983	15.0	8.7	23.7	10.2	33.9
1984	15.3	9.0	24.3	10.3	34.6
1985	15.4	9.2	24.5	10.7	35.2
1986	16.2	9.3	25.5	10.8	36.3
1987	16.0	9.8	25.8	11.1	36.9
1988	16.1	9.4	25.5	11.1	36.6

NOTE: Figures are those of the settlement basis, except for FY 1987 (revised budget base) and FY 1988 (initial budget base).
SOURCE: Ministry of Finance, *Fiscal and Monetary Statistics* (Tokyo: Government Printing Bureau, 1988).

from the tax collection system and become revenues of the social security special accounts. This discussion refers to them, however, because they are similar to taxes.

There are several reasons why the Japanese case is worth studying. First, the recent reform was a fundamental one as mentioned above. Until the introduction of the new consumption tax, Japan had no broadly based indirect tax. This tax raised strong opposition, and controversy surrounded almost all aspects of the tax system. Second, more than ten years were required from the time of the first proposal by the government until the adoption of reform. This time frame reflects the significance of the attempt to fundamentally overhaul the tax system. Third, as emphasized in this chapter, demographic conditions in Japan are expected to change significantly during the coming decades, with huge effects on social security expenditures. Future increases in the tax burden will accordingly be very large.

Among the many groups involved in the tax reform debates, the major ones have been the government, especially the finance authority (the Tax Bureau of the Ministry of Finance); the Liberal Democratic party (LDP), which has been the ruling party for more than thirty years; the opposition parties; the business community; labor unions; journalists; scholars; and other opinion leaders. The first step of a tax reform is usually a report of the Tax Council (*Zeisei Chosakai*), which is a formal advisory body to the prime minister. Since the council's activity is in effect managed by the Ministry of Finance (MOF), its report may be regarded as representing the finance authority's position. In recent years, the Tax Council of the LDP, a party committee, has also become quite influential in tax policy determinations. The views of business and labor union leaders on tax issues are frequently reported by the newspapers, TV, and other mass media. Opinion surveys are conducted from time to time by the government or by newspapers to find the attitudes of the general public.

Different groups give different reasons for supporting tax reform. From the point of view of the finance authority, the foremost goal is to obtain more revenues to reduce the budget deficit. Taxpayers, especially salaried workers, demand reform because they feel their tax burden has grown too heavy. They are also discontent with inequalities in the present system, which, they say, have been neglected for so long that they have reached an intolerable level. Business leaders claim that the corporate tax burden in Japan has become heavier than that in other countries in recent years. If the burden is not reduced, they warn, Japanese companies may lose their international competitiveness. Finally, the last reason for reform is the long-term outlook for revenue needs. As Japan's population grows older, revenue sources will have to be secured for a growing volume of social security expenditures. Thus the tax structure must be modified to accommodate a level of tax burden comparable to (or even higher than) that of European countries.

We will examine these and other issues in this chapter, beginning with a review of recent trends in the tax burden. Whether tax reform is in fact necessary for reducing the budget deficit is a matter of debate, and we will consider the arguments in the following section. Next, we discuss horizontal inequities in tax treatment and the issue of progressivity, and evaluate the measures adopted in the 1988 reform to address these areas. International factors play a role in determining whether the corporate tax burden is too heavy; we review the evidence on this issue and look at how the reform has affected corporate taxation and the taxation of interest income and capital gains. Another potential area of reform, which has been subject to little discussion, is the financing of future social security expenditures. The expected aging of Japan's population will lead to sharp rises in social security expenditures if the current system is not changed. Finally, we deal with two controversial issues: broad-based consumption taxes, which were adopted in the face of strong arguments on both sides, and taxes on land, which were not on the reform agenda but are currently thought to inhibit utilization and development of land.

Background: Recent Changes in the Tax Burden

Until the 1973 oil crisis, Japan's ratio of tax burden to national income was quite stable, at a level of around 19 to 21 percent. The ratio fell sharply in fiscal year 1975 because of a recession caused by the oil shock. However, it quickly recovered its previous level and is now much higher than the pre-oil-shock level: the ratio of total tax revenues to national income, which was 18.9 percent in FY 1970, rose to 25.5 percent in FY 1986. If social security contributions are included, the increase in government receipts is even more dramatic: their ratio to national income rose from 24.3 percent in FY 1970 to 36.3 percent in FY 1986.

The composition of taxes has also changed significantly. While the ratio of indirect taxes to national income in recent years has been about the same as it was in the 1960s, that of direct taxes has increased considerably during the past decade. The share of direct taxes in total tax revenue, which was about 50 percent in the 1960s, has risen to about 60 percent in recent years. A more distinct trend can be observed in national taxes. In FY 1970, the share of direct taxes in national taxes was 66.1 percent. In FY 1986, it had risen to 73.1 percent.

Among national taxes, income tax has increased the most sharply. In FY 1970, the ratio of income tax revenue to national income was 4.0 percent, whereas in FY 1986, it had risen to 6.4 percent. Social security contributions, which can be regarded as a kind of direct tax, have also increased dramatically. Their ratio to national income increased from 5.4 percent to 10.8 percent over the same period.

In the case of social security contributions, the increase in the burden was a result of explicit revisions in the system. For example, the rate of contribution of the employees' pension (*kosei nenkin*) was raised (in several stages) from 6.2 percent in FY 1970 to 12.4 percent in FY 1986 (including the employers' share).[1] The increase in the income tax burden in recent years, however, is not the result of explicit revisions in the income tax law. Rather, it was an "automatic increase,"[2] which occurs when a progressive tax structure is not indexed to offset inflation—as Japan's is not—or economic growth. Until the early 1970s, the income tax law was amended almost every year in order to prevent this mechanism from operating, but a significant change in this trend occurred after the first oil shock. Adjustments to the income tax law were not undertaken for seven full years from FY 1977 to 1984.

In spite of the recent increase, the tax burden is still low in Japan compared with European countries. The main reason is that the share of social security expenditures in national income remains small in Japan. This issue will be discussed again below.

Is a New Tax Necessary for Reducing the Budget Deficit?

The first thrust for tax reform came from the need to increase tax revenue to reduce the budget deficit, which grew significantly after the first oil crisis and was further enlarged by expansionary policies in the late 1970s. In its October 1977 report, the Tax Council recommended the introduction of a new tax. Modeled after the value-added taxes in European countries, this tax was called the general consumption tax (*ippan shohi zei*). In September 1978, the details of the tax were released in another report of the council. The Ohira administration, which took office in December 1978, declared that it would introduce the new tax in FY 1980. This proposal became the most important issue in the general election of October 1979.

The opposition parties argued that many steps had to be taken before introducing a new tax. In particular, they argued, reexamination of expenditure and correction of inequalities in the tax system were indispensable. Scholars and journalists were of the same opinion. For example, Noguchi (1980) pointed out that there were many items in the budget that had to be rationalized. It is worth noting that business leaders also strongly supported this view. In the background was a change in business leaders' opinions on the role of government. In periods of rapid growth, they usually demanded expansionary fiscal policy. In the 1980s, however, those who favored small government became predominant. This change was caused by their apprehension that further increases in fiscal burdens would fall on business in the form of increased corporate income tax.

Thus, although the LDP decided just before the election to repeal the decision to introduce a new tax, the general election resulted in a setback for the party. Since then, attempts to introduce a new revenue-increasing tax have become a political taboo, as was made clear in the first report of the Ad Hoc Council on Administrative Reform (*Rinji Gyosei Chosakai*), established in March 1983. The basic policy orientation established by the council was "fiscal reconstruction without tax increases"— in other words, the reduction of the budget deficit was to be achieved through expenditure cuts, not through tax increases. (During the 1980s, expenditure growth was severely suppressed. As a result of this suppression and the automatic increase in income tax revenue mentioned before, the budget deficit was reduced significantly.)

For several years after 1979, the government made no proposals for tax reform. In 1985, however, the Nakasone administration declared that it would undertake a fundamental tax reform. The Tax Council began its activity in April 1986 and released its report in October 1986. This time the reform was revenue-neutral, designed not to increase revenues but to change the tax structure. The major components of the reform were (1) reduction of income tax through a decrease in progressivity, (2) reduction of corporate income tax, (3) abolishment of the preferential treatment of interest income, and (4) introduction of a broadly based consumption tax, the *uriagezei* (sales tax).

The new tax again met with strong opposition, and the government was forced to repeal its reform bill. A revised bill containing only items 1 and 3 passed the Diet in September 1987. The Takeshita cabinet called for another round of fundamental reform and in 1988 proposed a new broadly based indirect tax called *shohizei* (consumption tax). Below we will review debates concerning these reform proposals.

Issues of Horizontal Equity: The 9-6-4 Problem

The Japanese income tax is based on comprehensive taxation—that is, all categories of income are added together and are subject to the same rate schedule. In spite of this, it is frequently pointed out that the burden of the income tax is unevenly distributed among different categories of income. In particular, the income tax burden of salaried workers is heavier than that of small business owners, the self-employed, and farmers of the same income.[3]

There are several reasons why this problem arises. One is the different treatment of income under tax law. The most important difference is that while deduction of actual expenses is allowed for business and agricultural income, only a fixed proportion determined by law can be deducted from salaried income. In the case of business income, avoiding progressive taxation is possible by splitting income among family members. Moreover, a double deduction of expenses is allowed for business income because the salary of the business proprietor may be deducted.[4]

Another reason is the difference in the actual assessment. While almost 100 percent of salaried income is captured by the tax authorities through withholding at the source, it is difficult for the tax authorities to capture all business or agricultural income, which is taxed according to taxpayers' self-assessments. (The probability of being audited has fallen considerably in the past decade, to only about 2 to 3 percent, because the number of taxpayers has grown significantly whereas the number of tax officials has remained almost unchanged). Thus, small business proprietors, the self-employed, and farmers often declare only a fraction of what they actually earn. This inequality in assessment is commonly called the 9-6-4 (or 10-5-3) problem, which means that the portion of income subject to taxation is 90 to 100 percent of actual earned income for salaried income, 50 to 60 percent for business income, and only 30 to 40 percent for agricultural income.

In Japan, this problem receives more attention than the vertical equity issue. In fact, it is usually regarded as the most serious problem of the present tax system. Although there is much casual evidence to support the existence of this inequality, it is difficult to rigorously prove its existence because most of the necessary data are unavailable. In fact, the government refuses to acknowledge the 9-6-4 problem. Ishi (1984: ch. 5) conducted an analysis by comparing tax statistics with national account statistics. Based on the assumption that the latter reflect true income, he concluded that the portion of income subject to taxation is almost 100 percent for salaried income, 60 to 70 percent for business income, and 20 to 30 percent for agricultural income. This result validates the popular belief. Honma, Atoda, Hayashi, and Hata (1984) obtained a similar outcome.

Another way to infer the extent of the 9-6-4 problem is to look at the chronological changes in tax burden. Noguchi (1986b) pointed out that the automatic increases in income tax mentioned in the previous section aggravated the uneven distribution of tax burdens. Over the 1970–1983 period, the ratio of withheld income tax to national income rose from 2.8 percent to 4.8 percent, while that of self-assessed income tax remained virtually unchanged (0.97 percent in FY 1965 and 1.26 percent in FY 1983). These figures indicate that the rising tax burden over the past years has fallen mainly on the shoulders of salaried workers[5] and that the differential between them and business entrepreneurs has widened.

In spite of the absence of definite empirical evidence, almost everyone believes that the 9-6-4 problem exists and agrees, at least formally, that it should be corrected. There are, however, differences in opinion as to what measures should be adopted for that purpose.

The government reform package allowed the deduction of actual expenses for salaried workers and introduced a new deduction for a spouse having no income. Although these changes have improved the situation, they are far from perfect solutions, and most agree that further steps should be taken.

One group argues that the solution should be found within the framework of the present income tax system. (For example, see Miyajima 1986, 1987 and Hatta 1988.) Labor unions and opposition parties take a similar position. Others argue that inequality in the income tax is to a large extent a reflection of differences between types of income, and hence the system's heavy reliance on the income tax should be modified. They believe that introduction of a VAT-type tax would improve the overall situation (see Noguchi 1985a, 1987a). However, the opposition parties disagree and labor unions are not persuaded by this argument.

Another problem related to horizontal equity is the treatment of two-earner households and working women. However, this issue is not seriously discussed in Japan.

Issues of Vertical Equity: Diminishing Progressivity

The progressivity of Japan's income tax is fairly steep. In the 1986 schedule, the marginal rate climbed from 10.5 percent for the lowest bracket to 70 percent for the highest bracket. Although it is true that the progressivity is not necessarily effective for those people whose income takes the form of business or asset income (Ishi 1979), the stipulated progressivity is almost 100 percent effective for salaried workers. Thus, there were demands for diminishing the progressivity, especially for those people with an annual income of around ¥10 million (about US$70,000). This movement was accelerated by the developments in the United States and Britain toward flat-rate income taxes.

Diminishing the progressivity thus became one of the most important elements of the income tax reform proposed by the government. In the first reform package of October 1986, the government proposed lowering the highest marginal rate to 50 percent and reducing the number of brackets from fifteen to six.

There were almost no objections to this proposal. Interestingly, the opposition parties and labor unions did not raise strong objections to lowering the higher marginal rates. Two reasons can account for this: (1) Japan is one of the countries in which income is most equally distributed, as demonstrated, for example, by Itaba and Tachibanaki (1987) and (2) the government did not raise the lower marginal rates, and hence the reform did not increase the income tax burden of any income class.

However, some taxes must be increased in order to finance this reform. In the government proposal, the consumption tax (and the abolition of the preferential treatment of interest income) bore this role. Since a consumption tax is generally regressive, this reform was relatively favorable for the middle and upper classes.

The total effect of the reform package depends on the effect of corporate income tax reduction on household income, which is an unsettled question. A report by the MOF made a certain assumption about this issue and concluded that the burden of every income class would be reduced. Honma (1986a) argued, without taking into account the effect of corporate income tax reduction, that the 1986 government plan would increase the burden of those whose annual income was lower than ¥5 million (about US$35,000). Opposition parties used the latter estimate for objecting to the sales tax, but not, interestingly, to the relaxation of progressivity.

Is the Corporate Tax Burden in Japan Too Heavy?

During the tax reform debates, business leaders asserted that the corporate income tax burden in Japan was higher than that in other countries, especially in the United States and the United Kingdom. They argued that in an international comparison of the corporate tax burden, special tax measures such as accelerated depreciation allowances and investment tax credits should be taken into account, and that the indices used by the MOF and the Tax Council were inaccurate in that they compared only the statutory tax rates. Debates on this matter took place between the MOF and the Keidanren, the group of big corporations (Keidanren 1985).

Nakatani (1985, 1987) argued that if the tax structure of one country is more favorable for investments than that of other countries, as was the case in the United States before the 1986 reform, that country tends to attract more capital from other countries than it would if tax structures were the same everywhere. This causes a distortion in the world capital market and a serious misalignment of exchange rates. Thus, the differences in tax structure in various countries have important implications on the workings of the international economic system, and it is necessary to coordinate tax policies among the major countries, especially between the United States and Japan.

Noguchi (1985c) examined the MOF-Keidanren debate and pointed out that Keidanren's argument overestimates the effect of accelerated depreciation since it neglects increases in tax in later years. He also pointed out that the tax burden is affected by the firm's borrowing, the growth rate of the firm's revenue (because the effects of various tax-free reserve provisions depend on the growth rate), and the inflation rate. He concluded that the cost of capital to Japanese firms has increased in the recent years, due to an increase in the corporate income tax rate, a reduction of tax-free reserve provisions, a fall in the debt-equity ratio, the economic growth rate, and the inflation rate.

Shoven and Tachibanaki (1988) included the tax burden at the household level in their analysis and concluded that the effective rate in Japan is lower than that in the United States, because of a lower marginal tax rate on asset income at the household level. Iwata et al. (1987), however, compared the tax burden in Japan with that in the United States using the framework developed by King and Fullerton (1984), and concluded that while the former was higher than the latter in 1983, the difference shrank after the 1986 U.S. tax reform. Ando and Auerbach (1988) examined financial statement data and concluded that although the before-tax cost of corporate capital was higher for U.S. firms than for Japanese firms, the market returns in the two countries were much closer. They rejected certain potential explanations including differences in corporate taxation.

With these discussions in the background,[6] the government included a reduction of the corporate income tax in its first fundamental tax reform package of October 1986. Opposition parties did not raise strong objections to this proposal, although they of course gave no positive support to a measure that "reduces the burden of large corporations." Journalists and labor unions held more or less the same attitude.

Issues of Taxation of Interest Income and Capital Gains

In Japan, interest income from both small savings accounts and the postal saving system has been subject to *maruyu,* or preferential treatment. Two arguments have been made against this system. One, based on equity, said that the system was abused by wealthy individuals who held numerous accounts in different banks and post offices (sometimes using false names) far beyond the legal limit. The other was based on its potential effect on saving. Some economists argued that the *maruyu* intensified economic friction with other countries (for example, Nakatani 1985, 1987). They asserted that favorable tax treatment caused the high savings rate of Japanese households, which in turn produced the massive current account surplus. The high savings rate could be reduced by taxing interest income, and, the argument went, this would compress the trade surplus. The Maekawa Committee, an advisory committee to the prime minister established to find measures for easing trade friction, supported the above argument in its 1986 *Report of a Committee for Adjustment of Economic Structure for International Harmony.*

The above arguments (especially the former) were widely supported by journalists and the general public and denied by banks and the Ministry of Post and Telecommunications (which manages the postal saving system). Opposition parties also raised objections on the grounds that the abolition of preferential treatment would imply an increase in the burden of low-income households, although the objection was not strong. The MOF took advantage of the general support and included the abolishment of the *maruyu* in the first reform package of October 1986. As mentioned, this part of the reform bill passed the Diet in September 1987.

It must be noted, however, that the distributional effect of the reform was the opposite of what the general public had expected. Since the new system imposes a flat-rate tax of 10 percent on interest income, those wealthy people who had previously been subject either to comprehensive taxation or to a withholding tax of 35 percent actually gained from the reform.

Also, the abolishment of the *maruyu* will not necessarily reduce Japan's trade surplus. Although the relationship between taxation and the savings rate is a controversial issue, and although there is no definite empirical evidence on this subject, economists are generally doubtful of the effect (for example, see Iwata et al. 1986). At the very least, it seems necessary to note that this system already existed when Japan was running deficits in its current account.

From the viewpoint of taxation principles, whether or not to tax interest income is related to the fundamental issue of income versus expenditure taxes. To the extent that a large part of interest income was exempted from taxation, the Japanese "income tax" had an element of an expenditure tax. In addition, the following measures, which still exist in the Japanese income tax system, can be regarded as features of an expenditure tax:

1. Capital gains are taxed on realization, rather than on accrual.
2. Imputed rents of owner-occupied houses are not taxed. (This can be regarded as an expenditure tax of the prepayment type).
3. Interest payments are not deductible from income other than business income.
4. Pension contributions are deductible from income, and pension benefits are taxable income.

In short, the Japanese income tax was in fact an expenditure tax as far as income from assets was concerned. The abolishment of the *maruyu* implied a fundamental change in this respect, as was pointed out by Noguchi (1986a) and Kaizuka (1987). These arguments, however, did not attract much attention in Japan.

In the Japanese system, capital gains from the sales of securities were virtually exempted from taxation. This treatment was long criticized as a preferential measure for the wealthy. Criticism has grown because of the recent remarkable appreciation in stock prices and the abolishment of the *maruyu*. Thus, the government included in the present reform bill a strengthening of capital gains taxation. Although some LDP politicians and securities companies showed discontent, scholars, journalists, and the general public welcomed the reform.

Financing Future Social Security

The tax burden in Japan is low compared to that of other countries because of a relatively low level of social security expenditure. This does not, however, imply that Japan's social security programs are less generous. On the contrary, improvements in the early 1970s made the Japanese social security system comparable, and in some respects even superior, to those of European countries, as explained by Noguchi (1986a). The main reason for the relatively low level of expenditure is that the ratio of elderly people in the Japanese population is still low and Japan's public pension system has not reached "maturity," meaning that as yet relatively few people have become eligible for the full pension benefits.

As the years go by, though, this state of affairs will inevitably change. The public pension programs will automatically mature. Moreover, the aging of the population is expected to take place rapidly in the future. These factors would increase social security expenditures considerably even if no improvements were made in the system.

According to an estimate made by the Economic Council in 1982, the ratio of social security transfers to national income will increase to 25.3 percent in the year 2000 and to 31.2 percent in 2010 (Economic Planning Agency 1982).[7] (Most of the increase will result from the growth of public pension payments: their share in national income will rise to 17.1 percent in the year 2010). According to a more recent estimate made jointly by the Ministry of Finance and the Ministry of Welfare in 1988, the ratio of social security expenditure to national income will rise from 15.4 percent in 1988 to 29 percent in 2010.[8]

Both the social security burden and the tax burden must therefore increase, since Japan's public pension system is managed essentially according to the pay-as-you-go method. The question, then, is what taxes should be used to collect the additional revenue required. Politically, the easiest way to increase the burden is to rely on the automatic increase of the income tax mentioned before. This solution, however, will aggravate the distortions in the tax structure, and wage earners are liable to end up bearing almost all of the additional burden. Instead, it can be argued that the introduction of a VAT-type tax is necessary to spread the high tax burden as fairly as possible (for an example of such an argument, see Noguchi 1987a). This idea seems to be rather broadly accepted, especially among scholars.

Of course, other scenarios can be envisioned. It has been assumed that the social security system will be maintained in its present form, but it is conceivable that steps will be taken to reduce benefit levels. In fact, this is where the debate on tax reform should have begun. If Japan keeps the present social security system intact and goes the route of the European welfare state, the goal of tax reform would be to create a system capable of raising taxes to the European level. If Japan rejects the European welfare state as a model and decides to revamp the social security system, assigning only limited welfare functions to the government, tax reform would naturally have different goals; for instance, it would need to offer incentives for people to save more for after-retirement life. This kind of debate, however, is seriously lacking in Japan.

Debates on Consumption Tax

There were no sharp divisions of opinion concerning the reduction of individual and corporate taxes, because the reform bill imposed no extra burden on anyone, at least directly. Regarding the introduction of a VAT-type broadly based consumption tax (hereafter referred to simply as a consumption tax), however, opinions were sharply divided.

Opposition parties objected to the idea of a new tax, as they did to any government proposal. Journalists, labor union leaders, and small business proprietors also raised objections. Leaders of big corporations generally supported the idea. Many non-Marxist scholars admitted the necessity of a new tax, especially from the long-run point of view.

Arguments supporting a consumption tax have already been reviewed above. Critics have raised a number of objections. The most common complaint is that this type of tax is generally regressive. (This issue was discussed in the earlier section on vertical equity.) Another objection is that a consumption tax (or indirect taxes in general) offers an easy means of raising revenues. They argue that an indirect tax, which people are relatively unconscious of paying, will make it possible to finance the growth of big government. This danger exists, at least potentially. Yet Noguchi (1987a) pointed out that it is easier to raise the burden of income tax than that of a consumption tax. In fact, as mentioned earlier, the Japanese government has increased the income tax burden substantially over the past ten years simply by not adjusting the tax law to offset the automatic increase. Nothing of this sort can occur in the case of a consumption tax.

A more specific complaint about a consumption tax was voiced by small business owners. Consumption tax is designed on the assumption that businesses will shift taxes they pay to their customers. But these people maintain that in practice it may be difficult for them to do so and that they must bear the tax burden themselves. In addition, they argue that the costs involved in complying with tax collection requirements will impose an undue burden on businesses. The extra expenses include the cost of making new forms, revising accounting slips, modifying computer software, and so forth.

Although these arguments deserve careful consideration, they are made largely to hide the true objection of small business owners: if a consumption tax is introduced, tax authorities will be able to obtain detailed records of their transactions (especially if the invoice system is used) and may utilize them to strengthen direct taxes (corporate income tax or tax on business incomes). Small business owners are actually resisting increases in direct taxes.

There were also discussions about the macroeconomic effects of a consumption tax. Some economists argued that the tax will inhibit consumption and hold down effective demand. There were also complaints from other countries, especially the United States, that a consumption tax is yet another move by Japan to limit domestic consumption.

It is true that even if the amount collected by a consumption tax is offset by a reduction in the income tax, the immediate effect will be to dampen consumption somewhat.[9] Although this short-term impact cannot be denied, a reduction of the corporate income tax may offset it. Moreover, it can be argued that replacing the income tax with a consumption tax has a favorable effect on the long-run performance of the economy, since the latter has no adverse effect on capital accumulation, as shown, for example, by a simulation analysis by Noguchi (1987b). However, this type of argument is not popular in Japan.

Debates on Property Taxes

Although not included in the government reform agenda, reform of property taxes is potentially an important issue, since the inefficient use of land is one of the most serious economic problems in Japan.

Many economists believe that taxes on landholding, such as the property tax, have the effect of promoting development and utilization of land, while income tax on realized capital gains has a "lock-in effect" and therefore tends to delay changes in land utilization. In Japan, the stipulated rate of the property tax is 1.4 percent. Yet since assessment values of land for tax purposes are significantly lower than market values, and since there are a number of special measures, the effective tax rate is much lower: the average effective rate measured by the ratio of the property tax revenue on land to the total market value of privately held land is now around 0.15 percent. For farmland in urban areas, the rate is still lower: about one-thirtieth of that for residential land. This implies that idle holding of land, especially farmland in urban areas, is not penalized by the property tax. Income tax on capital gains from the sale of land, however, is quite heavy: for short-term holdings, the tax rate is as high as 96 percent. It follows that the Japanese tax system hinders land utilization and hence aggravates the land problem. In fact, the real land problem in urban areas is not an absolute shortage of land, but rather a lack of effective land use: there still exists a large amount of farmland in urban areas, and lands converted for urban uses are not used efficiently.

Therefore, many economists advocate an increase in the burden of the property tax and a decrease in that of the capital gains tax (see, for example, Noguchi 1983, 1988). In particular, they argue that it is necessary to raise the effective rate of the property tax on farmland in urban areas to the same level as that for residential land. There is strong opposition, however, to increasing the property tax burden. Opponents argue that the property tax is a "cruel" tax since it imposes a burden on a basic necessity of living even when there is no cash income. Because of these objections, measures were taken to keep the burden of the property tax relatively stable in the face of rapid land price increases in the early 1960s. In the case of farmland, the absolute burden was kept virtually constant. As relief measures have accumulated since then, the effective rate of the property tax has fallen considerably.

Objections to a heavier property tax are still quite strong. There is no political party that advocates strengthening the tax. Even the Communist party insists upon the reduction of the property tax burden. Thus, faced with the extraordinary increase in land prices during recent years, the government adopted measures to further reduce the effective rate of the property tax.[10]

On the other hand, general opinion favors a high capital gains tax on the grounds that it reaches those persons who obtain large amounts of income and that a heavy capital gains tax on short-term holding discourages speculative holding of land.

Concluding Remarks

The necessity of tax reform is recognized by all, since no one is satisfied by the present system. Specifically, there is a fairly wide consensus on the following points: (1) unequal distribution of the tax burden among different occupations, with an especially heavy burden on salaried workers, should be corrected; (2) the income tax burden should be reduced through diminishing progressivity; (3) introduction of a new tax is not necessary to reduce the present budget deficit; and (4) some measures should be taken to cope with future increases in social security expenditures.

The major differences in opinion concern the relative weight attached to further reform of the present income tax on the one hand and the introduction of a new consumption tax on the other. Opposition parties, labor unions, and the majority of journalists argue that the unequal tax treatments must be corrected before a new tax is introduced. Others say a consumption tax is the key to remedying the present situation, since it distributes tax burdens evenly among people of different occupations.

The failure to introduce the sales tax in 1987 was not necessarily a result of the above argument, however. The core of the objection was small business owners' apprehension that their transactions would become transparent to the tax authorities. It was unfortunate that labor unions supported this objection, since there are many workers who would likely be the beneficiaries of the reform. There was, it seems, considerable misunderstanding regarding the nature of the reform.[11]

The opposition parties' debates in the Diet were myopic; they were too concerned with the immediate effects of the reform, such as the total amount of income-tax reduction or the reduction in the net burden of low-income people. Very few discussions took place on such questions as the desirable tax structure for Japan, the effects of taxation on economic activities, or the long-run level of the tax burden.

Although the consumption tax was initiated in the reform bill of 1988, the need for reform will not disappear, since there are many items that were not included or only insufficiently included in the present governmental proposal. As discussed in the previous section, reform of land taxation is an urgent task. The income tax should be improved in many respects, particularly with regard to correcting the unequal treatment of salaried versus business income. Taxation of income from assets should be reorganized through explicit consideration of taxation principles and the effects on economic activity. Finally, the consumption tax is by no means an ideal one, especially in that it does not use the invoice system. But these are issues for future debates.

Sweden: Tax Reform in a High-Tax Environment

With total tax revenue in excess of 50 percent of gross domestic product (GDP) and marginal effective tax rates on labor that average over 70 percent, Sweden has the highest taxes in the Organization for Economic Cooperation and Development (see Table 8.1). Swedish public opinion has generally favored such high taxes, together with public redistributional spending, as a way to provide all residents with an acceptable standard of living. Beginning in 1982, however, the country began to lower marginal taxes.

Because Sweden is an outlier, its experience can provide valuable information about the distortions that arise when taxes are high. The two most important distortions appear to be a reduced labor supply and a high level of tax arbitrage whereby individuals finance investments in lightly taxed forms of capital by borrowing. Interestingly, the impetus to curb this type of tax arbitrage has come not only from concern about efficiency but also from a feeling that arbitrage counteracts the intended distributional effects of a progressive income tax schedule. In broad terms, awareness of the distortions caused by high taxes has grown continuously throughout the past decade, resulting in a significant tax reform in 1982 and in plans for still more far-reaching reform in the early 1990s. Although publicity surrounding tax reforms in the United States and elsewhere has had some effect on Swedish

Financial support from the Bank of Sweden Tercentenary Foundation is gratefully acknowledged.

TABLE 8.1   Levels of Taxation in Countries of the Organization for Economic
               Cooperation and Development (OECD) (percentage)

	Average rate (total tax revenue/GDP[a])	Marginal effective rate on labor income[b]
Sweden	50.3	76.4
Norway	47.8	68.4
Belgium	46.6	65.5
Netherlands	45.5	63.1
Denmark	44.0	69.1
France	43.7	54.9
Austria	41.1	56.2
United Kingdom	39.6	52.9
Ireland	39.6	54.6
Italy	38.3	52.3
Luxembourg	37.7	54.2
Germany	37.3	56.4
Finland	36.6	64.0
Canada	34.9	45.2
New Zealand	33.6	49.1
Greece	31.9	47.1
Australia	31.0	43.2
Switzerland	30.9	41.8
Portugal	30.8	38.4
United States	30.5	44.5
Japan	27.2	29.5
Spain	25.3	43.8
Turkey	20.1	50.2

a. Average tax rates are for 1982.
b. Marginal rates on labor are for 1978 and include the effects of personal income, payroll, and indirect taxes.
SOURCE: I. Hansson and C. Stuart, "Why Are Taxes So High in Sweden?" Mimeo.

debate, much of the underlying pressure to reform the tax system is home-grown.

In Sweden, taxes are collected by the national government and one layer of local governments. The national government imposes a progressive tax on personal income while local governments impose proportional taxes on personal income at rates that equal roughly 30 percent in all jurisdictions (Figure 8.1 details the relative importance of different taxes as revenue sources since 1950). Although total (national plus local) marginal personal tax rates currently range to about 75 percent, a major feature of the 1982 tax reform was to reduce the marginal personal rate for most full-time workers to 50 percent. The national government also receives substantial receipts

FIGURE 8.1   Various Taxes' Share of GNP in Sweden, 1950–1986

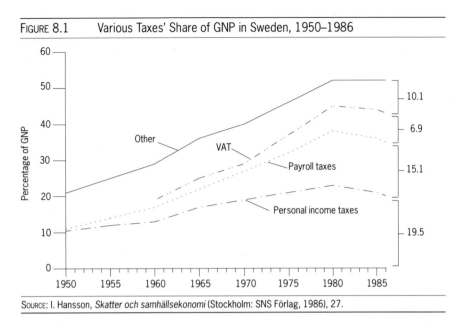

SOURCE: I. Hansson, *Skatter och samhällsekonomi* (Stockholm: SNS Förlag, 1986), 27.

from proportional payroll and value-added taxes. In addition, a corporation income tax is levied by the national government at a rate of 52 percent, but the presence of numerous corporation tax preferences has in recent years reduced the importance of the corporation income tax as a revenue source.

Here we report on the Swedish tax experience. We begin with an overview of Sweden's high-tax environment, noting the importance of the country's commitment to public redistribution. We then examine trends in taxation. Most notably, tax revenue has risen more or less continuously as a share of GDP in the postwar period reaching 55 percent in 1987, while marginal tax rates rose until 1982 but now appear to be falling. Next we discuss several of the problems created by high taxes that have led to support for a reduction in marginal rates. Thereafter we study the proposals Sweden considered and rejected in preparation for the 1982 tax reform; these include an expenditure tax, a cash-flow corporation tax, and a tax on real capital income. Distributional concerns were one reason for rejection of these proposals. Another is that as a small open economy, Sweden might face international tax arbitrage if it had implemented tax structures different from those in other countries. The following section examines the changes that were adopted in 1982. The tax reform lowered both marginal tax rates and the maximum relief provided for deductions; a novelty is that the tax system became asymmetric in that the maximum relief provided for deductions was reduced below the maximum marginal tax rate.

Sweden is currently planning another major tax reform, aimed at further reducing marginal rates and broadening the tax base. In the final section we consider proposed changes to corporation and personal income taxes and to indirect taxes.

The High-Tax Environment

The high levels of taxation in Sweden mirror a highly developed welfare state with substantial public redistributions in cash and in kind. It is useful to think of public expenditures as composed mainly of public goods and of redistributions, the latter including public provision of *private* goods. Expenditures on public goods in Sweden amount to roughly 10 percent of GDP, which is fairly normal compared with other OECD countries.

Redistributions in cash and in kind, on the other hand, amount to roughly 50 percent of GDP. A major example of redistributional spending is the social security system, which effectively guarantees each pensioner a level of disposable income equal to 78 percent of the per capita disposable income of the average Swede (including children). The 78 percent figure does not include all types of redistribution targeted to the elderly because it misses extensive publicly paid expenses for nursing homes and for medical care, which is provided to all residents in kind by the public sector and which is consumed disproportionately by pensioners. Redistributional spending is not limited to the elderly. For employees who become sick and must miss work, the public sector not only pays direct medical expenses but also provides cash transfers to replace lost employment income. The public sector also organizes and finances essentially all paid day care of children and education, including generous cash transfers for maternity and paternity leave that amount to the equivalent of roughly one year's employment income.

It is clear from Swedish political rhetoric that a major and generally accepted motivation for the observed level of redistributional spending has been to protect residents against economic events that might result in temporary or permanent low consumption. The overall impact of Swedish tax-and-transfer schemes on the distribution of consumption is difficult to assess precisely, however, because private insurance and private schemes for redistributing across the life cycle, which are naturally little used in Sweden, would doubtless have been more prevalent in the absence of public tax-and-transfer schemes. Nonetheless, data in Figure 8.2 indicate that Sweden is characterized by a relatively even distribution of disposable income and by high transfers from the public sector.

It is worth emphasizing that the *desirability* of using the public sector to organize life-cycle redistributions and to even consumption across individuals is an accepted principle in Swedish political debate. The revealed Swedish preference for public redistributional spending is a fundamental part of the environment in which taxes have risen in the past, and this preference continues to exert substantial force on the ongoing process of reform. In thinking about tax reform in this paper, we take the Swedish preference for redistributional spending as a given and do not ask the deeper question of why Sweden and other countries in northern Europe apparently have greater preferences for redistributional spending than do other OECD countries.

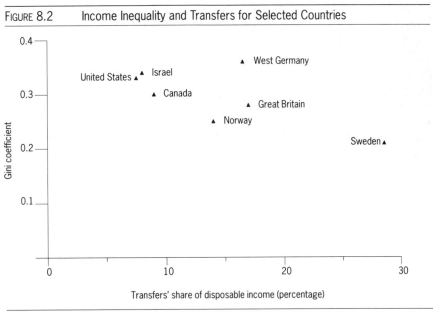

FIGURE 8.2   Income Inequality and Transfers for Selected Countries

NOTE: The Gini coefficient can vary between 0 and 1, with 0 representing equal income distribution and 1 representing maximally unequal distribution.
SOURCE: S. Ringen, "Svensk inkomstfördelning i internationell jämförelse, Expertgruppen för studier i offentlig ekonomi" (Ministry of Finance, Stockholm, 1966, mimeo), 12.

The Swedish Experience: Trends and Problems

Trends. The expansion of the Swedish welfare state involved a secular rise in taxes as a share of GDP from about 20 percent in 1950, which was fairly normal by international standards, to 55 percent in 1987.[1] The rise in the level of taxation was combined with increases in the progressivity of the income tax, with the result that taxes on marginal earnings have been very high throughout the 1970s and 1980s. Much of the impetus for increases in taxation came from a desire to even consumption across individuals and across periods in a single individual's life cycle. The proliferation of policies designed to even consumption was especially evident in the 1970s, when industrial subsidies amounting to between 1 and 2 percent of GDP were provided to protect workers in declining industries such as shipbuilding and steel production; these subsidies soon came to be seen as costly and ineffective in the long run and have since been curtailed. The importance of distributional considerations as a driving force behind the rise in taxation is perhaps brought out most strikingly by the fact that, especially in the 1970s, there was substantial feeling that high marginal rates were desirable per se as a device for preventing individuals with high incomes from consuming too much. Early in the period when taxes were increasing, the potential cost of high tax rates in terms of reduced economic performance was largely neglected. Part of the explanation may be that many of the behavioral adjustments to high marginal taxes were not immediately apparent but rather took several years to reveal themselves.

As the distortionary effects of high marginal rates on earned income have become more evident, public opinion has shifted toward the view that reductions in marginal rates along with other adjustments in the tax code to reduce distortions would be desirable. Thus the total taxation of marginal earned income averaged across the population, including marginal personal income, payroll, and indirect taxes and the taxlike effect of income-indexed transfers, reached a peak of 73.2 percent in 1982 and has since declined to 71.1 percent.[2] The development of this wedge on earned income, measured as the ratio between gross and net earnings, is shown in Figure 8.3. Current plans for more substantial reform of the tax system in the early 1990s include further reductions in income tax rates that should continue the downward trend in marginal taxation of earned income. Thus, Sweden may have reached its peak of (marginal) taxation in 1982.

Although high taxation of marginal earnings is now recognized by all of the major political parties as a serious economic problem, there is less consensus among the parties about the appropriate overall level of taxation. For instance, total taxes as a share of GDP have continued to increase from 50–51 percent in the early 1980s to 55 percent in 1987. A broad majority in parliament expresses a wish to return to a level close to 50 percent of GDP, but actions that would seriously limit the scope of the welfare state meet strong resistance from voters. Most voters continue to be willing to accept high taxes in order to maintain an extensive welfare state. Only the conser-

FIGURE 8.3   Ratio of Gross to Net Earnings in Sweden, 1955–1986

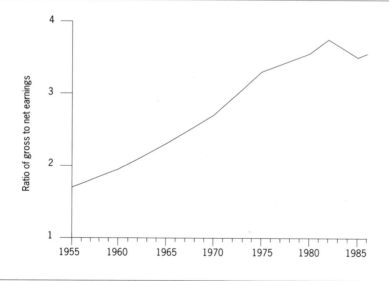

SOURCE: I. Hansson, *Skatter och samhällsekonomi* (Stockholm: SNS Förlag, 1986), 89.

vative party, which represents roughly 15 percent of the electorate, wishes to decrease taxes substantially below 50 percent of GDP.

Problems. Although high taxes in Sweden clearly have distorted resource allocation, the Swedish economy manages to maintain per capita GDP and consumption levels that are high by the standards of developed countries. Here, we review some of the specific experiences that have made the problems with high taxes more apparent and thereby have contributed to the current trend toward a reduction of marginal rates.[3] The first is bracket creep: the combined effects of inflation and nonindexed tax brackets have led to a situation in which nearly all full-time workers, including the blue-collar workers who make up a substantial portion of the support of the Social Democratic party, had for some time before 1982 faced marginal income tax rates far above 50 percent. The tax reform of 1982 then reduced the marginal tax rate for most full-time workers to 50 percent. Faced with these rates, individual workers have become aware of the adverse impact of high marginal taxes, as extra earnings from overtime work or increased wages largely have been taxed away. Such experiences have helped to instill a general feeling that overtime work does not pay and that reductions from full-time work are sometimes advantageous because only modest declines in disposable income result. As a consequence, there is now relatively broad support for changes that would raise the net reward for extra work.

Behavioral responses to high marginal rates on earned income may initially have been difficult to identify because of lags between increases in tax rates and changes in behavior, but these responses are now obvious to many voters. The main response has been a reduction in labor supply.[4] Recall that the peak aggregate marginal rate on labor income of 73 percent that occurred in 1982 implies that, in 1982, gross earnings were almost four times net earnings on the margin. Tax wedges of this magnitude discriminate strongly against taxed uses of time and effort. As revealed in Figures 8.4 and 8.5, average hours of work per working individual fell sharply from 1976 to 1981, and both average hours and total hours worked in the Swedish economy have risen since 1981. Declines in hours up to 1981 can be viewed at least partly as a response to high and increasing taxes on marginal earnings, and rises in hours since 1981 may partly reflect declines in marginal taxes.[5] Data in Rivlin (1986) provide a longer perspective. Work per citizen aged 25–64 in Sweden has decreased by 18 percent for men and 25 percent for women during the last twenty years while the corresponding figures for the United States are 6 percent for both men and women. Analyses using different empirical methods suggest that perhaps two-thirds of this decrease in Swedish labor supply can be attributed to increased taxes and government expenditures (see Rivlin 1986: 120–23).

Another widely noted problem is that high marginal taxes stimulate the use of tax-favored fringe benefits as a partial substitute for cash remuneration. This substitution is typically viewed as undesirable because it gives rise

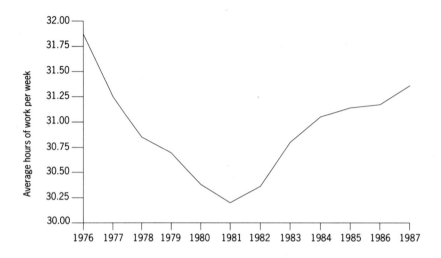

SOURCE: Ministry of Finance, Sweden.

FIGURE 8.5   Total Hours Worked Annually in Sweden according to National Income Accounts, 1970–1987

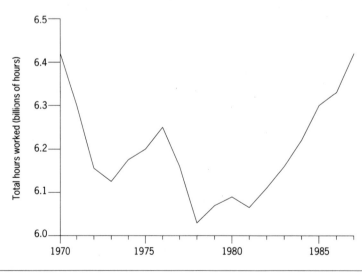

SOURCE: Ministry of Finance, Sweden.

to horizontal inequities and because it tends to counteract the intended distributional effects of the progressive rate structure.

Finally, high tax rates and nonindexed tax brackets are thought to contribute to inflationary wage-price spirals. In particular, most wages in Sweden are determined through central negotiations between labor and employer organizations. In these negotiations, labor typically argues that because of high marginal taxes, gross nominal wages must increase greatly in order to maintain constant real net wages. It is of course an open question whether high marginal taxes really contribute to inflationary spirals. Empirical analysis by Normann (1983), for instance, suggests that high progressivity may dampen wage increases by reducing distributional tensions. In any case, economists have pointed out that problems of excessive wage demands might be reduced by indexing tax brackets. Indexing was instituted in Sweden in the late 1970s but was not politically viable and was removed in the early 1980s. Many politicians today believe that reducing progressivity by lowering marginal taxes and (possibly) leaving total tax revenue constant would help limit upward pressure on wages.

Special problems in the taxation of capital. The taxation of capital income presents special problems in a high-tax environment, especially under inflationary conditions. Capital income in Sweden is taxed under the personal income tax and is treated formally on a nominal basis. At the same time, various provisions imply that capital is taxed *effectively* according to one of four distinct principles depending on the type of investment and the source of funds: taxation of nominal capital income, taxation of real capital income, outright exemption and implicit exemption by expenditure-tax treatment. On the other side of the income statement, all household liabilities are subject to a nominal principle of taxation. That is, consistent with the formal inclusion of capital income on a nominal basis, nominal interest expenditures are fully deductible.

On the income side, strict nominal taxation of capital income applies to returns from about 15 percent of household gross wealth, including interest on bonds and some bank saving. Owner-occupied housing, on the other hand, constitutes 39 percent of household gross wealth and gives rise to an imputed income that is included in the tax base of the personal income tax. This imputed income is 1.5 percent of assessed valuation in 1990 or about 1 percent of market value for nearly all owner-occupied housing, so income from owner-occupied housing is effectively taxed on a real basis. Returns on the remaining 49 percent of gross wealth are in effect not subject to income taxation. For instance, returns from savings in certain special bank accounts are exempt from taxation, as are implicit returns on consumer durables. A larger group of assets, which most notably includes pension insurance, are subject to expenditure-tax treatment whereby the taxpayer is allowed to deduct saved amounts from income and later counts benefits as taxable income when these are paid out. As is well known, this treatment means that the net rate of return equals the gross rate of return if the tax rate is constant over time, so assets with expenditure-tax treatment are approximately untaxed.

This mixture of principles of taxation has led to undesirable tax arbitrage that has become extreme in Sweden's high-tax environment. The fundamental mechanism for avoiding taxes is to invest in lightly taxed assets and to finance the investments by debt, for which interest payments are fully deductible. An important example is debt-financed investment in owner-occupied housing. Because taxable imputed income is 1.5 percent of assessed value and deductible interest payments currently run about 12 percent of the borrowed amount, such investments produce a net tax write-off equal to about 10 percent of the invested amount. The importance of this type of tax avoidance is revealed by the fact that, largely due to the amount of debt-financed home ownership in Sweden, personal taxation of capital income actually *decreases* tax revenue by 0.5 percent of GDP. That is, tax relief due to interest deductibility exceeds revenue from the taxation of capital in the form of interest income, dividends, and capital gains, so that abolition of the personal taxation of capital income would raise total tax receipts.

Tax avoidance by borrowing to purchase lightly taxed assets is especially attractive for high-income individuals with high marginal tax rates. Not surprisingly, such individuals hold a disproportionate share of tax-favored assets. This "tax-clientele effect" means that individuals and households with high incomes receive net tax relief through the taxation of capital income, while net tax payments are positive for individuals and households with low incomes (see Figure 8.6). Thus the taxation of personal capital income in Sweden at present redistributes in a way that counteracts the intended effects of progressivity in the personal income tax schedule.

Concern about the divergence between the "formal" progressivity built into the tax schedule and the actual progressivity of the tax system after individuals have adjusted their behavior to avoid taxes is a major aspect of current plans for tax reform. Until recently, a strongly progressive tax schedule was viewed as an efficient device for equalizing the distribution of income. Several systematic studies have revealed, however, what observers in Sweden might have suspected: although both the income tax and the tax system generally exhibit strong formal progressivity (Figure 8.7), actual tax payments are roughly constant as a fraction of total income (Figure 8.8). Increased awareness of deficiencies in the measurement of income and recognition of patterns of tax avoidance have undermined the support for high formal tax rates and have created a desire to institute creative rules to deal with tax avoidance that takes place through adjustment of portfolios of assets and liabilities.

In sum, there seems to be little disagreement among politicians that the taxation of capital under the personal income tax currently reduces tax revenue, counteracts the intended effects of high formal progressivity, distorts the allocation of investment, and complicates the tax system. The effects of nonneutral tax treatment are especially pronounced in Sweden's high-tax

FIGURE 8.6 Taxes Paid on Capital Income as a Share of Total Income in Sweden, 1982

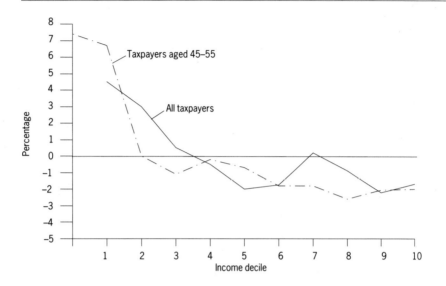

SOURCE: I. Hansson, *Skatter och samhällsekonomi* (Stockholm: SNS Förlag, 1986), 153.

FIGURE 8.7   Formal Tax Progressivity in Sweden, 1982

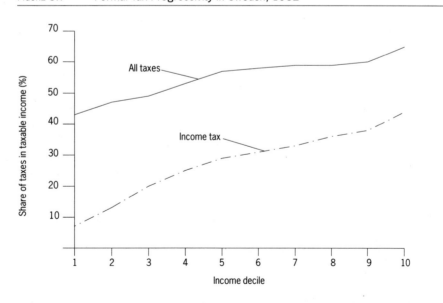

SOURCE: L. Calmfors et al., *Nya spelregler för tillväxt* (Stockholm: SNS Förlag, 1986), 88.

FIGURE 8.8   Actual Tax Progressivity in Sweden, 1982

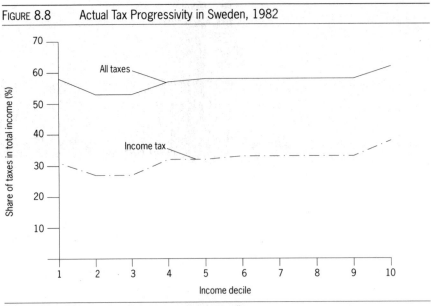

NOTE: Data are for individuals aged 45–55; taxes include payroll taxes.
SOURCE: L. Calmfors et al., *Nya spelregler för tillväxt* (Stockholm: SNS Förlag, 1986), 73.

environment, which is not surprising because the distortionary consequences of taxation typically increase more than linearly with tax rates.

Some Tax Reform Proposals That Have Been Considered and Rejected

In Sweden, tax reforms are initiated by appointment of a commission by the
government. In most instances, the commission consists of members of
Parliament and has a staff that typically includes academics from the social
sciences and law as well as officials from the Ministry of Finance. On the basis
of general instructions from the government, the commission issues a report
analyzing possible changes in the tax system and proposing reforms. Following review and critique of the report by interested groups, the government
may decline to undertake further action or it may accept or modify the
commission's proposals, which usually results in formulation of legislative
text that is submitted to Parliament. Unlike countries such as the United
States where bills are often modified extensively and rapidly during the
legislative process as a result of political negotiations, Sweden has a slower
and perhaps more careful bill-writing process, with little modification taking
place after submission to Parliament.

The expenditure tax. Partly because of academic arguments, the conservative-
middle government in power from 1976 to 1982 became interested in the

expenditure tax as a general solution to many of the problems encountered with capital taxation, and it thus assigned a parliamentary commission to study how such a tax could be implemented. The resulting commission report, *Progressiv utgiftsskatt* (Sweden 1976), resembles the *Blueprints for Basic Tax Reform* in the United States (1977) and the Meade report in the United Kingdom (1978). The report unanimously concluded that the expenditure tax would give rise to such serious problems of implementation that it could not be introduced in spite of the significant efficiency gains that such a tax would in theory generate.

The expenditure tax under consideration was the *Blueprints*-Meade type in which all savings are deductible and all dissavings are essentially taxed on a cash-flow basis. The expenditure tax would differ from the income tax primarily in that there would be a shift toward implicit public co-ownership of private wealth. For instance, marginal personal tax rates in Sweden are currently between 50 and 75 percent for most wage earners. Given expenditure tax rates in this range, private wealth of US$100,000 (about SEK 600,000) would support consumption of only US$50,000–25,000, with the remaining US$50,000–75,000 in effect publicly co-owned in the sense that the government would have to be paid that amount in taxes if the US$100,000 were dissaved.

The implicit government co-ownership of private wealth was perceived as the source of substantial difficulties. One set of problems involves transfers of wealth between taxpayers as a result of marriage, divorce, and death. (Note that partly as a result of high marginal income taxes, there is no joint taxation of income in Sweden—all income earners must file separately.) To prevent individuals with high marginal taxes from avoiding an expenditure tax by shifting assets to individuals with low marginal taxes, transfers of wealth would have to be taxed as dissavings for the donor and deducted as savings by the donee. If the donor and donee had constant but possibly different tax rates, such a rule for taxing transfers would give the same net tax liability as if the donee had accumulated the wealth by saving. With progressive tax schedules, however, tax avoidance through the shifting of assets and hence reported saving to individuals with higher marginal taxes would be possible unless transfers were taxed in a way that took account of all past marginal tax rates of the donor and the donee—which would be impossible in practice. Any method used to tax transfers would require some simple rule to fix the rates applied to donors and donees on the basis of one or several years' tax returns, which would allow individuals to avoid taxes either by concealing gifts or by manipulations that would lower the donee's marginal rates during the relevant years. Even if such taxation of transfers were technically possible, problems of liquidity and of taxpayer understanding and acceptance were thought to be substantial. For example, a transfer of an owner-occupied house from husband to wife at divorce or death would result in net tax payments as long as the husband's marginal tax rate exceeded the wife's rate.

Related problems would arise when wealth shifts status as a result of emigration or immigration. To prevent tax avoidance, it would be necessary to tax the wealth of emigrants when they leave the country, which would be difficult to implement in an open economy. To treat immigrants under an expenditure tax, it would be necessary to determine their wealth when they enter Sweden. If the wealth of immigrants were allowed to provide for future consumption on a tax-free basis, immigrants would have an incentive to overstate wealth, while if no such tax-free status were granted, immigrants would instead have an incentive to conceal wealth and later report it as saving.

The transition to an expenditure tax presents a similar and more serious set of problems. In order to prevent individuals from avoiding taxes by reporting low wealth at the transition, the expenditure tax would have to allow for untaxed future consumption equivalent to wealth at the time of the transition. This would permit taxpayers to postpone taxation by "consuming" old wealth and by "saving" current earnings. The implied amount of lost tax revenue during such a transition was estimated by the commission to equal approximately one year's GDP in Sweden. In principle, this sort of postponement could be prevented by special restrictions that would allow an individual to claim deductions for saving only to the extent that his or her net wealth had risen. Such restrictions could be circumvented, however, by concealing wealth at the transition or, in the case of related taxpayers, by arbitrage under which one of the taxpayers would report dissaving of old wealth and the other would report new saving. Because married couples must file separately in Sweden, restrictions that permit saving deductions only if net wealth had risen could be defeated by simple tax planning within a marriage.

Another concern with the expenditure tax was that it would tend to make personal bankruptcy after reported consumption of all wealth especially attractive. Such bankruptcy would amount to a relatively severe form of (intentional or unintentional) tax avoidance, because individuals would also in effect have consumed the share of capital "co-owned" by the government. An additional perceived problem is that under an expenditure tax with a progressive rate structure, tax liabilities increase as reported consumption becomes more uneven, regardless of whether actual consumption is smooth or uneven. Such unevenness in reported consumption would generally occur when taxpayers purchase cars or other expensive consumer durables and thereby report large dissaving. This would create distortions and complications by encouraging tax planning and would punish nonplanning taxpayers. Averaging schemes might help alleviate the problem, but these would also complicate the expenditure tax. Finally, the commission believed it would be undesirable to introduce tax rules that diverged from the rules used in other countries. Because Sweden is a small open economy, such divergence would encourage international tax arbitrage.

The commission also considered a "simplified" expenditure tax or earned-income tax under which the net rate of return on savings would be brought to equality with the gross rate of return by exempting capital income from personal income taxation. In the terms used in *Blueprints,* the simplified expenditure tax would apply the tax-prepayment method to all assets; that is, consumption would be taxed by imposing a levy on earned income when it is earned and not when it is consumed. Because tax payments would not be postponed and because capital income would be tax-exempt, nearly all of the problems noted above with the traditional expenditure tax would be avoided. The commission concluded that the earned-income tax was prefer-able to the traditional expenditure tax because implementation and transi-tion would be less complicated and because the simplified version would leave less scope for tax avoidance and evasion. In spite of its advantages, however, the commission rejected the earned-income tax on the judgment that ability to pay taxes should be measured by the sum of labor and capital income and not by labor income alone. The commission felt that although there are serious shortcomings in the measurement of income under the current income tax, income is a better measure of ability to consume than would be actual consumption as measured under an expenditure tax, and thus that income is the more equitable tax base.

Cash-flow tax on corporations. Regardless of whether income or some form of expenditure taxation is applied to private individuals, cash-flow taxation might still be used to eliminate the effective taxation of saving in firms and thereby to increase capital formation.[6] In fact, although an income tax (at a 52 percent rate) and not a cash-flow tax is currently imposed on corporations, the income tax tends to resemble a cash-flow tax because the tax base has been narrowed in recent decades by the introduction of tax breaks designed to stimulate investment. These tax breaks allow firms to postpone taxation. Thus as long as profits are not too high, many corporations report taxable profits and hence pay taxes only to the extent required for dividend pay-ments (Kanniainen 1988). Under a cash-flow tax, taxes would similarly be paid only as a result of dividend payments.[7]

A proposal to shift formally from income to cash-flow taxation of corpo-rations was recently examined and rejected by a parliamentary commission on corporate taxation. One perceived problem was that a shift to cash-flow taxation of corporations might result in substantial postponement of tax payments on corporate capital, which would be undesirable on equity grounds. The argument was that because taxation of capital gains on stocks occurs when gains are realized instead of when they are accrued, tax post-ponement can occur unless retained profits are taxed, as they are under a corporation income tax. Under this argument, a traditional corporation income tax acts as a tax-withholding device.

Several additional motivations for rejecting a shift to a cash-flow tax on corporations were related to international ramifications. One important consideration was that cash-flow taxation of corporations in Sweden would cause the Swedish tax system to deviate too much from tax systems applied in other countries. Such deviations could stimulate tax avoidance based on international tax arbitrage and might also hamper integration between Sweden and the European Community. It was also felt that cash-flow taxation in Sweden would complicate double taxation treaties. For instance, the cash-flow tax would differ fundamentally from the corporation income tax in the United States, which means that the United States would probably not allow tax credits for cash-flow taxes paid in Sweden by U.S. subsidiaries. A shift to a formal cash-flow tax on corporations might therefore create a disincentive for U.S. corporations to invest in Sweden because the shift would effectively raise the tax liabilities of the corporation to the U.S. government.

Taxation of real capital income. As noted earlier, the personal income tax currently applies four different principles of taxation: taxation of nominal capital income, taxation of real capital income, direct exemption of capital income, and indirect exemption due to expenditure-tax (or tax-expenditure) treatment. One way to reduce the distortions implied by application of different principles would be to replace taxation of nominal capital income with taxation of real capital income. In practice, the most important changes would be to base taxes on real rather than nominal interest income and expenditure, and to base depreciation allowances on indexed purchase costs.

This alternative was also examined by a commission, which recommended a shift to taxation of real capital income. One problem with such a shift, however, is that homeowners would no longer be allowed to deduct the inflation portion of their interest payments and hence would face liquidity problems. Because the government in Sweden subsidizes many home loans and is in a position to influence loan conditions, the commission also recommended that homeowners be offered indexed loans as part of the shift to real taxation. The proposal to provide indexed loans was necessary to make the package politically acceptable. Nonetheless, many reviewing agencies and politicians strongly criticized indexed loans, arguing that such loans would be difficult to understand and would place homeowners in a more precarious position than the existing system, because loan amounts would be tied to increases in the overall price level, which could easily exceed increases in housing prices. These considerations together with the fact that other countries generally tax nominal capital income contributed ultimately to rejection of a shift to real taxation of capital income.

The foregoing discussion of the tax reforms that were *not* implemented in Sweden reveals a significant difference between what academics generally view as the best tax system in a closed economy with perfect information and no costs of filing and auditing tax returns and the type of system that in fact can be implemented in an open economy with imperfect information and limitations on the complexity of tax returns. Of particular interest is that the design of tax systems may to an increasing extent be a matter of international policy coordination, especially from the perspective of a small open economy. In the case of Sweden, there has been a strong desire to avoid sharp deviations from the types of tax systems used abroad.

Tax Reforms That Have Been Implemented

Lower marginal tax rates and maximum tax relief for losses. Having rejected the fundamental tax reforms listed above, Parliament and the government tried to ameliorate the problems caused by high, nonneutral taxes through less far-reaching reforms. The first important step was the 1982 reform that mandated reductions in marginal personal income tax rates from a level of 60–74 percent for nearly all full-time employees to a level of 50 percent in 1985. The effect of the 1982 tax reform was to reduce the aggregate level of marginal taxation of labor income from 73.2 percent in 1982 to 71.1 percent in 1985 (Hansson 1986). This percentage-point reduction is roughly on a par with the effect on the aggregate rate in the United States caused by the U.S. Tax Reform Act of 1986. Because tax rates were substantially higher in Sweden to start with, the overall stimulative effect of the Swedish tax reform of 1982 might be expected to be as great or greater than the more recent U.S. Tax Reform Act.

An important feature of the 1982 reform was that to counter the redistributional effects of rate reductions and to dampen nonneutralities in capital income taxation favoring debt-financed consumption and investment, the 1982 reform limited the tax relief for losses to a maximum of 50 percent. In particular, taxpayers with marginal tax rates in excess of 50 percent who had negative capital income that was deducted from taxable labor income were no longer allowed benefits from these deductions equal to their marginal tax rates times their capital losses. The limit on the value of deductions means that capital income is treated asymmetrically, with positive capital income subject to the progressive rate structure of the personal income tax but with negative income resulting in tax relief of at most 50 percent. A noteworthy consequence is that tax relief on interest payments for owner-occupied housing is currently limited to 50 percent of interest payments.

The asymmetric treatment of capital income has been perceived as a viable innovation that has largely had positive effects and that may be extended in future tax reforms. Because the limitation of tax relief on interest expenditure arises only for individuals with marginal tax rates in excess of 50 percent, it is irrelevant for most taxpayers. Interest expenditures are still fully deductible against earnings for most voters, which doubtless contributed to the implementation of the reform and, given the strong distributional sentiments in Sweden, to the political attractiveness of taxing capital income asymmetrically.

In addition to the 1982 reform, a number of minor "loophole-plugging" changes have been made to eliminate existing forms of tax avoidance and to combat newly developed forms. Of note is that recent deregulation of financial markets has among other things removed limits on the amount of debt that can be issued by the banking system, which has tended to increase the extent to which individuals with high marginal tax rates can borrow to purchase lightly taxed assets. Legislation designed to combat new forms of tax avoidance has typically had the negative side effect of complicating the tax system.

Shifting from more troublesome to less troublesome tax bases. Much of the criticism directed at the current tax system in Sweden involves personal and corporation income taxes and focuses on tax arbitrage that is possible because of the mixture of different principles for taxing capital income. These problems do not arise under the traditional expenditure tax discussed above, which is a tax on consumption, or under an earned-income tax. Nor do these problems arise under consumption taxes such as the value-added tax or under labor income taxes such as payroll taxes, because capital income is not subject to consumption or labor taxes. Although abrupt shifts to progressive expenditure taxes have been rejected, more gradual but nonetheless significant shifts in the direction of proportional expenditure taxation have indeed taken place through the introduction of and increases in value-added and payroll taxes (see Figure 8.1). Further, although a combination of income, payroll, and value-added taxes may have complicated the tax system as a whole, the net result may still have been a less complicated system than would have resulted from attempting to correct for the nonneutralities that arise in raising revenue equal to 50 percent of GDP with only an income tax. In any case, recent tax reforms in Sweden have continued the trend of decreasing the relative importance of "troublesome" taxes such as the personal income tax and the corporation income tax while increasing the relative importance of less troublesome taxes such as value-added and payroll taxes, which are proportional and less subject to manipulation.

A Major Tax Reform in the Works

Preconditions. Sweden has been a world leader in the development of high average and marginal taxes, but the recent direction of tax reform in Sweden has been to reverse the trend toward greater marginal taxation. Discontent with the present Swedish tax system has been growing for some time, and the tax reform of 1982 that decreased marginal tax rates and made the taxation of capital income slightly more neutral seems to have been a clear first step. More recently, the highly publicized U.S. Tax Reform Act of 1986 has focused international attention on the problems of distortionary taxation, leading to tax reform movements in many other countries. This turn in the international tide has caught the attention of Swedish observers and increased the sense that a more fundamental reconsideration of Swedish tax policy is appropriate.

Accordingly, three parliamentary commissions have been appointed to suggest revisions to the personal income tax, the corporation income tax, and the system of indirect taxation. In broad terms, the goal is to develop a tax-reform package that lowers tax rates and broadens tax bases, as has been the thrust of recent reforms in other countries. The government's instructions to the commissions are that overall tax revenue is to be held constant but that shifts among different sources of revenue are possible. It thus appears that the trend toward less reliance on personal income taxation will continue: a likely outcome of reform will be to shift tax revenue amounting to roughly 2 percent of GDP from income taxes to taxes on consumption. More specifically, the government's instructions are to devise a tax reform that (1) lowers tax rates and broadens tax bases, especially for personal and corporate income taxation; (2) makes the taxation of different types of investment and savings more neutral; (3) increases household saving and decreases household borrowing; (4) simplifies the filing and auditing process; and (5) provides rules that can be applied for a long period of time. Given the broad consensus in Sweden about the problems with the current system for taxing income, a relatively far-reaching tax reform thus appears to be in the offing.

Personal income taxation. Marginal personal income tax rates are likely to be reduced from a range of 35–75 percent in 1988 to a range of 30–50 percent in the early 1990s. For most full-time employees, rates will be decreased from a current level of 50 percent to 30 percent.

Reform of the rules for taxation of capital income is of particular interest. Two restrictions apparently imposed by the political process are important. First, the majority of homeowners must be permitted to deduct nominal interest expenditures fully and to benefit from tax relief at the same rate as their marginal tax rates (30 percent). Quite simply, any tax reform that did not satisfy this restriction would alienate homeowners to a degree that politicians would not accept. Tax reforms in many other countries seem to face a similar restriction.

The second restriction is that tax relief from interest expenditures must not exceed 30 percent for the minority of high-income individuals who have marginal tax rates on earned income of greater than 30 percent. The reason is that it would be politically unacceptable for the net cost of debt-financed owner-occupied housing to be lower for high-income individuals than for the majority of homeowners. More generally, there is a political desire to limit the extent to which high-income individuals can derive benefits from the allowed deductibility of interest expenditures and from other income tax rules.

Together, these restrictions cannot be met under a traditional progressive income tax levied on the sum of labor and capital income. Instead, a choice must be made between two alternative systems, both of which are currently under consideration. One alternative is to extend the asymmetric rules for capital taxation mentioned above, subjecting positive capital income to a progressive tax schedule but limiting the rate of tax relief for negative capital income to 30 percent. The second alternative is to split the taxation of capital income from that of labor income, treating positive and negative capital income symmetrically by imposing a proportional tax on income from all capital, while retaining a progressive rate structure for labor income. Interestingly, Denmark now has both asymmetric rules for capital income and a split system for taxing capital and labor income.

Neither of these alternatives is problem-free. Asymmetric rules discriminate against risk taking and encourage tax avoidance by manipulations that reduce income taxed at the full marginal rate and also reduce the magnitude of negative capital income, which receives relief at a rate lower than the full marginal rate. A separate proportional tax on capital income means that the progressive rate structure would apply to labor income instead of to the sum of labor and capital income, conflicting with the notion that ability to pay is best measured by total income. A separate proportional tax would also create an incentive for high-income individuals to report labor income as capital income.

Since the overall level of taxation is high and will remain high in Sweden, these two alternatives may possibly be viewed as second-best (or third-best) options given that the majority of homeowners must be treated favorably and that equity considerations exclude rules in which gains from deductions of interest expenditure are greater for high-income individuals. Of course economists might argue that adequate public subsidization of owner-occupied housing, if it is to be given, would best be organized without entangling it with the income tax and then imposing special restrictions on the income tax. Experiences from Sweden and other countries suggest, however, that this advice is seldom followed. A possible explanation may be that support for owner-occupied housing via the tax system is relatively concealed from non-owners of housing and hence is easy to maintain, and that homeowners realize this and effectively block shifts to systems in which support is more explicit. Another possible explanation is that liquidity considerations, uncertainty, and money illusion make nominal and not just real interest expenditures and income important to individuals, leading to tax rules that treat wage earnings and nominal interest rates on the same basis for most individuals. A third possible explanation, which might be especially relevant in a small open economy, is that other countries typically base tax rules on nominal rather than real interest payments, and that if a country must treat some assets on a nominal basis in order to prevent international tax arbitrage, then the country may find it better to base the entire tax system on nominal rather than real rules.

Corporation income taxes. Current plans are to decrease the corporation income tax rate from 52 percent to about 30–35 percent and to finance the rate reduction by base broadening. Interestingly, the base broadening is largely to be accomplished by sharply restricting reserves that currently are untaxed, in effect moving from close to a cash-flow tax toward a more comprehensive income tax. These changes are similar in spirit to changes in the U.S. Tax Reform Act of 1986, which also reduced corporation tax rates and repealed investment incentives such as the investment tax credit.

Indirect taxes. Indirect taxes are to be increased to finance partially the decrease in personal income tax rates. The most important change is to broaden the base of the value-added tax to include most services, which for historical reasons have not been subject to value-added taxation. Much of the revenue to finance personal rate reductions will likely come from base broadening of the value-added tax.

Summary

To most Swedes, protecting residents (not just citizens) against temporary or permanent low consumption is a proper role of government. The Swedish political preference for redistribution has in the past forty years led Sweden to a position as the world's highest-tax country. The possible distortionary effects of taxes were given little thought until relatively recently. Poor economic performance during the 1970s prompted concern with levels of taxation in the 1980s, resulting in the 1982 tax reform that lowered marginal personal taxes. Although marginal taxes apparently reached their peak in 1982, the average tax rate measured as the proportion of GDP taken in taxes has continued to rise.

One problem caused by high marginal taxes has been tax arbitrage that occurs when individuals invest in lightly taxed forms of capital such as homes and pension insurance, and finance the investments by debt, for which interest payments are fully deductible. So extensive is such arbitrage that net receipts from taxes on capital income are negative except in the lowest three or four income deciles. This is seen by many Swedes as undesirable because it counters the intended distributional effects of a progressive rate structure.

Several proposals often advocated by economists for dealing with problems of capital taxation have recently been studied by government commissions and rejected. A shift from an income basis to an expenditure basis for progressive personal taxation was rejected because of numerous complications and opportunities for tax avoidance, because an expenditure tax would deviate from systems imposed in other countries (and might thus lead to tax arbitrage), and because the sum of labor and capital income was perceived to be a more equitable tax base than, ultimately, labor income alone. A simplified expenditure tax (i.e., an earned-income tax) was also rejected on the basis that it is more equitable to tax capital income. A cash-flow tax for corporations was rejected because taxes on capital can effectively be postponed under such a tax and because of fears of deviating from tax rules imposed in other countries. Finally, real taxation of capital income was rejected because it would hurt homeowners.

An interesting change in personal taxation implemented in 1982 was the asymmetric treatment of capital income whereby positive income is taxed at the taxpayer's marginal rate, which exceeds 50 percent for high-income individuals, but where negative income results in tax benefits at a rate of at most 50 percent. Distributional concerns account for some of the attractiveness of this change.

Major tax reform is currently in the planning stage. Further reduction in marginal tax rates is a clear goal of reform. Because tax reform is to be revenue neutral, this should reduce overall progressivity. Another clear goal of tax reform is to make the taxation of capital income more neutral. Much of the political pressure to reform the rules for taxation of capital income stems from distributional concerns—namely, from a desire to limit the extent to which high-income individuals can benefit from tax planning.

Tax Reform in the United Kingdom:
The Recent Experience

Since the election of the first Thatcher government in 1979, the tax system of the United Kingdom has undergone substantial changes. The incoming government was committed to reduce the overall tax burden and its disincentive effects, and these commitments have continued to be popular political issues for incumbents. Substantial rate reductions and some simplifications have been implemented in the income tax, but changes elsewhere in the tax system do not seem to form part of a coherent strategy for tax reform, and many anomalies have been ignored or even aggravated. Although the income tax reforms have undoubtedly reduced distortions affecting incentives to work and to save, excessive concentration on income tax has allowed problems in other areas of taxation to continue, or has even aggravated such problems.

The first section of this chapter briefly describes the U.K. tax system, emphasizing the importance of taxes other than income tax, which raises only around one quarter of total revenue. The social security tax, national insurance contributions, is the second-largest revenue raiser. Corporation tax in the United Kingdom has recently grown very rapidly, and is now an important source of revenue. The United Kingdom does have a value-added tax, which contributes roughly half of all indirect tax revenue, the bulk of the remainder coming from excise duties on tobacco, alcohol, and gasoline. Taxes on capital contribute very little revenue in the United Kingdom. In the second section we consider the evolution of the tax system. Next we examine the effects of the tax system on the distribution of income, showing the substantial progressivity of the system in the bottom half of the income distribution, contrasted with the nearly proportional nature of the system in the upper half of the distribution. This leads to a discussion of the country's income tax rate structure and of its indirect tax system. Here we also consider the recent proposals for fiscal harmonization within the European Community (EC). The following two sections discuss the corporation and capital tax systems. The tax treatment of married and unmarried individuals has been a source of controversy for most of the period since 1979. In 1988 the debate culminated in a set of proposals, which we analyze next. Local government in the United Kingdom raises less than 10 percent of total revenue, but is affected by controversial proposals to replace a property tax with a poll tax. We consider both the nature of local government funding in the United Kingdom and its reform. The next section examines two areas where unplanned interactions cause problems: the relationship between income tax and social security contributions and that between taxation and means-tested benefits. We then discuss the United Kingdom's highly complex system for taxing saving and the administration of the tax system. The final section assesses the changes made to the U.K. tax system in the 1980s.

The U.K. Tax System, 1988/89

Total tax revenue in the United Kingdom in 1988/89 was around £171 billion, equal to 37.5 percent of gross domestic product (GDP). The largest contributor to tax revenue is the personal income tax, which yields just under a

TABLE 9.1   Tax Revenues in the United Kingdom, 1988/89

	Billions of £	% of total tax revenues
Personal income tax	42.1	24.6
National insurance contributions	31.6	18.5
Corporation income tax	21.0	12.3
Capital taxes	5.0	2.9
Value-added tax	26.2	15.3
Excise duties	20.0	11.7
Other indirect taxes	6.0	3.5
Local authority rates	19.0	11.1
Total tax revenues	170.9	
Total GDP	456.0	

Source: United Kingdom, *Financial Statement and Budget Report 1988/89* (London: Her Majesty's Stationery Office, 1988).

quarter of the total (see Table 9.1). Personal income tax is levied at a basic rate of 25 percent, which is the marginal rate for almost 95 percent of taxpayers. There is a single higher rate of 40 percent.

Next in importance are national insurance contributions, a payroll tax levied on both employers and employees, hypothecated to certain elements of the social security budget. The normal rate of tax is just under 20 percent of earnings, with employees contributing slightly less than half of this total. The value-added tax (VAT) is a multistage general consumption tax, imposed at a standard rate of 15 percent on slightly over half of all consumer expenditure: food, fuel, and housing are the principal exclusions. Taken together, these three broad-based taxes—personal income tax, national insurance contributions, and VAT—total about 60 percent of U.K. tax revenue. This has been a relatively constant figure, although the income tax has had a diminishing share of the total and national insurance contributions and VAT, an increasing one.

Corporation income tax had diminished to almost insignificant proportions earlier in the decade, but revenues have recently grown rapidly as profits have revived. The figures in Table 9.1 include revenue from taxes on North Sea oil production, which have generated over 5 percent of U.K. government revenues during the 1980s; since the fall in oil prices in 1986, however, this is no longer a major source of revenue. The corporation tax is imputed to individual shareholders; a basic-rate taxpayer pays no further income tax on company dividends.

Among other commodity taxes, there are substantial excises on tobacco, alcoholic drinks, gasoline, and diesel fuel. Local authority rates are a property tax levied on both householders and businesses in the 450 local authority areas in the United Kingdom. There are three principal capital taxes, none of great revenue significance. Capital gains tax is imposed, at income tax rates, on indexed gains over £5,000. Inheritance tax is charged at 40 percent on estates over £110,000. Stamp duty is payable on transfers of property. The rate on securities is ½ percent and on real estate 1 percent.

Tax revenue as a share of GDP grew very rapidly in the 1960s (Figure 9.1), but has stabilized since then. A marked increase in the mid-1970s coincided with the oil crisis, recession, and the election of a Labor government in 1974, but this rise was quickly checked. There has been some fall in average tax levels since the present Conservative government came to power in 1979 but the reduction is not large.

The Evolution of U.K. Tax Policy

The development of Britain's present tax system may be traced from 1799, the year in which income tax was first introduced. The innovation was not universally welcomed. "It is a vile, Jacobin, jumped up Jack-in-office piece of impertinence—is a true Briton to have no privacy? Are the fruits of his

FIGURE 9.1   Tax Revenue as a Percentage of GDP in the United Kingdom, 1960–1988

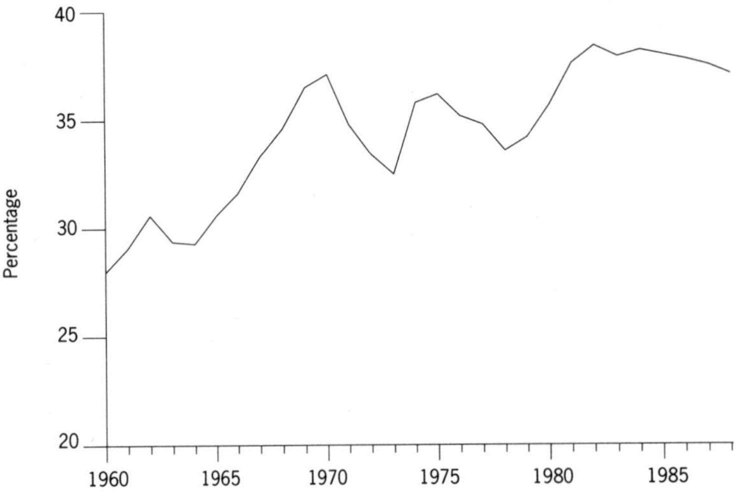

SOURCE: United Kingdom, *Financial Statement and Budget Report 1988/89* (London: Her Majesty's Stationery Office, 1988).

labour and toil to be picked over, farthing by farthing, by the pimply minions of Bureaucracy?" (Sabine 1966: 31). At least in part in response to such concerns, the income tax was completely restructured in 1803, taking on many of its modern characteristics. The most important innovation was probably the schedular system: incomes were classified as either Schedule A, B, C, D, or E, depending on their source. Thus the tax authorities would know the amount of income from each source but not the amount of an individual's total income. This feature persists and accounts for much of the administrative complexity of the British income tax. The schedules are still used, the most important being Schedule E, which covers income from employment, and Schedule D, which covers mainly profits, interest, and dividends. Income tax disappeared soon after the end of the Napoleonic wars in 1815, but reappeared in 1842 as Robert Peel restructured the system of import tariffs and excise duties. There has been an income tax in the United Kingdom ever since.

The next major milestone came in 1909 with Lloyd George's "People's Budget," which increased the progressivity of the system and imposed a surtax on incomes over £5,000 per year (over £150,000 at 1988 prices). This took the maximum rate to 8 percent but only in the face of enormous opposition. Soon, during the First World War, the top tax rate exceeded 50 percent, and although rates fell after the war, they remained far higher than had seemed feasible before 1914. Even so, before the Second World War there were only some 4 million taxpayers out of a working population of more than 20 million. By 1948 there were more than 12 million taxpayers. It was this growth in the coverage of income tax that led the Churchill government to institute the pay-as-you-earn (PAYE) system of withdrawal at source. By 1960 essentially the whole of the working population was covered by the income tax. There was a rationalization of the structure in 1973 when the surtax, which had been separately assessed and administered, was integrated into a single structure with basic-rate income tax.

The surtax, or higher-rate tax as it became after 1973, was never paid by more than a very small proportion of taxpayers. The maximum rate varied from time to time, but often reached absurd levels: George Bernard Shaw, facing a marginal tax rate of 97½ percent, once described his occupation as tax collector on 2½ percent commission. Even in 1978, the highest tax rate on earnings was 83 percent, which, with a 15 percent surcharge on investment income, took the top rate of income tax to 98 percent. In 1979 the first budget of the Thatcher administration reduced these rates to 60 percent and 75 percent. The investment income surcharge was subsequently abolished, and in 1988 the highest rate of tax on income of any kind was set at 40 percent. We discuss the changes in the income tax rate structure more fully below.

National insurance contributions have existed in some form since 1911 and were introduced as a comprehensive tax in 1948 in conjunction with postwar social security reforms. They were at that time flat-rate payments, but as the required level of social security expenditure grew, so did the necessary level of flat-rate payment. By 1960 further increases would have made payments unacceptably heavy for those on low incomes, so some element of earnings relation was introduced. By 1975 the contribution was entirely earnings-related. This shift from a flat-rate tax to a combined tax rate on earnings of almost 20 percent had a profound impact on the progressivity of the tax system.

The separate taxation of companies began in Britain only in 1947. Before that the taxation of profits was covered by the personal income tax: companies were taxed as individuals. In 1947 the rate of profits tax was increased, and individuals and partnerships were exempted from it, thus creating a separate tax on corporate profits for the first time. In 1965 a classical system of corporation tax was introduced. The company paid a flat rate of tax on taxable profits. Shareholders paid income tax on dividends and capital gains tax on gains arising from corporate retentions (or other sources). In 1973 the classical system was replaced by an imputation system, which alleviated the double taxation of dividends by giving shareholders credit for tax paid by the company to offset the individual's income tax liability on dividends. In the early 1970s companies faced severe liquidity constraints, largely as a result of the problems caused by inflation for a tax system based on historic cost profits. Allowances were provided for increases in the value of inventories (stock relief) and full expensing of expenditures on plant and machinery was permitted. In 1984 only about 65 percent of companies were paying any corporation tax. The reforms of that year abolished stock relief, cut the tax rate from 52 to 35 percent, and provided depreciation on a 25 percent declining-balance basis for most assets. The effects of these changes are assessed in a later section.

In 1965 capital gains tax was introduced as a separate tax, on nominal gains (some gains were already subject to income tax). In 1982 a first attempt at indexation was made, followed by a second attempt in 1985. In 1988 the capital gains rate, which had been a flat 30 percent, became the individual's marginal income tax rate. Probate duty on estates was introduced in 1694 and replaced in 1894 by estate duty. This duty in turn was replaced in 1975 by a capital transfer tax, which taxed gifts during life as well as gifts at death. Finally, in 1986 the tax on gifts during life was abolished, with the remaining tax on gifts at death renamed the inheritance tax.

Excise duties on drink and tobacco have been in force for almost as long as these commodities have been imported. A more general sales tax—the purchase tax—was introduced during the Second World War and imposed at the wholesale level. The replacement of this tax by the VAT, which covered a slightly wider range of goods and also included services, coincided with Britain's entry to the European Community in 1973.

The burden of local authority rates (local taxes) has grown steadily with the size of local government. Dissatisfaction with rates and with the system of local authority finance in general has been widespread, leading to government proposals to replace it with a poll tax. The debate and the effects of the reform proposed are considered below.

From 1979 to 1988, three major tax reform packages were introduced. The first, in 1979, came within a month of the election of the present Conservative government. Changes were confined to rates of existing taxes and the implementation of a promised shift from direct to indirect taxation. The basic rate of income tax was reduced from 33 to 30 percent, allowances were increased substantially, and the revenue lost was recouped by increasing the standard rate of VAT from 8 percent to 15 percent. The highest rates of income tax were cut by considerably more, with the maximum rate on earnings falling from 83 percent to 60 percent. The timing of these measures proved inopportune. In particular, the increase in the VAT—which in itself added almost 4 percent to the retail price index—coincided with an already accelerating inflationary trend. The annual inflation rate had, within a few months, risen above 20 percent. In the remainder of the first Conservative Parliament, tax changes were minor and the proposed switch from direct to indirect taxation was not pursued further.

The second round of reforms came in the first budget of the Thatcher government's second term of office, in 1984. The new chancellor of the Exchequer, Nigel Lawson, proclaimed a "tax reform budget." The rhetoric proved more substantial than the reality. Although the corporation tax underwent radical changes—which are described in more detail below—the structure of personal taxation was affected only by the withdrawal of a few minor tax expenditures, particularly partial relief for life insurance contributions. The warm reception the package initially received indicated, however—as governments in other countries were discovering—the potential popularity of tax reform. There were wide expectations that the 1985 budget would contain more radical measures. Interest groups who feared the consequences of measures to broaden the tax base began intense lobbying. It became apparent, however, that the chancellor's advisers had few ideas of how to maintain the momentum acquired in 1984. The 1985 budget contained no significant reforms.

At that time, it appeared that the drive toward tax reform in the United States would also run out of steam. When the U.S. Congress unexpectedly approved a reform bill in 1986, its effects were felt in Britain. Lawson was clearly wounded by suggestions that the institutions of the U.S. government had found the political courage and imagination that he lacked, and attempts to portray the 1984 changes as more radical reforms than they in fact were carried little conviction. The reelection of the Conservative government for a third term in 1987 and the reappointment of Lawson as chancellor set the stage for a third round of reform. The 1988 budget was the most radical of the decade, with the top income tax rate cut to 40 percent and the number of rate bands reduced to two. In subsequent sections of this chapter, we describe the measures adopted in greater detail and in the final section attempt an assessment of the whole reform process.

The Distributional Effects of the U.K. Tax Burden, 1948–1988

The U.K. tax system is markedly progressive in the lower half of the income distribution. In the upper half the average rate of tax increases only slightly with income (except, prior to 1988 and particularly prior to 1979, for the small group subject to significant amounts of higher-rate income tax). These patterns hold for taxes only (Figure 9.2) and for taxes and benefits together (Figure 9.3).

These distributional effects are a consequence of elements in the tax structure that we have outlined and will describe in more detail in later sections of this chapter. The main sources of progressivity are the benefit system and the virtually linear income tax. Benefits accrue overwhelmingly to those in the lowest deciles. The existence of a substantial tax-free allowance creates income tax progressivity in the lower parts of the income distribution, but the interaction of the income tax with national insurance contributions implies that the overall tax rate on income barely increases between average and twice-average earnings. We discuss this feature of the British tax system more extensively below.

This substantially linear structure makes the evolution of the distributional effects of the British tax system over time comparatively easy to describe. The progressivity of the tax system increased steadily from the late 1950s to the early 1980s. This was primarily the result of the switch from lump-sum social security contributions to a tax proportional to earnings.

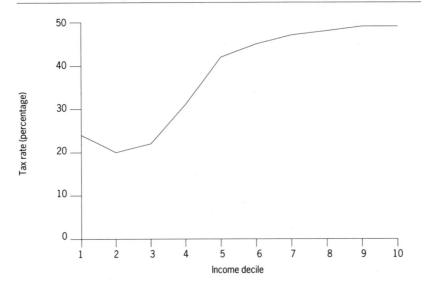

FIGURE 9.2   Average Tax Rate Paid in the United Kingdom, 1984

NOTE: Data for this figure cover the whole U.K. population.
SOURCE: Institute for Fiscal Studies (London), based on Family Expenditure Survey data.

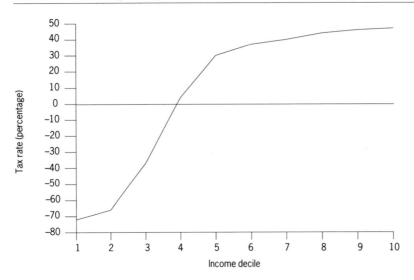

FIGURE 9.3   Average Tax and Benefit Rate in the United Kingdom, 1984

NOTE: Data for this figure cover the whole U.K. population.
SOURCE: Institute for Fiscal Studies (London), based on Family Expenditure Survey data.

Estimates of the overall marginal tax rate are 48 percent for 1958 and 61 percent for 1983 (see Dilnot, Kay, and Morris 1983 for details of the methodology involved). Since 1983 tax rates have fallen in the United Kingdom, and with them the degree of progressivity.

The Income Tax Rate Schedule

For many years, a distinctive feature of the U.K. tax system has been the very wide basic rate band, which meant that most taxpayers faced the same marginal rate of tax. In the 1980s, other countries have substantially reduced the complexities of their rate schedules, and the wide basic rate band is less unusual.

Table 9.2 shows the income tax schedule that operated in four postwar years, with thresholds reflated to 1988 levels by the change in average earnings. The apparent complexity of this table is misleading; in practice the effects of the schedules were quite simple. In 1948/49, there were two reduced rates for those with low taxable incomes, then a very wide band up to £30,000 where the basic rate applied. Although there were thirteen rates, almost everyone paid 36 percent. In 1966/67 the same was broadly true, although higher rates began slightly earlier, at a taxable income of £15,300. In 1978/79 higher-rate tax became due on taxable earnings in excess of

TABLE 9.2   Income Tax Rates and Thresholds in the United Kingdom, 1948–1989

1948/49		1966/67		1978/79		1988/89	
Rate (%)	Threshold (£)	Rate (%)	Threshold (£)	Rate (%)	Threshold (£)	Rate (%)	Threshold (£)
12	750	15.5	750	25	1,750	25	19,300
24	3,750	23.3	2,380	33	18,600	40	
36	30,000	32	15,300	40	21,000		
55	37,000	43	19,150	45	23,000		
57.5	45,000	46	23,000	50	26,000		
62.5	60,000	51	30,600	55	29,000		
67.5	75,000	61.5	38,300	60	33,000		
72.5	90,000	67	46,000	65	37,000		
77.5	120,000	72.5	61,000	70	43,000		
82.5	150,000	78	77,000	75	56,000		
87.5	180,000	83.5	92,000	83			
92.5	225,000	89	115,000				
95		91.5					

NOTE: Rates and thresholds have been reflated in line with 1988/89 average earnings. The average earnings for a male full-time worker in the United Kingdom in 1988/89 were £12,500.
SOURCE: Authors' calculations.

£18,600, and was paid by 3.6 percent of the population. By 1988/89 only one higher rate of income tax was left, paid by 5 percent of the population.

Reducing the level and number of higher tax rates was an important objective of the Thatcher government. In the first Conservative budget in June 1979 the top rate of tax on earned income was cut from 83 percent to 60 percent (see Table 9.3). The number of taxpayers paying rates of 40 or 45 percent, however, actually increased. No further major changes to higher rates occurred between 1979 and 1988. Then all but one of the higher rates was abolished, leaving a two-rate system with a 25 percent basic rate and a single higher rate of 40 percent.

TABLE 9.3	Percentage of U.K. Taxpaying Population Paying Tax Rates over 40 Percent, 1978/79 and 1983/84	
	1978/79	1983/84
Rates in excess of		
40	3.62	4.43
45	2.52	2.53
50	1.76	1.49
55	1.35	0.71
60	0.95	0.36
65	0.69	
70	0.48	
75	0.33	
83	0.16	
Total	3.62	4.43

Source: Inland Revenue, *Inland Revenue Statistics*, various years.

VAT and Indirect Taxation

The value-added tax is by far the most important indirect tax in the United Kingdom, accounting for around one-half of total indirect tax revenue. All traders whose annual turnover exceeds £22,100 are liable to VAT on their output; however, registered traders may recover any VAT that has been charged on their purchases. Thus intermediate transactions are effectively free of VAT and the incidence of the tax falls on final consumption.

There are three ways goods and services can be treated under the U.K. VAT. Sales are liable to tax at the standard rate of 15 percent unless either zero-rated or exempt. For goods that are zero-rated or exempt, no tax is due on output. But a zero-rated trader can recover tax paid on inputs while one who is only exempt cannot. Sales of a zero-rated commodity are therefore free from VAT, while exempt items bear tax to the extent that it is imposed on goods and services used as inputs in their production. This effective tax rate varies widely across different exempt commodities, depending on the proportion of inputs that are subject to tax. Exemption thus creates distortions in the pattern of production and trade.

The principal zero-rated items are food (except for restaurant meals, ice cream, confectionery and chocolate products, all drinks other than tea and coffee, potato chips, prepared nuts, prepared pet food); water; books, newspapers, magazines, news services, newspaper advertising, maps; fuel and power; public transport; children's clothing and footwear; and prescription drugs.

The primary exempt items are postal services, education, insurance, transactions in money and securities, betting and gaming, rent and land, health services, and funeral services.

The VAT was introduced in 1973 at a standard rate of 10 percent. In 1974 the government reduced the rate to 8 percent in the hope of controlling inflation, then around 25 percent. A year later, a higher rate of 25 percent was introduced on a group of commodities perceived as luxuries, such as electrical durables, cosmetics, private boats and aircraft, and fur coats. Following protests from the industries affected, the higher rate was cut to 12½ percent one year later. In 1979 the higher rate was overtaken when the standard rate was raised from 8 percent to 15 percent as part of a shift from direct to indirect taxation in the first Conservative government. This was accompanied by a reduction in the basic rate of income tax from 33 percent to 30 percent and substantial increases in personal allowances for income tax. The standard rate of VAT has remained unchanged at 15 percent since 1979.

Changes to the scope of the tax since its introduction have been comparatively minor, and all significant adjustments have involved extending rather than restricting the coverage of the tax. The most important of these changes have been reductions in the number of food and construction activities that attract the zero rate.

The most controversial issue related to the VAT at present is fiscal harmonization within the European Community (EC). Proposals currently being considered by the EC would involve far-reaching changes to indirect taxation in EC member states. In the case of the VAT, the European Commission is proposing that member states set their tax rates within two bands: a standard rate of between 14 and 20 percent for the majority of goods and services, and a reduced rate of between 4 and 9 percent for a limited number of basic goods and services, such as food, public transport, domestic energy, and books and newspapers. Excise duties on alcoholic drinks, tobacco, and mineral oils would be set at uniform rates throughout the EC, in most cases at the average of member states' existing duty rates.

In the United Kingdom, these proposals could mean that most zero-rated goods would bear VAT at the minimum rate of 4 percent; the one exception would be children's clothing, which would be included in the standard rate band, but is at present zero-rated. Changes in some excise duties would also be substantial: the tax on a bottle of spirits would fall by about £2.30, and on a bottle of wine by seventy pence. The average tax on a packet of twenty cigarettes would fall by twelve pence, and the duty on a gallon of petrol would rise by over twenty pence.

The Commission claims that its proposals are the "minimum changes" to indirect tax rates that are needed to permit the abolition of frontier formalities and controls, planned for 1992. These frontier controls do impose costs on industry, by causing trucks, drivers, and goods to stand idle at borders and raising the bureaucratic costs of trading goods within the EC. However, if fiscal controls and documentation at frontiers are abolished, it does not necessarily follow that member states' indirect tax rates must be fully harmonized. Certainly, the technical problems of operating VAT once frontier controls have been abolished are not greatly affected if VAT rates differ between member states. In addition, the method of operating the VAT proposed by the commission will continue to ensure that different VAT rates do not give an unfair cost advantage to producers in low-tax member states. Thus the main justification for EC control of indirect tax rates when frontier controls are abolished is to keep the problem of cross-border shopping by individuals within acceptable bounds. Yet if this is the main problem, we should note that most of the costs of cross-border shopping are borne by those EC member states that set higher tax rates than their neighbors. If they choose to do this, the decision is surely for them to make; EC action is needed merely to set a lower bound for tax rates to restrict the scope for competitive undercutting. By seeking to set a ceiling for tax rates as well as a floor, the commission is going beyond what is needed. It is also creating unnecessary problems of budgetary adjustment for higher-tax member states—indirect tax receipts in Denmark, for example, could fall by almost a quarter if the commission's proposals are implemented in their present form.

As yet, there are few signs that the U.K. government intends to act in accordance with the EC proposals. During the 1987 election campaign Margaret Thatcher pledged that the VAT would not be imposed on food or children's clothing, and it is unlikely that she will bow to EC pressure for such a change.

Corporation Tax

Corporation tax was introduced in Britain in 1965. The model used was a classical system, so that dividends were taxed under both corporation and personal income taxes. In 1973 this was changed to an imputation system, which continues to the present day. Companies must pay advance corporation tax (ACT) at a current rate of one-third of any dividends paid. Shareholders receive a tax credit of this amount, which can be offset against their own tax bill. With a basic rate of income tax of 25 percent, this system exactly eliminates any liability for a basic-rate taxpayer, and the rate of advance corporation tax is regularly adjusted with the basic rate of income tax so as to maintain this relationship. The company itself can set its payment of ACT against its own payment of corporation tax on profits.

The changes in the corporation tax base implemented at around the same time were probably of more practical significance. Depreciation provisions were made steadily more generous, culminating in 100 percent immediate write-offs for plant and machinery and 75 percent for industrial buildings. Relief was given for increases in the value of stocks over the period of account. The result was that by the end of the decade around half of all companies were tax-exhausted—that is, they paid no mainstream corporation tax (other than ACT)—and finance leasing developed as a means of transferring unused reliefs from non-taxpaying to taxpaying companies.

This system was radically revised in 1984 (see Table 9.4). The primary objects of the change were to reduce the incidence of tax exhaustion and the discrimination between different kinds of investment, while lowering the effective marginal rate of tax. As Table 9.5 shows, these purposes were broadly achieved, at the price of some discouragement to investment.

The transitional period provided a substantial positive incentive to invest, since allowances were available at the higher rates of tax, while returns on investments would be received when the tax rate had fallen to 35 percent. This situation seems to have had some effect on company behavior, with dramatic increases in investment in the transitional years. As shown in Devereux (1988), however, the 1984 reforms increased the wedge between pre- and post-tax costs of capital on average. The pre-1984 system required the pre-tax rate of return to exceed the real rate of interest by 1 to 2 percent.

TABLE 9.4   Main Features of the 1984 Reforms to the U.K. Corporation Tax (percentage)

	Fiscal year			
	1983	1984	1985	1986
Statutory rate of corporation tax	50	45	40	35
Capital allowances				
Plant and machinery				
Initial allowance	100	75	50	0
Writing-down allowance	25	25	25	25
Industrial buildings				
Initial allowance	75	50	25	0
Writing-down allowance	4	4	4	4
Stock relief: abolished March 13, 1984.				

NOTE: The writing-down allowance for plant and machinery is on a declining-balance, or exponential, basis. For industrial buildings it is on a straight-line basis. Both are based on historic cost values.
SOURCE: Authors, based on U.K. tax schedule.

TABLE 9.5   Distribution of Taxable Profits in the United Kingdom, 1982–1988

	Taxable profits of taxpayers (billions of £)	Taxable profits of non-taxpayers (billions of £)	Percentage of tax-exhausted companies
1982	3.1	–4.3	35.5
1983	4.1	–4.5	30.0
1984	5.7	–4.3	22.2
1985	8.3	–3.9	19.9
1986	11.4	–3.9	14.9
1987	14.1	–4.1	11.1
1988	15.2	–4.4	11.6

SOURCE: M. P. Devereux, "Corporation Tax: The Effect of the 1984 Tax Reform on the Incentive to Invest," *Fiscal Studies* 9, no. 1 (1988): 62–79.

The post-1984 system, once fully implemented, increased this wedge by some 1 percent.

Capital Taxes

Estate duty, a tax levied on the value of property left at death, has long been avoided on a massive scale. It is probable that the largest amount of tax ever paid in the United Kingdom was that paid on the death in 1953 of the fourth duke of Westminster. Increasingly, estate duty became a tax on those whose means were neither modest enough to enable them to remain below the threshold nor substantial enough to make avoidance—particularly through trusts or inter vivos gifts—an activity sufficiently rewarding to offset the costs and loss of immediate control of family assets.

In 1969 an attempt was made to tackle some of these difficulties, and in 1974 more radical measures were taken with the introduction of the capital transfer tax. The CTT included lifetime gifts within the scope of the tax and sought to raise more revenue through lower rates of tax on a broader base. The results were not successful. Avoidance continued on a substantial scale, interest group pressures eroded the remaining base, and the share of CTT in total tax revenue continued the declining trend begun by the estate duty. In 1982 the charge on gifts was limited to the cumulative total in any ten-year period and in 1986 it was abolished altogether; the emasculated CTT was renamed the inheritance tax. It does not appear that the charge on gifts ever raised material amounts of revenue. In 1988 the elaborate schedule of inheritance tax rates rising to 75 percent was reduced to a single rate of 40 percent on estates over £110,000 (the value of a modest house in southern England).

Since the acceleration of inflation in the 1970s the government had been under pressure to allow indexation of capital gains. Daunted by perceived administrative difficulties, authorities instead raised the threshold of gains at which tax became payable. This threshold, tied to the retail price index, had reached £5,000 per annum by 1982. The government's introduction of its own index-linked securities forced the issue on indexation; in 1982 a complex scheme of partial indexation was introduced and was rationalized to full indexation three years later. Indexation applied only to the period since 1982. In 1988 pre-1982 gains were relieved of tax altogether, the exemption level was reduced from £6,600 in 1987/88 to £5,000, and the remaining gain was taxed at the individual's marginal income tax rate.

Stamp duty on transfers of property is one of the oldest of British taxes. It was for many years levied at 2 percent of the value of the property purchased, with reduced rates for domestic property, so that average houses would attract only a ½ percent or 1 percent rate while more valuable ones would be subject to the full charge. With the internationalization of securities markets, there has been growing concern that a turnover tax of this magnitude would lead taxpayers to conduct an increasing proportion of transactions offshore. As a result the rate has twice been halved—once (for all transactions) from 2 percent to 1 percent, and subsequently (for transfers of securities only) from 1 percent to ½ percent.

The Taxation of Husband and Wife

Reform of the current tax treatment of married couples has been on the agenda in the United Kingdom for well over a decade, although successive governments have found it much easier to identify the need for change than to implement it. The government first produced a Green Paper (discussion document) on the subject in 1980. This was followed by vigorous debate but no action. Another Green Paper was produced in 1986 but was so badly received that its proposals were abandoned. Finally, the 1988 budget made proposals for change in 1990 that now seem certain to be introduced.

The present system reflects the nineteenth-century origins of the income tax structure as a whole. Essentially, a married woman has no independent status as a taxpayer. Her income is treated as that of her husband and aggregated with his. The wife is given a personal allowance equal to the single person's allowance against her earnings (but not her investment income), and the husband receives an enhanced personal allowance. The resulting structure of allowances is shown in Table 9.6.

Although most couples are financially better off married than they would be unmarried, a small minority faces financial disincentives to marriage. Most of these disincentives result from the aggregation of income and the restriction of certain tax reliefs to one per taxpayer unit. Since the incomes of husband and wife are summed for tax purposes, the higher rates of income tax are more likely to affect a two-income married couple than a similar unmarried couple. In 1988/89 the basic rate band stretches from taxable income of £0 to £19,200. Very few single people pay tax at higher rates, but the joint income of two people is much more likely to exceed this limit. If a

TABLE 9.6   Income Tax Allowances under Current U.K. System

	Tax allowance (£)	Ratio to single allowance
Single person	2,605	1
Single-earner couple, married	4,095	1.57
Two-earner couple, married	6,700	2.57
Single-earner couple, unmarried	2,605	1
Two-earner couple, unmarried	5,210	2

SOURCE: United Kingdom, *Financial Statement and Budget Report 1988/89* (London: Her Majesty's Stationery Office, 1988).

couple's income puts them in the higher rate bracket, they can elect to be taxed separately, in which case they forgo the enhanced married man's allowance. This option, however, is helpful only if the wife has earned income, since all investment income is treated as the husband's regardless of whether the couple opts for separate taxation.

The 1980 Green Paper was an inconclusive survey of alternatives, pointing tentatively toward minimalist reforms. In 1986, the government proposed a scheme of transferable allowances that would give everyone a single allowance but would permit a partner who had insufficient income to use his or her allowance fully to transfer it to his or her spouse. The scheme was criticized for its disincentive effect on working women and for its generosity, relative to the present system, to single-earner couples in which the wife chooses not to work (rather than being detained at home by family responsibilities). It was abandoned (see Symons and Walker 1986).

The 1988 proposal removes the appearance of sex discrimination while retaining the substance of the present system. The most important element in the package is a system of independent taxation of all income, including that from investments. Every adult will receive the same allowance and be taxed separately on his or her total income. This allowance will not be transferable. The second element is a new allowance, called the married couple's allowance (MCA). The MCA has been set equal to the difference between the existing married man's allowance and the single allowance. The MCA will be given initially to the husband, but where the husband cannot make full use of it, it can be transferred to the wife. The most significant fact about the reform is that for almost everyone there will be no practical effect (see Table 9.7).

Local Government Finance

Local government expenditure accounts for some 20 percent of total government expenditure in the United Kingdom. At present around one-half of local government revenue is derived from government grants, one quarter

TABLE 9.7   Ratios of Current and Proposed U.K. Income Tax Allowances to Single
             Allowance

	Current	Proposed
Single person	1 (SA)	1 (SA)
Single-earner couple, married	1.6 (MMA)	1.6 (SA + MCA)
Two-earner couple, married	2.6 (MMA + WEA)	2.6 (SA + SA + MCA)
Single-earner couple, unmarried	1 (SA)	1 (SA)
Two-earner couple, unmarried	2 (SA + SA)	2 (SA + SA)

SA = single allowance. MMA = married man's allowance. MCA = married couple's allowance. WEA = wife's earnings allowance.
SOURCE: United Kingdom, *Financial Statement and Budget Report 1988/89* (London: Her Majesty's Stationery Office, 1988).

from local authority rates, or taxes, on nondomestic property, and only one quarter from rates on domestic property. Property tax rates are based on the "ratable value" of a property—an official estimate of the amount for which a property would be rented in the open market. Revaluation last occurred in 1973, and as there has been no real market in rented property in the United Kingdom, either before or since then, the base of the tax has become increasingly arbitrary.

In 1976 the Layfield Committee of inquiry into local government finance reported that there was a growing problem posed by the imbalance between local revenue sources and local expenditures. It argued that there was need for either greater scope for local authorities to raise their own taxes to finance their own expenditures, or for greater central control of local activities, clearly preferring the former solution. It predicted growing tension and frustration in the relations between local and central government unless this issue was resolved. The committee's recommendations were ignored and their predictions have been more than adequately fulfilled.

In the 1986 Green Paper *Paying for Local Government*, the government argued that the key problem was that accountability in local government was "blurred and weakened by the complexities of the national grant system and by the fact that differences arise among those who vote for, those who pay for, and those who receive local government services." The Green Paper went on to argue for reforms that would improve the link between voting for local services and paying for them: "If people can understand the costs of the different services provided to them, and if the costs are fairly distributed, then they can make sensible choices not only about the balance between local priorities but also about the overall level of spending." The proposals contained in the 1986 Green Paper, which will be introduced in England and Wales in 1990, aim to remove this perceived failure of accountability.

This lack of accountability was not the only criticism made of the old system. Domestic property rates themselves have long been unpopular. The most frequent criticism made of them is that they are inequitable. Since these rates are a tax on the estimated market rental value of a house, they take no account of potential or actual income. Thus, a single elderly woman will pay the same in rates as a family of four with two wage-earning adults, provided they live in identical houses.

In response to these and other problems the government produced its 1986 Green Paper, followed by legislation based on the paper. The center-piece is the so-called community charge, a flat-rate poll tax on everyone over the age of eighteen, which is to replace domestic rates. As with domestic rates at present, the level of the community charge will be under local authority control. However, the government intends to withdraw local control over the level at which nondomestic rates are set. In the future, these will be levied at a uniform national poundage and will become an earmarked national tax, with the revenues distributed in the form of a per capita grant to local authorities. The central government's contribution to local authority spend-ing will be provided in the form of a fixed block grant, unrelated to the level of local spending.

The government sees the poll tax as a way of extending the number of local taxpayers from the 15 million householders currently liable for rates to the 35 million adults currently entitled to vote at local elections. The government's view is that residents who are not householders, or whose income is so low that they receive a 100 percent rebate of any rates they pay, have little interest in the level of local taxation, and are therefore inclined to vote for councillors promising higher expenditures, from which they will benefit, funded by higher taxes that they will not pay. In addition to sending poll tax bills to every adult, the government set the maximum local tax rebate at 80 percent, thus ensuring that everyone would pay something toward local government services.

The withdrawal of local control over business rate levels is another response to the desire to increase accountability. Since business taxpayers have no voting power, the government sees no reason to allow local author-ities power over the level of business tax. Finally, by moving to an entirely lump-sum grant system, with the grant related to an assessment of need but entirely unrelated to expenditure, the government will succeed in restricting local authority control to the 25 percent of finance raised by the poll tax. Any change in the level of expenditure must be funded by a change in the level of the poll tax, and will therefore be transparent to the local electorate.

The scheme has been unduly criticized on the grounds that the dis-tributional effect of the change will be regressive. Although true, this is in fact not the central issue. Not only is progressivity best seen as characteristic of the tax system as a whole, rather than of individual components of it, but the distributional neutrality of the poll tax is perhaps its principal virtue. The view of some local authorities that they can offset the disliked distributional policies of the central government by high levels of local spending financed by progressive local taxation is one of the sources of the present tension between central and local government.

It is, at present, very unclear how the measure will actually work. The legislation is vague about the precise definition of liability for the tax and the means by which the identity of potential taxpayers is to be established, leaving both matters largely in the hands of local registration officers.

But the change is, in any event, largely irrelevant to the theme of accountability. The limitation of local tax rebates, the abolition of local control over nondomestic rates, and the requirement that local taxpayers pay the full cost of any change in local spending, have nothing to do with the poll tax, and could easily be implemented within the framework of the present rating system. A more careful analysis would begin from the Layfield position and from the experience of other countries, most of which have handled the universal problems of local-central government relations rather more successfully and none of which have adopted a poll tax. If real local autonomy is to be preserved, one obvious possibility is a local income tax, which would allow at least as much accountability as a poll tax, while avoiding some of its distributional and administrative problems. More fundamentally, little consideration appears to have been given to the appropriate scope of local government activity. In the United Kingdom, almost half of total local government expenditure is accounted for by education, in which real local autonomy has been substantially eliminated and is in process of final erosion. Were this to be paid for directly by central government, many of the problems of local government finance would be substantially reduced.

The Relationship between Income Tax, National Insurance, and Social Security

As a result of the long history and independent development of taxation and social security in the United Kingdom, the system today suffers from a number of unplanned interactions between taxes and social security benefits. The worst example of this is probably the incoherent marginal and average direct tax rate schedule that results from the combination of income tax and national insurance contributions. There is also considerable concern for the disincentives created by the high marginal tax rates imposed on those with low incomes by the tax and social security systems.

We begin with the effect of the combined income tax and national insurance schedule. National insurance contributions were initially a flat-rate charge, but soon became earnings-related, and are now simply a second tax on income. While the income tax schedule applies different rates to each successive band of income, the national insurance (NI) contributions schedule allows the overall income band to determine the rate at which the whole of income is taxed. This creates substantial discontinuities in the rate schedule; there are three different levels of income at which these discontinuities occur. At the same time, there is a ceiling beyond which no further NI contributions are due that lies below the beginning of the higher rate of income tax. The marginal rate of direct tax therefore falls from 34 percent (25 percent income tax and 9 percent NI) to 25 percent, before rising again to 40 percent when the higher income tax rate applies.

Consider first the effects of the jumps in NI liability at low earnings levels. When earnings reach the NI floor, or lower earnings limit (LEL), of £41 per week in 1988/89, NI contributions are due not just on the excess of earnings over £41 but on the whole of earnings. Thus at earnings of £40 a week no NI contribution is due, while at earnings of £41 a week NI contributions of £4.10 a week are due, £2.05 from the employee and £2.05 from the employer. A similar jump occurs from £69.99 to £70, when weekly NI contributions jump from £7.00 to £9.80 as the rate rises from 5 percent of all earnings to 7 percent of all earnings for both employer and employee. A further jump comes at £105 when the rate rises from 7 percent to 9 percent, with joint payments from employee and employer rising from £14.70 to £18.90. This pattern is shown in Figure 9.4, which illustrates the relationship between earnings and employees' NI contributions (see Blinder and Rosen 1985 for a discussion of the effects of such discontinuities in the budget constraint). The pattern for employers' NI contributions is similar, but with a further jump at £155 where the contribution rate rises to 10.45 percent.

FIGURE 9.4   Current U.K. National Insurance Contribution Schedule

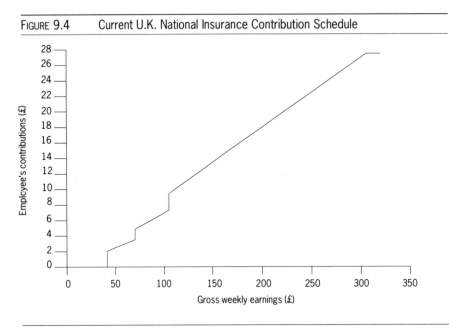

SOURCE: Authors, based on U.K. tax schedule.

FIGURE 9.5   Marginal Tax Rates for Married Men in the United Kingdom, 1988/89

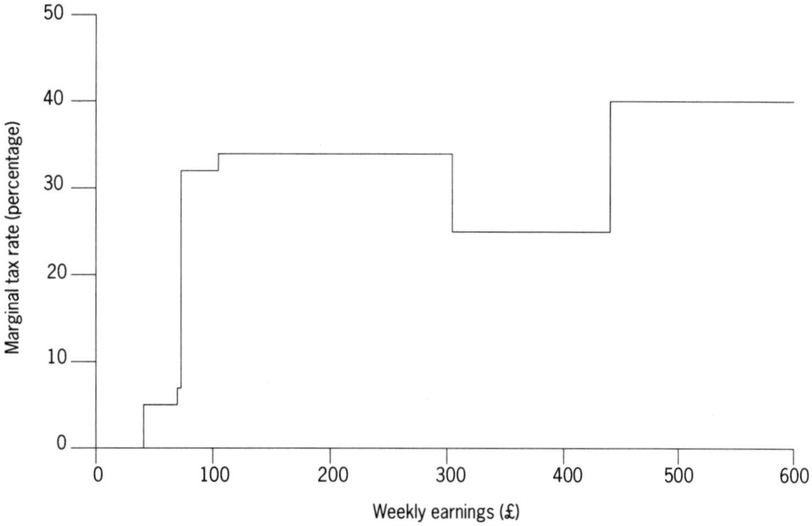

SOURCE: Authors, based on U.K. tax schedule.

Figure 9.5 shows the marginal tax rates, including both income tax and NI contributions, for a married man. At weekly earnings above £41 only NI contributions are paid and the marginal rate is 5 percent; this rate rises to 7 percent at £70 per week, and 32 percent at £78.75 per week, when income tax becomes payable at 25 percent. At £105 per week the NI rate rises to 9 percent, implying a combined rate of 34 percent. This rate is constant up to earnings of £305 a week, beyond which point no further NI contributions are due, so the rate drops to 25 percent. The higher rate of income tax at 40 percent becomes due at weekly earnings of £450.

Figure 9.6 traces average tax rates for married men, including income tax and employees' NI contributions, and shows that the average tax rate actually falls between weekly earnings of £305 and £450. As shown earlier in this chapter, these irrational relationships between taxes now dominate the overall distributional effect of the British tax system.

The interaction between the tax and benefit systems may also have major effects on work incentives at the lower end of the income distribution. There are two frequently cited "traps": the poverty trap and the unemployment trap. The poverty trap affects those workers who find that an increase in their wage could leave them little or no better off as a result of the combination of higher tax liabilities and lower benefit entitlements. The unemployment trap affects those who find that the income they receive while unemployed is as high, or nearly as high, as the net income they would receive if they were employed. Both of these problems have been seen as creating undesirable disincentives to work and self-help, and they were central issues in the social security reforms that became fully effective in 1988. As Table 9.8 shows, the reforms reduced marginal tax rates on low-income families to below 100 percent, but not by much.

FIGURE 9.6   Average Tax Rates for Married Men in the United Kingdom, 1988/89

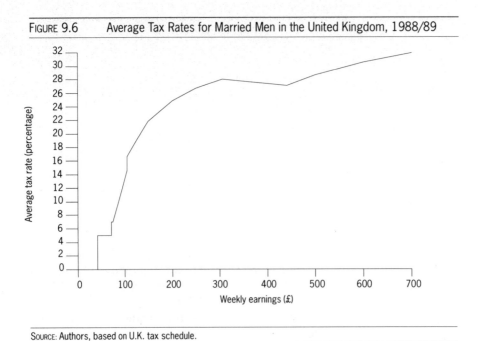

SOURCE: Authors, based on U.K. tax schedule.

TABLE 9.8   Marginal Tax Payments under Old and New Benefit Systems in the United Kingdom (£)

	Withdrawal per additional pound of gross income	
	Old system	New system
Income tax	.25	.25
National insurance contribution	.07	.07
Family income supplement[a]	.50	.48
Housing benefit	.23	.17
Total withdrawal	1.05	.97

a. Under the new system, this benefit is known as a family credit.
SOURCE: Authors' calculations.

Taxation and Savings

In Britain, as in many other countries, the rate of return on savings has come to depend at least as much on the tax treatment of the assets concerned as on the profitability of the underlying investment.

Table 9.9 illustrates for three groups of income taxpayers the degree of fiscal privilege (DFP) of several forms of saving. The DFP is an index developed by Hills (1984) to examine the impact of the privilege or penalty on different assets. The DFP is the difference between the investor's marginal income tax rate and the effective rate of tax on the asset in question. Thus a DFP of 0 implies that the tax system is neutral; a DFP of 100, that the tax privilege is worth 100 percent of the real pretax return; and a DFP of –50, that the tax penalty is worth 50 percent of the real pretax return.

The table assumes a 3 percent real return before taxes and an estimated inflation rate of 4 percent for 1988/89. The most striking feature of the table is the dispersion of DFPs. Looking first at the column for basic-rate taxpayers, we find that the most tax-privileged assets are those that generate deductions against income tax. Contributions to private pensions and mortgage interest relief are tax deductible. Direct share ownership is shown only slightly tax penalized, because although any inflation compensation in the dividend is

TABLE 9.9   Degree of Fiscal Privilege of Assets for Three Groups of U.K. Taxpayers, 1988/89

Asset	Zero-rate taxpayers	Basic-rate taxpayers	Top-rate taxpayers
Pension contributions (10 years)[a]	–2	48	83
House with 50 percent mortgage[b]	36	17	67
Pension contributions (25 years)	–2	33	56
Tax-exempt assets	0	25	40
Life insurance contract (5 years)[c]	–29	–4	11
Direct share ownership[d]	–2	–2	–2
Low-coupon gilts[e]	0	–10	–16
Building society deposits[f]	–54	–29	–50
Interest-bearing assets	0	–33	–53

a. That is, contributions into a pension scheme with ten years to maturity.
b. The value of the mortgage is assumed to be below the current ceiling of £30,000 for tax relief. The stamp-duty calculation assumes a move to a new house every seven years. It is also assumed that a move to a more expensive house will produce a higher local rates bill. Specifically, it is assumed that for a given percentage increase in the value of the house owned, the rates bill will increase by half of that proportion.
c. It is assumed that the fund invests in equities only and that these yield a dividend of 3 percent.
d. The dividend yield is 3 percent. The stamp-duty calculation assumes that one-tenth of the investor's portfolio is turned over each year.
e. These are government securities whose interest rate (or "coupon") is low relative to their value at redemption. In consequence, most of the return to this form of saving comes as a capital gain.
f. Building societies are savings banks that specialize in home loans.
SOURCE: J. Hills, *Savings and Fiscal Privilege*, Report series no.9 (London: Institute for Fiscal Studies, 1984).

taxed in full, we have assumed that the bulk of the return comes in the form of capital gain. Building society deposits are heavily tax-penalized, since the full nominal return is subject to income tax, albeit at a slightly reduced rate, known as the composite rate. Other interest-bearing assets are similarly penalized, again because of the taxation of nominal rather than real interest. The pattern for top-rate taxpayers is similar, but the DFP is typically larger in absolute terms.

FIGURE 9.7   Degree of Fiscal Privilege for Selected Assets in the United Kingdom, 1978/79 and 1988/89

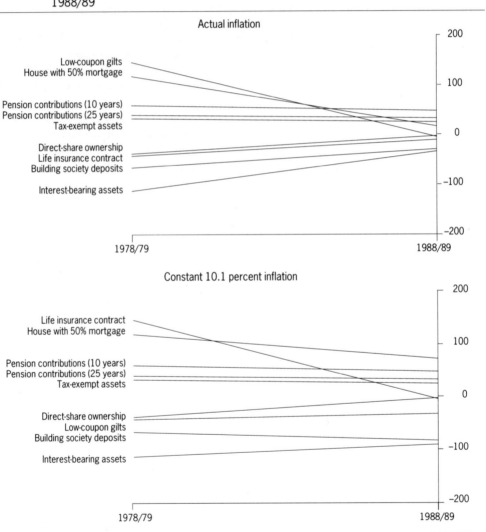

NOTE: Data are for basic-rate taxpayers.
SOURCE: M. H. Saunders and S. J. Webb, "Fiscal Privilege and Financial Assets: Some Distributional Effects," *Fiscal Studies* 9, no. 4 (1988): 51–69.

Figure 9.7 shows the DFP for selected assets at actual inflation in 1978/79 and in 1988/89. There has clearly been a substantial reduction in the dispersion of DFPs. The figure also shows the DFP in 1978/79 and 1988/89 assuming a constant rate of inflation. The convergence has clearly as much to do with the reduction in the rate of inflation as the effect of structural changes in the tax system. Nonetheless, some reforms have also been important.

- Rates of income tax have fallen considerably, from 33 percent to 25 percent for basic-rate taxpayers and from 98 percent to 40 percent for top-rate taxpayers. These reductions in rates reduce the value of reliefs.
- The introduction of indexation for inflation in the capital gains tax (CGT) in 1982 and its extensions in 1985 and 1988 have reduced the penalty arising from the taxation of purely inflationary gains.
- Following the 1988 budget, the rate of CGT faced by an investor is the same as his or her marginal income tax rate. Previously, there was a flat-rate CGT at 30 percent.
- In 1984 tax relief on life insurance premiums was abolished for new contracts, substantially reducing the tax privilege for this asset.
- Stamp duty on houses has fallen from 2 percent to 1 percent and on shares from 2 percent to ½ percent.

This list contains changes that have both increased and reduced fiscal privilege, and there have been others. The most important have probably been the business expansion scheme (BES), which gave substantial tax advantages to investment in new business, and the personal equity plan (PEP), which provided a new privileged tax regime for direct share ownership.

Tax Administration

The essentials of the structure of income tax in the United Kingdom are remarkably simple. The rate structure is uncomplicated and, in comparison with the United States or many other Western countries, the range of allowances available is very limited. The administration of this system is, however, peculiarly cumbersome, and the average taxpayer's understanding of how income tax works correspondingly limited.

There are two primary reasons for this. One is the schedular system, by which different types of income are taxed according to different principles, assessed separately, and collected at different times and in different ways. As we indicated above, this scheme was created for the express purpose of causing confusion, at a time when it was thought that the possession of too clear a picture of an individual's affairs by the agents of government might pose a threat to personal liberty. It is difficult to take this argument seriously now, and given the confusion caused to the individual as well as to the Inland Revenue, the structure may reasonably be thought to have outlived its purpose.

The second aspect is the cumulative pay-as-you-earn (PAYE) system. In the United States, and in all other major countries (except the Republic of Ireland, which follows the British system), withholding of tax from income, including employment income, is undertaken on a fairly rough and ready basis. It is expected that some end-of-year adjustment of liability will prove necessary, and the system is designed to include a mild degree of excessive withholding to encourage the submission of tax returns and streamline the process of adjustment. In Britain, however, the withholding system attempts to collect the exact amount of any liability and minimize the need for end-of-year adjustment. It is this, rather than the economic merits of a linear schedule, that has motivated the wide basic rate band in the income tax system, since it is only easy to withhold from secondary income sources on this basis if most taxpayers have the same marginal rate of tax. It is also necessary to keep records by reference to a taxpayer's employer and to link each employment with any previous or concurrent employments.

Although this system has some advantages, and aspects of it are sometimes viewed with envy by other tax authorities, none has seriously considered adopting it and it is clear to us also that its disadvantages outweigh its merits. It is expensive—administration costs are around four times as much per pound or dollar collected as they are in the United States, for example. It restricts the design of the tax structure in a large and growing number of ways, of which the constraint on the rate schedule is only one of the least important. The taxpayer has little understanding of how tax is collected from him, and the accuracy of the collection of liabilities is low. The situation has been greatly aggravated by the substantial delays in implementing computerization. Although there is some political interest in administrative reform and widespread popular dissatisfaction with the mechanics of tax collection, concern for the machinery of the tax system rather than its effects remains limited, although in our view such concern has become a necessary preliminary to more substantive change.

Assessment

Whatever else might be said about changes to the tax system in the 1970s and 1980s, most observers of the British fiscal system would agree that there have been a great many of them. In evaluating those of the 1980s, our assessment is that they have been beneficial, but that the results are slight relative to the volume of activity that generated them.

Perhaps the most remarkable feature of the period—and it is a change that has not, of course, been confined to the United Kingdom—has been the adoption of economic neutrality as an objective. In his 1988 pamphlet "Tax

Reform: The Government Record," the chancellor of the Exchequer wrote that one of the objectives of the government had been "to see that, as a general rule, people's choices are distorted as little as reasonably possible through the tax system" (Lawson 1988). A decade ago, such a statement would have been widely seen as an esoteric academic argument: the political assumption was that the function of the tax system was to promote the good and discourage the bad, to reward the deserving and to penalize the undeserving, and although there might be political disagreement as to who or what the good, bad, deserving, and undeserving were, the approach was common across the spectrum of opinion.

But to the extent that progress in achieving these new objectives has been made in Britain—and some has been made—it has been the result of reductions in the rates of tax rather than of improvements in the structure. These reductions have indeed been spectacular—in income tax, from 98 percent to 40 percent; in inheritance tax, from 75 percent to 40 percent; and in corporation tax, from 52 percent to 35 percent. But the effects even of these rate changes should not be exaggerated. In the main, these cuts in rates were little more than political gestures and never touched more than a small minority of the population—and in reality, because avoidance was readily possible and endemic, touched even that minority more lightly than might be thought. None of these comments are meant to deny that the reform process is a welcome one, but its significance can be, and has been, exaggerated.

We should note that the reductions in income tax have not been confined to the higher rates—the basic rate of tax has fallen from 33 percent to 25 percent. For the bulk of the population, however, this drop has been broadly offset by increases in the ordinary rate of national insurance contribution from 6½ percent to 9 percent and in VAT from 8 percent to 15 percent over the same period.

Where structural changes have been needed, the record is disappointing. Improvements to the income tax schedule have been more than eroded by the increasingly convoluted structure of national insurance contributions, which are now a tax of almost equal significance. The corporation tax has been restructured, although in an unimaginative way that leaves underlying problems of disappointing investment performance, vulnerability to renewed inflation, and the increased internationalization of the world economy largely intact. Having a broad-based sales tax is a limited achievement if you do not have a broad base for it, and the government has been persistently unwilling to tackle this issue. There have been improvements in the interaction of taxes and social security as a result of changes to the benefit system; palliative adjustments to the tax system have been resisted. The taxation of husband and wife has been reformed, but in a cosmetic rather than a substantive way. The previously incoherent regime for taxing savings is, if anything, slightly more incoherent. And the proposed reform of local government finance must rank as one of the most bizarre proposals in the history of public finance.

The primary reason for this mixed record has been the absence in British reform of any cohesive view of the tax structure as a whole, of the kind that motivated more effective reform proposals in other countries such as the United States and New Zealand. Nor has there been any evidence of the attempt—successful in both these countries—to defeat specific interest groups by winning a consensus for a comprehensive package of reforms. A style of government—characteristic of Britain in the 1980s—that is at once secretive and decisive may be effective if you have solutions, but is self-defeating if you are still in search of them.

The U.S. Tax Reform of 1986:
Is It Worth Copying?

The political process that produced the 1986 Tax Reform Act in the United States began in 1984 with the goal of designing a tax system promoting economic neutrality and efficiency, economic growth, fairness, and simplicity. Although the resulting reform has been hailed by some as landmark legislation and the realization of the impossible dream, not everyone sees it that way. From my perspective, the 1986 tax bill gets decidedly mixed grades on these early design criteria. I would give it a B or B– on efficiency and neutrality, an F on economic growth, a B on fairness, and a gentleman's C on simplicity.[1] With a report card like that, it is worth looking at what happened and what went wrong. Given the early kudos that accompanied passage of the bill, it is also important to explain these low grades. That is the purpose of this chapter.

What We Did

The Tax Reform Act of 1986 was certainly the most sweeping change of the tax code since 1941. I can describe only the major features of the new law. The actual tax reform document exceeds 1,000 pages. Detailed presentations and analyses are available from several sources (see, for instance, Prentice-Hall 1986).

For individuals, the previous schedule of fourteen marginal tax rates ranging from 11 to 50 percent was replaced with only two statutory rates, 15 and 28 percent. Personal exemptions were increased from US$1,080 in 1986 to US$1,950 in 1988, and the standard deduction was increased to US$3,000 for single individuals and US$5,000 for married couples. The result of the increases in the personal exemption amounts and the standard deduction is that married couples with incomes under US$8,900 are not subject to taxation, and couples with two children do not begin to pay tax until their income exceeds US$12,800. The tax thresholds in 1986, before the new law, were US$6,060 for married couples and US$8,300 for a traditional family of four. The significant increase in the threshold amounts removed six million households from the tax rolls. This feature alone accounts for much of the progressivity achieved by the reform and a good deal of the simplification.

Despite the fact that the top statutory rate is now 28 percent, many upper-middle-income taxpayers face a marginal tax rate of 33 percent. This bit of trickery comes about because the 15 percent rate for some income and the personal exemptions are "taxed back" with what amounts to a 5 percent surtax beginning at US$43,150 of taxable income for individuals and US$71,900 for joint returns. This feature allows the average tax rate on taxable income to reach the full 28 percent for high-income households (rather than asymptotically approach it), but it has the undesirable result that upper-middle-income households actually face higher marginal tax rates than the very rich.

The reduction of the personal marginal tax rates and the increase in the tax thresholds was made possible by sharply curtailing tax shelters, limiting itemized deductions, and increasing corporate taxes. The taxation of nominal long-term capital gains was increased by eliminating the 60 percent exclusion. The top rate of taxation for long-term capital gains went from 20 percent in 1986 to 33 percent in 1988. The new law eliminates the US$100 dividend exclusion, curtails the tax advantages of individual retirement accounts, raises the thresholds for the deductibility of many itemized deductions, and tightens the restrictions on interest deductibility. Tax shelters are attacked on many fronts: depreciation deductions are decelerated, the investment tax credit is eliminated, the deductibility of interest costs and losses on passive investments is limited, and the alternative minimum tax is strengthened.

The relatively low grade that I assigned the 1986 tax reform on simplicity is largely due to the complicated distinction introduced between passive and active income. Passive investments include all real estate holdings and other investments not actively managed by the taxpayer. In practice, the distinction is not as clear-cut as this implies. The new law is difficult to characterize, but basically it limits the deductibility of losses on passive investments to other passive investment income. Unused net passive losses can be carried forward (without interest) to be used against future passive income.

The simplicity goal was also harmed by forcing many more taxpayers, both corporate and individual, to compute their tax obligation under two separate tax programs: the regular income tax and the alternative minimum tax (AMT). The AMT is a kind of admission that, despite all the effort, the income tax is still poorly designed and that the only way to get at the income that somehow otherwise escapes the regular tax system is to set up a second tax system. It is surprising that we are now relying on the AMT more rather than less after all of the effort to bring the regular income tax closer to a tax on economic income. It is also revealing that Treasury I proposed repealing the AMT for both the personal and the corporate income tax, whereas the Congress found it necessary to strengthen the AMT in the 1986 Tax Reform Act.[2]

What We Didn't Do

The new tax law looks much worse if we concentrate on what we didn't do rather than on what we did. We did not address this country's totally inadequate level of national saving. We did not move to a consumption tax in order to improve intertemporal neutrality. We did not index the definition of income for inflation in order to tax real income. We did not integrate the personal and corporate income tax systems in order to equate the taxation of corporate and noncorporate investments. We did not reduce the tax preferences for debt over equity in order to slow the alarming increase in corporate leverage in the United States. We did not enact measures to reduce the U.S. cost of capital or to reduce the tax wedge between the marginal product of capital and the return to investors. These were missed opportunities. They are particularly frustrating when one recognizes the validity of the argument that taxpayers deserve a break from tax reforms and that we should leave the law untouched for a few years. We changed the law dramatically, but I believe we missed many, perhaps most, of the big opportunities. I will now elaborate on my list of omissions.

The failure to promote saving. Probably the primary problem facing the U.S. economy is the inadequate level of aggregate national saving. In the past few years, net aggregate saving has fallen to about 2 percent of gross national product (GNP), which is consistent with a long-run rate of growth for real wealth of well under 1 percent and a constant, stagnant level of per capita wealth. Clearly the United States cannot remain a leading economic power in the long run with such an anemic saving rate. Aggregate net investment in the economy is running at the more adequate level of 6 percent of GNP. This is only possible because two-thirds of U.S. net investment is financed with foreign investment, which probably cannot be maintained in the long run. This rate also implies that while production in this country may grow at an acceptable rate, income and consumption will not be able to keep up. Indeed, it is fair to say that the U.S. saving rate is inadequate according to both historical and international measures.

Given that low national saving is the overriding economic problem facing the country, it is ironic that the 1986 tax reform did nothing to address it. In fact, an objective assessment finds that the reform made the problem worse. It certainly failed to encourage private saving, and it did nothing to reduce federal government dissaving.

In terms of private saving incentives, the tax reform greatly reduced the advantage of individual retirement accounts (IRAs), 401K accounts, and other supplementary retirement accounts for middle- and high-income taxpayers. This change seems counterproductive in that the best evidence we have (Venti and Wise 1988) indicates that roughly half of IRA saving was incremental private saving. The full taxation of capital gains also amounts to an extra tax burden on equity saving and can be expected to weaken saving somewhat. The removal of saving incentives at the household level was not offset at the corporate level. In fact, the net tax advantage of debt for corporations (over equity) may encourage firms to reduce retained earnings and finance investments with debentures or junk bonds. The net effect is likely to be a reduction in corporate saving.

The aspects I have mentioned (IRAs, capital gains, the tax advantage of debt) are details. There were two larger missed opportunities to encourage saving. One was the failure to replace the income tax with a consumption-based tax, which I will discuss at some length later. The other massive mistake was not to address the government's negative contribution to national saving. The federal deficit is a huge contributor to the weakness in national saving and to our need for foreign capital. The initial design guideline of revenue neutrality, when the government had roughly a US$200 billion deficit, is hard to justify. The deficit today is still around US$200 billion if one allows social security to have a separate account and permits it to build up a surplus designed to allow the system to deal with the retirements of the baby boom generation.[3] Not only did the reform not address the need to reduce the deficit, but the official projections predict the reform to be revenue-losing after the first five years. It can be characterized as revenue-neutral only because it uses some front-loaded revenue devices. Some of those (such as the one-time treasury windfall in 1986 as a result of the massive amount of capital gains realized before the end of the exclusion) have already run out of steam.

There seems to be a near consensus among economists that a tax increase is necessary to bring the deficit under control and to permit the economy an adequate level of saving. The only arguments deal with the timing and nature of the tax increase and the political problems in enacting one.

The failure to index inflation. The 1986 Tax Reform Act and all of the treasury proposals that preceded it attempted to design a fair and efficient broadly based income tax. If we accept that goal in order to judge the reform on its own terms, it still has at least one major failing: the failure to index the definition of income for inflation.

Inflation is a fact of life in the United States. The absence of indexation thus presents an enormous problem, particularly for capital gains. Nominal capital gains are not even a reasonable approximation of real capital gains. Martin Feldstein and Joel Slemrod (1978) found that individuals paid tax on US$4.6 billion of nominal capital gains on corporate stocks in 1973. The US$4.6 billion total of realized nominal gains translated to a total US$1 billion real loss on these transactions. Even the sign of the nominal magnitude was wrong (relative to the correct inflation-adjusted number) in the aggregate and doubtless for many individual cases. In most years, nominal returns are at least twice real returns on safe assets, meaning that full taxation of realized gains, even with the deferral advantage, usually implies an overtaxation of real gains. Taxation of nominal capital gains thus acts more as a random wealth transactions tax than an income tax. The old 60 percent exclusion was clearly a very crude instrument for converting nominal to real gains, but it probably was better than nothing.

Within the framework of an income tax, the proposal of Treasury I was about as effective as it is possible to be in dealing with inflation and the definition of income. For capital gains, the correct indexation requires restating the cost basis in terms of today's dollars. This was precisely what Treasury I suggested, and its proposal was not overly complex.

Once one admits that nominal capital gains are not even an approximation of real gains and accepts the need to index cost bases, it is necessary to index the definition of income throughout the code. For instance, taxing only real gains and allowing full nominal interest deductibility opens enormous opportunities for arbitrage. Treasury I recognized this and proposed a useful, though imperfect, formula for separating real and nominal interest expenses. It would have permitted only the deduction of real interest costs. Symmetrically, Treasury I would have taxed only real interest receipts.

The correct calculation of real capital gains and real interest income and expenses is an important aspect of "fairness," although one that does not receive much attention. It should be noted, however, that the gain that indexation achieves on fairness comes at an inescapable cost in terms of adding complexity, for taxing real economic income is necessarily very complicated.

If one attempts to tax real income and leave a separate corporate income tax in place, then the definition of corporate income needs to reflect the effects of inflation. Here as well, Treasury I had it right, but the 1986 Tax Reform Act did not. Depreciation allowances, interest costs, and cost of goods sold (or inventory accounting) must all be adjusted for corporate income. The failure to adjust depreciation deductions is made even more costly in that depreciation lifetimes were extended for many assets and set at approximately economic lifetimes. I do not see anything desirable in doing this in the absence of indexation.

The failure to integrate the personal and corporate income tax. The 1986 Tax Reform Act transfers roughly US$24 billion per year (for the first five years) in tax burden from households to corporations. This shift permits the misleading claims that 80 percent or more of households would pay less tax with a revenue-neutral reform. Such claims ignore the personal burden of the corporate income tax. The first principle of tax incidence theory is that all taxes are ultimately borne by households. Nonetheless, roundabout taxes (such as the corporate tax) have political appeal because their incidence is well hidden from the general public.

The corporate income tax is more than just an indirect means of taxing wealthy households. It distorts the allocation of assets in the economy in that it only applies to the return on corporate assets (and not to such important categories of physical assets as housing and most farms). Moreover, it only applies to equity-financed corporate assets, since interest payments to debt holders are deductible from the corporate income tax base. In my opinion, the fact that debt payments escape the corporate income tax is a major factor in the merger and acquisition wave in the United States as well as in the numerous leveraged buyouts, share repurchases, and corporate restructurings. The tax code strongly favors highly leveraged companies.

The United States is one of the only countries in the world that does not at least partially offset the double taxation of corporate equity investments. The double taxation occurs because equity income first faces the corporate income tax and then the remaining income faces personal taxation (immediately if the money is distributed as a dividend, and when realized if the funds are retained and result in capital appreciation). Tax reform actually significantly increased double taxation because of the elimination of the long-term capital gains exclusion and the dividend exclusion. Many other countries usually reduce the double taxation through light taxation of capital gains and/or light taxation of dividends. Some give credit on a personal level for the corporate tax paid.

Treasury I proposed substantial relief from the double taxation of corporate equity income by allowing a deduction of 50 percent of dividends paid. That deduction, in combination with the Treasury I proposal for taxing only real capital gains, would have been a big improvement over the 1986 Tax Reform Act. Unfortunately, the dividend deduction was reduced to 10 percent in Treasury II and was eliminated in the actual bill.

The tax reform process was accompanied by a great deal of discussion of putting various investment activities on "a level playing field." The idea was to eliminate many tax-preferred tax shelters and to tax all investments equally so that self-interested investors would allocate their resources according to economic productivities. The idea was a good one, but difficult to accomplish. Although the reform may have brought about a more even-handed treatment in the taxation of various categories of business plant and equipment, it failed to equalize the treatment of housing and other business assets and to level the treatment of debt- and equity-financed investments.

The failure to stimulate growth and investment. The combination of decelerating depreciation deductions, the elimination of the investment tax credit, and the lowering of the marginal corporate tax rate from 46 to 34 percent has the somewhat perverse effect of increasing the taxation of new investments and decreasing the taxation of old capital. Table 10.1 shows that over the first five years of the new law, the taxation of existing capital is reduced by US$68.3 billion, whereas the taxation of new investment is increased by US$188.4 billion. The same conclusion is reached in the cost-of-capital studies of Hendershott (1988), Fullerton, Henderson, and Mackie (1987), and Bernheim and Shoven (1987). Each of them find that the new law increases the cost of capital facing firms on new investment.

Although it is difficult to quantify the effects of these measures, the increased taxation of new equity-financed investment surely will hurt the level of investment in the United States, its international competitiveness, and its economic growth rate over the next couple of decades.

TABLE 10.1 Changes in Corporate Tax Revenue in the United States, 1987–1991 (billions of U.S. dollars)

	1987	1988	1989	1990	1991	1987–1991
Change in revenue from:						
Taxes on old capital	0.8	−8.6	−17.1	−20.1	−23.3	−68.3
Taxes on new investment	24.3	32.5	39.6	43.5	48.5	188.4
Total change in coporate tax revenue	25.1	23.9	22.5	23.4	25.2	120.1

NOTE: Taxes on new investment include capital cost, minimum tax, and some accounting provisions of the 1986 act. The other changes (decelerating depreciation deductions, elimination of investment tax credit, lower marginal rate) are treated as applying to old capital.
SOURCE: Lawrence H. Summers, "Should Tax Reform Level the Playing Field?" NBER Working Paper no. 2132 (Cambridge, Mass.: National Bureau of Economic Research, 1987).

The failure to establish consumption as the basis for taxation. In almost all of the discussion to this point, I have accepted the idea that the tax reform was attempting to institute an improved income tax. If that was the target, then Treasury I would have gone a long way toward reaching it. In the several important respects I have just covered, the actual reform act is far inferior to the income tax proposed in Treasury I.

However, it is not at all clear we should move our hybrid tax toward an income tax instead of toward a consumption tax. The consumption tax potentially offers high grades on intertemporal neutrality, promotion of growth, simplicity, and fairness. Such a tax would be neutral between present and future consumption, rather than penalizing future consumption as does an income tax. Several analysts have found significant efficiency gains for the economy in moving to a consumption tax. Ballard, Fullerton, Shoven, and Whalley (1985) estimate that a consumption tax (and corporate tax integration) could be designed to increase economic efficiency by more than 2 percent of the value of GNP plus leisure. As total tax collections are no more than 20 percent of GNP plus leisure, these are extremely significant gains for the economy. Relative to today's U.S. economy, we are speaking roughly of a pure efficiency gain of US$100–US$150 billion per year. A similar magnitude is found in Auerbach and Kotlikoff (1987), who emphasize the important distinction between consumption taxes and wage taxes.[4]

A consumption tax, be it a value-added tax (VAT) or a direct expenditure tax such as Bradford's "X-tax" (Bradford 1986), is inherently simpler than an income tax. By directly or indirectly calculating consumption expenditures, the tax avoids the complexities of computing real capital income. The issues of inflation adjustment, for instance, become far less difficult.

The potential for fairness results not only from the progressivity that one could build into the rate structures of a direct expenditure tax, but also from the nature of the tax base itself. A household's consumption represents its withdrawals from the aggregate social product, while its income (under strong competitive and technological assumptions) represents the value of its marginal contribution to the social product. I feel that this distinction alone makes consumption the fairer basis for taxation.

Many U.S. trading partners rely on consumption taxes of some type. According to Shoven and Tachibanaki (1988), Japan's tax system is essentially a labor income tax because it taxes capital income very lightly at the personal level. They found that the Japanese government received (through taxes) approximately 7 percent of the return on a new, marginal, domestically financed investment, whereas the U.S. government got around 37 percent for a similar U.S.-financed American investment. While the Japanese are considering a modest increase in personal capital income taxation, they are also proposing to introduce a consumption-based value-added tax. Overall, Japan will retain a tax system that presents a smaller tax wedge between the return on investments and the return to investors (see, for example, King 1987) and is more conducive to saving and economic growth.

European countries rely heavily on value-added taxes. Ballard, Scholz, and Shoven (1987) have found that a value-added tax can be a remarkably efficient means of raising revenue. We found that the marginal cost of raising funds via higher income tax rates (from their pre-1987 levels) was as much as 25 percent higher than the cost of raising them through a new VAT. The value-added tax has the advantage that it offers static efficiency by taxing alternative sources and uses of funds equally and has dynamic neutrality in taxing present and deferred consumption on an even basis.

A Review of the Grades

Economic efficiency and neutrality. I give the new law a B– on efficiency and neutrality. It levels the playing field in the narrow sense of taxing various business investments more similarly. However, it does not alter the discrimination against saving, against equity-financed corporate investments, or in favor of owner-occupied housing.

Economic growth. The reform must get an F for economic growth. It is clearly anti-saving and anti-investment. Its tax breaks go to existing capital rather than to additions to the capital stock. Finally, it does nothing to address the government's dissaving.

Fairness. Tax reform has had some positive results in terms of fairness, and I give it a B. By ensuring that almost all rich individuals and big profitable companies now pay taxes, the reform certainly improved the perception of fairness. And perceptions are important, particularly for compliance with a system based on self-reporting. Many of the tax shelters that eliminated the tax burdens of rich households and large businesses were both unfair and inefficient. So, there is a case to be made that the reform was largely successful on the criterion of fairness.

But it does not deserve an A. It is not fair to tax individuals on fictitious income (due to inflation). Further, the indirect corporate tax is less fair than a direct tax on households.

Simplicity. I would give the reform a C for simplicity. Those who had simple returns before ended up with even simpler returns (or perhaps no returns). However, many of those with complicated returns found that the new law made things worse. Taxing real income is very complex. The failure of this law is that taxation has become extremely complicated and still does not tax real income. The real missed opportunity in terms of simplicity is lack of a consumption tax.

Should We Retake the Course?

I have found myself wavering on the issue of whether we should leave the tax system alone for about ten years or whether we should admit that we did not succeed and try to fix it again. I am increasingly convinced that this is not a good tax system to maintain for the rest of this century. Its failures on saving and growth are simply too important not to correct.

My feeling, then, is that we should begin to study thoroughly a complete overhaul of the tax system. There is no rush. In fact, it would be preferable to take four or five years to consider the change. But this time, let's be bold and move to an integrated consumption tax that scores well on the efficiency, growth, fairness, and simplicity criteria. In the meantime we must address the enormous federal deficit and the low level of private saving. Increased gasoline, liquor, and cigarette taxes and the reinstatement of a liberalized individual retirement account would be appropriate steps in this direction.

Part IV

Tax Reform and Developing Countries

Economic Reform in the
People's Republic of China, 1979–1988

During 1979–1988, the People's Republic of China introduced bold and sweeping economic reforms, extending the power to make many economic decisions from the central government to local governments, firms, and individuals. Many aspects of these reforms were remarkably successful, stimulating several other socialist countries to experiment with similar changes.

These reforms were accompanied, however, by a growing inflation rate and growing distortions to relative prices and relative incomes, given the remaining government controls on prices and wage rates in a number of sectors. The resulting drop in real incomes in these sectors[1] and the increase in corruption as individuals tried to circumvent the distortions may have been partly responsible for the political turmoil that occurred during April–June 1989.

I would like to thank Lili Liu, Michelle White, other contributors to this volume, and especially Xiaohong Chen for helpful comments on earlier drafts of this paper. I would also like to thank various officials of the Chinese Academy of Social Sciences, the Chinese State Planning Commission, and a manufacturing firm in Beijing for helpful discussions on the characteristics of the recent economic reforms. Finally, I would like to thank the students I taught in the Economics Training Program at People's University in Beijing in 1986, who themselves taught me much about the functioning of the Chinese economy.

The reforms were far too fundamental to be referred to simply as tax reform, though one important aspect of the reforms was to create a tax system. Before the reforms started in 1979, the government in one way or another directly controlled virtually every aspect of the economy. Production decisions were made directly by the government, while individual consumption patterns were in large part determined by rationing. Prices, and therefore taxes, played little role in determining the allocation of resources.[2] There is now a variety of explicit income taxes, sales taxes, and property taxes, which are relatively similar in form to taxes used in Western countries. Unlike Western governments, however, the government in China continues to affect the allocation of resources in many ways other than through the tax system. The government still has substantial control over wages and many prices, and still must approve many allocation decisions. Under the reforms these powers have been reduced and decentralized so that local and provincial governments now make many of these decisions, but these governmental powers still exist.

Given the more comprehensive nature of the reforms in China, the focus of this chapter must necessarily be broader than that of other chapters in this volume. The first and simplest set of questions, addressed in the first section, is simply descriptive. How much revenue does the government receive, how much does it spend, and how have these figures changed under the reforms? This provides one view of the importance of the role of the government in the economy. Based on the size of tax revenues, the government in China is not particularly large by Western standards, and revenue has been falling quickly under the reforms. Expenditures have not fallen as quickly, however, leading to a growing deficit and worsening inflation.

A second and important focus of the chapter is the effect of the economic reforms on the efficiency of resource allocation. Many studies of Western economies assume that the sole reason for inefficiency in the economy is taxes. The second section examines how the incentive structure set up by the Chinese government under the reforms, in all its aspects, has affected the efficiency of the allocation of resources. The policy changes led to dramatic growth rates in both agriculture and rural industry. It would appear, though, that these two successes occurred for quite different reasons. Under the "responsibility system" introduced in agriculture starting in 1979, farmers could grow what they wished and sell it themselves at market prices. Most of their tax payments were nondistortive lump sums, and the few taxes that were not lump sums caused only minor distortions. Therefore, it is not surprising that agricultural output grew quickly. In contrast, rural industry faced heavy and often arbitrary tax rates. Since the local governments kept most of this revenue, however, they had the incentive and the ability to encourage rapid development of rural industry.

The reform of state-owned enterprises has proven to be far more difficult. The government transferred the power to make many decisions to firm managers, but still imposed very heavy tax rates on these firms. The results have not been particularly encouraging. Tax rates have been high enough that firms normally preferred to pay out retained earnings to workers rather than reinvest them, leading to a consumption boom. Given the low interest rates on loans and the favorable treatment of debt in the tax system, however, firms found it extremely attractive to borrow to finance new investment, leading to excess demand for loans. As a result, the government or the banks have been forced to make many of the investment decisions, undoing this aspect of the attempted decentralization. Faced with the high tax rates, firms also have a strong incentive to evade taxes. They have been sufficiently successful at doing so that the government has imposed minimum tax payments on firms.

The reforms also increased the scope for individual decision making, particularly in rural areas. Before the reforms individuals were assigned jobs, housing, and ration coupons for almost all consumer goods, leaving little room for individual decisions. Approval was even needed for marriage partners and childbearing. Under the reforms rural households have been free to make virtually all economic and consumption decisions. Almost a quarter of households have shifted from agriculture to rural industry, often financing needed investment out of their own savings. In urban areas, free markets have opened for food and consumer goods. However, jobs are often still assigned, and firms control access to housing and a variety of consumer durables. Although much has changed, important government controls remain.

One issue not addressed in this chapter concerns the distributional effects of the Chinese fiscal system. While of much interest in light of the claims that China has achieved a remarkable degree of equality in living standards, this question seemed too difficult to answer properly. For example, distributional analyses in Western economies in principle involve estimating the incidence of the entire tax system by constructing a general equilibrium model of the economy, then forecasting how the welfare of different types of individuals would differ if lump-sum taxes were used instead. Attempting to forecast the distribution of welfare in China if the government were to eliminate all controls on the economy is simply out of the question. As seen in response to the relaxation of controls in rural areas starting in 1979, the resulting changes in the economy can be pervasive and in many ways unexpected. Even assessing the current distribution of welfare in China is difficult given the large price distortions and the degree to which consumption levels are not closely tied to income levels, but depend on controlled access to many scarce goods and services.

Size of the Government in China

Describing the importance of the government in China simply in terms of the size of its revenue or expenditures is very misleading, given the government's power to control many of the decisions made and financed by firms and individuals. However, any discussion of the role of the government should start with an examination of the financial flows *directly* controlled by the government.

Before the reforms, central government revenues in China were about a third of national income,[3] which is not particularly large compared with the equivalent figure in other countries. Yet over half of the government's revenue was used to finance new capital investments in state-owned enterprises. Government expenditures on goods and services were small by Western standards, leading to a poor transportation network, poorly financed schools, and shortages of electricity.

Under the reforms, the relative size of government revenues shrank quickly. There were several reasons for this. To begin with, much of the growth in the Chinese economy under the reforms occurred in sectors that were less heavily taxed, particularly agriculture. In addition, the government explicitly allowed firms to retain a higher fraction of their profits in order to provide added incentives. Finally, revenues from the taxation of profits did not grow as quickly as might have been expected, in part because firms could easily understate their income given the complicated barter transactions that occur between firms.

Government expenditures did not drop as quickly as revenues, however, leading to a growing deficit.[4] The deficit has been financed partly by debt and partly by growth of the money supply. The resulting inflationary pressure has created severe problems for the economy. Some prices respond quickly to the inflationary pressure, while other prices are held fixed by the government. As a result, there are growing distortions to relative prices, increasing shortages of goods whose prices are pegged, and rising subsidies by the government to maintain production of those goods in short supply. The growing gap between pegged prices and black-market prices has also created a greater incentive for corruption, which has become a major political problem.

The reform process has therefore led to an increasing macroeconomic imbalance. The resulting higher inflation rate has created growing microeconomic distortions, which themselves add to the government deficit.

Efficiency of the Chinese Economy

The various policy changes in China during 1979–1988 had major effects on the allocation of resources. This section focuses first on the changes that took place in production in rural areas, which started in 1979, and then discusses the changes occurring in urban industry and commerce. Finally, it describes the increasing flexibility that individuals faced under the reforms in making economic decisions.

Rural reforms.

Agriculture. Before 1979, agricultural decisions were almost entirely controlled by the government. The government assigned individuals to particular farms, allowing virtually no mobility; it chose the crops to be planted, with a heavy emphasis on grains (regardless of climate); it procured all output not to be consumed by the local farmers and supplied this output to consumers located elsewhere by rationing; and it determined the consumption levels of farmers according to work points, but not true individual productivity. The agricultural sector was barely even part of a monetary economy, since consumption levels were tied directly to work points based on certain allocation rules.

In 1979, there was a major shift in policy, introducing what has been known as the responsibility system. Individual families were assigned plots of land, eventually for a fifteen-year period at a fixed rental payment, and given quotas of particular crops that they were required to sell to the government at prespecified prices at the end of the growing season.[5] Excess production could be sold on the "free market" at unregulated prices. The prices paid by the government for grains and oil were originally about half of the free-market prices, but because of the low quality of crops obtained as a result, the government gradually raised its procurement prices.[6] Procurement prices for other crops were much closer to market prices.

Families also faced an average tax rate on the projected harvest of grains, oil, and cotton of 15.5 percent, paid in kind before 1985 and in cash since then;[7] the tax rate on production of other crops was about half this rate. Harvest projections were based on the average yield of each plot over the previous five years and were recalculated every five years. Farmers faced no further government restrictions. They have recently even been allowed to sell use of their land at a controlled price.[8]

The results for agricultural output were quick and dramatic. Not only did outputs increase substantially, but more important there was also a major shift in the crop mix. Output of cotton, vegetable oils, fruit, meat, and fish increased very quickly in response to the new flexibility in crop choice. There was, in addition, much more specialization of production according to local climate and soil conditions. Quality of produce increased substantially, according to many accounts. On net, per capita income of farmers tripled between 1978 and 1986, because of the combined effects of increases in output, a shift toward more profitable crops, and rising prices for agricultural goods.

One persistent problem is that the government remains committed to making grain available to urban residents at very cheap prices, to insure that all individuals have enough to eat regardless of their income level. But the government cannot afford to purchase the desired quantity of grain at market prices, and then resell it at such a large discount. As a result, the government continues to impose grain production quotas on farmers, and pays too little for this grain to make the production voluntary. Grain production is sufficiently unprofitable that there are stories of farmers going into the cities to buy ration coupons for grain from urban residents, and then using the grain obtained to fulfill the quota for grain sales to the government.[9]

Another problem is that since the prices of most other goods are still controlled to some degree by the government, agricultural prices are much more sensitive to inflationary pressures than are other prices. The recent large government deficits have led to sharp increases in the relative price of food, creating political pressure for some sort of price control on food as well.

The limited term of the lease of land to farmers may eventually present difficulties. Initially, the term was only five years and the resulting short-term behavior was obvious, causing the term of the lease to be extended to fifteen years. To what degree behavior is still too short-term is unclear. It is likely to become more so as the term of the lease nears its end.

Rural industry and commerce. The agricultural reforms also made it far easier for individuals to leave agriculture and work in rural community enterprises set up by local governments, or work independently in small, privately owned firms. The resulting rapid growth in rural community enterprises has probably been the most important effect of the reforms, and it is one that was quite unexpected. Between 1978 and 1986, income of rural community enterprises grew at over 20 percent per year. Virtually a fifth of the rural labor force has shifted from agriculture to commerce and industry since the reforms started. This rapid growth has occurred in spite of strong preferential treatment given to enterprises owned by the national or provincial governments in access to scarce or imported inputs, skilled labor, and cheap credit.

This rapid growth at first appears surprising since these enterprises have been subject to heavy taxation and are under strong local government control. Before 1985, community enterprises had to pay virtually all their profits to the various levels of government. Starting in 1985, measured profits have been subject to a progressive income tax, with a 55 percent maximum rate. However, supplementary fees of various sorts often claim a large fraction of any profits that remain. These combined tax rates are high enough that self-financed investments should rarely be profitable.[10]

In addition, managers of community enterprises are normally appointed by the local government and depend on local government support for further career advancement. The government can further influence a firm's economic decisions through its control over access to low-interest loans and subsidies to scarce inputs.

Given the high tax rates and continuing government involvement in economic decisions, rural enterprises would seem to have little incentive or ability to become such a dynamic sector of the economy. Why have these rural enterprises been so successful? The answer seems to be that the local governments, which in practice make the bulk of the economic decisions regarding rural enterprises, face relatively undistorted incentives and few restrictions on their ability to respond to these incentives. Much of the tax revenue collected from community enterprises remains with the local government,[11] which therefore sees its effective tax rates solely as the rates paid to higher levels of government. Since these tax rates are generally very low, the local government faces minimal distortions when making economic decisions regarding community enterprises.[12]

There are essentially no restrictions imposed on local governments concerning the operation of these community enterprises. Pricing decisions and the internal organization of the firms are flexible; trade, at least within the province, is unhampered; and the choice of outputs is unrestricted. Communities are generally too small to play an important role in the market for most goods, so there is every reason to expect a competitive market structure to develop in this sector of the economy.

Of course, there has to be some question concerning the local governments' objectives. During the reform period, the national government has had little control over the behavior of local governments. The initial presumption must certainly be that local governments attempt to maximize some measure of the welfare of local residents.[13] Given the local governments' virtually complete control over the revenues of rural enterprises, one must therefore presume that local governments attempt to allocate local resources efficiently.

One remaining problem was that firms that generated less tax revenue for local governments, perhaps because their prices were set too low by the national government or because the national government's share of the profits tax was larger, seemed to receive less generous support from local governments. Investments in such activities as roads, education, electricity, and communication seemed particularly neglected. Distortions created by the national government's share in tax revenue certainly had an effect.

Another problem was that the local governments were not in a very good position to judge the relative merits of different types of investments. Western firms have designed a variety of ways to decentralize decisions within a large enterprise, so that decisions are made by those with the best information yet are still made in the interests of the larger organization.[14] Perhaps with more time, local governments in China will come up with an equivalent mechanism, though ideological controls on interest rates may make this difficult.

In spite of these problems, the community enterprise sector became large enough to cause political leaders to ask how large it should be allowed to get within a socialist economy. During the first few months after the military crackdown in June 1989, about 5 percent of rural enterprises were closed, and remaining firms faced new restrictions.

Under the reform, community enterprises in China remained much more important than private enterprises. Yet private enterprises faced relatively similar tax rates. Private enterprises were also subject to the turnover tax and to a progressive tax on income, with a maximum rate of 60 percent. While individual incomes have been subject to tax at rates as high as 45 percent, the tax phases in at a high enough income level that few people are directly affected. Perhaps the extreme stigma attached to private enterprises during the Cultural Revolution lingered enough that individuals avoided setting up private enterprises in fear of possible future retribution.[15] An additional explanation is that local governments do not provide any assistance to private enterprises, so that the high tax rates do in practice discourage the growth of this sector.

Reform of state-owned enterprises. The reform in the control of state-owned enterprises has been much slower. Before 1979, all major decisions concerning the behavior of state-owned enterprises were made by the government, and virtually all profits (or losses) went to the government. In particular, the government provided the needed capital and material inputs to the firms, assigned workers and managers to the firms, and took delivery of the firms' output at prices set by the government. Workers' wages were normally based on national norms and had no relation to individual or even firm productivity. The career path of managers depended on their success in fulfilling the stated output targets for the firm. As a result, managers had a strong incentive to obtain excess inputs to ensure their ability to meet any output targets and to avoid overfulfilling output targets so as not to face more ambitious targets in the future.

The initial reforms gave managers somewhat more power to make internal decisions concerning technology and output mix. Faced with the need to find inputs or sell outputs directly, there was much more pressure to match the technology and the product mix to the demands of the economy. In addition, firms were allowed to retain as much as 20 percent of the profits they generated, making profits a much more important factor in their decision making.

By 1984, the government set up an explicit tax system for state-owned enterprises, taxing away some fraction of a firm's accounting profits and requiring the firm to use 50 percent of retained profits for new investment,[16] 30 percent for bonus payments to workers, and 20 percent for noncash benefits to workers.[17] Firms could also apply to newly created banks for loans at very low interest rates to finance new investments.[18]

The top marginal profits tax rate (including both the income tax and the adjustment tax) varied by firm from 55 percent up to 68.5 percent, being higher for firms that had more profits per worker in 1983, and there was an additional tax payment based solely on 1983 profits.[19] The variation in rates was intended to equalize retained profits per worker, at least based on the situation prevailing in 1983, so that workers' compensation would not be tied to arbitrary differences in allowed prices, access to cheap inputs, or access to better technology. However, it also equalized pay in spite of past differences in worker productivity. Anticipation of future attempts to re-equalize retained profits per worker likely dampened incentives on firms to increase productivity.

The definition of accounting profits is generally similar to that used in Western countries. However, both interest and principal repayments on bank loans are deductible when calculating taxable profits. As a result, the tax system provides a slight net subsidy to debt-financed new investments, above and beyond the incentive created by the low interest rate charged on bank loans.[20] Depreciation rates are generally slower than in Western countries, and they differ less across types of capital. Another interesting difference is that the deductible expenses for labor are fixed by the government through its control of the basic wage rates. Supplementary bonuses and benefits are not normally deductible expenses.

An important problem faced under the tax system was tax avoidance and evasion. For example, the value of payments in kind are not generally reported in accounting profits. As a result, taxable income would be reduced by selling output at a reduced price in exchange for cheap consumer goods for the firm's employees. Firms also had some discretion in reclassifying various nondeductible worker benefits as deductible production costs and in repaying loans more quickly. In addition, auditing of firms in China has been limited, making misreporting quite feasible.[21]

The next major policy, started on an experimental basis in 1985, was the contract responsibility system.[22] This system was designed to protect the government against undue erosion of its tax revenue. In its original form, firms contracted to make a fixed tax payment each year to the government, based on their forecasted profits and their normal tax rate.[23] The firm was not constrained in its use of any retained profits. During the contract period, the tax was lump sum, but that period was short enough (often one year in the initial experiments) that firms would need to be concerned about the provisions of the next contract. As a result, the effective tax rate on new investment still seemed to be viewed as very high, leading to a low reinvestment rate.

Many contracts signed in 1987 therefore specified a time path of both tax payments and new investment.[24] In one contract I examined closely, the guaranteed tax rate was 69.5 percent of forecasted profits, but extra profits were taxed at only 36.3 percent up to a specified profit level 5 percent larger than the original forecast, and at only 28.1 percent above that level.[25] In addition, the contract specified a guaranteed level of investment in each year of the contract and designated the impact of increased after-tax profits on new investment, before-tax payroll,[26] and after-tax worker benefits.[27]

The decision-making powers of firms remain quite circumscribed, compared with the situation faced by Western firms. Most firms are heavily overstaffed, having been assigned workers in the past against their will. In practice, they cannot fire excess workers.[28] While firms have more flexibility than before to base pay and promotions on productivity, pressure from workers still leads to a much more compressed distribution of pay than would be expected with a free labor market.[29] In particular, unskilled workers seem generally to be paid much more than their marginal product—it is not uncommon for firms to report having 15 percent to 40 percent more workers than they need for production, yet having difficulty getting skilled workers. In effect, each firm is assigned responsibility for providing financial support to some fraction of the otherwise unemployed.[30]

In addition, new investment projects of any size must be approved by some level of government, regardless of the source of finance. Economists at the State Planning Commission claim that the government is primarily concerned with undoing the distortions created by the mispricing of goods, exchange rate controls, and interest rate controls. As a result, projects must be attractive to both the firm, at existing prices, and the government, at (its perception of) undistorted prices. Projects that are attractive to the government but not to the firm would not be proposed, and so not undertaken. To compensate for this, the government provides special subsidies, particularly approved access to bank loans and inputs at cheap prices,[31] to projects that it finds attractive but that might not otherwise be undertaken. The gain from qualifying for these subsidies is large enough that firms have the incentive to forgo many profitable projects, at least temporarily, in hopes of eventually receiving subsidies to help finance them.

While pricing decisions still generally require government approval, there appears to be more flexibility than in the past. Traditionally, prices were set equal to average costs in the industry plus a certain percent markup, and output was sold to a government procurement agency regardless of demand.[32] It is now much more common for firms to sell directly to other firms or individuals, increasing substantially the incentive for firms to cut back production of goods in excess supply. Shortages are still common, however. In one industry looked at closely, the largest firms still set their prices based on the fixed markup rule, using the average per-unit cost of all firms in the industry. However, the smaller firms in the industry had substantial flexibility in setting their prices.

It is not entirely clear what the objectives of firms have been when making use of their extra decision-making powers under the reforms. Managers are subject to a variety of pressures from both the government and the workers. The concerns of the government could include the growth rate of the firm, employment, size of tax remittances, and profitability. In order to understand the behavior of firms in China, it is therefore essential to understand not only the incentives created by the contract system or the tax system but also the incentives created by the particular form of supervision of the firm—there is no equivalent to a board of directors pushing to maximize share values.

Although many possible objectives for the firm might be hypothesized, probably the objective that best rationalizes the observed behavior of firms during this period is the maximization of the welfare of existing workers.[33] In general, firms have had two responses to the reforms. First, they have tried to pay out as large a fraction as they could of retained earnings as bonuses or benefits,[34] which one would not expect if the objective of the firm were to maximize growth, profits, or tax payments. Second, they have demanded bank loans and government grants for new investment far in excess of supply. This is hardly surprising since the interest charges on such financing are pegged at very low levels and since the tax system subsidized debt-financed investments.[35] Since central government control of the banking system has been loose, there has been a continuing risk of excess investment financed by printing money. During 1984 in particular, control was so limited that money supply expanded by over 50 percent, owing to excess investment loans to firms. Since then, the government has imposed direct controls on new investment, by requiring government approval of larger projects before the investment can be undertaken.

Several clear problems have developed under the contract system. To begin with, since there is no labor market, large and arbitrary differences in pay between workers at different firms can easily develop, creating political objections to the current reform process. In principle, workers receive bonuses and benefits in proportion to increases in the firm's profits. These gains can result from price changes as well as from increased worker effort. Even if they arise from increased worker effort, the firm with the largest improvement, and so the highest wages, need not be the firm with the most productive workers, given the initial inequality in productivity when the contracts were first signed. In addition, the contracts specify the total payroll and not the pay per worker, creating a perverse incentive to reduce the work force in order to raise pay per worker.[36] Since workers cannot be fired, this effect will show up slowly, as firms fail to replace workers who retire or transfer to other firms. But it will inevitably create a growing difference in the pay of those lucky enough to have obtained permanent jobs in state firms and those who have not, presumably because they were too young. Since the firm's payroll is related to both sales revenue and profitability, yet future tax payments are likely tied to profitability, there may also be a perverse incentive to raise sales but lower profitability in order to both raise current wages and reduce future taxes.

There is also a sizable number of goods that either are not marketed at all (for example, land and housing) or are in excess demand. Since a market-clearing price cannot officially be paid for these goods, other ways have inevitably developed to clear these markets. A common approach is to buy goods in excess demand either with other goods in excess demand or with goods sold at below market-clearing prices.[37] As would be expected under this type of barter system, much time seems to be spent trying to find a coincidence of needs between groups of firms.

To some degree, firms still face a soft budget constraint, creating a variety of other inefficient incentives. While there have been a few demonstration cases of firms allowed to go bankrupt, the government normally reimburses losses when they occur so as to keep firms in business.[38] Even in those cases when firms did go bankrupt, the workers were protected from significant financial loss. As a result, firms may well face a financial incentive to generate losses in order to qualify for transfers from the government. For example, selling goods at a reduced price in exchange for cheap consumer goods for the firm's workers aids the workers directly and may generate government transfers which are of further value. It would appear from the government statistics that a large amount of revenue is being spent reimbursing such losses.

The limited term of existing contracts also creates strange incentives. A firm's presumption must be that any subsequent contract will again tax profits, as forecasted at the end of the existing contract, at a very high rate. Initial contracts based their forecasts of future profits on the actual profits earned during the previous three years. If managers presume that the same procedure will be used to forecast profits under the next contract, then high profits during the last three years of the existing contract not only are subject to immediate taxation, but also are likely to lead to heavier taxation through-out the life of the next contract. Taking these various effects of higher profits on the present value of taxes into account, the marginal tax rate on higher profits during the last three years of the existing contract can easily be over 100 percent.[39] Uncertainty about the future policy regime also leads to a fear of heavy taxation of profits after the current contract ends, or greater diffi-culty in using these profits to aid the firm's workers, creating an incentive to pay out as much to workers now as is feasible.[40]

Another commonly cited problem that has plagued the entire reform process is that provincial governments try to protect local firms by restricting imports of goods from firms in other provinces that compete with local production. This behavior is easily understood. Most of the tax revenue received by provincial governments comes from taxation of the profits of local firms. Given the lack of alternative sources of revenue, the local gov-ernments need to raise profits in order to raise revenue and so have the incentive to increase the market power of local firms. This perverse incentive would be much weakened if provincial tax revenue were based on the consumption of local residents,[41] since then tax revenue would not depend on where goods were produced but only on the level of local consumption.

One other continuing problem is that the average time between the start and the completion of investment projects is very long. This problem likely arises from the political nature of the approval process for new investment— it is politically far easier to approve a project but provide inadequate funding than to reject a project outright. Also, once a project has been started, a firm has a much stronger claim on future (subsidized) financing. The problem is likely to remain important as long as loans and grants for investment are at very low interest rates. There will be excess demand for these loans, requiring a political allocation of funds, and firms will try to manipulate this political process by seeking to initiate large projects that will have a strong claim on future financing.

Recently, in reaction to the success of rural community enterprises, the government has started to sell or lease small state enterprises. Whether this policy will be as successful as the changes affecting community enterprises is subject to question, however. City governments are likely to be much less supportive of these firms than rural governments have been of community enterprises. The presumption is that the small enterprises will not have access to government loans, implying that they will have a much harder time obtaining financing for new investments, and any repayments to creditors will not be deductible from taxable income. Given the high tax rates faced by these small state enterprises, new investment incentives will be very weak.

Increased scope for individual decision making. Before the reforms, individuals in China had little scope for decision making. People were assigned jobs, often in the same firm that one of their parents worked in. Pay was based on seniority but rarely on the individual's own productivity. Housing was assigned by the firm, again based heavily on seniority. Most consumption goods were rationed, with alternative supplies often difficult or impossible to find. What savings occurred was often by fiat, with the government requiring workers to purchase particular bonds or to deposit money in a bank. Approval was even needed for marriage and childbearing. It is difficult to talk about a tax system during this period, since prices played little role in the economy.

This system has changed more in the rural areas than in the cities under the reforms. Individuals can now move relatively easily from agriculture to rural collectives or private enterprises. Those that remain in agriculture have virtually full discretion in making economic and consumption decisions. Many consumer goods are available without restriction. Not only can individuals save through bank deposits, but they can also save through purchase of housing or consumer durables, through investments in farm equipment or in new collectives, or through more education for themselves or their children. Their ability to save by having more children is more restricted than before, however, because of the government's effort to reduce the population growth rate. In addition, since the financial return to more education remains quite limited owing to the compressed wage distribution, the reforms have made education less attractive. Perhaps as a result, financial saving has been growing quickly in rural areas.[42]

In urban areas, the reforms have opened up new food and consumer goods markets through the growth of free markets, implying that extra monetary income has more value. Because of price controls, however, it is difficult to purchase more than the rationed allocation of many goods, though black markets have become much "grayer" since the reforms. Housing, in particular, is still assigned by the firm. The only readily available outlet for savings, in addition to consumer durables, is bank accounts, which pay extremely low interest rates.[43] As a result, savings by urban residents are limited.

Labor mobility remains extremely limited. Transferring from one firm to another requires the approval of *both* firms, leading to potentially complicated negotiations. Those who already have adequate housing could well end up waiting several years until they are assigned equivalent housing by a new employer. Most university graduates are assigned to their initial job, where they must remain for a certain number of years.[44]

In the wake of the reforms, therefore, it is possible to look at the effects of tax distortions on the behavior of rural households. Urban households, however, still seem to face important direct controls on their choices, making an analysis of the effects of the government on their behavior more complicated.

Conclusions

Only since the economic reforms that started in 1979 has it begun to be possible to consider the effects of the government on the behavior of individuals and firms in China through the government's control of an explicit or implicit tax system. Previously, the government directly controlled virtually all economic decisions. The reforms have involved extensive decentralization of decision making, partly from the national government to local governments, but also from the government to firms and individuals. Judging the degree of decentralization that has occurred is not easy, however, since many decisions still require government approval. The clear impression is that the approval process has become much more pro forma.

The reform process has involved repeated attempts at decentralization followed by partial recentralization after the government recognizes that its mechanism for controlling the decisions of firms and individuals is inadequate.[45] There has been continual experimentation with alternative incentive mechanisms, as the government searches for an approach that allows decentralization to proceed smoothly. This experimentation is still actively under way.

Understanding the full incentive effects of any particular mechanism that has been attempted or proposed is not straightforward. For example, state-owned enterprises now have explicit contracts with the government that carefully describe how their tax payments will be determined during the five-year period of the contract. But firms must still negotiate with the government for access to foreign exchange, skilled labor, loans at below market interest rates, or inputs at cheap prices, as well as over permitted output prices. In addition, there are no explicit rules determining the characteristics of the firm's next contract with the government. Realistically, the probability that the policy regime itself will remain unchanged by the time contracts are subject to renewal is quite low, making it very difficult to infer the implicit incentives faced by firms.

The results of particular attempts at decentralization have often been dramatic. Encouraging the development of collective firms in rural areas has resulted in a more than 20 percent annual growth rate in the income of such firms from 1978 to 1986. Not all dramatic effects have been favorable, however. Allowing state-owned firms to invest without direct government approval in 1984 and to finance these investments with either retained earnings or bank loans resulted in an unsustainable explosion of new investment financed by new money. Early in 1988, rumors of a major price reform, leading to higher prices, seem to have caused a dramatic drop in new bank deposits.[46]

The next decade promises to be a critical one for the Chinese economy, as it searches for a viable way to decentralize decision making without violating various political constraints that the economy remain socialist and relatively egalitarian. Whether it will be able to overcome the current economic and political problems that have arisen under past reforms and move further toward a market economy is an open question.

Tax Reform in an Inflationary Environment: The Case of Colombia

After two decades of continuous reform, Colombia has in recent years taken important steps to establish an inflation-proof tax system. In late 1986 the country enacted legislation that disallows income tax deductions for the inflationary component of interest expense; it also extended a similar exemption of the inflationary component of interest income found in prior law. At the end of 1988 it enacted a two-stage transition to a sophisticated "integrated" system of inflation adjustment patterned after that used in Chile. During the first stage, from 1989 through 1991, Colombia will continue to rely on ad hoc methods to compensate for inflation in the measurement of income from business and capital. Contrary to the recommendations of a study commissioned by the government (McLure, Mutti, Thuronyi, and Zodrow 1988), Colombia did not replace its system of accelerated depreciation allowances with one based on economic depreciation when it introduced inflation adjustment of depreciable assets. In choosing the integrated system of inflation adjustment, Colombia rejected a radically new tax system based on consumption rather than on income. This chapter examines the recent evolution of both the theory and the practice of inflation adjustment in Colombia. Not only is it a fascinating story; it may offer insights that will be useful for other countries as they consider inflation adjustment.

Many countries that have experienced protracted periods of inflation have modified their tax systems in an attempt to immunize them from the effects of inflation.[1] Until now countries that have introduced comprehensive systems of inflation adjustment have been characterized by what might be called "chronic inflation"—high rates of inflation extending over long periods of time. Under such circumstances there is really no alternative to an explicit system of inflation adjustment; ad hoc approaches, including periodic adjustments of personal exemptions and bracket limits, simply are not adequate to deal satisfactorily with the problem. By comparison, it has generally been thought possible—and even desirable—for a country with a relatively low level of inflation to "muddle through" with such ad hoc measures and thereby avoid the complexity of inflation adjustment. After attempting such an approach, beginning in 1974 Colombia, a country with a well-deserved reputation for its attempts to improve its tax system, decided that it must move to reduce the vulnerability of its tax system to inflation— even rates of inflation that are relatively low by LDC standards.

Rarely, if ever, has the transition to an inflation-proof tax system been made in one or a few discontinuous jumps. The more common pattern is one of experimentation and groping, as first one adjustment and then another is added to the system or substituted for some previous scheme subsequently found to be inadequate.[2] This has certainly been the case in Colombia.

The past twenty years have seen the following evolution of thinking and public policy regarding inflation adjustment in the tax system of Colombia: at first inflation adjustment was totally rejected on policy grounds. Then it was instituted on a partial basis for personal exemptions, the rate structure, and other items fixed in nominal amounts; only subsequently was it allowed fully for these nominal amounts. Inflation adjustment of basis in the measurement of capital gains and some forms of interest income was provided under certain circumstances.

In 1986 inflation adjustment was extended to all interest income and expense, but not to depreciation (and similar) allowances or to cost of goods sold from inventory. Acceleration of depreciation allowances and last-in, first-out (LIFO) inventory accounting have provided ad hoc substitutes for explicit adjustment in the measurement of income, but at the expense of guaranteeing understatement of asset values for the purpose of the net wealth tax.

A recent report by foreign advisers offered the government of Colombia two alternatives that would either move the country to a more comprehensive and consistent system of inflation adjustment or eliminate the need for such adjustments. At the end of 1988, acting on the basis of that report, the government adopted the above-mentioned two-stage approach to inflation adjustment.

After a brief explanation of the need for inflation adjustment, this chapter traces and analyzes Colombia's experience in dealing with inflation in its income tax from the work of the Taylor and Musgrave missions of the 1960s (*Fiscal Survey of Colombia* 1965 and Musgrave and Gillis 1971, respectively) through the 1988 reforms based on the recent report on the taxation of income from business and capital (McLure, Mutti, Thuronyi, and Zodrow 1988), much of which is devoted to the inflation issue.[3] It considers both the relatively simple question of the indexation of nominal amounts and the much more complex issues of adjusting for inflation in the measurement of income. Moreover, it considers the impact of inflation on the measurement of net wealth, which is subject to separate taxation in Colombia and also serves as the basis for a presumptive measure of income (in June 1989, the net wealth tax was repealed, effective in 1992). The final section pulls together lessons from the Colombian experience in deciding whether and how to deal with the effects of inflation. This experience is instructive for developed countries, as well as for other countries in the third world.

Two Types of Inflation Adjustment

Inflation causes two types of problems, unless explicit measures are taken to prevent them.[4] First, it causes the erosion of the real value of amounts fixed in nominal (monetary) terms in the tax law, such as personal exemptions and the limits of rate brackets in a graduated-rate income tax. Second, it causes income from business and capital to be measured inaccurately.

Indexation of nominal amounts. As a result of the erosion of the real value of personal exemptions, low-income families, including those below any reasonable definition of the poverty limit, may be brought into the tax net, with adverse effects on both equity and tax administration. Because of bracket creep, taxpayers with a given real income may be pushed into ever higher marginal rate brackets and therefore pay increasing fractions of their income in taxes. As this happens, the view of vertical equity that underlay the pre-inflation pattern of graduated rates is compromised and economic incentives are blunted.

In theory this process could continue until all nominal values have, in effect, been reduced to near zero in real terms and far too many taxpayers are subject to the top marginal tax rate on most of their income. In fact, political opposition to the playing out of this extreme scenario usually results in action being taken periodically to increase the nominal amounts in question. Of course, even if some target pattern of exemptions and real rate structure is restored in this way, considerable inequities and disincentives may have occurred in the meantime, especially if the inflation rate has been high. Moreover, the impression that the tax system is unfair created by the interaction of inflation and an unindexed income tax may give a psychological justification to those who practice tax evasion. Perry and Cárdenas (1986: 175–76) suggest that this happened in Colombia following the 1974 decision to provide only partial indexation of nominal amounts and the basis of capital assets.

The solution to this problem is relatively straightforward. Important nominal amounts specified in the tax law can simply be adjusted by the percentage increase in a general price index over some period.[5] Since new income tax forms, instructions, and rate tables are commonly printed each year, there is little administrative difficulty in making this inflation adjustment annually. This type of adjustment need cause little inconvenience or confusion for the taxpayer, since all the calculations of the new nominal amounts are made by the government and reported to the taxpayer.[6]

Inflation adjustment in the measurement of income. The type of inflation adjustment just described (indexation of nominal amounts) would be desirable even in an economy with only labor income, that is, one in which there is no saving and investment and therefore no income from business and capital. By comparison, the second type of inflation adjustment, that related to the measurement of real income, would be necessary only in an economy in which there is income of the latter type, because inflation generally causes real income from business and capital to be mismeasured. It would be desirable even in a system in which no nominal amounts were specified in the tax law and there were no graduated rates—for example, in a simple system consisting of application of a flat-rate income tax to all income, with no personal exemptions. The two types of inflation adjustment are thus conceptually quite distinct. Of course, the first type of adjustment would generally be desirable, even if the measurement of the tax base were indexed.

Mismeasurement of income resulting from inflation can usefully be considered to fall into two categories: that applicable to financial assets and liabilities (involving essentially interest income and expense on unindexed debt) on the one hand and that involving real assets (actually, income and expense involving assets whose values are not set in nominal terms, including capital gains, depreciation and similar allowances, and cost of goods sold from inventories) on the other. Real interest income and expense are overstated by a system that taxes the entire amount of nominal interest income and allows a deduction for the full amount of nominal interest expense, with no recognition that inflation reduces the real value of outstanding principal. (Under such circumstances, the inflationary part of "interest" payments is, in effect, repayment of principal.)

Similarly, capital gains are overstated if no allowance is made for the increase in prices that has occurred since the time an asset was acquired; tax may even be paid on nominal gains when real losses have occurred. Income will also be overstated to the extent that no allowance is made for inflation in the calculation of depreciation (and similar) allowances or the cost of goods sold from inventories.

The mismeasurement of income that results from the combination of inflation and an unindexed tax system can lead to either distortions or inequities, depending on whether the inflation was anticipated or unanticipated.[7] If inflation is unexpected, it creates windfall gains for debtors and windfall losses for creditors. The taxation of the full nominal amount of interest income and the deduction of nominal interest expense aggravates these effects. By comparison, if inflation is expected, it is likely to be reflected in market interest rates; thus the inequities associated with unanticipated inflation may be largely absent. In an economy closed to international capital flows, if borrowers and lenders are in the same marginal tax bracket, inflation will have no effect on real variables (borrowing, lending, etc.); interest rates will simply adjust. Financial decisions may, however, be distorted if borrowers and lenders are in different tax brackets; high-income taxpayers can be expected to prefer to finance their operations with debt instead of equity, and low-income taxpayers may have a tax-created incentive to lend. Moreover, if the future course of inflation is uncertain, both borrowers and lenders may be reluctant to engage in long-term debt contracts.

Unanticipated inflation also creates windfall losses for those who can only deduct (or depreciate) the historical cost of assets, rather than the inflation-adjusted value, in calculating capital gains, depreciation allowances, or cost of goods sold from inventories. If inflation is anticipated, it combines with an unindexed tax system to cause disincentives against investing in depreciable (and similar) assets, inventories, and assets expected to yield capital gains. Of course, in any given situation the lack of inflation adjustment generally causes both inequities and distortions.

Solutions to the mismeasurement of income. Contrary to the simplicity of the provisions required to deal with the erosion of nominal amounts, the inflation adjustments required to avoid mismeasurement of income from business and capital are inevitably quite complicated. As a result, most countries have understandably been reluctant to embark on a course of systematically indexing the measurement of income. Rather, they tend to follow a fairly standard pattern of groping toward this type of inflation adjustment, first by using ad hoc substitutes for inflation adjustment and then by adopting piecemeal, but explicit, adjustments; only after such a period of experimentation (if at all) have most come to a comprehensive and consistent system.[8] This pattern has been followed in Colombia.

The ad hoc substitutes for inflation adjustment commonly employed are quite predictable. (All of these techniques may also be justified on grounds other than inflation adjustment.) Accelerated depreciation is commonly provided in lieu of explicit inflation adjustment of the depreciable basis. LIFO inventory accounting is often allowed, rather than the conceptually preferable indexed first-in, first-out (FIFO) method. Capital gains may be partially exempt or taxed at preferential rates.

Since all these approaches reduce the tax bases of the taxpayers who use them, they find ready proponents in the private sector, as well as among public policy advocates who are concerned about the inequities, distortions, and disincentives for saving and investment created by an unindexed tax system. It may or may not be recognized that such ad hoc measures as accelerated depreciation and preferential treatment of capital gains generally compensate for only a given rate of inflation, and are either too generous or not generous enough at any other rate.

Even public policy advocates may not realize that providing adjustments for real assets, without extending them to financial assets, can accentuate inequities and distortions. (They may recognize the inequity of failing to index financial assets, but see this primarily as a distinct issue to be contrasted with proposed adjustments for real assets; even worse, they may confuse the type of inflation adjustment needed for accurate measurement of income with those for amounts fixed in nominal terms. Both phenomena are illustrated by the recommendations of the Taylor mission reported below.) Of course, while taxpayers may advocate exclusion of the inflationary component of interest income, they can hardly be expected to favor the corresponding inflation adjustments of financial obligations (which may involve partial disallowance of deductions for interest expense) that are logically required if adjustment is made either explicitly or implicitly for real assets.

As a result of these influences, it is fairly common for ad hoc adjustments first to be made for depreciable assets, capital gains, and inventories; for some (or all) of these to be replaced by explicit inflation adjustments; and then for inflation adjustment to be extended to interest income and expense. In some countries there is further movement to an integrated approach (to be described briefly in the section "The 1988 Report") that brings logical consistency to a piecemeal system. Colombia has generally followed this progression, although interest indexing has been introduced before explicit adjustment of depreciation and inventories.

The net wealth tax. In Colombia the existence of a net wealth tax from 1935 to 1989 introduced another element into the inflation adjustment story that is not encountered in many countries.[9] If net wealth is to be measured reasonably accurately, it is necessary to index the basis of capital assets and inventories. Otherwise, inflation will cause the value of such assets to be understated. Moreover, the use of accelerated depreciation and LIFO accounting as substitutes for explicit inflation adjustment accentuates the problem, by reducing the remaining basis of depreciable assets too rapidly and assigning the most outdated values to inventories. Similarly, according preferential treatment to the taxation of realized nominal capital gains, rather than indexing basis and taxing only real gains, leaves the value of such assets understated for net wealth tax purposes. The existence of a net wealth tax thus strengthened considerably the case for using explicit inflation adjustment instead of ad hoc substitutes.

The Taylor and Musgrave Reports

During the 1960s the tax system of Colombia was the subject of two tax reform missions staffed primarily by foreigners. These two missions are commonly called the Taylor and Musgrave missions, respectively, after their directors, Professors Milton Taylor and Richard Musgrave. Their reports (*Fiscal Survey of Colombia* 1965; Musgrave and Gillis 1971), especially that of the Musgrave mission, have become classics in the area of taxation in developing countries and have cast long shadows over the tax reform process in Colombia.[10]

It will thus be useful to consider the recommendations of the Taylor and Musgrave missions regarding inflation adjustment in some detail. Before doing so it will be convenient to have a thumbnail sketch of relevant aspects of the Colombian tax system as it was in the early 1960s and of the inflationary experience of the country over the past several decades.

The early 1960s tax system. There was no adjustment of nominal values for inflation in Colombia's tax system in the early 1960s. Moreover, essentially all calculations of the income from business and capital were based on historical values. An important exception was the provision that allowed accumulation of a tax-free reserve for the replacement of machinery and equipment acquired before June 1, 1957. Annual accruals to this reserve were calculated as 15 percent of net commercial profits but could not exceed 15 percent of the historical cost of assets; accumulated reserves could not exceed 100 percent of historical cost. The Taylor report indicates that this provision was designed "to compensate for the higher costs of replacing depreciable assets due to inflation." Under the system in place at that time, straight-line depreciation was allowed for 90 percent of the cost of assets, using lives of twenty years for real property, five years for automobiles and airplanes, and ten years for other assets (*Fiscal Survey of Colombia* 1965: 83).[11]

Capital gains were not taxed before 1960. Starting in 1960 gains on real estate accruing after that year were taxed, but taxable gains were reduced by 10 percent for each year assets had been held (including the period before 1960). Gains on other assets remained legally exempt. Before 1974 Colombia did not tax the interest paid on bonds issued by the state and certain parastatal organizations, and there was no indexation of interest.

Colombia levied a net wealth tax at graduated rates on the wealth of individuals from 1935 to 1989 and continues to use net wealth as the base of the presumptive income tax. Ownership shares in corporations and limited liability companies are included in the net wealth of the owners. Where shares are not publicly traded, taxable values are the pro rata share of the net worth of companies. Many of the asset values included in the base of the tax are real estate.

Inflationary experience. Inflation has been much higher in Colombia during the past fifteen years than before. From 1972 to 1985 the average inflation rate (as measured by the percentage change in the consumer price index) was 21.6 percent. By comparison, from 1958 to 1972 it was only 10.5 percent, and if three years of extraordinarily high inflation are omitted, the average rate in this earlier period was barely 7 percent. (See column 1 of Table 12.1.) This experience—and especially this large shift in the rate of inflation—plays an important role in explaining Colombia's reaction to the perceived need for inflation adjustment in its tax system.

TABLE 12.1   Inflation and Indebtedness of Companies in Colombia, 1950–1985

		Debt as percentage of debt plus equity	
Year	Change in CPI (1)	All companies (2)	Manufacturing (3)
1950	n.a.	24.0	n.a.
1955	n.a.	29.0	n.a.
1960	4.1	37.0	34.2
1961	7.8	37.0	35.9
1962	3.6	40.0	37.9
1963	31.6	40.0	40.0
1964	17.3	43.0	42.5
1965	3.4	43.0	42.8
1966	19.7	45.0	45.7
1967	8.3	44.0	44.1
1968	5.9	44.0	44.5
1969	10.4	46.0	n.a.
1970	6.5	43.9	42.5
1971	9.5	47.4	46.8
1972	13.0	49.8	49.0
1973	20.9	53.7	52.7
1974	24.5	57.0	57.0
1975	22.6	60.5	59.9
1976	20.2	62.1	61.5
1977	33.2	61.6	60.4
1978	17.8	61.1	59.4
1979	24.6	65.1	63.5
1980	26.6	73.0	n.a.
1981	27.5	71.2	n.a.
1982	24.5	71.7	n.a.
1983	19.8	71.2	n.a.
1984	16.1	n.a.	n.a.
1985	24.0	n.a.	n.a.

n.a. = not available.
SOURCE: Column (1): International Monetary Fund, *International Financial Statistics* (1986), 278–79; Column (2): Mauricio Carrizosa S., *Hacia la Recuperación del Mercado de Capitales en Colombia* (Bogota: Editorial Presencia, Ltda., 1986), 32; Column (3): Ricardo Chica A., "La Financiación de la Inversión en la Industria Manufacturera Colombiana: 1970–1980," *Desarrollo y Sociedad,* Centro de Estudios sobre Desarrollo Económico, vol. 15–16 (September 1984, March 1985), 232–33.

The Taylor report. Both the Taylor and Musgrave missions considered the case for inflation adjustment and rejected it. The Taylor report (*Fiscal Survey of Colombia* 1965: 65) argued that personal exemptions were higher than appropriate for Colombia. Thus, rather than favoring indexation of exemptions, the report thought it desirable that "the exemptions are reduced automatically as inflation continues."

After acknowledging that Colombia was "a society in which inflation has been chronic," the Taylor report noted, "Another problem with respect to taxing capital gains is their illusory nature under inflationary conditions. . . . Therefore, it could be argued that capital gains, to be taxed equitably under the income tax, should be discounted by the increase in the price level." It went on to conclude, however:

> Inflation has a variable impact on different groups. Its effect on the value of assets is relatively extreme and unique, but wage earners also suffer from inflation by a lag in their wage increases and by a reduction in the real exemption limits of the income tax. If no adjustment of the income tax is to be made for wage earners and others, should one be made for taxpayers realizing capital gains? And should an adjustment be made for the illusory character of capital gains when these gains in the most part redound to an economic class that uses investment in assets as a hedge against inflation? Would not such an adjustment only reward and encourage this activity all the more? These issues, it would seem, are sufficient to discourage the use of any adjustment factor for the illusory aspect of capital gains [p. 79].

It is interesting to note that in making this argument, the Taylor mission made no distinction between inflation adjustment of nominal amounts and inflation adjustment to avoid mismeasurement of real income from capital.

Using very much the same reasoning, the Taylor mission also rejected inflation adjustment for depreciation allowances, arguing that "replacement cost depreciation is not warranted unless inflation is particularly severe" (p. 83).[12] In addition to the argument quoted above, it noted the technical difficulties of replacement cost depreciation and then argued:

> If inflationary pressure is to be contained, certainly it is not desirable economic policy, in general, to remove its penalties through automatic adjustments. *A more therapeutic method is to permit the painful effects of inflation to be manifested for whatever beneficial effects these will have as a restraint on inflationary pressures* [p. 84; emphasis added].[13]

The Taylor report opted instead for more liberal depreciation allowances, noting, among other things, that "this policy, in itself, is a compensation for higher replacement costs" (p. 85). The report advocated a system of triple declining-balance depreciation.

The Taylor report did not consider the possibility of inflation adjustment for interest income and expense. After contrasting a situation involving an investment in a fixed asset with one involving investment in an interest-bearing bond, the mission concluded:

> Thus, depreciation based on replacement cost discriminates against persons who own non-depreciable assets and who depend on fixed incomes. . . . It is undesirable to give tax relief to some and not to others during a period of inflation. *Since it is impossible to give relief to everyone, why select any particular group for special treatment?* [p. 264; emphasis added].

There was apparently no appreciation of the economic distortions that can result from the combination of accelerated depreciation and deduction of the entire amount of nominal interest expense.

The Musgrave report. Although the Musgrave report suggested that personal exemptions should be increased to allow for previous inflation, it said, in words reminiscent of those used by the Taylor mission in another context:

> we do not propose that an automatic inflation adjustment, such as that used in Chile and other high-inflation countries, be built into the exemption level and the limit for rate brackets. Such a system might be needed if inflation rates became exceedingly high. But short of this situation, *provision for automatic adjustment tends to remove resistance to inflation and to institutionalize a high inflation rate.* These effects are detrimental to sound economic development. . . . Although Colombia would be left with some degree of inflation, the distorting effect upon exemptions and the rate structure could be adjusted for periodically as necessary, rather than regularly and currently [Musgrave and Gillis 1971: 51, 53; emphasis added].

The Musgrave mission was more sympathetic to the inflation adjustment of capital gains.[14] It proposed two alternative schemes for consideration by the government. Under one the entire nominal gain would be subject to tax, but at preferential rates. Under the second, the basis of assets would be increased by some fraction of the percentage increase in the general price level (p. 49). It is worth noting that Musgrave himself favored the second plan (p. 71).

Although its analysis of the problem was somewhat more sophisticated than that of the Taylor mission, the Musgrave mission rejected inflation adjustment of depreciation allowances for many of the same reasons as the previous mission: loss of economic discipline, with detrimental effects on development, administrative difficulty, and the inequity of applying adjustments only for depreciable assets. It is noteworthy that the Musgrave mission explicitly made the important link between inflation adjustment of depreciable assets and debt on the same balance sheet, as well as in comparisons across taxpayers. Yet, like the Taylor mission, the Musgrave mission noted that "similar objectives might be accomplished, and more effectively, by liberalizing depreciation allowances based on historical costs" (p. 82).[15]

The 1974 Reforms

In 1974 Colombia carried out an extremely far-reaching reform of its tax system.[16] These reforms clearly reflected the influence of the two missions discussed earlier, especially that of the Musgrave mission. Included among these reforms, however, were important provisions for inflation adjustment, changes that neither the Taylor nor the Musgrave mission had supported.

The 1974 reforms provided for the annual adjustment of personal exemptions, bracket limits, and other magnitudes fixed in pesos at 8 percent per year. According to Perry and Cárdenas (1986: 24, 177–78), the government chose a fixed adjustment because it believed that it would be possible to return to inflation rates in the pre-1970 range of 7 to 10 percent and that this goal could be achieved more easily if full allowance were not made for inflation.[17] Thus the 1974 reforms took a middle road between the recognized need for indexation and the "no indexation" advice of the Taylor and Musgrave missions.

General taxation of capital gains (defined as gains on assets held more than two years) was also introduced in 1974. The 10 percent exemption of gains for each year of ownership was repealed, except for owner-occupied housing. It was replaced with a novel provision under which the tax rate to be applied to "occasional gains" (a concept that included gifts and inheritances, as well as capital gains) was determined by deducting 10 percentage points from the marginal rate that would result from adding 20 percent of such gains to ordinary income. Annual revaluation of assets (in addition to a one-time revaluation to 1974 values) could be made for the purpose of calculating capital gains; reflecting the considerations described above, adjustments were limited to 8 percent per year. In an interesting and logically consistent move, the 1974 reforms required that such revaluations must also be used for purpose of the net wealth tax and the newly enacted presumptive income tax (described below). Any adjustments not made in a given year could not be made subsequently.

In addition, the treatment of interest income was rationalized somewhat. Essentially all interest (except that on certain pre-1974 governmental obligations) was made taxable. But in the case of constant purchasing power bonds, the inflation premium was exempt, again up to a rate of 8 percent. Nominal interest expense remained fully deductible.

A somewhat puzzling and logically inconsistent provision—but one that complied with the Taylor and Musgrave recommendations—denied the general use of inflation-adjusted values for the calculation of depreciation allowances. Instead, the 1974 act introduced a system of accelerated depreciation based on application of the double declining-balance method to 100 percent of cost for assets with lives of at least five years. (Under previous law a nondepreciable salvage value was required.) Ordinary depreciation rates could be increased by 25 or 50 percent, respectively, for assets used two or three shifts. Moreover, the depreciable basis of assets acquired through the issuance of debt denominated in foreign currencies or domestic securities of constant purchasing power could be adjusted for the increase in the peso value of such debt.

As in most developing countries, tax evasion is a serious problem in Colombia. In 1973, following the suggestion of the Taylor and Musgrave missions, a provision to tax agriculture on a presumptive basis had been enacted (though not implemented). The 1974 reforms extended the use of a presumptive measure of income to all taxpayers. Under the "presumptive income tax," the taxpayer's income was presumed to be at least 8 percent of net wealth.

The 1974–1985 Period

The period immediately following the 1974 reforms was one of "counter-reforms," as those powerful interests that had been hurt used their political influence to reverse many of the 1974 measures. This in turn was followed by repeated episodes of reform and counterreform, culminating in the major reforms enacted in 1986.

Several important changes were made in the provisions for inflation adjustment during this period. Indexation of nominal amounts, which had initially been only 8 percent, was raised to 14 percent for 1977, set at 60 percent of the actual rate of inflation for 1978, and then made complete beginning in 1979.

A similar pattern was followed in raising the optional inflation adjustment available for capital gains, and by 1983 only real capital gains were legally taxable. (In addition, extremely generous features of the counter-reforms passed in 1979 essentially eliminated the taxation of capital gains at the taxpayer's option, in addition to reducing the tax rates applied to taxable gains, at least for high-income taxpayers. See McLure 1988.)

Beginning in 1983, 60 percent of the monetary correction on indexed debt issued by financial institutions (and 40 percent of that on other indexed debt) was made exempt from tax.

Colombia further liberalized depreciation allowances in 1976, by giving the taxpayer greater latitude to choose depreciation methods for personal property (that is, property other than buildings), as long as no more than 40 percent of cost (or 50 or 60 percent, respectively, for property used two or three shifts) was written off in one year. Explicit inflation adjustment was still not allowed.

In 1983 the cadastral value of real property that is used in the calculation of the net wealth tax, and therefore the presumptive income tax, was indexed for inflation. The potentially important benefits of this reform were reduced by a provision that limits the value of real estate for the purpose of the presumptive income tax to 75 percent of cadastral value.

The 1986 Reforms

Late 1986 saw yet another major reform of the Colombian income tax. Among the most important features of this reform were the abolition of the individual income tax on dividend income and the extension of indexing to all interest income and expense. The inflationary component of most interest income was excluded from the tax base of individuals, effective immediately; by comparison, disallowance of deductions for interest expense was to be phased in over a period of ten years, as was the exclusion of the inflationary component of interest income of companies. (When an individual has both interest income and expense, only net interest income can be excluded immediately.) The inflation adjustment is calculated as the fraction of the nominal interest rate represented by the inflation rate. Exchange rate gains and losses are to be treated in the same way as interest income and expense for purpose of these adjustments. Financial intermediaries were exempted from interest indexing, creating some discrimination in their favor and giving rise to the use of a variety of "gimmicks" to beat the system.[18]

Complete inflation adjustment was provided for capital gains. For some assets any adjustments not made annually could not be made at the time of disposition. But in the important cases of real estate, shares in companies, and partnership interests, adjustments need be made only at the time of disposition, and therefore would not affect the bases of the net wealth and presumptive income taxes.

No change was made in the tax treatment of depreciable assets or inventories. However, the 1986 legislation provided authority for the president to change the system of inflation adjustment for up to two years following enactment; it was widely presumed that the president's authority would be used to introduce inflation adjustment of depreciation allowances. In response to this authority the government of Colombia commissioned a detailed study of inflation adjustment and related issues; this study is discussed in the following section. The remainder of this section comments briefly on the reasons given for introduction of interest indexing and the elimination of the shareholder tax on dividends.

Recent years have seen the increasing "decapitalization" of the Colombian economy. The second and third columns of Table 12.1 provide indicative data on the change in the ratio of debt to total capital for all companies and for manufacturing companies over the period 1950–1985. Whereas this ratio stood at about 25 percent in 1950, it had risen to 50 percent by the early 1970s and had reached 70 percent by the beginning of the 1980s. It has been asserted that the increased reliance on debt finance can be attributed in part to the failure to provide indexation of interest expense and to the "double taxation of dividends" (Carrizosa 1986: 19). In addition, the shortening of the term structure of debt in response to greater uncertainty about the course of inflation rates can be seen in Table 12.2; between 1970 and 1980 the ratio of short- to long-term debt increased from roughly 30/40 to about 50/25 (see

TABLE 12.2	Term Structure of Debt of Manufacturing Companies in Colombia, 1970–1980		
Year	Short term	Medium term	Long term
1970	30.95	28.19	40.86
1971	27.21	28.03	44.76
1972	21.00	24.84	54.16
1973	27.51	21.87	50.62
1974	31.89	20.70	47.41
1975	32.26	21.24	42.50
1976	43.74	21.40	34.86
1977	45.83	26.06	28.11
1978	46.01	27.40	26.59
1979	47.59	25.53	26.88
1980	49.94	26.98	23.08

SOURCE: Ricardo Chica A., "La Financiación de la Inversión en la Industria Manufacturera Colombiana: 1970–1980," *Desarrollo y Sociedad*, Centro de Estudios sobre Desarrollo Económico, vol. 15–16 (September 1984, March 1985), 220.

Chica 1984–85). There is little doubt that concerns of this type played an important role in explaining the exemption of dividend income and the adoption of interest indexing in 1986.[19]

The 1988 Report

The discussion up to this point makes it clear that policy on compensation for inflation in the tax laws of Colombia has developed in a rather uneven and haphazard manner. The relatively simple step of fully indexing nominal amounts evolved fairly quickly, despite initial opposition, and has been resolved satisfactorily for almost ten years. By comparison, the much more difficult issues of avoiding mismeasurement of income from business and capital have proven more problematical, despite almost a decade and a half of experimentation and groping toward a solution. A report submitted to the government of Colombia in 1988 (McLure, Mutti, Thuronyi, and Zodrow 1988) represents an attempt to help the government grapple with this second set of problems in a systematic manner.

The 1988 report examines two alternative plans that might reasonably be considered by any country contemplating moving from an income tax that is largely unindexed to one that would avoid inflation-induced mismeasurement of income. The first alternative is a conventional indexed income tax; the second is a more radical shift to a direct tax system based on consumption, rather than on income. These two plans are described briefly.

The indexed income tax. The purpose of an indexed income tax is to produce, for tax purposes, a calculation of real income that is not vulnerable to inflation. Perhaps the most extreme version of this approach is the integrated system employed in Chile. Under it the value of all real assets and liabilities appearing on the balance sheet, including net worth (and indexed debt, to the extent of indexation), are adjusted to reflect inflation. In contrast, financial assets (those whose value is fixed in nominal terms) are not adjusted. In this way the balance sheet is made to reflect reality more closely than one based on historical costs—an important advantage in a country such as Colombia that has a net wealth tax and a presumptive income tax based on net wealth. Depreciation allowances, capital gains, and cost of goods sold from inventories are then based on these inflation-adjusted values. The adjustments to the balance sheet are also reflected in the calculation of income for tax purposes. The net result is a measure of real income that is not sensitive to inflation.[20]

An alternative approach achieves much the same results through essentially ad hoc adjustments to income statement items, rather than systematic adjustments of the balance sheet. Thus part of nominal interest income and expense is disregarded under this approach, whereas under the integrated approach there is no explicit adjustment of these items. For political reasons it is almost axiomatic that no more than 100 percent of interest will be disregarded, even though in theory an inflation rate in excess of the nominal interest rate should result in a negative figure for real interest income or expense; the integrated approach, by comparison, has no lower bound on the implicit real interest rate. No adjustment to balance sheet figures for unindexed debt would be appropriate (or occur) under either approach.

There appear to be no inherent differences in the treatment of depreciable assets, inventories, and capital gains under the two approaches. The ad hoc approach could be used to produce only inflation-adjusted income statements, while leaving the balance sheet on a historical cost basis, but there seems to be no obvious reason not to. Thus it does not seem necessary to adopt the integrated system just because a country imposes a net wealth tax.

The 1988 report concluded that, on balance, a discrete shift from an unindexed system to an integrated system such as that used in Chile may be inadvisable. Experience suggests that it may be a good idea to gain experience with ad hoc adjustments before attempting to move to an integrated system. This is the judgment of other experts who have examined this issue. For example, Milka Casanegra has written about the Chilean experience:

> It is doubtful whether the private sector and the tax administration would have been able to cope with this sophisticated mechanism if they had not previously had lengthy experience with simpler profit adjustment schemes [Casanegra 1984: 29].

Also:

> The Chilean experience shows that comprehensive profits adjustment schemes can be administered, provided the tax service and the private sector have had previous experience with such schemes and they are based on

indexation of assets and liabilities rather than on indexation of income and expense flows [Casanegra 1984: 34].[21]

This conclusion is reinforced by the fact that the inflation rate in Colombia has been substantially below that in Chile, especially at the time Chile adopted the integrated system.[22] As noted below, Colombia chose to use the ad hoc approach for several years and then shift to the integrated system in 1992.

The consumption-based alternative. The second approach considered in the 1988 report would convert the Colombian income tax to a consumption-based direct tax. This approach would be substantially simpler than the income tax—so much so that it was called the Simplified Alternative Tax or SAT.[23]

The SAT would consist of two essentially separate taxes, one on individuals and one on businesses. The base of the individual tax would be only labor income; that is, dividends, interest, capital gains, and other nonlabor income would be exempt. Personal exemptions, graduated rates, and itemized deductions could be employed to tailor the tax base to the individual circumstances of taxpayers.

The business tax would be levied at a flat rate (presumably the top rate of individuals) and would apply to all businesses, whether organized as corporations, partnerships, or proprietorships; business losses could not be used to offset individual income. All business purchases would be immediately deductible, whether for current operating expenses, additions to inventories, or depreciable assets. Interest and dividends would not be deductible expenses, and interest and dividends received from other businesses would not be taxable.

The SAT would avoid both the difficulties associated with the inflation adjustment required for inflation-proof measurement of real income and the timing issues that plague implementation of an income-based tax.[24] It would therefore almost certainly be simpler than the other alternative, an indexed income tax. Moreover, any consumption-based tax has well-known advantages of horizontal equity and neutrality toward the saving-consumption choice. Finally, the SAT would equalize the competition for investment funds between Colombia, which taxes capital income earned domestically but has difficulty in taxing foreign-source income of its residents, and developed countries, many of which do not tax the return on investments by foreigners.[25] There are, however, several potentially negative considerations.[26]

First, the 1988 report argued that the substitution of the SAT for the income tax would be acceptable on distributional grounds only if the net wealth tax were retained. Yet there would be no direct link between net wealth and the base of the SAT, as there is between the income tax and the net wealth tax. Beyond that, net wealth could not be used as the basis of a presumptive measure of the base of the SAT, as under the income tax. Thus it would be difficult to maintain the progressivity of the present tax system.

Second, it is commonly asserted that financial accounting in Colombia is often abused by unscrupulous business people. Requiring conformity between the accounting used for tax purposes and financial accounting would probably improve both. This could be done under an inflation-adjusted income tax, but not under the SAT, which uses very different concepts.

Third, there is considerable doubt whether the SAT and any withholding taxes that might accompany it would be eligible for the foreign tax credits of the United States and other countries that offer such credits. Whether this is an important consideration depends in part on the extent to which potential investors in a country considering adopting the SAT are in an excess foreign tax credit position.

Finally, there is the natural reluctance of any country to be the first to adopt a new method of taxation; this can be an extremely important consideration to politicians.

The Government's Response to the 1988 Report

After careful consideration of the 1988 report, the government of Colombia, in a pair of decrees issued on December 26, 1988, acted to modify the system of inflation adjustment introduced in 1986.[27] This section details the most important provisions of the 1988 law relating to inflation adjustment, evaluates them, and discusses the political process that led to their choice.[28]

The reforms. Deciding against the radically different Simplified Alternative Tax, the government took a two-stage approach to the problem of introducing more complete inflation adjustment. For the period from 1989 through 1991, Colombia will continue to use an ad hoc system, extending the inflation adjustments already found in the law to depreciable assets; then beginning in 1992 it will switch to an integrated system of inflation adjustment patterned after that employed by Chile.

Eligibility/requirements. All taxpayers are eligible to use the ad hoc inflation adjustment of depreciable assets, provided such adjustments are also employed for financial accounting. Beginning in 1992, companies in the for-profit sector are required to use the system; individuals generally are not.[29]

Depreciable assets. Inflation adjustment was to be extended to depreciable assets beginning in 1989; inflation-adjusted values were to be used for the calculation of net wealth, as well as taxable income. However, the accelerated depreciation found in prior law was not replaced with a system more closely approximating economic depreciation, as proposed in the 1988 report.

Inventories. Beginning in 1992 replacement cost can be used to value ending inventories: until 1999, LIFO will continue to be available as an option to provide an ad hoc substitute for inflation adjustment. Between 1992 and 2002 differences between replacement cost of inventories and book values of inventories will gradually be reflected in net wealth, but without being subject to income tax; this provision will primarily affect taxpayers who have previously used LIFO.

Interest. During the 1989–1991 transition period the basic provisions for inflation adjustment are the same as under prior law. Upon introduction of the integrated system in 1992, explicit inflation adjustment of interest expense will no longer be necessary; the proper adjustment "drops out" of the adjustment of net wealth and real assets (and indexed financial assets and liabilities).[30] Financial assets and liabilities denominated in foreign currencies will be revalued to reflect changes in the particular exchange rate involved.

Stock shares. Shares in corporations traded on a stock exchange will be revalued at the market price. Those in limited liability companies (*limitadas*) and corporations not traded on exchanges are to be valued on the basis of the value of the company after it has made its inflation adjustments.

Appraisal of the reforms. Most of the 1988 reforms are appropriate and consistent with the recommendations of the 1988 report, such as the required conformity between tax and financial accounting. Yet a few are clearly questionable on policy grounds.[31]

The failure to provide a less accelerated system of depreciation while introducing inflation adjustment for depreciable assets is clearly inappropriate. The marginal effective tax rate on income from depreciable assets is now well below the statutory rate; by comparison, the failure to adjust for inflation under prior law roughly offset the benefits of accelerated depreciation at an inflation rate of 20 percent (see McLure and Zodrow 1989). This glaring omission was almost certainly dictated by political considerations; it helps to offset the cost to taxpayers of the indexation of interest expense introduced in 1986.[32]

The decision to adjust the value of inventories to replacement cost, instead of using inflation-adjusted FIFO, and to use changes in particular exchange rates, rather than the rate of domestic inflation, to revalue assets and liabilities denominated in foreign currencies is a major departure from the recommendations of the 1988 report. While these two decisions will produce a more accurate measure of net wealth, they are much more complicated to implement and they will produce a less accurate measure of taxable income (see McLure, Mutti, Thuronyi, and Zodrow 1988: ch. 7).

The decision-making process. Constitutional and political concerns were probably as important as economic considerations in explaining the decisions (1) not to adopt the Simplified Alternative Tax and (2) to introduce the integrated system in the way chosen.[33] It was feared that the Supreme Court would not interpret the extraordinary powers granted to the president in the 1986 law as allowing reforms as far-reaching as adoption of the integrated system of inflation adjustment; the even more fundamental change to the SAT would be even more problematical. If the use of the emergency powers to introduce the integrated system is found to be unconstitutional, however, the 1988 changes in the ad hoc system would presumably survive.[34]

Even had these constitutional concerns not been dispositive, it is unlikely that Colombia would have adopted the SAT in the 1988 reforms. The English version of the 1988 report was first made available in Colombia only in mid-September; the Spanish version was not available until mid-November. It would have been extremely ill-advised for the government to have attempted to use its extraordinary powers to introduce a new and radically different tax system with no more public discussion than was possible before the powers expired at the end of the year.

This does not, of course, mean that Colombia will never adopt the SAT. One thing that has become apparent from observation of the fiscal history of Colombia is that new ideas create an intellectual ferment that often leads to the eventual adoption of proposals initially viewed as impractical or politically infeasible.

Whether Colombia would have opted for a one-stage shift to the integrated Chilean system of inflation adjustment in the absence of concern about a possible constitutional barrier is not clear. Acting as a consultant to the government, Santiago Pardo, the most recent past director general of Internal Taxes, had visited Chile to assess for himself the relative merits of the Chilean and ad hoc approaches to inflation adjustment and apparently came away convinced that the former was really no more complicated than the latter. Yet, transitional problems apparently would have been greater in moving directly to the Chilean system. Not the least of these problems would be the need to educate many taxpayers who had no experience with inflation adjustment before 1987. The two-stage process chosen provides an opportunity for both such education and public debate before the 1992 shift to the integrated system.

Concluding Remarks: Lessons of the Colombian Experience

The history of tax analysis and tax policy in Colombia over the past quarter century provides instructive lessons for those contemplating how a country might deal with the interaction of its tax system and inflation.[35]

First, it clearly indicates a tendency to move in short tentative steps, rather than venturing out in sharp, discontinuous steps. Even the indexing of nominal amounts was introduced gradually over several years, rather than suddenly. Trial and error has played an even more important part in the more complicated area of inflation adjustment in the measurement of income from business and capital. Thirsk (1988) has written:

> The policy reactions to a particular tax issue can best be described as being a sort of fiscal tatonnement, or process of government groping, in which policymakers never quite manage to get it right the first time but gradually, and sometimes after a few false starts, converge on a satisfactory solution to a problem. Partial, indirect and incomplete tax remedies are replaced by more direct and comprehensive tax measures that work better.

Second, the perceived desirability of inflation adjustment clearly depends on the expected rate of inflation. The 1970s began with the belief that Colombia might soon return to the relatively low rates of inflation experienced before 1970. During the period covered by this survey policy makers have become less sanguine about inflation and have therefore introduced increasingly far-reaching measures for inflation adjustment.

Third, it is apparent that some of the hesitancy with which Colombia has moved in this area reflects the state of academic thinking on inflation adjustment, as well as the accumulated experience of other countries. As Thirsk (1988) has noted, "The power of ideas and the prevailing intellectual climate is apparent in explaining why certain tax measures were adopted at the time." In the 1960s influential foreign advisers urged that inflation adjustment be rejected because they emphasized the role taxation plays as an automatic stabilizer. More recently, less emphasis has been placed on the stabilizing effects of fiscal policy and more on the inequities and distortions that result from an unindexed income tax. Perry and Cárdenas (1986: 177–78) note that in accentuating the stabilizing characteristics of an unindexed income tax, Colombia was following the conventional wisdom of the day— wisdom that was increasingly repudiated when the developed countries experienced the double-digit inflation of the 1970s.

To some extent the increased attraction of inflation adjustment may be traceable to the fact that in 1984 the U.S. Treasury Department proposed a system of inflation adjustment for the United States that included a proposal for interest indexing somewhat similar to that enacted in Colombia in 1986. This may have given inflation adjustment an aura of respectability it had lacked before; after all, inflation adjustment had previously been employed primarily by countries with extremely high rates of inflation—countries that Colombia did not necessarily want to be seen to emulate.

This shift in emphasis, in turn, reflects developments in thinking about the effects of taxation, especially during periods when inflation has occurred or is expected. The Taylor report says essentially nothing about the need to combine inflation adjustment of depreciation allowances with interest indexing if distortions and inequities are to be avoided. The Musgrave report notes explicitly the importance of this link between the two sides of the balance sheet, but without any detailed analysis; indeed, its proposal for accelerated depreciation can be interpreted as being quite inconsistent with its failure to propose inflation adjustment of interest expense. The 1988 report focuses strongly on the need for consistency in the treatment of real and financial issues in inflation adjustment. In this it employed the analysis of marginal effective tax rates, a methodology that did not exist at the time of the Taylor and Musgrave missions. Of course, the 1986 legislation that provided interest indexing had already been based on a clear recognition of the need for interest indexing or its equivalent.

A final academic development that has recently influenced policy advice in Colombia, if not yet tax policy, is the increasing interest in consumption-based direct taxes. At the time of the Taylor and Musgrave missions a consumption-based tax was thought to be administratively infeasible, though perhaps attractive on economic grounds. By 1988 the economic advantages of such a tax had taken second place to the perceived administrative advantages of the SAT, which many tax experts consider to be substantially easier to implement than an income tax, especially one adjusted for inflation. For reasons described in the previous section the government of Colombia decided against the SAT.

Colombia has one of the best income tax structures in Latin America. This is especially true now that it has adopted an integrated system of inflation adjustment for implementation beginning in 1992. (The recent decision to repeal the net wealth tax is, however, in the minds of many, an unfortunate step backward.) Historically, the quality of its tax administration has lagged behind that of its tax structure. As a result, the tax system has not been as good in practice as on paper. Despite administrative reforms taken since 1986, the next step in Colombian tax reform would appear to be increased focus on administrative matters.[36]

Tax Reform and the Value-Added Tax: Indonesia

In the 1970s and 1980s, value-added taxes became prominent features in the tax systems of dozens of less-developed countries (LDCs), particularly those classified as middle-income nations (World Bank 1988b: Appendix Table 1). Indeed, successful revenue results from comprehensive tax reform in LDCs have been strongly associated with implementation of value-added taxes (VATs) in a very high proportion of cases (Gillis 1989b). Moreover, value-added taxes as implemented in more recent tax reform programs have tended to be simpler in structure than was the case for VATs adopted by LDCs in the late 1960s and early 1970s.

The case of Indonesia is relevant for a volume on tax reform for several reasons. First, a value-added tax was the cornerstone of the far-reaching tax reform adopted in that country in 1983. Second, the tax, imposed at a flat rate of 10 percent and initially with no provision for exemption by product category, is one of the simplest types of VAT ever adopted anywhere. In fact, the law establishing VAT prohibits use of more than one flat rate of tax. Third, the revenue performance of the VAT has, in its first three years of existence, easily fulfilled original expectations. Fourth, the Indonesian experience with the VAT thus far provides yet another example of the lower vulnerability of the tax-credit type of VAT to the corrosive effects of rent-seeking behavior, relative to other types of VAT and to income taxes. Fifth, the Indonesian case illustrates one of the many paradoxes of the VAT: extending the base of the tax may not always result in increases in revenue.

Finally, the Indonesian case is of some interest precisely because it illustrates how a VAT may be deployed to enhance chances of success for comprehensive reform of entire tax systems. In 1983 thoroughgoing changes were also adopted in business and individual income taxes. These changes remained essentially intact through 1989. The new income tax law applies to the income of all business firms and individuals. Whereas the old, separate income tax laws provided for progressive rates of tax reaching 50 percent for individuals and 45 percent for firms, the new unified system involves a maximum rate of only 35 percent. Although income taxes still account for more than three-fifths of total revenues, three-quarters of all income tax collections flow from foreign oil companies, so that the VAT is by far the most important source of nonoil tax revenue. The new property tax law applies at a single rate on all types of property and at present low rates has not become a major revenue source. The relative importance of taxes on foreign trade has been declining steadily since 1980: combined import and export duty collections were only marginally more important in the revenue structure than tobacco and alcohol excises and so-called "nontax" revenues (timber royalties and dividends paid to the government from state-owned firms). Together, taxes on foreign trade, nontax revenues, and excises account for less revenue than the VAT. Excises as well as taxes on foreign trade were scheduled to further decline in relative importance after 1987, while the shares of nonoil income taxes and property taxes are due to rise. Reform of this latter group of direct taxes was enacted in the expectation that a substantial gestation period would be essential before significant returns from basic changes in direct taxes would be forthcoming. This expectation, based primarily on recognition of weakness in tax administration, has proven largely correct.

This chapter first depicts the Indonesian VAT against the broader backdrop of the first two decades of worldwide experience with this form of sales tax. It then discusses the factors precipitating tax reform and the decision to enact a VAT in Indonesia. The third section reviews the first three years of experience with this fiscal instrument. Finally, the chapter attempts to identify lessons that might be distilled from this particular episode in tax reform.

Worldwide Experience with the VAT

The VAT may not represent the wave of the future in worldwide tax reform, but it is clearly the wave of the present. Nearly sixty countries have chosen one or another form of VAT since it was first adopted in its comprehensive retail form in Brazil in 1967 (Gillis, Shoup, and Sicat 1989). (Both Colombia and France, however, utilized manufacturer's-level value-added taxes before that time.) Adoption of the comprehensive VAT in Brazil was followed in short order by adoption in Denmark (1967) and Uruguay (1968), and was subsequently made a condition for entry into the European Community (EC) by all original members of the EC. Thus for later entrants to the EC, the VAT was a requisite for membership in an organized trading community; the forty-odd less-developed countries that had adopted the tax by 1987 did so even in the absence of such an incentive.

Preference for the VAT in indirect tax reform proposals over the past two decades has been striking. In industrial countries over that period, only Australia (1985) rejected the VAT option in favor of another form of sales tax, in this case a single-stage retail tax that itself was ultimately rejected. In 1988 both Canada and Japan were actively considering adoption of the VAT. For middle-income LDCs, the recent predilection for the multiple-stage VAT in tax reform programs has been almost universal: there are virtually no examples of adoptions of single-stage sales taxes in LDCs over the past two decades. Moreover, the VAT has been an integral part of very recent tax reform proposals for Jamaica (1986), Pakistan (1987), and Malawi (1988). Table 13.1 provides a chronology of adoption for the VAT in twenty-five selected LDCs, as well as information on the share of the tax in both GDP and total tax revenues.

By 1987, somewhat more than half the LDCs now using the VAT and all but two countries included in Table 13.1 (Indonesia and India) employed the comprehensive form of the tax (Gillis, Shoup, and Sicat 1989). But at least two of the countries now utilizing the comprehensive VAT first employed the cruder manufacturer-importer level VAT of the type used by Colombia from 1966 to 1984 and France from 1954 to 1968.

Otherwise, the value-added taxes adopted by LDCs since 1968 have tended to share three common features. First, all such taxes have employed the tax-credit method of collection, the administrative advantages of which have been partly responsible for decisions to choose VAT over other forms of sales tax.[1] Second, an overwhelming majority of LDCs have chosen the consumption-type VAT, as opposed to the income or gross product types of VAT. Finally, all value-added taxes employed in LDCs are, like those of the EC, imposed upon the destination principle.[2]

Reasons for Widespread Adoption of the VAT

Rationales for adopting the VAT have of course varied greatly among countries. But by the late 1970s, the VAT had acquired an international reputation that made it an attractive option in a large number of tax reform programs. Four widely perceived, and often overstated, advantages of the tax seem to have been particularly significant in influencing policy makers in LDCs to opt for the VAT: revenue-generating capability, administrative advantages, and implications of the tax for economic neutrality and export promotion.

TABLE 13.1   Two Decades of Value-Added Taxation in Selected Developing
Countries, 1966–1988

Country	Year VAT first introduced	VAT as % of GDP[a]	VAT revenue as % of total tax revenue[a]	Basic VAT rate (%)	Other VAT rates (%)
Colombia	1966[b]	2.1	27.0	10	0, 4, 6, 20, 35
Brazil	1967	6.5	28.7	17	
Uruguay	1968	4.6	23.5	20	12
Ecuador	1970	1.3	12.4	6	
Bolivia	1973[b]	n.a.	n.a.	10	
Chile	1975	8.1	37.4	20	0, 0.5, 33, 35, 50, 90
Costa Rica	1975	3.7	17.4	10	
Argentina	1975	1.9	14.9	18	5, 23
Nicaragua	1975	2.8	10.4	10	25
Honduras	1976	1.5	12.2	5	6
Panama	1977	1.9	9.1	5	
Korea	1977	4.0	25.1	10	0, 2, 3.5
Mexico	1978	3.2	19.7	15	0, 6, 20
Haiti	1982	1.1	11.5	10	
Peru	1982	4.3	31.2	6	
Guatemala	1983	1.6	24.8	7	
Dominican Republic	1984	0.9	9.9	6	
Madagascar	1984	3.2	26.4	15	
Turkey	1985	3.1	21.9	10	
Indonesia	1985[c]	2.9	16.7	10	
Niger	1986	n.a.	n.a.	25	15, 35
Portugal	1986	n.a.	n.a.	16	0, 8, 30
Taiwan	1986	n.a.	n.a.	5	
India	1986[c]	n.a.	n.a.	n.a.	
Malawi	1988[c]	n.a.	n.a.	n.a.	

n.a. = not available.
a. 1983 data, except Indonesia (1987).
b. Introduced initially as a manufacturer's-level VAT, later converted to a retail VAT.
c. Manufacturer's-level VAT.
SOURCE: Adapted from Milka Casanegra de Jantscher, 1989, "Problems of Administering a Value-Added Tax in Developing Countries," *The Value-Added Tax in Developing Countries*, edited by M. Gillis, G. Sicat, and C. Shoup (forthcoming).

The VAT as money machine. The record of the VAT in generating large amounts of revenue quickly, and in comparatively painless fashion, has given it a reputation as a "money machine." This reputation has been questioned (Stockfish 1985) insofar as it stems from experience in European countries, but the record in LDCs does lend some credence to the alleged revenue advantages of the VAT relative to the taxes it has replaced. In all LDCs that adopted the VAT before 1981 (except for the first Bolivian VAT adopted in 1973) the VAT as a percentage of GDP was appreciably higher in

1983 than in the year it was first introduced (Gillis, Sicat, and Shoup 1989). In Indonesia, the share of VAT in GDP in 1987, at 4 percent, was nearly three times that garnered in 1983 by the taxes it replaced (see Table 13.2). And for half of the nineteen LDCs in Table 13.1 for which revenue data were available, the share of VAT in GDP was higher than 3 percent; in all but two of these cases, the VAT constituted at least 20 percent of total tax revenue. Still, in four of the countries listed in Table 13.1, VAT revenues were equal to or less than 1.5 percent of GDP. But in three such cases, the basic rate of VAT was appreciably lower than the average utilized elsewhere. Notwithstanding the marked revenue success of the VAT in nations such as Brazil and Chile (Table 13.1), its reputation as a money machine appears to have been at least slightly overstated.

Administrative advantages. While claims, common twenty years ago, that the VAT was largely self-administering are now heard rarely, it is nevertheless true that certain features of the tax-credit type of VAT do offer three principal advantages over single-stage sales taxes in limiting the scope for evasion. These are (1) certain of its self-policing aspects, (2) audit improvements possible from the cross-check of invoices, and (3) the fact that the VAT involves collection of a major portion of revenues before the retail stage.

The self-policing feature of the VAT, while limited, stems from the fact that underpayment of the tax by a seller (except, of course, a retail firm) reduces the tax credits available to the buying firm. Even so, firms also subject to income taxes have incentives to suppress information on purchases and sales in order to avoid not only VAT, but income taxes as well. Also, this putative administrative advantage of the VAT is diminished when evasion at the final (retail) stage of distribution is endemic. Cross-checking of invoices—through matching invoices received by purchasers against those retained by sellers—when not carried to extremes, as it is in Korea, is a valuable aid in audit activities (Hutabarat and Lane 1989). But it is no substitute for true, systematic audit (Due 1963: 130–40). Finally, the fact that a large share of the VAT (all VAT revenues for preretail types of VAT, as in Indonesia) is collected prior to the retail level is an advantage, particularly given the abundance in most LDCs of small-scale retail firms that do not keep adequate records. In sum, the administrative advantages of the VAT are very real, if sometimes exaggerated.

Economic neutrality. A neutral tax system is one that raises the desired amount of revenue in such a way as to leave economic decisions unaffected, except by the effects of taxes in reducing real income and wealth. In recent years neutrality has become a more commonly sought goal than was the case in the 1950s and the 1960s (Gillis 1989a). The VAT, or at least a uniform-rate VAT, offers some minimal advantages in approaching neutrality relative to other forms of sales tax and to income taxes.

TABLE 13.2 Indonesia's Tax Structure before and after Reform

	1983			1986			1987 (preliminary)		
	Billions of rupiah	% of total tax revenue	% of GDP	Billions of rupiah	% of total tax revenue	% of GDP	Billions of rupiah	% of total tax revenue	% of GDP
Internal indirect taxes	1,670	10.9	2.3	4,129	27.0	3.9	4,704	23.4	4.0
Sales taxes (after 1984, VAT)	830	5.4	1.1	2,942	19.2	2.8	3,375	16.7	2.9
Excises	775	5.1	1.1	991	6.5	0.9	1,106	5.5	0.9
Stamp duties and other	65	0.4	0.1	196	1.3	0.2	223	0.1	0.2
Taxes on foreign trade	661	4.3	0.9	885	5.8	0.8	1,122	5.6	1.0
Import duties	557	3.6	0.8	820	5.4	0.7	938	4.6	0.8
Export duties	104	0.7	0.1	65	0.4	0.1	184	1.0	0.2
Income taxes	12,331	80.5	16.7	8,019	52.4	7.5	13,034	64.4	11.0
Taxes on oil/liquefied natural gas firms	10,398	67.9	14.1	5,559	36.4	5.2	9,716	48.1	8.2
Nonoil income taxes[a]	1,785	11.7	2.4	2,189	14.3	2.0	2,838	14.0	2.4
Interest, dividends, and royalty tax	148	0.9	0.2	271	1.8	0.3	480	2.3	0.4
Property taxes	132	0.9	0.2	238	1.6	0.2	260	1.3	0.1
Nontax revenue[b]	520	3.4	0.7	2,022	13.2	1.9	1,102	5.5	0.9
Total revenue	15,314	100.0	20.8	15,293	100.0	14.3	20,222	100.0	17.0
Nonoil revenue	4,916	32.2	6.7	9,734	67.3	9.1	10,506	52.0	8.8

a. Includes both individual and corporate income taxes. For nonoil income taxes, the share for corporate income taxes in 1986 GDP was 1.4 percent. The share of individual income taxes was less than half as high, at only 0.6 percent of GDP.
b. Primarily dividends from government-owned enterprises for 1983. The 1986 figure includes temporary windfall from surplus on domestic oil operations.
SOURCE: Ministry of Finance, Republic of Indonesia.

First, a value-added tax is imposed upon something that no firm would try to maximize (Shoup 1969). Second, the consumption-type VAT is superior to other forms of sales taxes in freeing producer goods from tax (Gillis 1985b). Finally, as noted just below, the tax-credit type of VAT, unlike single-stage taxes, offers a small but important advantage in achieving neutral treatment of traded goods.

Exports and the VAT. One frequently voiced argument for replacing other forms of broad-based indirect taxes with a tax-credit type of VAT is that exports can easily be freed of tax under the latter but not the former. This may be done under the VAT merely by zero-rating all exports.[3] This capability has been an important consideration in countries utilizing fixed exchange-rate systems and also seeking expansion of manufactured exports. The superiority of the VAT in freeing exports from tax is well established and in fact was the principal argument employed in support of a shift from a single-stage retail tax to a VAT in Sweden in 1969 (Cnossen 1975: 514).

The VAT as Cornerstone of the Indonesian Tax Reform of 1983

Planning for reform. The decade 1971–1981 was a period of unprecedented economic prosperity for Indonesia. Real GDP had grown at an average annual rate of 7.9 percent; GDP per capita rose 5.5 percent per year. Nonoil exports, stagnant for the early part of the period, were growing rapidly following a successful devaluation in 1978, and the inflation rate had settled to 7 percent, not far above world inflation. Two successive booms in the world oil market had led to a seventy-eight-fold increase in oil and gas export earnings over the period. By 1980 oil accounted for 71 percent of exports and two-thirds of tax collections; government spending as a share of GDP in 1981 was, at nearly 24 percent, 60 percent higher than in 1971 (Gillis 1984).

World oil prices peaked in January 1981, at a time when many financial institutions were projecting continued strength in the world oil market through the rest of the decade (World Bank 1981). While a budget deficit of 2.5 percent of GDP was projected for the year, inflows of project aid were expected to be more than sufficient to cover this shortfall. In sum, revenue pressures for tax reform were entirely absent. Nevertheless, the minister of finance, supported by influential colleagues in the national planning agency, decided in January 1981 to initiate preparations for fundamental tax reform, to be implemented sometime before the middle of the decade.

This group of decision makers viewed tax reform as essential with or without continued boom conditions in world oil markets. On the one hand, the prospect of another decade of high petroleum prices was seen as propitious for tax reform. Under these conditions, revenue risks from fundamental changes in the revenue structure would be negligible. Continuation of the oil boom would also vastly reduce the political risks of tax reform. Thus, reform could focus heavily on base broadening and tax simplification, because the cushion provided by oil revenues would allow for substantial reduction in tax rates in income and sales taxes. Sustained inflows of oil taxes, then, would present an opportunity for fundamental restructuring of an antiquated, corruption-ridden, and inordinately complex tax system.

On the other hand, the ministers did not share widespread optimism about the future of the world oil market, particularly in the medium term. Any considerable weakening in the world oil market before the middle of the decade would present grave problems for economic management; a collapse in the market would be ruinous. This vulnerability existed because the sharp rise in government spending had been accompanied by a palpable slackening in the efforts of the tax administration to collect domestic nonoil taxes. By 1981 the ratio of nonoil taxes to GDP had slipped to 6.1 percent (see Table 13.3) or about 26 percent of total government spending. Tax rate increases in the outmoded revenue system in place in 1981 could not be

TABLE 13.3   Domestic Tax Revenues in Indonesia as Percentage of GDP, 1967–1987

Year	Nonoil domestic tax receipts[a] (1)	Tax receipts on oil and liquefied natural gas exports (2)	Total domestic tax receipts (1) + (2)
1967	6.2	0.9	7.1
1968	6.0	1.2	7.2
1969	7.3	1.7	9.0
1970	8.3	2.0	10.3
1971	8.7	3.0	11.7
1972	8.7	4.3	13.0
1973	9.2	5.1	14.3
1974	7.4	9.0	16.4
1975	7.9	9.8	17.7
1976	8.4	10.4	18.8
1977	8.4	10.2	18.6
1978	8.8	10.2	19.0
1979	7.9	13.7	21.6
1980	7.2	15.8	23.0
1981	6.1	15.0	21.1
1982	6.8	12.2	19.0
1983	6.7	14.1	20.8
1984	6.1	14.6	20.7
1985	8.0	11.8	19.8
1986	9.1	5.2	14.3
1987[b]	8.8	8.2	17.0

a. Nonoil tax revenue includes surpluses from domestic oil operations in 1986 and 1987: 1986 = 977 billion rupiah; 1987 = 114 billion rupiah.
b. Preliminary figures.
SOURCE: 1967–1979: Malcolm Gillis, "Episodes in Indonesian Economic Growth," in *World Economic Growth*, edited by Arnold C. Harberger (San Francisco: ICS Press, 1984), Table 3; 1980–1987: Ministry of Finance, Republic of Indonesia.

expected to generate collections anywhere near that which would be required in the event of even a moderate fall in oil prices, much less the precipitous drop that actually occurred in 1985–1986. In 1981 decision makers therefore viewed fundamental tax reform as essential, whether or not oil prices remained high.

The old tax system. The tax system in place before reform was extremely complex, primarily because of decades of attempts to manipulate tax bases and tax rates to achieve nonrevenue goals. Complexity was compounded by ad hoc measures required to compensate for revenue losses due not only to fiscal fine-tuning but also to tax evasion facilitated by widespread corruption in tax administration.

Indirect taxes. The internal indirect tax system in place before 1984 consisted of three principal elements: a sales tax of the cascade, or turnover, type extending through the manufacturing stage; sumptuary excise taxes on tobacco, beer, sugar, spirits; and assorted stamp duties. These taxes accounted for about 11 percent of total tax revenues, or about 2.3 percent of GDP, with the sales tax making up nearly half of that (see Table 13.2). The excise system, the fourth-largest source of overall tax revenue, was working reasonably well; accordingly, a decision was made to leave these levies unchanged. Stamp taxes, insignificant revenue sources in any case, were to be abolished except for a small number that were easily enforced. Other indirect taxes were import duties, which by 1983 had become a minor source of revenue, owing both to the effects of high protective tariffs and growing reliance on such nontariff barriers as quotas. Import duties were but 3.6 percent of total tax revenues and less than 1 percent of GDP. The principal focus of indirect tax reform was to be upon the sales tax.

The antiquated, cascade-type manufacturer's tax utilized in Indonesia had been discarded by virtually all countries well before 1980. The numerous inherent defects of this form of sales tax (Due 1957) were compounded in Indonesia by its eight different tax rates ranging from 1 percent to 20 percent. Largely because of a complicated structure of exemptions, the tax was also an unproductive source of revenue. Whereas in other LDCs sales taxes typically account for 20 to 25 percent of revenue (Ahmad and Stern 1987: 6) and 4 percent to 5 percent of GDP (Tait, Gratz, and Eichengreen 1987: 147), Indonesian sales tax revenues were but 5 percent of total tax collections and about 1 percent of GDP. Further, the structure of the sales tax provided ample scope for corruption and evasion: under the system of multiple tax rates, sales could easily be understated and/or misclassified. Finally, the impossibility of determining the sales tax element in export prices gave rise to an inordinately complicated and costly export rebate system that was subject to both official and taxpayer abuse.

Income and property taxes. The old systems of income and property taxes, as well as those emerging from the process of tax reform, have been depicted in detail elsewhere (Gillis 1989c) and are described here only in outline form.

Income taxes other than those collected from foreign oil companies were not major sources of tax revenue before the reform. Nonoil income taxes were but 2.4 percent of GDP in 1983. Personal income tax revenues by themselves were less than one-half of 1 percent of GDP (see Table 13.2). Moreover, little corporate tax was collected from private domestic and foreign firms: state-owned enterprises typically accounted for between two-fifths and one-half of corporate tax collections. The poor revenue performance of the income taxes was attributable partly to major structural defects and partly to severe administrative shortcomings (Gillis 1989c). The tax on individuals was imposed at steeply progressive rates beginning at 5 percent and rising to 50 percent on all income in excess of US$14,000. The base was riddled with exemptions and exclusions. The tax on business firms was also applied at graduated rates of 20 percent, 30 percent, and, on profits above US$39,000, 45 percent. The base of the corporation tax, like that of the personal income tax, had been narrowed by all manner of exclusions, chiefly those related to tax incentives promoting industry, exports, regional development, the stock market, and taxpayer use of public accountants. A special tax regime applied to the operations of foreign oil companies, with methods for determination of tax liabilities spelled out in contracts between the foreign firms and the government oil enterprise. The essence of taxes on foreign oil companies was that all levies combined were intended to capture 85 percent of their *net* income (after deduction of all allowable costs).

Property taxes, primarily collected in rural areas, were truly insignificant sources of revenue, accounting for less than 1 percent of total tax revenues and only 0.2 percent of GDP (see Table 13.2). The extensive fine-tuning that characterized income taxes was carried over into the multiple-rate property tax, the system was permeated with exemptions, and land valuations were seriously out of date (Gillis 1989c).

Objectives of the Indonesian tax reform. Four principal objectives were uppermost in the minds of decision makers as preparations for tax reform began in 1981 and 1982. These goals are grouped under four general headings: revenue, income distribution, economic neutrality, and tax administration and compliance.

From revenue neutrality to revenue enhancement. Although decision makers began their work with the goal of revenue neutrality (that is, of maintaining the current level of tax revenues), it became clear by late 1982 that the reform of nonoil taxes would have to be revenue-enhancing in order to avoid massive budget deficits in 1984 and thereafter. Oil export prices began to weaken in 1982, in a gradual process that continued until late 1985, by which time prices per barrel were 25 percent lower than in 1981. Abrupt collapse of the market in 1986 sent prices to as low as US$10 per barrel by mid-year or less than 30 percent of the 1982 peak. The steady weakening of the oil market through 1983 was itself enough to cause the government to move quickly to implement a series of five major policy reforms across a wide front. These drastic measures were designed to restructure the economy so that Indonesia would be positioned not only to cope with the effects of lower oil prices, but to capitalize on the recovery expected in the world economy in 1984–1985. These 1983 policy reforms included a sharp reduction in government subsidies on domestic consumption of oil in January, a 28 percent devaluation of the rupiah in March, cancellation or postponement of several large capital-intensive government projects involving several billion dollars in mid-May, and fundamental liberalization of financial policy in June. The tax reform, initially planned as a stand-alone adjustment to be implemented at a time when the treasury was flush with oil revenues, instead became the last in a series of measures intended to deal with the dislocations caused by the post-1981 collapse in oil prices.

Income distribution. Income distribution issues have occupied the attention of economic policy makers ever since Indonesia declared independence in 1945. But whereas income distribution policies before 1966 focused primarily on reducing relative impoverishment (uneven distribution of income across income classes), since 1966 they have emphasized alleviation of absolute impoverishment—in other words, raising living standards for the poorest 40 percent of society, especially for the millions of poor rural households, particularly in Java (Gillis 1989c: ch. 4).

Policy makers have seen the budget as playing a significant role in rectifying problems of income distribution, but they have placed emphasis almost wholly on the expenditure, not the tax, side of the budget. In the case of the 1983 tax reform, the decision makers expected the tax system to provide growing revenues to finance programs dealing with poverty, particularly rural poverty, but they did not regard tax instruments per se as useful in reducing relative impoverishment by leveling down high incomes. Pessimism about the role of taxation in income redistribution stemmed primarily from widespread recognition of serious and long-standing weaknesses in tax administration. Moreover, empirical studies conducted as part of the research program preceding tax reform indicated that decades of emphasis on redistributive tax policies had accomplished little in the way of income redistribution in Indonesia. For example, the effective rate of income tax for the richest 5 percent of the population was only 4 percent in 1981, although the nominal tax rate applicable to income for this group was 50 percent (Gillis 1985a: 234).

The ineffectuality of the tax system in promoting redistribution was also a consequence of defects in tax structure. Income, sales, and property taxes prevailing before the 1983 reform were replete with exclusions and exemptions. Although proponents of many of these provisions sought to justify them on grounds of reducing income inequality, the effects were generally otherwise. Income items excluded or favored under the income tax—housing and auto allowances, free use of vacation homes, physicians' fees, interest income, and salaries of civil servants—went overwhelmingly to the wealthiest one-fifth of the income distribution.

The failure of progressive rates of income and sales taxes to secure significant income redistribution was apparent from an incidence study carried out in 1982–1983 for the reform program. Although this study, like all incidence studies, suffered from significant methodological and data limitations, it was nevertheless the most comprehensive ever undertaken for Indonesia. Results indicated that the poorest third of the population paid 5 percent of their income in taxes, a share not much below that of all higher income groups up to the richest decile. And even in the richest decile, taxes were only 9 percent of income, except for the top quarter of this group (the top 2 percent of the income distribution) for whom the effective tax rate was estimated at 13.6 percent. It is to be noted that this figure for the topmost 2 percent was largely a consequence of the assumption that the *entire* burden of both personal income taxes *and* export taxes was borne by this most affluent group (Gillis 1985a: 236).

In view of Indonesian fiscal experience since 1966, and in light of such conclusions on fiscal incidence as were available, policy makers came to view the appropriate income distribution goal for tax reform as insuring that changes in taxation would not make the poor worse off, primarily by placing low-income households outside the tax net, to the extent possible. The tax side of the budget, then, was not to be used as an active tool for redressing problems of relative impoverishment.

Economic neutrality. Indonesian tax policy in the three decades before 1984 was purposely nonneutral. The tax system was viewed not only as a means of raising revenues and redistributing income, but also as a useful tool for guiding private consumption, investment, and employment decisions to ends sought by the state. Tax exemptions and differentiation of sales and income tax rates were the preferred techniques for securing desired nonneutralities. Favored activities or pursuits were provided tax incentives, primarily in the form of reduced rates, often equaling zero. Disfavored activities and products were ineligible for such incentives, or in some cases subjected to special rates of income and sales tax higher than those generally applicable to taxed undertakings.

By 1981 thirty years of active pursuit of nonneutralities in taxation had yielded a tax system so interlaced with complex tax incentive arrangements as to be almost inadministrable. By then, it had become clear to many within the government that whatever useful social purposes were served by efforts to fine-tune the tax system—and there is scant evidence that useful purposes were in fact served—the attendant costs had become unacceptably high. These costs were measured not only in terms of tax revenues forgone, but in terms of the administrative difficulties involved in operating a system overloaded with incentives (Gillis 1985a: 245–49).

By 1982 decision makers were in any case already predisposed to discard as unworkable most of the elaborate system of tax preferences that had evolved over the previous two decades. By 1983 this predisposition had changed to a strong preference for economic neutrality in the tax structure, owing to results of several studies of tax preferences undertaken for the reform. Those studies revealed the wastes and complexities of not only the more bizarre types of tax incentives (the incentive for firms to "go public" and thereby promote a rudimentary stock market, the incentive for using public accountants), but the most hallowed incentive of all: tax holidays for promotion of foreign and domestic investment (Gillis 1986: 247–48).

Accordingly, economic neutrality was a central emphasis of the reform package as presented to the Parliament in late 1983. Stress on neutrality was most evident in the shift toward greater uniformity in sales and income tax rates, the complete abandonment of tax incentives, and the broadening of the sales and income tax bases. In turn, these measures made possible the general lowering of income and sales tax rates, further advancing the goal of neutrality and the reduction of economic waste.[4]

Administration and compliance. The impetus for tax reform in Indonesia did not originate within the tax administration itself. On the contrary, there was initially no significant support for reform among any of the senior officials responsible for assessment and collection of taxes. Heavy inflows of oil tax revenues from 1973 to 1981 meant minimal pressure for better tax collection performance. Moreover, tax administrators had few incentives for undertaking changes of any kind, as large numbers of them had come to enjoy financial prosperity well beyond that supportable by official salaries for civil servants. Except for the most senior officials, installed in 1981, the tax administration remained ambivalent if not hostile to the reform program right up to the time it was implemented.

Nevertheless, the relevant decision makers in the Ministry of Finance and in the rest of the cabinet were acutely conscious of serious shortcomings in the tax administrative machinery. A major objective of the reform was therefore to improve tax administration and facilitate taxpayer compliance, and in the process curb needless costs of collection as well as reduce the scope for corruption. The means adopted for achieving these objectives were threefold:

1. drastic simplification of tax laws
2. establishment of a new, computerized tax information system for both sales and income taxes
3. reform of tax procedures (such as rules and regulations governing filing, penalties, assessments), with stress on the need for depersonalization of tax administration

Simplification would have been a significant emphasis of the 1983 reforms even in the absence of any explicit decision to seek fundamental improvements in tax administration and compliance. The decision to de-emphasize the role of the tax system in income redistribution, as well as the shift toward greater economic neutrality in taxation, would by themselves have reduced the complexity of tax laws and regulations. In addition, simplification was seen as a *sine qua non* for major improvements in tax administration. Decision makers expected simplification to narrow the scope for corruption, since complexities and ambiguities in tax law were used by tax collectors and taxpayers alike to cloak their transgressions. Simplification was also expected to foster improved taxpayer compliance by increasing certainty in tax collections.

Finally, simplification of income and sales tax law was required to facilitate the task of revamping and modernizing the tax information system. Efforts to computerize some of the operations of the Ministry of Finance had begun as early as 1971. All those initiatives were stillborn, however, partly because they were seen as threatening to some groups within the tax administration and partly for a purely mechanical reason. Some upper-level tax administrators had long opposed installing a computerized system because many compromised officials feared that the system would not only be accessible to, but under the control of, other agencies within the ministry rather than the tax department, thereby increasing the risk that corruption might be exposed. Further, the cash registers used to record taxpayer payments at local treasury offices around the nation had space for only nine digits, an insufficient number to allow utilization of a workable system of taxpayer identification numbers. This argument against computerization was finally negated by a fortuitous 1981 decision to purchase new electronic cash registers capable of handling sixteen digits, more than enough to accommodate the system of taxpayer identification numbers. The government then decided to make substantial investments in hardware, software, and foreign expertise in the construction of a new computerized tax information system that would allow not only vastly improved master tax files, but speedier and more systematic monitoring of collection performance.

Reform of taxpaying procedures for sales and income was not viewed as a critical need in the initial stages of preparation for the tax reform. But as the architects of the reform came to understand the interplay between tax procedures and tax administration, this too became an important priority. Tax procedures include provisions specifying how taxpayers shall comply with their tax obligations as well as the administrative structure governing the execution of responsibilities of tax officials. The procedures concern, for example, assessment and refund of taxes, timing of payments, filing of returns, collection of arrears, objections and appeals, and fines and penalties.

These procedures varied from tax to tax, and many had gone unrevised for decades. Further, the levels for many fines and penalties had been set in the 1950s and 1960s, and inflation had eroded any deterrent effect they once may have had (for example, a transgressor might face six months in jail or a fine of 1,000 rupiahs—US$0.75). Other penalties were set at such unrealistically high levels as to be unenforceable. The government began to see a completely new law, consolidating all procedures for all taxes, as an essential complement to reforms governing income and sales tax structure. Two themes were to shape the new law on procedures: simplification (also planned for the tax structure) and depersonalization of tax administration. Depersonalization involved a general reduction of discretionary authority in the hands of tax officials and a decline in the number of direct contacts between taxpayers and tax officials. Instead, greater reliance would be placed on withholding methods and on electronic data processing of taxpayer information sent to district offices. Finally, depersonalization required a shift from the decades-old tradition of official assessment of tax liabilities to self-assessments by taxpayers. The move toward self-assessment also supported other aims of procedural reform. With self-assessment, the number of personal contacts between taxpayers and officials—and therefore the number of opportunities for collusion—is fewer. Also, the shift toward self-assessment would reduce the routine workload on tax officials, allowing for more and better audits of cases promising high revenue payoffs.

The reformed system. The new tax laws were adopted by Parliament in 1983 and implemented in 1984–1986. The new system reflects the view that the four objectives cited above are best served by a vastly simplified tax system oriented primarily toward raising revenues. Accordingly, the reform heavily stressed simplification of both tax structure and tax administration. Simplifying the tax structure required extensive broadening of the base of both income and consumption taxes, with reliance upon an unprecedented degree of uniformity in tax rates.

Income tax reform was implemented first, effective on January 1, 1984. The new VAT, which was to replace existing sales taxes, was initially scheduled to be in operation by June 1984, but this starting date was postponed until April 1985 because of inadequate preparation within the tax administration. Property tax reform was implemented in 1986. The centerpiece of the reform, certainly from a revenue standpoint, was, however, the VAT. The radical transformations of the income[5] and property taxes, described elsewhere in some detail (Gillis 1985a, 1989c), reflect the same principles as those guiding sales tax reform: simplification flowing both from marked broadening of tax bases and from the use of sharply lower and more uniform tax rates.

The VAT formulated to replace the archaic multiple-stage manufacturer's tax was, as initially implemented, the simplest VAT ever adopted anywhere. The VAT option was chosen over other forms of sales tax for essentially the same reasons, described above, that virtually all LDCs have selected the VAT in tax reform programs since 1968: its reputation, deserved or not, as a money machine, its perceived administrative advantages relative to single-stage retail and preretail taxes, its neutrality advantages, and its efficacy in freeing exports from tax.

While the new sales tax law allows extension of the VAT to the wholesale and retail levels, immediate coverage of these stages of distribution was deemed infeasible, primarily on administrative grounds, principally because of the severe difficulties that would be involved in bringing hundreds of thousands of wholesale and retail firms within the scope of the tax. The VAT will be extended to these stages of distribution once authorities decide that tax administration is equal to the task, and certainly not before the year 2000. From 1985 to 1989, the tax was confined to the manufacturer-importer level.

The VAT is imposed at a uniform rate of 10 percent on all taxable goods, whether imported or produced domestically. The reformed sales tax law prohibits the use of differentiated tax rates. However, the minister of finance is empowered to raise or lower the uniform rate within a band of 5 to 15 percent, depending on revenue needs. The tax is assessed on the tariff-inclusive value of imports. Initially all imports were subject to tax in the customs house, but by 1988 a limited number of capital-good imports and raw materials had been awarded special treatment: VAT on these items may be postponed until a later date, typically when the project commences operation. This means, of course, that importation of capital equipment gives rise to no tax credits against taxes due on sales. In other cases, VAT liability is "suspended" on imports. And in a very limited number of cases, the VAT on the delivery and/or importation of certain taxable goods is borne by the government; as a practical matter such imported goods bear no tax as long as they are not resold to other firms.[6]

The Indonesian VAT, like those used in the European Community, is imposed on the destination principle, employs the tax-credit method of collection, and is intended to be a levy on consumption. The implications of each of these features are discussed at length in other sources (Gillis and Conrad 1984; Gillis 1985a).

Finally, the Indonesian VAT as adopted in 1983 differs from all those utilized by other countries (except Bolivia) through 1987 in one very important respect: the VAT law allows neither exemptions nor zero-rating of any locally manufactured products consumed domestically.[7] (The Bolivian VAT also allows no exemptions.) It is important to note, however, that the base of a manufacturer's tax such as that used in Indonesia does not extend to such items as unprocessed food or other staples that do not go through a manufacturing stage. Since such items are outside the tax base, and inasmuch as up to half of the consumption of the poorest 60 percent of households has been in the form of unprocessed food, the application of a uniform tax rate involves little risk that the VAT, as now constituted, imposes a significant burden on the poor. This is particularly true as long as agricultural producers do not make use of significant amounts of taxable inputs other than fertilizer, the sale of which is highly subsidized through the budget.[8]

Indonesia's VAT contains few of the features, such as differentiated rates, that have bedeviled sales tax administration elsewhere. The absence of exemptions by product category and the reliance on a uniform rate virtually eliminate uncertainty as to what is taxable under the VAT, and at what rate.

The prospects for successful operation of the new VAT were aided immensely by the fact that nearly 60 percent of the base of the tax passes through three bottlenecks that are easily accessible to the tax administration: the customs house, sales of refined petroleum products by Pertamina (the state oil enterprise),[9] and the 200-odd government-owned, and relatively large, enterprises whose sales would be taxable under the new tax law. Given these bottlenecks, the tax administration is in a position to collect more than half the potential VAT revenues with minimal expenditure of administrative resources, thereby enabling enforcement efforts to be focused on the remaining, less accessible portions of the tax base.

Administrative feasibility was a critically important consideration in adoption of a relatively simple tax, since it was intended that the VAT furnish at least 60 percent of any incremental revenues expected from tax reform. But policy makers recognized that whatever the administrative, revenue, and neutrality arguments in favor of a flat-rate tax with virtually no exemptions, the political acceptability of such a tax would be limited; belief in the efficacy of rate differentiation in taxation was simply too widespread to ignore.

Accordingly, in order to improve the political acceptability of the reform package, a special, separately administered "luxury" sales tax was devised to complement the VAT. This tax applies to sales of a very limited number of income-elastic products at rates of 10 and 20 percent; luxury taxes cannot be credited against the VAT. Taxable products include stereo sound systems, autos, firearms, aircraft, cameras, and yachts. These items are subject to the VAT as well, so that luxury items carry an indirect tax burden two to three times higher than nonluxuries. Altogether, the items subjected to the special higher rates of luxury tax constitute much too small a proportion of total consumption to generate substantial tax revenues (luxury tax collections were less than 6 percent of VAT revenues in 1985–1987) and account for too low a share of the spending of the rich to achieve much income redistribution. Nevertheless, the luxury tax has thus far served to protect the integrity of the uniform-rate VAT, and for that reason its political role in the success of the reform has been much larger than its limited revenue significance.

Indonesia's Experience with the VAT: The First Three Years

By mid-1988, there was enough evidence on the impact of the VAT on revenues, economic stability, and tax administration to allow some preliminary generalizations. Several more years will be required before informed

judgments can be made about the income distribution and resource allocation implications of the tax.

Revenues. As expected, the VAT has been the revenue mainstay of the tax
reform; within three years, VAT collections were nearly 3 percent of GDP,
almost three times that of the taxes it replaced (see Table 13.2). Moreover,
VAT revenues as a percentage of GDP had surpassed by 21 percent combined
collections of the personal and nonoil business income taxes. The strong
revenue importance of the VAT is all the more remarkable for two reasons.
First, the tax rate is very low relative to value-added taxes employed elsewhere. Most of the twenty-odd LDCs using the *retail* VAT employ a standard
rate of between 10 and 15 percent (Table 13.1), and in those countries the
share of VAT collection in GDP has typically been between 2 and 4 percent.
The Indonesian tax, however, is a manufacturer's VAT levied at a rate of 10
percent. The retail equivalent of this rate is about 5 or 6 percent, since a
manufacturer's-level tax does not generally include wholesale and retail
distribution margins. Even so, the share of the Indonesian VAT in GDP is not
much lower than in several countries imposing higher (retail-equivalent)
rates, and higher than in a few nations with (retail-equivalent) rates of 10
percent and more (Table 13.1). The simplicity and uniformity of the Indonesian VAT may indeed account for much of its strong revenue performance
relative to value-added taxes used in many other LDCs.

Second, strong rates of revenue growth for the VAT have continued in
spite of the fact that a very large part of the VAT base did not grow at all after
the tax was adopted in 1985. Domestic sales of refined petroleum products
by the state oil firm Pertamina initially constituted about one-fifth of the base
of the VAT. Historically, the nominal value of sales of refined petroleum
products grew at about 12 percent per year over the period 1971–1982. From
1985 through 1988, however, nominal consumption of these fuels rose hardly
at all, partly because subsidies on refined products were drastically reduced

TABLE 13.4	Sales Tax and VAT Revenues in Indonesia, 1984–1987						
	Overall sales tax or VAT revenues		Revenues from refined oil products[a]		Revenues exclusive of refined oil products		Domestic
Year	Total (billions of rupiah)	Percentage change	Total (billions of rupiah)	Percentage change	Total (billions of rupiah)	Percentage change	inflation rate (%)
1984[b]	878		0		878		
1985	2,260	257	498		1,762	201	4.4
1986	2,892	28	500	0	2,392	36	9.1
1987	3,374	17	502	0	2,872	20	9.3

Blank cell means not applicable.
a. Gasoline, diesel fuel, kerosene, aviation gas, fuel oil.
b. 1984 reflects the old sales tax, including sales tax on imports.
SOURCE: Ministry of Finance, Republic of Indonesia.

in 1983 and 1984. Table 13.4 shows that overall VAT collections managed to grow at a healthy clip despite virtually zero growth in fuel sales.

Largely as a consequence of the very strong revenue performance of the VAT, nonoil taxes as a percentage of GDP were nearly one-third higher in 1987 than in 1983 (see Table 13.2).

Economic stability. In retrospect, the tax reform could not have come at a more propitious time. With another precipitous decline in oil prices in 1986–1987, the absence of reform would have required even steeper cuts in government spending beyond the draconian measures implemented in those years or would have resulted in substantially larger deficits than actually occurred. Through tax reform, combined with sizable cuts in spending, the overall budgetary deficit was reduced from nearly 4 percent of GDP in 1983 to a much more manageable 2.2 percent in 1987 (see Table 13.5).

The contribution of the VAT to revenues was not the only way it contributed to economic stability. The VAT was implemented with almost negligible effects on the price level, contrary to the predictions of many businessmen, as well as economists, who claimed that introduction of the VAT would accelerate inflation. In this respect, the Indonesian experience with the adoption of the VAT was not inconsistent with that of nearly three dozen other countries for which studies of price effects of the VAT have been made (Tait 1989).

In fact, neither the introduction nor the implementation of the VAT in Indonesia had any noticeable effects on the price level. The introduction of the VAT in April 1985 coincided with a decline in the consumer price index in April and May. Moreover, domestic inflation for the next twelve months was well below that for the previous year.

Decision makers had announced with some confidence in January and February of 1985 that the price-level effects, not to mention the inflationary

TABLE 13.5   Government Spending, Revenue, and Deficits in Indonesia before and after Tax Reform

Year	Government spending as % of GDP	Total domestic tax receipts as % of GDP	Total foreign grants as % of GDP[a]	Budget deficit as % of GDP
1971	14.8	11.6	0.3	–2.9
1981	23.8	21.1	0.2	–2.5
1982	22.9	19.0	0.1	–3.8
1983	24.8	20.8	0.1	–3.9
1984	22.1	20.7	0.1	–1.3
1985	23.7	19.8	0.1	–3.8
1986	20.9	14.3	0.2	–6.4
1987	19.2	16.8	0.2	–2.2

a. Excludes project aid and all loans.
SOURCE: Ministry of Finance, Republic of Indonesia; GDP figures from World Bank, *Indonesia: Adjustment, Growth, and Sustainable Development* (Washington, D.C.: World Bank, 1988).

impact, of the switch to VAT would be nil. This confidence was due to two factors. First, they recognized that the VAT was to be substituted for a cascade tax that itself may have had some price-level effects. Second, policy makers were well aware that the rate of monetary expansion in the first quarter of 1985 had decelerated; they knew from long experience that, particularly in economies without extensive indexation of contracts, domestically generated inflation arises from monetary expansion, not tax adjustments.

Administration. It may be argued that the administration of taxes in Indonesia has improved since enactment of fundamental tax reform, in that with the introduction of the highly simplified VAT, tax evasion has likely declined. Much of the decline in evasion is attributable to structural and procedural simplification and the fact that sales tax reform was designed to take advantage of such "tax handles" as the domestic sales of the state oil monopoly, the customs house, and the larger government-owned manufacturing enterprises. It is difficult to misapply a uniform rate VAT to these easily accessible collection points. There has been, however, little evidence of improvement in administrative practices in the tax department, particularly in income taxation. And while a newly installed computerized tax information system will ultimately enable significant gains in collection and enforcement, its potential had barely begun to be exploited by 1988. The system is still unfamiliar to most officials, and its implementation has been plagued by coordination problems as well as some residual resistance from within the tax administration and legal restrictions on audit activities.[10]

Consequently, the revenue potential of the VAT was placed in jeopardy in the first few months of its existence by administrative slippages and oversights. All taxable firms were required to register for the tax by April 1, 1985, but only 25,000 did so by that date. Concerted efforts were undertaken to rectify the problem, and by September 1985, 51,000 taxable firms had registered, about the number anticipated for the first year. But only 36 percent of registered firms were by then complying with the monthly filing requirement, and no audits of any VAT taxpayers, even the largest thousand firms, had begun by 1986. However, decision makers in the cabinet continued to apply pressure on the VAT administrators to improve performance through 1986 and 1987. By early 1987, progress was notable; the number of registered firms had increased by more than 50 percent over 1985, to 76,756. Moreover, plans were announced for expansion of VAT audits, to enable collections to increase by at least 20 percent for the year. By March of 1988, 81,141 firms had been brought within the scope of the tax.

Still, actual VAT collection may be less than 60 percent of potential collections, and even many large firms were not in full compliance. Compliance rates for the 750-odd largest private domestic firms were particularly low: 58 percent as compared to 83 percent of the 375 largest foreign firms and 69 percent for the 70 largest state-owned firms (Cnossen 1985: 3).

Some aspects of VAT structure have led to avoidable difficulties in tax administration. Chief among these has been the attempt to include all construction in the base of this nonretail tax. Only about one-third of construction firms filed VAT returns in 1987, a filing ratio only half as high as that for firms in the industrial sector (World Bank 1988a: 41). The low filing ratio for construction firms is traceable to the administrative difficulties involved in the attempt to tax large numbers of small contractors.

The interaction between the VAT and the separate luxury tax has also led to problems, partly because of the way the tax administration has chosen to interpret both laws. The sales tax law does prohibit the crediting of luxury taxes against VAT liability. The law also provides that luxury tax shall be collected only once from the manufacturer or importer of luxury goods. In practice, however, several so-called luxury items are taxed twice under the luxury tax, while some items subject to the luxury tax escape it entirely.[11] These problems suggest that in the presence of a VAT, special indirect taxes on "luxuries" are best avoided in most LDCs unless they are vital for insuring the political acceptability of a uniform-rate VAT, particularly when, as in Indonesia, luxury tax collections are quite small relative to the VAT (the luxury tax has been responsible for less than 5 percent of VAT revenues).

A final problem in the first years of experience with the VAT has been administrative acquiescence to pleas for special treatment. While the number of such instances has been limited through 1988, not many more will be required to severely complicate the operation of the tax. Measures included under this heading include those cited earlier regarding suspension of VAT liability for certain imports (particularly capital equipment) and government payment of tax on such items as low-cost housing, purchases by the armed forces, sales of taxis, imports of cattle and poultry feed, and water.

The damage from this type of backsliding on the VAT has, however, been limited by two factors. First, the tax authorities have continued to adhere to the principle that outright exemptions may not be granted. Second, all VAT revenue losses from such special treatment, including government payment of tax, are treated as tax expenditures, in the sense that VAT revenues are reported gross of amounts not collected for these reasons. Thus, the costs of providing tax relief are explicit and transparent. This is fortunate, since by 1988 the various forms of VAT relief granted for purposes cited above involved a revenue cost equal to 12.4 percent of total VAT revenue.[12]

Opportunities for base broadening in the near to medium term. The first three years of experience with the VAT indicate that while the tax should generally remain at the manufacturer-importer level for another decade or so, it may be feasible and desirable to extend coverage of the tax to certain services not ordinarily included in the base of a nonretail tax. Three particular candidates for inclusion in the VAT base are telecommunications, electricity, and domestic air travel. All three of these services are supplied largely by government-owned enterprises; in the cases of electricity and telecommunications, the enterprises occupy near-monopoly positions in the relevant markets. The revenue implications of extending VAT to these services would not be substantial; arguments for including these items in the tax base would therefore have to be based on considerations relating to tax neutrality, tax administration, and income distribution.

The primary reason for limited revenue gains from taxing these activities under the VAT is that the government-owned firms supplying electricity, telecommunications, and domestic air travel already pay substantial amounts of VAT on their purchases, particularly purchases of capital goods. Inclusion of these highly capital-intensive services within the VAT base would mean that taxes paid on inputs for such services would be credited against taxes due on sales. In the case of electric power, the net revenue gain would likely be zero or even negative, not only because of the above reason, but because the smallest residential users would almost certainly be exempted, for income distribution and/or political reasons.[13]

Application of the VAT to telecommunications services and domestic air travel would involve some increase in revenues, both because a lower proportion of the inputs used to produce them are subject to VAT, and because exemptions would probably not be necessary for either income distribution or political reasons. Still, overall net revenue gains from including these services in the tax base would only be on the order of Rp 150 million, or about 5 percent of 1987 VAT collections.

Limited revenue gains notwithstanding, extension of the VAT to electricity, telecommunications, and air travel appears, on balance, advisable. The goal of tax neutrality would be served primarily because inclusion of electricity and telecommunications in the base would reduce the indirect tax content of exports. Firms, especially exporters, utilizing both services would then be able to claim as credits or receive as refunds taxes paid on such purchases.

Extension of the VAT base to cover these services would also facilitate tax administration, particularly in the cases of electricity and telecommunications. These services are purchased primarily by industrial and commercial firms (only 30 percent of electricity is sold to residential users). In such circumstances, exemption of these services breaks the chain of tax credits that has proven elsewhere to be a valuable, if somewhat overrated, aid to VAT administration.

Inclusion of domestic air travel provided by the three government-owned airlines may also be desirable on administrative and income distribution grounds. Business travelers would be able to credit the VAT on air travel against taxes due on sales. Nonbusiness travelers are, in Indonesia, primarily the affluent.

Lessons

The VAT in Indonesia has largely lived up to its advance billing as a potent provider of tax revenues that offers some neutrality and administrative advantages relative to other broad-based taxes. The Indonesian experience suggests that these advantages are best seized by adoption of a uniform-rate VAT imposed upon as broad a base as is feasible. In addition, the VAT has played at least a small role in a virtual explosion of manufactured exports since 1983,[14] given that zero-rated exports may now leave Indonesia with little or no indirect tax content.

The VAT has also displayed two largely unheralded strengths as it has operated in Indonesia since 1985. Both concern the benefits arising from the use of the tax-credit method of collection.

First, the very structure of a tax-credit VAT forces policy makers to focus more carefully on important trade-offs in taxation: trade-offs between revenues and ease of administration, between revenues and efficiency in resource allocation, and between revenues and income distribution. Because of the tax-credit mechanism, the tax does not work like other taxes (indeed, paradoxes are not uncommon under a VAT of this type). Exemptions, so eagerly sought when single-stage taxes are used, become largely valueless or even harmful for preretail firms under the tax-credit VAT. On the other hand, extending the tax to a hitherto untaxed activity (for example, electricity) may, contrary to expectations under other taxes, not only not increase net VAT revenues, but actually decrease them.

Second, relative to other indirect taxes, the VAT narrows the scope and the rewards of rent-seeking activity, precisely because it is less vulnerable to pressures for tax relief. If, as argued by Stern (1987: 26), indirect taxes are in general less vulnerable to manipulation by wealthier rent seekers than are direct taxes, the VAT appears to claim advantages in this regard over both other indirect taxes and direct taxes. Firms accustomed to lobbying for tax exemption as a means of tax relief quickly find that, under the VAT, exemptions are not generally in their interest, unless they happen to have few taxable inputs. The only sure route for securing beneficial tax preferences under the tax-credit type of VAT is through award of zero-rating privileges to the favored activities or firms. But zero-rating of locally consumed goods, while common in many value-added taxes in Europe, is out of the question in Indonesia, on administrative grounds alone. Therefore, traditional methods of seeking rents through tax favors are rendered ineffective under the Indonesian type of VAT.

This leads to the final lesson to be drawn from the Indonesian experience with the VAT. When traditional paths for securing tax preferences are blocked, rent seekers will sooner or later devise new methods: the "termite principle" is operative upon all tax systems at all times. In Indonesia, new methods for gaining tax advantages appeared within one year of enactment of the tax. However, the Indonesian experience also shows that policy makers are not necessarily helpless when it comes to measures suitable to limiting damages from operation of the termite principle: explicit identification of the costs of tax relief, through reporting of both gross and net VAT revenues, has clearly curbed the growth of special privileges under the VAT.

Tax Reform Issues in Mexico

Mexico's experience with tax reform is a lesson in the effects of administrative and human limitations on the ideal tax system. Policy makers made changes to the tax system with the goals of keeping taxation simple, avoiding an excessive tax burden, maintaining confidence in the economy, and globalizing the taxation of income (in other words, extending coverage of the system to include all sources of net wealth). These goals, however, often conflicted with the administrative capacity and revenue needs of the central and local governments.

Since the 1970s Mexico has witnessed several extensive changes in its tax system, beginning with sharp increases in excise taxes and continuing with a wide-ranging structural reform centering on the value-added tax and on attempts to nudge the system toward global income taxation. While Mexico simplified its myriad local indirect taxes by introducing a turnover sales tax and later a value-added tax, the VAT itself grew ever more complicated as the number of rates proliferated to meet political demands.

Likewise, when Mexico indexed its corporate income tax in 1987 to avoid losses of tax revenue resulting from high inflation, the system was simplified. The transition to the new tax, however, was characterized by extremely complex procedures. Corporations were required to use two different accounting systems to calculate their taxable income and still another method to calculate the profits to be shared with workers.

The opinions expressed in this paper are the sole responsibility of the author.

Global income taxation, in particular, faces many practical obstacles, and the partial globalization of income taxation, which Mexico achieved, creates severe distortions and inequities of its own.

This chapter begins with an introductory section detailing the history of Mexico's tax system until the early 1970s, followed by a discussion of the objectives of Mexican tax authorities. The next section analyzes Mexican tax policies and reforms during the various administrations from 1970 to the present. A "true" global income tax was the goal of the legislative changes during President Echeverría's government, and this section presents their implications. (A reminder of the practical shortcomings of such a tax is useful in a discussion of Mexico's reforms and appears in the appendix.) The improvements to indirect taxation made by President López Portillo's administration through the introduction of the VAT are considered next. President de la Madrid, entering office during the debt crisis of 1982, faced a particularly severe shortage of funds and high inflation. He raised tax rates and extended the process of indexation to the corporate income tax; the section concludes by examining those changes and their results.

Historical Background

Mexico's earliest taxes were those imposed by the last Spanish viceroys in the colonial period. The financial needs of the Spanish Crown, which was seriously indebted and militarily threatened, led to a heavy burden of taxation on the colonies, and these high taxes had a role in encouraging the Mexican independence movement.

Interestingly, the colonial tax system at the beginning of the nineteenth century included a personal income tax, one of the earliest in existence.[1] The tax was so comprehensive it included the rent imputable to owner-occupied housing, although it allowed the deduction of losses incurred from damages on real estate perpetrated by the independence fighters (Col 1975).[2]

The most important legacy of the colonial tax system, however, was the fiscal weakening of the Mexican government as a result of the sour taste left by the high taxes and fiscal excesses of the Spanish Crown (Tenenbaum 1985). After independence was achieved in 1811, Mexican governments therefore faced political limits to taxation. Besides, the richest tax source momentarily disappeared when the silver mines were flooded during the fight for independence. Tax-weak governments limped throughout the 1800s, acquiring debts and losing wars and territory. The thirty-five-year Porfirio Díaz presidency and dictatorship (1876–1911) changed all this temporarily, but the long-lasting Mexican Revolution (1911–1920) again required the rebuilding of Mexico's tax system.

The postrevolutionary governments maintained lean administrations from 1921 to 1971. A moderate degree of intervention in the economy backed by sound budgetary responsibility allowed the government to keep a small and simple administrative structure. A minuscule military budget (less than 1 percent of gross domestic product in the past forty years) after the revolutionary armies were gradually disbanded contributed to the success of this arrangement.

As the economy was mostly agrarian and the population generally rural up to 1940, taxation relied heavily on foreign trade and on oil royalties. From the 1940s onward, manufacturing and services gained in importance, as did sales and income taxation (see Table 14.1). In contrast to the ambitious and probably unrealistic income tax of the Crown, the modern income tax was for many years largely a tax on corporate profits and on wages in the formal sector.

Until 1973 the personal income tax was based on progressive schedules that differed according to the source of income (corporate income tax had been schedular up to 1965). In some cases progressivity was simple, as in financial interest payments to individuals, which were taxed from 1965 to 1971 according to a schedule that ranged from rates of 2 percent to 10 percent.

Later, in 1973, interest rates below a certain threshold were exempted on the probably rightful presumption that mostly lower-income people held such deposits. At the same time a two-tiered interest-withholding tax was introduced with a lower rate for those who wished to cumulate their interest income with other income.

In the case of family firms, their profits were (and are) taxed progressively by a schedule not unlike the personal income tax schedule. Large corporations, however, were taxed on paid dividends via a noncreditable dividends tax.

The federal sales tax was introduced in 1948 to replace part of the stamp tax, a relic of colonial days whose remaining elements persisted until the reforms of 1979. It was a turnover tax, with all the distortions and random

TABLE 14.1   Structure of Mexico's GDP, 1930–1987 (percentage)

	1930–39	1940–49	1950–59	1960–69	1970–79	1980–87
Agriculture, livestock, fishing, and forestry	21.3	18.9	17.8	14.1	10.7	9.2
Mining[a]	7.4	5.3	4.9	4.8	2.5	3.8
Manufacturing	12.9	15.9	17.8	20.7	24.3	24.4
Construction	2.7	3.0	3.8	4.2	5.2	4.8
Electricity	0.8	0.7	0.9	1.3	1.3	1.5
Commerce, restaurants, and hotels[b]	30.7	23.3	31.4	31.5	25.7	25.3
Transport and communications	2.5	2.9	3.4	3.2	5.9	7.4
Services	21.5	20.9	19.8	19.8	24.1	23.3

a. From 1930 to 1969, mining includes petroleum processing; from 1970 on, petroleum processing is included in manufacturing.
b. From 1930 to 1969, figure does not include restaurants and hotels, which are included in services.
SOURCE: For 1930 to 1969, Banco de México, *Indicadores Económicos*; for 1970 to 1987, Instituto Nacional de Estadística, Geografía, y Informática, *Sistema de Cuentas Nacionales*.

incidence associated with such schemes, but it was simple to administer in an environment where illiteracy was still rampant. A few excise taxes were also gradually adopted on goods or services that had low elasticities of demand and were easy to administer, such as gasoline, alcohol, beer, tobacco, and telephone services. Excises were imposed even on nonconsumer goods when there were only one or two manufacturers nationwide, such as automobile tires and glass.

From 1941 to 1962 Mexico also had an inheritance tax, repealed by Congress in the latter year because it was felt that in practice the tax was bearing mostly on the lower middle class. This social stratum had wealth to turn around, mostly in real estate, but little legal sophistication to avoid the tax as most everyone else was doing.

From 1940 to 1970 the tax burden increased from 6.4 percent of gross domestic product (GDP) to 9.9 percent (see Table 14.2). This 3.5 percentage point increase was the result of (probably) better administration, the streamlined turnover tax introduced in the 1940s, and rising income tax schedules. The changing structure of the economy in the direction of more manufacturing and services away from the primary nonminerals sector also made an important contribution toward increasing the ratio of taxes to GDP. Foreign trade taxes gradually lost importance, not because of lesser protection but because quantitative controls were preferred to tariffs.

The Tax Goals of Mexican Administrations

Practical and administrative considerations were the common denominator of taxes from the 1940s to the mid-1970s. Mexico was changing and modernizing its tax structure, but the pace and direction were inspired by the related goals of keeping the system simple and avoiding an excessive burden. The latter was feasible because the government succeeded in keeping its size small.

Treasury authorities were keen on making only gradual changes and on preventing their moves from affecting confidence. An example of the caution of tax authorities occurred when Mexico first flirted with the idea of a value-added tax (VAT). In the mid-1960s there was great excitement in the business sector because the treasury was considering a value-added tax to replace the turnover tax and an ample assortment of excises.

Private sector representatives and tax experts from both sides of the issue traveled to Europe to observe first-hand the experiences of countries that had introduced the VAT, and produced a document asserting that the new tax would be inflationary. To the consternation of the treasury specialists who had worked on the project, expecting it to be sent to Congress, the treasury decided to shelve the idea.

This episode illustrates the extent to which price stability, with its concomitant effect on the soundness of the currency, was prized. The country had attained an enviable record of low inflation for a fast-growing economy. From the mid-1950s to the early 1970s, inflation had been held at a rate equal to that of Mexico's trading partners, while GDP had grown at an average annual rate of 6.5 percent. Price stability had been attained after the spurt in prices provoked by the 1954 devaluation of the peso, after which the nominal parity of the peso had remained fixed. Mexico had thus achieved a respectable period of growth-cum-stability. Its record of 3.5

TABLE 14.2   Federal Government Tax Revenues and Social Security Contributions in Mexico, 1940–1988 (as a proportion of GDP)

| | | | | | Indirect taxes | | | |
| | | | | | | Trade taxes | | Other |
	Total fiscal burden	Social security contributions	Total tax revenues	Direct taxes	Total	Import taxes	Export taxes	indirect taxes[a]
1940	6.4	n.a.	6.4	0.8	5.6	1.3	0.9	3.4
1945	6.3	0.3	6.0	1.5	4.5	0.8	1.0	2.7
1950	7.9	7.4	1.9	5.5	5.9	1.1	1.3	3.1
1955	8.3	0.6	7.7	2.3	5.4	1.1	1.8	2.5
1960	7.5	1.1	6.4	2.3	4.3	1.2	0.7	2.2
1965	8.3	1.8	6.5	2.3	4.2	1.3	0.4	2.5
1970	9.9	1.8	8.1	3.5	4.6	1.4	0.2	3.0
1971	10.0	2.0	8.0	3.4	4.6	1.2	0.2	3.2
1972	10.7	2.4	8.3	3.7	4.6	1.2	0.2	3.2
1973	11.3	2.5	8.8	3.8	5.0	0.9	0.1	4.0
1974	12.0	2.7	9.3	4.0	5.3	1.0	0.2	4.1
1975	13.7	2.9	10.8	4.4	6.4	0.9	0.1	5.4
1976	13.0	3.0	10.0	4.8	5.2	0.9	0.2	4.1
1977	15.0	3.4	11.6	5.1	6.5	0.6	0.3	5.6
1978	15.3	3.3	12.0	5.7	6.3	0.6	0.1	5.6
1979	16.2	3.5	12.7	5.6	7.1	0.9	0.1	6.1
1980	18.3	3.3	15.0	5.8	9.2	1.0	(0)	8.2
1981	18.1	3.2	14.9	5.8	9.1	1.1	(0)	8.0
1982	18.4	3.4	15.0	4.9	10.1	0.9	(0)	9.2
1983	20.1	2.8	17.3	4.2	13.1	0.5	(0)	12.6
1984	19.1	2.6	16.5	4.2	12.3	0.5	(0)	11.7
1985	19.1	2.8	16.3	4.1	12.2	0.6	(0)	11.6
1986	17.5	2.7	14.8	4.3	10.4	0.7	(0)	9.7
1987	17.8	2.5	15.3	3.9	11.3	0.7	(0)	10.6
1988[b]	21.6	2.6	18.5	4.8	13.6	0.4	(0)	13.2

n.a. = not available. (0) = not meaningful.
a. It includes revenues from taxes on fuel, tobacco, alcohol, telephone, production, and services. Up to 1979 it includes the turnover sales tax and since 1980 the value-added tax, natural resources, and others. From 1977 on, revenues from taxes on domestic consumption and on oil exports have not been included in the natural resources tax; rather they are included in this column.
b. Estimated.
SOURCE: Banco de México, with information from *Estadísticas de Finanzas Públicas*, Treasury Department; International Monetary Fund, *International Financial Statistics*; and Office of the President, Mexico, *Miguel de la Madrid Quinto: Informe de Gobierno*, Apéndice Estadístico.

percent annual inflation was not to be disturbed, even if it meant adding only 2 or 3 more percentage points to the price index in the introductory year of the VAT.

The policies of that period were a coherent whole (Gil Díaz 1984), directed toward acquiring and preserving the confidence of Mexicans in their own economy, an especially difficult and delicate task in a country with an unstable past and with the proximity of the goods and financial markets of its economically giant northern neighbor. But virtue and persistence paid off. The financial requirements of the public sector had been limited to amounts financeable by the economy and by a dynamically static foreign debt (it grew at approximately the same rate as GDP). The currency had remained consistently stable for many years, and the financial system had deepened as a consequence of currency stability and real returns to depositors. Public revenues were scarce and so were the funds available for investment, but those limited funds were prudently managed to obtain good returns on investments in infrastructure.

The bottom line, with strong implications for tax policy, was that growth and equity were to be achieved by maintaining confidence, an active but compact public sector, and a tax system that was simple and as comprehensive as possible (and indeed real wages and employment grew more than ever before or since). The negative reaction of the treasury to the introduction of a VAT is understandable in this context. Its desire to avoid taxing wealth and even to eliminate the unfair inheritance tax can also be understood. Unfortunately, many of these achievements were gradually disassembled in the 1970s.

The tax system had been built up pragmatically, without an adequate guiding philosophy. Its supposed goal was global income taxation, so its lack of coverage could not be justified on a priori or philosophical grounds. The authors asserted that their practical achievements represented an appropriate tax system but did not have a realistic framework within which to justify their position. On the contrary, the tax system was confronted continually with the ideal of global taxation and found wanting by its critics. Its authors could respond only with weak or incorrect defenses. For example, although interest income was taxed, if anything, at an excessive rate if the inflation tax is considered in calculating the full resource appropriation by the government (Gil Díaz 1987), the government presented the situation as one of a deliberately low tax to promote savings (Ortíz-Mena 1969). Likewise, the government justified subsidies like accelerated depreciation as a means of promoting investment. But the argument was unnecessary: faster depreciation was never taken, because the law made it complicated enough to prevent its use.

Nonetheless, it would be unfair to fault public officials for their lack of theoretical cohesiveness. The understanding of fundamental tax matters was weaker than today, or perhaps the knowledge of the scope of ignorance was smaller. Henry Simons's impossible dream of taxing net increments of total wealth reigned supreme, and many people worked toward the perfect globalization of the income tax.

The Goals and Achievements of Mexican Tax Policy from the Early 1970s to the Present

The lifetime equity aspects of consumption taxation and its advantages in terms of efficient resource allocation, plus the innumerable and perhaps insurmountable practical difficulties presented by a global income tax (see the appendix), have convinced many modern economists of the superiority of the consumption tax.[3] However, the goal of Mexican policy makers was to produce a global income tax that was as comprehensive as possible. Until 1970 a practical compromise between the half-hearted ideal and the limitations of reality was followed, but no theory supported it. On the contrary, it seemed as if a reasonable goal had remained beyond reach and that reforms should be introduced to achieve it. The problem with this approach is that although the global tax is desirable on horizontal and vertical equity grounds, the practical impossibility of globalization has probably made it more inequitable than simpler alternative arrangements. Partial globalization, like partial indexation, may produce highly distortive and inequitable results.

President Echeverría's tax reforms, 1970–1976. During the election campaign of Luis Echeverría, there were passionate discussions about the need for a radical tax reform (its details were not spelled out, but income redistribution would be tackled through taxation). The debate continued throughout his first two years in office, but common sense generally prevailed in ruling out radical options. From all the pushing and shoving emerged two basic reforms: one in the direction of more comprehensive income taxation and the other in the form of high excises.

The first reform touched financial interest income and was largely cosmetic. It established a higher withholding tax while leaving a lower rate for those who opted to cumulate their interest income with other income. Nearly all taxpayers opted for the first formula, since the threshold at which it paid to voluntarily globalize interest income was at such a low income bracket that no one was really affected.

The effect of the higher tax on interest was to further reduce the real yield from financial interest in a period when rising inflation required higher nominal rates. It thereby contributed to a leveling off of the sharply rising trend that financial intermediation had shown in the previous fifteen years. One remedy might have been to fully gross up the higher tax into a higher gross interest rate. In such a case financial intermediation would probably not have suffered as much.[4] The best option, however, would have been not to tax interest income at all.

If interest is grossed up, savers have a higher gross income but their net income is the same and the incidence of the tax is borne by the users of credit or, most probably, by the consumers of nontraded goods and services. If an incidence measure does not take this effect into account, the bearing of the tax by savers will be merely illusory.

Further, in Mexico the net revenue from the tax is nil or perhaps even negative. The government was and is a prime borrower of internal funds, so the higher tax will be reflected in higher costs on its internal debt. If the government's debt utilizes half of the country's loan funds, an average of one-half of the higher tax boomerangs as government expenditures, as long as the profit margin of banks remains constant. If the other half of loan funds is lent to corporations, half of the increase in the grossed-up interest rate ends up as a lower corporate income tax. In such circumstances the government obtains a net of only one-quarter of the tax increase. In more recent times, because of the federal tax reserve sharing formula with the states and because the government is a more intensive user of financial savings (75 percent), the tax on financial interest income probably has had a net negative effect on federal finances.

The tax increases on financial interest during President Echeverría's administration thus gained little revenue and partially choked the main internal source of funding for the government and for the private sector: the deposits made to domestic financial intermediaries. The result was a greater level of foreign borrowing by both sectors.

The second income tax reform concerned the globalization of rental income from housing. The assessment of this change is more complicated. Rents had been taxed as part of the schedular system; they were subject to a separate tax according to a tariff whose maximum marginal tax rate was 10 percent. In 1973 rents were made cumulative to income. There is no information to document whether taxpayers paid higher or lower taxes on rental income after the reform. Since the schedular tax could not be evaded as today's global tax can (by fragmenting income among several minors such as children and grandchildren), it is not unlikely that they paid a higher tax before the reform.

However, the presumption that the yield from rental income fell because it was subject to higher marginal and average tax rates has been used by private sector analysts to argue that the decline in the stock of rental housing in Mexico's growing economy is the result of this tax measure. The allegation seems plausible since the tax reform coincided with the drop-off in investment on rental housing. Besides, the tax base was enhanced in subsequent years because, since rental housing is generally an unleveraged investment, it was affected by the advent of high inflation rates that considerably lowered the real value of depreciation allowances. But the lack of investment continued into the 1980s despite reforms introduced in 1979 that allowed a full indexation of depreciation allowances for past and future inflation or, alternatively, permitted a blind deduction of 50 percent of gross income if the investor preferred not to itemize deductions. The low investment is thus probably due not to higher taxes but to the coincidence of the high inflation of 1972 onward with a legal structure that makes the real maintenance of rents practically impossible (Creel 1988).

Here, as in other income items, the ambitions of the law contrast with administrative capacity, although it is arguable that in this area better administration is, at least in principle, within reach. The fact is that the ever-smaller supply of rental housing in the three large Mexican metropolitan areas (Mexico City, Guadalajara, and Monterrey) is preferably diverted to foreigners, whose movements in and out of the country diminish considerably the possibility that a renter will be "locked in" to a contract. On the other hand, these transactions are easier to hide from the tax man, since the eventual departure of the foreigner makes a noncontract rental or a contract that does not reflect the actual paid value reasonably safe to operate from a legal standpoint.

Aside from administrative considerations, if the situation prevailing in rental housing is compared with the ideal comprehensive income definition, the biggest inequity and distortion is probably found in the exclusion from the tax base of the rental income from owner-occupied housing.

In sum, the most important reforms to the income tax base in President Echeverría's administration were the inclusion of income from rented property in the tax base and the changes to taxation of financial interest income.

In addition, the tax rates for individuals were raised from a 35 percent maximum marginal rate to 50 percent. Despite a progressive schedule for corporate income, the tax rate was in practice a flat 42 percent. Bracket creep because of inflation raised the tax on individual cash income considerably.

These were delicate times from a confidence standpoint and it was difficult or foolhardy to push for additional income globalization, so the government prudently went no farther.[5] However, there were important reforms in indirect taxation. The introduction of a new turnover sales tax (TST) led to the coordination of federal and state sales taxes and eliminated the mosaic of rates and treatments that had spread over time across the thirty-two federal entities (the Federal District and the states). The existence of the new tax-sharing system also paved the way for the introduction some years afterward of a federal value-added tax, which required such a system.

The TST functioned by leaving to each state a portion of the tax collected by it (the administration was shared but collection was in state hands). Under the TST revenue-sharing agreement, regional sales by a firm located in a particular state were allocated to the other industrial states according to the distribution of sales. Under VAT a huge redistribution of revenue would have taken place in favor of the states where the value added is concentrated; hence a different system had to be designed. When the VAT was introduced, therefore, it was extremely convenient and important to have some years of "history" of revenue sharing among states, based on the regional distribution of sales, in order to design a sharing system acceptable to the states.

The reform on revenue sharing was also far-reaching in that for a centralized government such as Mexico's—where regional authorities are based in Mexico City and where the dominant party has won every gubernatorial election for more than sixty years—it is more convenient for interstate resource allocation and for individuals' long-term planning to have a harmonious or, better yet, unified tax system.

In the current political system (led by a dominant party), without harmonized taxes, a governor may ignore the long-term negative political impact for the party and adopt an excessively high tax in order to finance a spurt in spending (which may in itself be a poor decision). Or a governor may spend heavily and tax little, trusting that the central government will bail the state out of debt because of the governor's good federal connections. In short, the local success of the party may sometimes not be felt to depend on local politics.

Equal tax rates across the nation and a legally limited tax base to prevent the abuses mentioned above represented considerable steps toward fiscal harmonization, at least in the revenue area.

It was not easy, of course, to get thirty-one governors to agree to surrender their taxing powers, but they were offered an enticing carrot. Most big states had a local TST rate of 1.2 percent (they also had the highest rates), and the federal government had a rate of 1.8 percent. The legislative initiative proposed that all governors set a federal TST rate of 4 percent, to be shared almost equally between the states and the federal government. States that did not wish to adjust their local taxes were entirely free to do so, but would not share in the federal tax and would have to superimpose on the new tax, now higher than the previously combined rates, their own local taxes. In these circumstances, it is not hard to understand why every state entered the new system while federal and local finances were reinforced.

Federal tax revenues and social security contributions increased considerably during this administration. The rise totaled 3.1 percent of GDP, an amount equal to the gain obtained in the previous thirty years, thanks mostly to the increase described in the TST and in excise taxes on goods such as beer, soft drinks, alcoholic beverages, telephones, cigarettes, and electricity. Both the TST and excises had been extremely low by international standards and probably remained so even after these substantial adjustments. The only exceptions were some Lafferian luxury rates of 30 percent that provided less revenue after being imposed.

President López Portillo's tax reforms, 1976–1982. Despite the tax improvements during President Echeverría's presidential term, falling real public sector prices and rapidly rising public expenditures kept the public deficit on the increase. The inability to finance the fiscal disequilibrium led to a balance of payments crisis and to a devaluation in 1976. The incoming government of President José López Portillo (December 1976) quickly stabilized the economy through a combination of luck (oil revenues were starting to pour in), greater confidence (the new president made conciliatory gestures to the whole nation, including the private sector), and an initial macro-economic adjustment (the budget was tightened).

By 1978 the economy was growing rapidly and inflation was under control, even though a rapid pace of public expenditures contributed to a quicker fall in the real exchange rate than in the previous devaluation (1954). The level of public spending had attained truly dizzying heights in 1981, leading to an appreciation of the real exchange rate in early 1982 somewhat larger than that attained before the September 1976 foreign exchange crisis. Contrary to some widespread notions, however, the economy on the whole had been adequately managed up to the end of 1980. The increase in public expenditures had been matched by even faster increases in revenues, thus permitting—regardless of ever-increasing foreign debt financing of the fiscal gap—an improvement in the external and internal public debt ratios to GDP.

This was Mexico's macroeconomic setting: a strong, growing economy that was virtually persecuted by foreign bankers wishing to lend. With such ample resources to finance public and private deficit needs, one may ask, why trouble with a tax reform? In fact, such a favorable revenue environment made it politically difficult to sell an increase in the tax load or even a merely "structural" tax reform. But a political commitment had been carried forward in part from the days of President Echeverría's administration, and there was also a circumstantial and catalyzing element: the treasury secretary combined a grasp of economics and ability as a negotiator. Without this strategic combination it is doubtful that for purely structural reasons the far-reaching tax reform that occurred would have been implemented. Political reasons and the globalization ideals were also present, but no one, except for some close advisers, was pressing them on the president. The treasury secretary understood that there was a political window, perhaps unique, to carry through a structural reform that would simultaneously fulfill the goal of income globalization and achieve a tax system less distortive for resource allocation.

There was another crucial human element in this equation. The position of undersecretary of the treasury, combining the administrative and inter-pretative functions of the U.S. Internal Revenue Service with the tax policy role of the U.S. treasury, was also occupied by an economist who understood the goals posed by the secretary and was able to translate the array of policy options into administratively viable proposals. This situation also repre-sented an unusual combination of circumstances, since policy formulation and the administrative acceptance of new policies, especially those designed to set administrators on an entirely different tack, are often tempestuous marriages at best. A similar human equation would be decisive to push through the reforms of 1987 discussed below.

The reforms were carried out in various stages from 1978 to 1982. Some important changes to the income tax of individuals and corporations were introduced in 1978 to go into effect in January 1979. The VAT and the sweeping changes to excises designed to simplify them and to incorporate them into the VAT, together with the new act on tax coordination with the states, were approved by Congress and scheduled to go into effect one year later.

The purpose of the delay was to allow taxpayers to become acquainted with the new laws and to perform the accounting, computer, and administrative adaptations required by the new tax. Lawyers, accountants, and tax administrators themselves were to take advantage of this respite, but they did not exploit the time available to the fullest. The private sector was convinced (erroneously but perhaps understandably) of the government's ultimate lack of resolve to put the tax in place and lobbied again to prevent its adoption. Outside the treasury, the administration itself was divided over the proposals.

The arguments presented by the private sector against the VAT were the same as on the former occasion, but the international experience with new VATs was by this time so rich that the treasury was convinced that the effect of the tax would be at most a slight once-and-for-all increase in the price level. However, the well-known benefits related to revenue and evasion control of the new indirect taxes were considered of overriding importance by the treasury, which throughout the year and to the last moment was presenting position papers, international evidence, and comparisons to persuade different sectors both inside and outside the government of the worthiness of the proposal.

It is true that at various times the proposal almost fell through. This was probably perceived by the private sector, because professional tax groups and firms were generally not ready for the new tax at the end of 1979. It was only at the very last moment, when they came to believe in the imminent entry of the VAT, that everyone scurried belatedly to adjust to the mechanics and legalities of the new system.

In the end it was the treasury secretary's ability to persuade the president that the inconveniences were outweighed by the advantages that carried the day. But doubts lingered and the inflation that ensued (26.3 percent in 1980 compared with 18.2 percent in 1979) was popularly attributed to the new tax. This perception also contributed to an eventual weakening of the original scheme, as we shall see. Another vulnerable point of the new Mexican VAT is that, unlike modern European versions, the law required the tax to be shown separately from the price of the merchandise on sales slips. This feature made the public more resistant, especially when the rates had to be increased.

Diverse groups were interested in how the new tax would affect them, and separate negotiations were conducted both before the law was enacted and in the year before it went into effect, taking various points of view into consideration and to make necessary amendments.

Perhaps the most important and protracted discussion involved the general rate of the VAT. The new rate had to make up the revenue that was going to be lost through the elimination of the 4 percent TST, the 30 percent luxury rates, and the 25 federal and 300 state excises. The best estimate by the treasury was an equivalent general VAT rate of 12.7 percent, which it was willing to lower to 12 percent in response to private sector demands that it be set at 10 percent. When the treasury realized that this was going to be the most contentious point and that the reduction of tax evasion through the new system would very likely compensate for the lower rate, it agreed to set the rate at 10 percent, eliminating the biggest negotiating obstacle.

Other issues involved (1) the credit for taxes embodied in previous investment, (2) the reduction in excises in order for a pyramided VAT to have the same incidence as the previous rate, and (3) the negotiation with the states regarding a revenue formula, since the old system, giving them a share of the amount they collected, was considered impossible to calculate under the VAT. Of these issues, the most interesting and important is the question of revenue sharing.

Negotiations resulted in the creation of a general sharing fund, calculated as a percentage of total federal tax collections. In the first year each state would share in a percentage of the fund equal to federal transfers received over the past three years divided by total federal transfers to the states in the same period. The federal government had been sharing almost 50 percent of the TST plus varying percentages of certain excises.

After the one-year transition period with shares allocated through constant coefficients, a new formula was to go into effect: those states whose collection efforts produced a greater percentage increase in collections than the average percentage increase would be rewarded with a larger coefficient in the following period. However, the constant coefficients applied during the transitional period were later almost impossible to eliminate, because the fund was a fixed percentage of federal revenues. This zero-sum game induced the states who had good reason to expect their coefficients to fall to withhold information, for example, on the regional distribution of sales of interstate firms, thereby short-circuiting the process.

Such behavior sent the revenue-sharing system into a yearly crisis, since the states that had been cooperating understandably wished to be rewarded. The solution adopted was to raise the overall percentage (the size of the fund) to keep everyone happy while maintaining the system of constant coefficients. This naturally led to a complacent administrative attitude in most states and to an increasing hemorrhage of federal funds, as the amount of federal transfers to the states went from 11.2 percent of federal tax revenues in 1979 to almost 20 percent in 1986.

The lack of tax collection efforts contributed to the laggard performance of the VAT in the years after the transition (1982–1986), but since these were also years of high inflation, lower imports, and higher exports, all of which contribute to a relative loss of value-added taxation, it is difficult to disentangle the contribution of lower collection efforts by the states from the other effects (see Table 14.3).

TABLE 14.3   Real Revenue from the VAT in Mexico, 1980–1988

	Real receipts (millions of 1978 pesos)	Increase from previous year (%)
1980	80,262.7	n.a.
1981	83,219.1	3.7
1982	72,877.9	−12.4
1983	87,200.4	19.7
1984	93,026.1	6.7
1985	92,612.6	−0.4
1986	84,245.3	−9.0
1987	90,763.6	7.7
1988[a]	96,123.2	5.9

n.a. = not available.
a. Estimated.
SOURCE: Banco de México, *Indicadores Económicos*, various issues.

The zero-sum formula was finally corrected by the 1987 reforms. The states were given 30 percent of the VAT they collected without holding this part of their share to a ceiling. Their response was immediate, and brought new vigor into their collections.

The administrative complications of the VAT naturally arose because of the peculiarities of Mexico's tax arrangements, in which the states relinquished their right to local sales taxes in order to participate in a federal tax. It would have been extremely difficult politically to have them relinquish their administrative responsibilities as well, since their role as collectors gave them authority and presence with their constituents. Therefore the solution had to include some administrative role for the states as well as an incentive. This made the solution more complex but probably unavoidable in situations where a national VAT has to coexist with strong local governments keen on keeping some of their tax prerogatives.

The rate structure of the VAT went through three stages. The first, adopted at the VAT's introduction, was a relatively elegant one. It included a basic rate of 10 percent, a zero rate for some agricultural goods and some basic foodstuffs, and a 6 percent rate for the northern frontier strip, to take into account the level of sales taxation of neighboring U.S. cities. Unfortunately, the legitimacy of the new tax was eroded by an exemption (but not a zero rate) given to sales through union stores.

The second stage, which began only one year after the introduction of the tax (1980), extended the zero rate to more foodstuffs. The indecisiveness with which the new tax was adopted made the government only too eager to please those who felt that inflation had been fueled by the VAT and that the real income of low-income people could be improved through tax-rate tailoring.

The third stage came about as a response to the fiscal deterioration of 1981–1982, which was countered through strong income and expenditure measures in the 1983 fiscal year by the entering de la Madrid government.

On this occasion the basic rate was raised from 10 to 15 percent. A symbolic luxury rate of 20 percent and a lower (6 percent) rate on medicines and on some food items were thrown in to make the higher rate politically more palatable.

The income tax also underwent a gradual change. From the beginning, the three objectives of income tax reform were to increase its scope, reduce its distortive effects on resource allocation, and adjust it to inflation.

With regard to base broadening, dividends were made cumulative to personal income with the introduction of an integration scheme that allows full credit for the corporate income tax. Capital gains were also included in the individual income tax base, with the exception of gains on stock-listed shares.

A long-lasting struggle by tax policy makers to bring areas of "special treatment," such as agriculture, newspapers, trucking, and construction, under normal tax rules was successful only for the construction industry. Although just a first step, it was an important accomplishment because it ended the possibility of overinvoicing through construction industry receipts: construction firms had been taxed through the application of a fixed percentage (3.2 percent) of their gross income. This procedure enabled them to inflate construction receipts and thereby provide other firms an income tax saving of 42 percent (the tax on profits of firms outside the construction industry was 42 percent). If the 8 percent profit sharing with workers was included, the net tax evasion was 46.8 percent of the artificial mark-up in construction expenditures.

Broadening the tax base by eliminating special treatment is probably the most effective reform possible, since it achieves several objectives simultaneously: it improves equity by bringing a lower-paying sector into the tax base; it decreases tax fraud and hence tax evasion; and it leads to better allocation of resources as they move out of the previously lower-taxed sector into, on the average, higher-taxed sectors with a higher social rate of return (tax included).

The inflation adjustments, while incomplete especially in the corporate income tax, were far-reaching and prepared the way for full indexation. However, in light of the high rate of inflation in 1982–1987 (President de la Madrid's administration), too much revenue was lost before full inflationary corrections were made on the tax base. Corporate income tax revenue fell from 2.7 percent of GDP in 1980 to only 1.5 percent in 1985.

The exceptions to the late timing in inflation adjustment were excises, where the elimination of specific taxes coincided with the 1980 entrance of the VAT. The new ad valorem rates entered just in the nick of time to prevent a substantial loss in revenues from inflation. Such a loss can only be compensated imperfectly through a continuous increase in the specific quotas, since annual adjustments would have to allow for imperfect forecasts of inflation while monthly or quarterly adjustments would have been administratively cumbersome. Besides, specific taxes tend to be "quality regressive" within a category. A per liter tax on beer, for example, fell proportionately less on the highest-priced containers (aluminum cans) purchased by well-to-do consumers. The same can be said for tobacco, wine and spirits, and other goods.

The inflationary adjustments introduced in the income tax were related to the "cost" of assets sold (capital gains) and to the "unleveraged" portion of depreciable assets. To prevent indexing contagium of other contracts in the economy, a table constructed with the price indices of many years—a sort of inverse price index—was published in the law. Explicit indexation would be necessary in later years when full indexation of the corporate income tax was introduced in 1987. In the individual income tax, the elimination of itemized personal deductions in favor of a single personal deduction equal to an annual minimum wage also introduced the indexation of deductions. Finally, the income tax schedule was adjusted every year to account for inflation.

President de la Madrid's tax reforms, 1982–1988. The entering government of Miguel de la Madrid would have faced a fiscal crisis of major proportions even had foreign credit been available. But there was in general a suspension of foreign credit throughout this presidential term, despite Mexico's structural adjustment changes that went beyond the goals agreed upon with international multilateral lending institutions. Fresh money was supposedly provided with each negotiation, but foreign banks provided resources with one hand and took them away with the other.

In the first five years of this administration (and the preliminary figures for 1988 only confirm the story), Mexico's total foreign debt went from US$95 billion at the end of 1982 to US$98 billion at the end of 1987. The US$98 billion are equal to US$83 billion in real 1982 dollars, a fall of 14 percent in real terms. If the foreign debt is measured net of international reserves, the nominal amounts were US$93 billion at the end of 1982 and US$85 billion at the end of 1987. The real net foreign debt is in this case US$71 billion, a fall of 24 percent in real dollar terms over the same period.

Faced with such a paucity of funds, the de la Madrid administration slashed government expenditures and increased considerably the level of taxation. The new rate structure of the VAT was already discussed above. From a not-so-simple structure of a zero rate on some items, a 6 percent rate on the northern border, and a 10 percent basic rate, the new VAT went to a structure of 0, 6, 10, 15, and 20 percent rates. This new arrangement further complicated the administration of this novel tax, straining capability of some of the less advanced states and increasing the ease with which fraudulent claims of excess credits were collected.

Nonetheless, since the basic rate was rising from 10 to 15 percent and since so many other taxes also had to be raised, it was felt that the VAT needed a more "political" presentation— in other words, greater progressivity. Even so, the so-called increased progressivity of the structure is minuscule compared to the administrative inconveniences the complex structure introduced. Besides, the new general rate is probably high enough to make tax evasion extremely profitable, especially given the fragmented administration of the tax.

The rates of excise taxes were also substantially raised, while a temporary surtax of 10 percent was imposed on the personal income tax.

The reforms on indirect taxation were perhaps still short of the rates and coverage prevalent in most other countries, but they were a move in the right direction, judging from an international comparison of ratios of excise tax revenue to GDP that shows an extremely low reliance by Mexico on indirect taxes (Gil Díaz 1987).

Despite the substantial increases in the rates of excises, their contribution to revenue did not increase commensurately. The ratio of excises to GDP was 1.81 percent in 1982 and increased to only 2.39 percent in 1983. The figures from 1984 to 1987 averaged 2.41 percent. The explanation lies partly in the zero rating of exports. Excises are not generally paid on exports, and there is a full rebate on the excises and on VAT paid in previous stages. As nonoil exports increased from 2.4 percent of GDP in 1982 to 8.49 percent in 1987, with imports lagging behind, the taxable base of excises and the VAT contracted.

Inflation is also to blame. Excise taxes and VATs were paid monthly, twenty days after the end of the month. Although this was a rather short delay, the average lag actually came to thirty-five days when one considers that there was already an average fifteen-day lag by the end of the month. With inflation often averaging 5 percent per month in 1986–1987, the Olivera-Tanzi effect amounted to approximately a 6 percent loss in revenues. To aggravate the situation, the partial indexing introduced in 1979 to allow reflated depreciation expenditures to the extent firms were unleveraged was also gnawing at the tax base (see Table 14.4).

Corporate income tax revenue also lost considerable ground. It fell from 2.6 percent of GDP in 1981 to 1.7 percent in 1982, and averaged 1.6 percent through 1983–1987. This outcome is a result partly of the Olivera-Tanzi effect,

TABLE 14.4   Effect of Inflation on Mexico's Tax Revenues, 1980–1988

	Inflation rate (%)	Loss of revenue because of inflation (% of GDP)
1980	29.7	0.41
1981	28.6	0.40
1982	98.8	1.04
1983	80.7	0.88
1984	59.1	0.68
1985	53.3	0.73
1986	105.7	0.78
1987	159.1	0.82
1988	51.7	0.40

SOURCE: Banco de México, *Informe Anual 1988*.

because the tax was collected in three payments annually, and partly of the deductibility of nominal interest expenditures. Since interest expenditures balloon when inflation goes up, mostly because they contain an amortization component (to compensate for the inflationary loss in the real value of the principal), the deduction of these payments erodes the base of the income tax considerably.

Although the corporate income tax revenue fell by an average of 1 percentage point of GDP through most of President de la Madrid's administration (it rose during the last year), the peso debt of firms net of their peso financial assets went from 12.8 percent of GDP in December of 1980 to barely 1.1 percent in December of 1987 (see Table 14.5). Thus, 7 percentage points of GDP or about 63 percent of the net corporate private peso debt as of December 1981 (just before the financial crisis) can be explained by the reduction in the corporate income tax from 1982 through 1987.

While such a debt cleansing was welcome, especially to strengthen corporations for the trade opening that took place from mid-1985 to 1987, the fall in corporate taxes further weakened the ailing public finances, which had to face the 1982 suspension of foreign credit as well as a precipitous fall in the country's terms of trade.

Thus, despite the complexities involved, the inflationary bleeding of taxes had to be stopped. Although indexation would complicate even more the administration of small and middle-sized firms, it was obvious that a complete inflationary correction of the corporate income tax base was absolutely necessary. The base of the tax had not eroded still further because of the drastic fall in the net debt of firms.

To increase revenues, two important corrections were introduced. The first was a drastic reduction in the payment period. In the middle of 1986, firms were required to make twelve payments annually of the corporate income tax, instead of the previous three, and payments had to be made only ten days after the closing of the month. The value-added tax and excise tax

TABLE 14.5   Domestic Debt and Taxes of Mexican Firms, 1980–1987

| Year | Net domestic credit to private corporations | | | Corporate income tax (% of GDP) |
	Billions of current pesos	Billions of 1980 pesos	% of GDP	
1980	549	549	12.8	2.7
1981	650	505	11.1	2.6
1982	869	340	9.2	1.7
1983	890	192	5.2	1.5
1984	1,400	190	4.9	1.6
1985	2,925	243	6.4	1.6
1986	4,086	165	5.1	1.7
1987	2,085	32	1.1	1.6

SOURCE: For net domestic credit, Banco de México, Dirección de Investigación Económica; for corporate income tax, Banco de México, *Indicadores Económicos*.

payment days were also moved ahead, from the twentieth to the eighth working day after the end of the month.

These reforms reduced the Olivera-Tanzi effect as much as was practically possible, but they also represented a considerable increase in administrative and accounting costs. An alternate, less costly, and fully corrective formula was also studied, but could not be implemented because of legal difficulties: the payment of the tax on the same date as before, along with a representative monthly nominal interest rate times a number related to the average days of delay. In the case of the VAT, for instance, the tax would have been paid on the twentieth day of the following month, plus the tax times i $(1 + \frac{1}{6})$, where i is the previous month's nominal monthly rate of interest.

The second correction involved either fully indexing the corporate income tax or introducing an entirely new concept based on consumption for corporate taxation: cash-flow accounting (see McLure 1988). This new definition would have eliminated completely the problems posed by inflation on the tax base and would have been extremely simple to administer by taxpayers and authorities. Moreover, taxpayer representatives favored it strongly over the fully indexed alternative. The only defect of the new scheme was that it was not a standard income tax, and therefore foreign investment would not be able to obtain a credit for it against its tax liability abroad. This unfortunate fact left indexation as the only alternative. But part of the road toward cash-flow taxation was traveled.

In order to make indexation simpler, it was combined with some of the elements of the cash-flow scheme. The greatest simplification was to permit the simple deduction of all purchases. This procedure eliminates all the complications of inventory costing, which are difficult even without inflation. Another simplification was to allow the immediate deduction of the present value of otherwise depreciable investments. A real interest rate of 7.5 percent was used to bring depreciation expenditures to the present. An otherwise twenty-year linear depreciation structure in housing, for instance, was converted into an instant deduction of 56 percent.

These simplifications, however, did not bring instant administrative relief to the taxpayer. To prevent large gains and losses among taxpayers, the new system had to be introduced gradually. After arduous negotiations it was finally agreed that 20 percent of the new tax would be put into effect each year, beginning in 1987. In 1987 a firm would pay its corporate income tax taking 20 percent of the tax generated by the new base and 80 percent of the old unindexed base. In 1988, 40 percent of the new base was considered and 60 percent of the old, and so on.

In addition, the corporate tax rate was reduced from a flat 42 percent to a flat 36 percent, bringing it into line with current international levels.

If the new indexed base with its cash accounting of purchases and instant depreciation had gone into effect immediately and in lieu of all previous legislation, it would have brought considerable simplification, despite the complications from the monthly inflationary corrections on profits derived from firms' net monetary positions. Unfortunately, the system's entry was not that simple.

As explained above, the smoothed entry of the new base entails the coexistence of both accounting systems for a number of years. But there is one more complication: when partial indexation was introduced in previous years, the unindexed base was maintained for calculating the profits shared by law with the workers (8 percent up to 1987, 10 percent afterward). Profit sharing is based on the old nominal notion of taxable income, but it is not a tax law as such; it is derived from a law proposed to Congress by a special commission set up every ten years. Therefore, even when the new system is fully operative, corporations will still be bound by the old system, with its own complications (mostly inventory costing). Even more unfortunate, from 1987 to 1990 three sets of methods are simultaneously needed to calculate taxable income.

Thus the transition period, plus the old base of the profit-sharing law, has created instead of a simple code an extremely complicated set of rules that have to be calculated every month, together with the ever more complex VAT and, in some cases, monthly excises.

Individual income taxation was adjusted for inflation as well. Despite budgetary vicissitudes, there was a full inflationary adjustment every year in the schedule of the personal income tax starting in 1978 (SHCP 1988). In 1987 the schedule was automatically indexed by making brackets a multiple of the minimum wage. However, notwithstanding the important downward adjustment performed on average tax rates in the 1979 reforms, the schedule before inflation had started from a rather high level, judged from an international standpoint. For example, a taxpayer with an income equivalent to twenty times the national average minimum wage, US$26,000 in 1988, paid an average tax of 37 percent in that year. The marginal tax rate for this bracket was 50 percent. Therefore, the present average and marginal tax levels calculated over money income are still high and quite likely to stimulate high levels of tax avoidance and evasion. The average impact of the tax is lessened, however, if income includes untaxed fringe benefits. In the past few years this concept has been continuously broadened in an effort by taxpayers to lower the tax burden and by unions to achieve a partial indexing of wages. Table 14.6 shows how nonsalary income has increased from one-quarter of income in the late 1970s to one-third in the late 1980s.

If the average tax is calculated including fringe benefits in income, the result would of course be a lower average tax. But a design that leaves so many categories of income out of the tax base tends to force sharp increases in the marginal rates and to distort labor-leisure choices in occupations where the tax is unavoidable.

The personal income tax schedule has evolved from a maximum marginal rate of 55 percent in 1979, when it was raised from 50 percent, down to 50 percent in 1988, and to 40 percent in 1989.

TABLE 14.6	Share of Wages and Salaries and Fringe Benefits in Total Labor Income in Mexico's Manufacturing Sector, 1978–1988 (percentages)	
Year	Wages and salaries	Fringe benefits
1978–1980	73.8	26.2
1981–1983	70.1	29.9
1984–1986	69.5	30.5
1987–1988	66.7	33.3

Source: Treasury Department, "Evolución de la Carga Fiscal del Impuesto sobre la Renta a las Personas Físicas: 1978–1980," internal document.

Concluding Remarks

Mexico's recent protracted and arduous experience with tax reform has taught us that the earnest pursuit of a global personal income tax faces constraints such as capital and population movements, administrative limitations, and assorted practical considerations.

The international movement of capital means that financial interest income cannot be taxed, except to the extent interest is grossed up. In such a case, however, the incidence is not on the saver, while the costs of servicing the public debt may exceed the revenues collected through this tax. If the tax is not established, however, firms can easily circumvent the corporate income tax through "back-to-back" operations.[6] Therefore, the existence of a corporate income tax ends up necessitating the establishment of a tax on interest income, despite its inconveniences.

Because of practical and administrative limitations, the personal income tax is quite distant from the Simons (1938) ideal and will remain so, yet legislators and tax specialists behave as if the horizontal and vertical equity goals of the tax are being or can be achieved. The gulf between reality and the ideal tax, combined with the widely accepted superiority and greater simplicity of a consumption tax, is another important issue raised by our recent experiences.

The need to prevent the double taxation of profits accruing to foreign investment requires a corporate income tax with provisions similar to those established in foreign countries. This requirement leads to a system of at least two layers of taxpayers—one capable of dealing with the administrative chores of the tax and the other outside of the system, sometimes ignored and often evading the tax, while providing evasion outlets to those within the tax base. This is, of course, a source of great inequity. Besides, the need to prevent the double taxation of dividends (that is, to integrate the personal and the corporate income taxes) combined with the myriad adjustments required by recent inflation and the transition to full inflationary accounting, have turned the corporate income tax into an administrative nightmare. The resulting system accentuates the duality of the system and prevents the tax from having a truly broad base to provide ampler revenues to the treasury. A simpler cash-flow system would be welcome in a developing country like Mexico, if the crediting of the tax by foreign corporations could be agreed upon with foreign treasuries.

Meanwhile, the pre-1970s Mexican income tax system of schedular taxation does not look at all bad in retrospect, although a consumption tax combined with a federal tax on real estate (and/or net assets of firms[7]) would still seem a preferred alternative. A schedular tax remains an aspiring global income tax and shares with it some of the practical inequities.

Regarding indirect taxes, the VAT greatly improved upon the cobweb of former taxes, but its lack of political salability has weakened the government's resolve to maintain its original simplicity. The new set of taxes is far better in many aspects than the old, but there has clearly been a problem with its decentralized administration by the states. Furthermore, the many rates now in operation have turned a simple tax into a complicated one.

Finally, perhaps the most pressing issue raised by Mexico's recent experience is inflation, which represents a substantial leech on government revenues, thus increasing the deficit and in turn contributing to an inflationary spiral. The reforms of 1987 and 1988 have shown, however, that despite the multiple complications that arise from indexing, inflationary corrections are necessary. Thanks to the reforms, corporate tax revenues, for instance, will provide 2.4 percent of GDP in 1988, not far below their peak of 2.7 percent in 1980.

These conclusions also set the agenda for other reforms:

1. The corporate income tax should be simplified, especially for tax-payers with scant administrative capacity.
2. A unified VAT rate would be welcome, perhaps with fewer exemptions and a lower general rate.
3. The administrative and legal coordination rules with the states on the VAT need to be modified.
4. Special tax bases need to be eliminated, since their existence allows the effortless shifting of tax bases from the taxed to the untaxed sectors.
5. Features that allow the averaging of taxation through time, such as special savings accounts whose income is not taxed and whose contributions would be deductible from taxable income, would bring the present personal income tax closer to a consumption tax.

Substantial reforms along these lines were enacted in the 1989 and 1990 tax reforms of the new administration of Carlos Salinas. Since describing and analyzing these reforms would require another chapter of equal length, this chapter leaves them for future consideration.

Appendix 14

Some Implications of the Global Income Tax

Attempting to tax the net real annual accretion of wealth presents several complications. These issues are well known to tax specialists (and might seem obvious in another context). Moreover, some tax specialists, aware of the deep practical limitations and related inequities of global income taxation, prescribe it anyway. Since, however, global income taxation has been one of the goals of the Mexican tax authorities, it will be useful to consider some of the important issues surrounding this method of taxation as they relate to Mexico's tax policy.

Global income is defined as a detailed and comprehensive measure of the net (of liabilities) increment of all possible sources of wealth—parrots, dogs, and flower pots included. But even if a comprehensive measurement is possible, how should the income of the spouse be taxed? For a family expenditure of 2 pesos, 1 peso may come from one person's gross income of 2 pesos and the other peso from another person's (the wife's, probably) gross income of, say, 1.20 pesos. Obviously the tax is distortive when applied individually because the same amount of revenue could be obtained with a lesser tax on the husband and a greater tax on the wife. A tax based on family income would lead to a greater effort by the husband, who would, for example, take in more patients or legal cases, and more leisure for the wife. Society would gain since the higher-valued gross output of the husband would expand while the lower-valued output of the wife would contract.

The tax based on the separation of each individual's income is also unfair. If two families have the same gross income, but one family's income is the result of only one party's working while the other family's income is generated equally by each member of the family, the progressivity of the tax schedule implies that the couple with one working member suffers a greater tax. However, if the family is used as the unit to be taxed, it will be cheaper to "live in sin" if both family members work.

There are other problems associated with the definition of family income:

1. One must consider housework. Housework, whether or not it is included in the national accounts, is income. Its exclusion from taxation distorts choices in its favor. Its inclusion would mean no distortion and a fairer distribution of the tax load.
2. Then there are the children. Are they consumption or producer goods? How should individuals be taxed if their education continues into adulthood, entailing large direct expenditures as well as forgone income?

3. One should not fail to include the imputed rent from owner-occupied housing. An easy way to exemplify the consequences of omitting imputed rentals is to imagine a renter who moves from an owned house, which he then rents, to another similar property, perhaps in another city, for which rent is exactly equal to his rental income. Obviously, the rental income from the house owned will be taxed and will therefore be less than the gross of tax rent paid to the owner of the other house.

4. All other conventional and monetarily measurable concepts of income should be included, as well as capital gains, preferably when accrued. Income originating out of the country should also be dutifully reported.

One need not go much further to realize how far the measurable reality in developing countries is from this Holy Grail. Even in developed countries, reality is a caricature of the ideal. No developed country taxes income from owner-occupied housing, although some have briefly tried and abandoned it. Some have a wealth tax applied hypocritically (no wines nor works of art in France, please) and inequitably. Almost all tax financial interest income lightly if at all. Some try to globalize household income, or at least income from labor, and end up taxing the institution of marriage. None of course has dared to include the imputed income of housework. How should one distinguish between the diligent housewife and the slob? How does one measure the forgone income of wildly different housewifely backgrounds?

The inclusion of capital gains varies, but in general such gains are not well weasured when included, nor, for practical reasons, are all potentially taxable items in the base. Furthermore, should averaging be performed? For how long? What about the ultimate complication: lifetime averaging to eliminate all the inequities that progressivity would impose on income lumps from any source?

If there is inflation, even slight or creeping inflation as is the modern norm even in stable countries, only real gains should be taxed, otherwise it is likely the principal value of the asset will be taxed. A tax on the principal would overstep the original purpose of the income tax while distorting asset allocation and producing inequities.

For the corporate income tax, indexation is a must, otherwise the deductibility of higher inflationary nominal interest expenditures will easily evaporate its base. But taxing real value is administratively complex, especially if one attempts full indexation when inflation is above moderate levels.

Another complication is that taxpayers in a truly global system will tend not to declare capital gains but to fully deduct capital losses. An inflationary environment will accentuate the revenue effects of the asymmetry.

To understand one of the main parameters of Mexican tax policy, international capital mobility must be considered. Except for a sad three-month interlude in 1982, Mexico has maintained no exchange controls for many decades. Capital needs open markets if it is to return, and Mexico–United States border linkages make controls on international currency movements a practical impossibility.

There are currently 275 million two-way crossings per year over the Mexico–United States border. It would take only US$109 per Mexican (half of the total trips are assumed to be by Mexicans) per trip to deplete a high level of international reserves of US$15 billion. There are other channels for capital flight, of course, such as foreign trade and tourism. The experiences of other countries are also quite eloquent about the ease with which money moves internationally despite and often because of controls. Therefore, international capital mobility creates an additional source of inequity and lack of tax coverage that probably starts with the middle class and becomes even more serious for the richest families.

Finally, it is important to mention, in this review of the most glaring absurdities of global income taxation in practice, that the taxation of wages is in many countries so high that organized workers able to obtain payment in kind have thereby sheltered a substantial portion of income from the tax base.

Part V

Conclusion

Appraising Tax Reform

Writing about the prospects for tax reform in the United States, John Witte had this to say in his 1985 book *The Politics and Development of the Federal Income Tax*: *"There is nothing, absolutely nothing in the history or politics of the income tax that indicates that any of these schemes have the slightest hope of being enacted in the forms proposed"* (emphasis in original; p. 380). Less than two years after the publication of those words, the United States had enacted the Tax Reform Act of 1986, which many believe to be the most important reform of the U.S. income tax since its inception three-quarters of a century ago. It seems safe to bet that similarly pessimistic prognostications were confounded in many countries during the 1980s, which could with reason be called "the decade of tax reform."

This chapter is an attempt to provide both an update of the rapidly evolving experience with tax reform and a summary appraisal of that reform for the eleven countries covered in this volume. The preceding chapters can be divided into three groups: conceptual or normative pieces (tax principles for developing countries, by Arnold C. Harberger, and international tax principles, by Joel Slemrod), chapters on tax reform experience in seven developed countries (Australia, Canada, Israel, Japan, Sweden, the United States, and the United Kingdom), and chapters on tax reform in four developing countries (China, Colombia, Indonesia, and Mexico).

Of necessity, this discussion must be selective; it is not intended to be exhaustive in either its updating or its appraisal of experience. Arnold

Harberger's chapter, though addressed explicitly to the problems of developing countries, provides a useful framework against which to appraise much of the experience reported here, since, for the most part, his guidelines are probably subject to general agreement among most economists working on tax reform in both advanced and developing countries. The discussion here, however, concentrates more on apparent explanations for failure to follow the Harberger guidelines than on instances of compliance with those guidelines.

No effort is made to tell how each of the countries surveyed has handled each of the issues covered in the Harberger chapter. (Since the country chapters do not deal with questions of trade policy, Harberger's views of the desirability of a uniform import tariff are not considered further.) Moreover, many fundamental changes (such as changes in the taxation of capital gains in many countries, Australia's taxation of fringe benefits, and the attacks on tax shelters in Australia, Sweden, and the United States) that would deserve greater attention in longer and more detailed discussions of tax reform in particular countries are neglected. This chapter does consider rate reduction, however, an additional criterion that does not appear in Harberger's guidelines but is consistent with their general thrust.

Finally, it makes little sense to apply the Harberger criteria systematically to the tax system of China. After all, in a command economy in which prices play little allocative role and the state owns a substantial portion of economic assets, taxes serve a very different—or at least a more limited—set of objectives than in a free market economy. In a free market economy taxes play an important role in determining the distribution of income and the allocation of resources, as well as in stabilizing the economy (helping to assure full employment and price stability). As Roger Gordon's chapter on China indicates, in a command economy the stabilization role of taxation is relatively more important, income distribution and resource allocation being more strongly influenced by state ownership and allocation of resources, pricing rules, limitations on labor markets, and other state controls.

What follows reports on some developments that have occurred since completion of the chapters of this book and draws on experience not reported in the country chapters. (Some of this more recent experience is reported in Whalley 1989. See also Tanzi 1987 and Pechman 1988. For the most part no references are given to points discussed in earlier chapters.) No effort has been made, however, to provide a comprehensive and up-to-date description of tax policy in the countries surveyed.

Similarly, this chapter does not attempt to trace the "paternity" of the tax reform that has been sweeping the world. Tax reform in some countries was obviously stimulated by that in the United States. But just as obviously, tax reform in other countries preceded that in the United States and influenced reform in both the United States and elsewhere. For example, the 1984 tax reforms in the United Kingdom, in which investment incentives were eliminated and rates were reduced, were extremely important in convincing

U.S. Treasury Secretary Donald Regan of the wisdom of proposing similar reforms for the United States. Moreover, to some extent the ubiquity of tax reform reflects the power of the common intellectual case for reform. (See also Whalley 1989 and Tanzi 1987 and references cited therein.)

Value-Added Tax

Harberger repeats the standard litany of well-known benefits of a value-added tax (VAT) with the now-conventional features: destination principle, consumption base, and credit method. Sweden (since 1968) and Colombia (since 1965, but only at the manufacturing level before 1983) have long had such a tax. (Even now Colombia does not allow immediate credit for taxes paid on purchases of some capital goods.) The United Kingdom introduced a VAT in 1973 as a condition of entry into the European Community (then the European Economic Community), and Israel has levied a VAT since 1976. Indonesia introduced the VAT in 1985 (after a delay due to administrative problems) as the keystone of the reforms reported in the chapter by Malcolm Gillis, and Mexico adopted a VAT in 1980, as noted in the chapter by Francisco Gil Díaz.

The experience with VAT—or even proposals for a VAT or other form of general sales tax—has not been so positive in the other countries surveyed. Japan introduced a 3 percent VAT in 1989, but has been under strong pressure, especially from housewives, to repeal it. Australia considered adopting a retail sales tax, but decided not to do so. For many years Canada studied the desirability of replacing its highly defective wholesale-level sales tax with either a retail-level sales tax or a federal VAT. After flirting seriously with a subtraction-method levy as a way of avoiding problems with the provinces it has finally decided to introduce a credit-method VAT. Whether this will soon occur is, however, subject to considerable doubt, as the plan is being attacked from all sides, especially by small business.

This leaves the United States as the only country considered here that does not have a VAT and has never had one seriously advocated in a government-sanctioned document. The United States Treasury Department, in its 1984 tax reform proposals to President Reagan, devoted an entire volume to the analysis of the VAT, but did not propose its enactment. Among the reasons the United States has no VAT (or other form of federal sales tax) are the fear of federal encroachment on the fiscal preserve of state and local governments, the fear of conservatives that it would turn into a "money machine" that would fuel the growth of public spending, and the fear of liberals that it would be regressive. (One observer has noted that an American VAT will have a political chance once liberals realize it is a money machine and conservatives realize it is regressive.) Some have seen this as the most likely and appropriate way to reduce the troubling federal budget deficit, despite President Bush's promise of "no new taxes." Recent events in

Eastern Europe, and the possible reductions in defense spending they portend, cast some doubt on this view.

Income Tax Issues

Rate reduction. The reduction of income tax rates is probably the most dramatic manifestation of the wave of tax reform that swept the world during the 1980s, as well as perhaps the most important. Rate reduction is important for several reasons. It reduces the adverse incentive effects of taxation on work effort, saving, and investment. Any nonneutralities and inequities that remain after reform are less important at low rates. Pressures on tax administration and compliance are lessened by rate reduction. Finally, people may feel that the system is better if low rates are levied on a broad base than if high rates are levied on a narrow base.

All the countries surveyed here have cut rates substantially. The rates in these countries—both before and after reform—are given in Table 15.1. For this group the average top marginal tax rate applied to the income of individuals has been reduced from 60 percent to 40 percent. The comparable reduction for corporations is from 46 to 35 percent. (Median tax rates are not reported since in all cases they fall within one percentage point of the average rates. China is not included in these calculations for reasons indicated earlier.)

Integration. Harberger notes that it makes no economic sense to levy a separate tax on the income of corporations, just because they are legal "persons." Rather, corporate and individual taxes should be integrated, either by taxing the income of corporations as if earned by a partnership or

Table 15.1	Tax Rates in Selected Countries, before and after Tax Reform	
Country	Top marginal rate for individuals (old/new)	Corporate rate (old/new)
Australia	60/49	46/39
Canada	34/29	36/28
Colombia	49/30	40/30
Indonesia	50/35	45/35
Israel	60/48[a]	53/48
Japan	70/50	42/37.5
Mexico	55/40	42/36
Sweden	75/50	56/30
United Kingdom	80/40	52/35
United States	70/28 (+5)[b]	46/34

NOTE: China is omitted because tax rates have little meaning in a command economy.
a. Assumes scheduled elimination of surcharge at end of 1989.
b. The additional 5 percent represents a surcharge faced by upper-middle-income taxpayers.
SOURCE: Previous chapters and Whalley (1989).

by providing relief only for double taxation of dividends. An integrated system is fairer, because combined corporate-personal taxation reflects the personal rate structure more closely than does separate taxation at both levels. It is also more neutral with regard to economic decisions, since it does not discriminate against the corporate form of business and products of the corporate sector. Finally, it does not favor debt financing, as does the separate taxation of corporate equity income at the firm level and of dividends at the individual shareholder level.

For administrative reasons, no country has attempted to provide partnership treatment of large corporations, though some do so for small corporations with relatively simple capital structures, and the recently enacted Australian system may, at the option of the corporation, approximate full integration. Among the countries surveyed here, Canada and the United Kingdom have long provided shareholders credits for the corporate taxes attributable to the dividends they receive, Mexico began to do so in 1979, and Australia (1987) more recently joined this group. Colombia, in its 1986 reforms, eliminated the tax on dividends, thereby providing a sort of ad hoc relief for double taxation of dividends that was thought to be appropriate to its administrative capabilities, even if not conceptually satisfactory. It did this in part to prevent the further "decapitalization" of its economy.

The United States is among the few developed countries that provide no relief from double taxation of dividends. During the past dozen years it has considered both the partnership method and two ways of providing dividend relief. (See U.S. Department of the Treasury 1977 and 1984 and U.S. Office of the President 1985.) None of these has ever received much support, for various reasons, including large revenue losses—which are matched by windfall gains to present owners of corporate shares, many of whom are in high income groups. The corporate managers who might be expected to support such a change have shown a marked lack of interest in it, presumably because they do not like the increased pressures for distribution of profits dividend relief would imply. They preferred instead to keep—but ultimately lost—other corporate tax benefits that were threatened by tax reform.

As this is being written there is a strong possibility that the U.S. Treasury Department will soon propose a system of full integration as part of efforts to encourage capital formation. According to rumors, the Treasury Department is rejecting dividend relief because of the incentive it gives for paying dividends. There is at least some possibility that business will be more favorably disposed to full integration than it was to dividend relief in 1985. This is true in part because business, having already lost many of its tax preferences, might as well accept this benefit. Moreover, by reducing the advantage of debt finance, integration would lead to more sensible financial policies and reduce the threat of leveraged buyouts and other forms of debt-financed corporate takeovers.

Japan recently decided to shift from a split-rate system (lower rate on distributed profits than on retained earnings) to a classical (unintegrated) system, perhaps to avoid giving the benefits of dividend relief to foreign investors. (Whalley 1989 suggests this was the motivation behind this change.)

Tax incentives. The income tax systems of most countries have been cluttered with a variety of tax incentives ostensibly intended to encourage such "worthy" goals as saving and investment, the production of selected goods, and the development of poorer regions. Actually, incentives encourage rent-seeking behavior and thereby create inequities, undermine the perception of fairness, distort the allocation of resources, and complicate tax administration and compliance. One of the striking developments of the 1980s is the elimination or substantial reduction of incentives in many countries.

Colombia eliminated almost all such incentives in 1974 and continues to have a relatively "clean" income tax, despite occasional retrogression. In the fundamental reforms enacted in the United States in 1986 much of the revenue necessary for rate reduction in a revenue-neutral context came from repeal or substantial reduction of a long list of incentives, including the investment tax credit (ITC) and accelerated depreciation; nonetheless, the U.S. tax code still contains a variety of incentives, especially for oil and gas. Accelerated depreciation was also withdrawn or decelerated in Australia, Canada (which also eliminated its ITC), Japan, and the United Kingdom. Indonesia eliminated incentives in order to reduce opportunities for corruption, as well as for the reasons identified above. Israel continues to provide a variety of tax incentives. The depreciation schedule adopted by Mexico, while more rapid than economic depreciation, is substantially less generous than the cash-flow alternative it would have preferred.

Inflation adjustment. There are two conceptually distinct forms of inflation adjustment of income tax systems. One—and the easier, by far—is the adjustment of amounts fixed in nominal (monetary) terms, including personal exemptions, standard deductions, and bracket limits. These adjustments are needed in order to prevent bracket creep, the tendency for inflation to cause taxpayers with a given real income to pay increasing effective tax rates.

The other type of adjustment, which is quite complicated, is the adjustment of the measurement of income from business and capital. If the measurement of income is not protected from the effects of inflation, taxable income will be either understated or overstated. Understatement of income occurs to the extent that full deduction is allowed for nominal interest expense, without adjustment for inflation. Income is overstated if taxable income is based on first-in, first-out inventory accounting, economic depreciation, and full taxation of capital gains and interest income, without inflation adjustment. Inflation adjustment is thus needed in order to provide both equity and neutrality.

Inflation adjustment in the measurement of income from business and capital can be accomplished on an ad hoc basis by adjusting various items on the income statement, most notably depreciation allowances, cost of goods sold from inventories, the basis of capital assets, and interest income and expense. More satisfactory is an integrated system based on adjustments to the balance sheet, which are then reflected in the income statement. Chile has perhaps the most sophisticated system of inflation adjustment in the world; it is based on this integrated approach.

Colombia has adjusted nominal amounts for inflation partially since 1974 and fully since 1979. Mexico has adjusted its rate schedule since 1978, and Israel has provided partial adjustment since 1976. By comparison, the United States adopted this minimal reform only in 1981, to take effect for 1985. Canada does not index nominal amounts. The federal government undertook an evaluation of indexation options at both the personal and corporate level in 1981 but decided not to proceed. The other countries surveyed do not index nominal amounts. Sweden briefly enacted indexation but repealed it for political reasons. Porter and Trengove cite bracket creep resulting from the lack of indexation as a primary cause of the relative growth in personal income taxation in Australia.

Colombia has by far the most comprehensive and most sophisticated system of indexing the measurement of income of any country covered by this survey; until 1992 it will continue to use an ad hoc system first introduced in 1986 and expanded in 1988, and then switch to an integrated approach patterned after that used in Chile.

Mexico considered a system of expensing (deduction of the entire purchase price of capital goods in the year investment is made), but rejected it for reasons to be specified below. Instead, it adopted a system in which corporations are able to claim in the year of investment deductions equal in present value to future depreciation allowances. This "first-year depreciation" system effectively isolates depreciation from the effects of inflation.

The United Kingdom and Australia provide inflation adjustment in the calculation of capital gains. Canada, Sweden, and the United States provide no indexation in the measurement of income, though they have considered it.

In its 1984 tax reform proposals to President Reagan, the U.S. Treasury Department (1984) recommended the adoption of an ad hoc system of adjustment. This proposal never received serious attention and, except for capital gains, was dropped from the proposals Reagan submitted to the Congress. Among the reasons for disinterest in inflation adjustment were its revenue cost, its complexity, the subsidence of inflation, the preference of the business community for accelerated depreciation based on historical costs, and its dislike for indexation of interest expense.

Consumption (Cash-Flow) Taxation

Over the years Colombia, Mexico, Sweden, the United Kingdom, and the United States have all considered moving from the traditional income tax to a system of direct taxation based on consumption or (in the case of Mexico) to a more limited cash-flow tax for corporations. As yet none has adopted such a tax, though Mexico is now moving in the direction of adopting a cash-flow tax for small business.

There are two ways of implementing a direct tax on consumption. (For more details, see Zodrow and McLure 1988 or McLure et al. 1989.) Both provide expensing (immediate deduction) for investment in both capital goods and inventories. They differ in their treatment of debt and interest. Under one, which is truly based on cash flow and the use of so-called qualified accounts, the proceeds of borrowing are taxable and the repayment of debt is deductible; as under the income tax, interest income is taxable and interest expense is deductible. The base of such a tax is clearly consumption.

Under the second "prepayment" approach debt transactions have no tax consequences and interest is neither taxable nor deductible. Under certain (admittedly unrealistic) assumptions the bases of the two consumption-based taxes are equal in present value. But the prepayment system is simpler to implement than the cash-flow approach.

Economists have commonly advocated the consumption tax because it is neutral toward the choice between saving and consumption, rather than penalizing saving, as the income tax does. Business has liked the consumption tax for a similar reason; it would be more favorable toward capital formation. More recently, an additional important reason for a consumption-based tax has been noted; in many ways it is much simpler than an income tax. This argument in favor of the prepayment approach figured especially prominently in a report done recently for the government of Colombia and described in my chapter on experience in that country. Ironically, one of the reasons the consumption tax has almost always been rejected is the perceived difficulty of implementation. Such a view fails to take account of recent work on implementating a consumption-based tax.

Mexico clearly wanted to adopt a cash-flow tax for all corporations. It was, however, stymied by fear that the United States would not allow foreign tax credits for such a tax. It thus opted for the first-year depreciation system described above and has more recently adopted a cash-flow system for small business.

In Sweden, as elsewhere, the combination of fully deductible nominal interest expense and exempt capital income gives rise to opportunities for tax arbitrage, borrowing on a tax-deductible basis in order to make tax-preferred investments. On balance the taxation of capital income in Sweden may actually result in a net loss of revenue. Sweden has considered adopting a consumption-based tax for more than ten years. It has been most concerned about implementation problems inherent in the qualified accounts approach to consumption taxation and has suggested that the prepayment approach is preferable on administrative grounds. Like Mexico and Colombia, Sweden has been concerned about the creditability of a cash-flow corporate tax.

Colombia did not adopt a consumption-based tax in its 1988 reforms for several reasons, including the fact that no other country has yet gone down this road, the uncertainty hanging over the creditability issue, the fear that such a move would not pass constitutional muster as being consistent with the emergency powers allowing the executive to change the provisions for inflation adjustment, and the extremely short time available to consider such a fundamental reform between release of the 1988 report on the taxation of income from business and capital and the expiration of the emergency powers. Given the history of tax reform in Colombia, one would not be surprised to see Colombia eventually replace its income tax with a consumption-based tax.

International Issues

Most of the country chapters do not consider explicitly the many complex international issues raised by Slemrod (and in less detail by Harberger). The most obvious exceptions are (1) the concern with international competitiveness found in the chapters on Canada and Japan, (2) Canada's fear that it would be swamped by deductions for interest expense if it did not lower its corporate rates to the level of postreform U.S. rates, and (3) the creditability issue just discussed in conjunction with consumption-based taxation. To some extent this neglect reflects the focus of the tax reform debate in various countries. In the United States, for example, there was not much careful analysis of international issues; much of what passed for analysis during the debate was simply wrong, or at least incomplete (see McLure 1989). Slemrod points out that the United States may have inadvertently stumbled onto a policy stance that, if not optimal, is at least broadly consistent with national self-interest.

Concluding Comments

It is impossible to summarize the appraisal of the tax reform experience of eleven countries in the limited space that remains. It is, however, interesting to note the grades Harberger might give two countries, Colombia and the United States. (It might be noted that John Shoven's assessment U.S. tax reform is based on a view of what constitutes good tax policy that closely resembles Harberger's.) Several preliminary comments are, however, worth making explicit before turning to the two report cards.

First, many important aspects of tax reform have not been tabulated or even considered in this chapter. For example, the proliferation of tax shelters during the 1980s was almost unique to the United States; the elimination of most opportunities for shelters constitutes a major achievement of the 1986 U.S. tax reform. It helped restore the perception of equity that had been so seriously damaged by the growth of shelters, as well as improving the actual equity and neutrality of the system.

Second, the fact that a given country has not adopted all the Harberger guidelines does not necessarily mean that policy is wrong-headed—though in some cases it clearly is. Economic and political circumstances simply differ in important ways across countries. This is perhaps nowhere seen more clearly than in the case of inflation adjustment. A high-inflation country can hardly be said to have a tax on net income if it does not index the measurement of income from business and capital. By comparison, in a low-inflation country the complexity cost of indexation may exceed its benefits.

It is interesting to note (if a little self-serving, given the author's long-term involvement as an adviser on tax policy to the government of Colombia) that the tax policy of Colombia is clearly more consistent with the Harberger guidelines—supplemented to include rate reduction—than that of any of the other countries considered. Colombia has a VAT (although one that does not allow immediate credit for all taxes on investment goods), it provides comprehensive indexation for both nominal amounts and the measurement of income, it has eliminated virtually all important investment incentives, it has eliminated double taxation of dividends, and it has reduced its corporate rate and its highest marginal rate on individual income to 30 percent.

It is also interesting that the United States has taken relatively few of these steps, despite all the hoopla over the Tax Reform Act of 1986. Though it has reduced its tax rates almost as far as any nation—to 28 percent (33 percent including the middle-income surcharge) for individuals and 34 percent for corporations—it has no national sales tax, it does not provide any indexation in the measurement of income, it allows no relief from double taxation of dividends, and it still provides substantial incentives for selected economic activities. The absence of a national sales tax is especially noteworthy, given its federal budget deficit.

Many of the other countries reviewed here would not fare much better than the United States in this grading. Most now have VATs, most (but not necessarily the same ones) now provide dividend relief, most have made progress in curtailing tax incentives, and most have reduced marginal rates. Most have not, however, made substantial progress in insulating the measurement of income—or even nominal amounts—from the effects of inflation.

Notes and References

Chapter 2   Joel Slemrod, "Tax Principles in an International Economy"

Notes

1. This point is developed in McLure (1987) and Slemrod (1988a).

2. See Slemrod (1988b) for a further discussion of the tax arbitrage possibilities opened by international capital mobility.

3. The GATT does attempt to regulate internal taxes, but only those that discriminate against imported goods in favor of domestic goods. Income taxes are excluded from the scope of GATT.

4. I refer to the Multinational Convention on Mutual Assistance in Tax Matters, developed by the Organization for Economic Cooperation and Development, which standardizes procedures for sharing of tax information among countries. Open to signature beginning in 1988, it has as of this writing been signed by few.

References

Gersovitz, Mark. 1987. "The Effects of Domestic Taxes on Foreign Private Investment." In *The Theory of Taxation for Developing Countries*, edited by D. Newbery and N. Stern. Washington, D.C.: Oxford University Press.

Lessard, Donald, and John Williamson. 1987. *Capital Flight and Third World Debt*. Washington, D.C.: Institute for International Economics.

McLure, Charles E., Jr. 1987. "U.S. Tax Laws and Capital Flight from Latin America." Hoover Institution, Stanford University, Stanford, Calif., unpublished paper.

McLure, Charles E., Jr., and Jack Mutti. 1988. "Notes on the Creditability of Personal Consumption Taxes." Paper presented at the National Bureau of Economic Research Taxation Program meeting, Cambridge, Mass., March.

Slemrod, Joel. 1988a. "A North-South Model of Taxation and Capital Flows." University of Michigan, Ann Arbor, Mich., unpublished paper.

———. 1988b. "Taxation with International Capital Mobility." In *Uneasy Compromise: Problems of a Hybrid Income-Consumption Tax*, edited by H. Aaron, H. Galper, and J. Pechman. Washington, D.C.: Brookings Institution.

Chapter 3   Arnold C. Harberger, "Principles of Taxation Applied to Developing Countries: What Have We Learned?"

Notes

1. For example, in Chile during the 1950s and 1960s one would usually find three or four taxes separately noted on a restaurant bill, each identified by the number of the legislative act that imposed it. In that particular case, the proliferation of little taxes arose mainly from the practice of instituting separate taxes earmarked for specific spending programs. As the years passed, the number of separate taxes originating from this process became totally unmanageable.

2. Alternative methods of assessing a value-added tax are the "subtraction" method and "addition" method. The subtraction method is just like the credit method except that it does not insist on an explicit record of tax paid at an earlier stage in order for the firm to claim a deduction. The firm pays simply on the basis of its sales minus its purchases of inputs (including investment goods) during the period in question. Deduction is given for input purchases regardless of whether or not they came from firms that are members of the valued-added network. Clearly, evasion is much easier under the subtraction method while administration is much simpler (owing to the ease of leaving out small tax-paying entities while still collecting tax at a later stage) under the credit method. Small wonder, then, that the credit method is overwhelmingly preferred among tax experts and administrators.

The addition method computes the base of the value-added tax, not by working back from final sales, but by building up from the different components of cost. Thus, costs of inputs and of capital goods are not counted in this buildup, but the other principal cost items—wages, salaries, interest, and profits—are. I know of no real-world system that is administered via the addition method. It has, however, been seriously considered as a possible way of dealing with the special problems of including the financial sector in the VAT network.

3. Rarely does one find a uniform rate of VAT outside the range of 5 to 20 percent.

4. This argument correctly identifies so-called Ramsey taxation as the exercise of monopoly and/or monopsony power on the part of the government. Such taxation would tend to change with every major shift in demand or supply of a commodity, particularly if demand and/or supply became significantly *less* (or more) elastic. Supporters of the argument contend that a government should not engage in the exercise of monopoly or monopsony power vis-a-vis its own citizens.

5. When we work with a single rate of VAT, the measurement of welfare costs and benefits becomes very easy. Consider placing a tax at the rate T on good y, with x being the output of the previously taxed sector, and z the output of the previously untaxed sector (apart from y). Measuring changes in output in dollars' worth at initial prices (i.e., choosing units so that all initial prices are \$1), we have a welfare change arising out of the market for y equal to $(\frac{1}{2})\, Tdy$. This is a negative welfare change (a positive cost) because the quantity of y falls (dy is negative) as a result of shifting y to the taxed category. The fall in y is compensated by rises in x and z, such that (if z is defined comprehensively enough, so as, for example, to include the leisure time of workers as an untaxed activity) $dy = -dx - dz$. Offsetting the loss $(\frac{1}{2}\, Tdy)$ in welfare due to the tax on y, there is an indirect gain equal to Tdx. There is a net gain from the whole operation (of shifting y from the untaxed to the taxed category) so long as dx is greater than or equal to $-(\frac{1}{2})dy$; that is, so long as the x sector ends up absorbing at least half the resources ejected from y when the tax is imposed on y.

6. If τ_j is the nominal rate of protection on final product j, τ_i that on input i, and a_{ij} is the fraction of the cost of j accounted for (at international prices) by input i, domestic resources costs can extend up to the domestic currency equivalent of

$$(1 + \tau_j) - \sum_i a_{ij}\, (1 + \tau_i)$$

per dollar's worth of final product displaced. The net saving of foreign currency obtained in the process is equal to

$$1 - \sum_i a_{ij}.$$

This pattern of protection therefore allows for domestic resource costs of up to

$$[(1 - \sum_i a_{ij}) + (\tau_j - \sum_i a_{ij}\, \tau_i)] / (1 - \sum_i a_{ij})$$

per net dollar of foreign exchange saved. This implies a rate of *effective* protection of

$$[(\tau_j - \sum_i a_{ij}\, \tau_i) / (1 - \sum_i a_{ij})].$$

It is easily seen that this rate of effective protection will be equal to τ_j, whenever all the relevant τ_i are also equal to τ_j. This says that the effective protection of a final product will be equal to its nominal protection whenever the relevant imported inputs into its production have tariffs equaling (or averaging) the rate that applies to the final product. Thus if all final products and all imported inputs carry the rate τ^*, then all domestic value added receives protection at that same rate.

7. In the formula for effective protection (see above, note 6), the inputs i should in principle cover all *tradable* inputs, not just those which are imported by a country. If some part of the local supply of an export product is used as an input into an import substitute, that much less of it (the export product) will be available to be actually exported. Hence the use of an exportable as an input typically entails just as much of

a drain on the country's available supply of foreign exchange as does the use of an import good.

8. Most countries that introduce investment tax credits impose statutory minima on the economic lives of the assets to be covered. This eliminates the most exaggerated cases of bias, but investment choices remain greatly distorted.

9. To have a special incentive implies that there are favored activities that policymakers want to stimulate. What I here call "rational" incentives all have the property that for each level of the incentives (for example, the 40 and 30 percent tax rates in the above example) there corresponds a critical expected gross-of-tax yield (for example, $16\frac{2}{3}$ and 14.3 percent, respectively) on the investments covered by the incentive. Rational investors operating under the incentive will tend to accept projects promising greater than the critical yield, and will tend to reject those whose expected yield is below the critical level. In no case would such a "rational" incentive lead to the acceptance of, say a 12 percent investment, while simultaneously leading to the rejection of a different, similarly covered investment with, say, a 17 percent yield.

10. Here there is a credit of $\alpha\tau(PVY + PVD)$ followed by a tax of τ applying to $[(Y + D) - (1 - \alpha)D]$. In present-value terms the net tax is $\tau(1 - \alpha) PVY$. That is, the ordinary tax rate of τ has been reduced by the incentive scheme to $\tau(1 - \alpha)$.

11. From the accounts of the firm we have $RA + NA = RL + NL + CS$, where RA and RL represent real assets and liabilities, NA and NL equal nominal assets and liabilities and CS equals capital and surplus. Inflation at the rate π brings about a loss on all nominal assets and a gain on all nominal liabilities. The net gain is $\pi (NL–NA)$. This of course equals $\pi (RA–RL)$ minus πCS.

Chapter 4   Michael G. Porter and Christopher Trengove, "Tax Reform in Australia"

Notes

1. The PAYE system is intended to encompass all wage and salary earners and involves withholding of tax at source (that is, by employers).

2. Section 26(e) of the act required the value to the taxpayer of all allowances, gratuities, benefits, or bonuses—whether received in cash or in kind—to be included in assessable income.

3. The Australian Constitution prevents state governments from taxing commodities. Since, under an agreement entered into during World War II, these governments have also handed over the income tax instrument to the central government, they are now somewhat restricted in the forms of tax they may use.

4. The conclusions are summarized in House of Representatives Standing Committee on Expenditure (1986).

5. In common with its counterparts in many other countries, the agency responsible for administering the tax system (the Australian Taxation Office) has only a minor involvement in matters of overall tax design. The department most concerned with the development of taxation policy is the treasury.

6. Malcolm Fraser's government held office from November 1975 until March 1983.

7. The ill-fated Australia Card proposal, which was to serve a variety of bureau-cratic purposes including taxation, social security, health insurance, and immigration, has now been replaced by a much more modest scheme to be applied only to taxation.

8. Except for taxpayers falling below a threshold level of income, a gross rate of 1.25 percent is payable by all residents in the form of a levy, which is designed to partially fund the system of national health insurance.

9. Thus, although the treasurer insisted when presenting the 1988/89 budget that tax cuts could not at that time be responsibly given (supposedly for reasons of demand management), this in reality implied a substantially increased impost on payers of personal income tax.

10. This restriction, however, means that some imputation credits paid to resident taxpayers go unused.

11. The Family Income Support (FIS) scheme paid amounts of around $A17 per week for each dependent child for low-income families. The FAS scheme extended this by raising the income levels at which amounts began to be withdrawn, by paying larger benefits, particularly for teenage children, and by paying additional benefits to those living in rental accommodation.

References

Asprey, K. W. 1975. *Taxation Review Committee: Full Report*. Canberra: Australian Government Publishing Service.

Campbell, J. K. 1981. *Australian Financial System: Final Report of the Committee of Inquiry*. Canberra: Australian Government Publishing Service.

Commonwealth of Australia. 1985. *Reform of the Australian Tax System: Draft White Paper*. Canberra: Australian Government Publishing Service.

House of Representatives Standing Committee on Expenditure. 1986. *A Taxing Problem: Review of 5 Auditor-General's Efficiency Audit Reports into the Australian Taxation Office*. Canberra: Australian Government Publishing Service.

Mathews, R. L. 1975. *Report of the Committee of Inquiry into Inflation and Taxation*. Canberra: Australian Government Publishing Service.

Chapter 5   John Whalley, "Recent Tax Reform in Canada: Policy Responses to Global and Domestic Pressure"

Notes

1. See Canadian Tax Foundation 1988: Table 7.8.

2. See Canadian Tax Foundation 1988: Table 7.29.

3. See Canadian Tax Foundation 1988: Table 3.1.

4. This section draws on Hamilton and Whalley (1989a) who provide similar documentation of the 1987 Canadian tax changes to that contained here. See also other papers on Canadian tax reform contained in the edited collection by Mintz and Whalley (1989).

5. Under other changes in CCA, the rates for satellites went from 40 to 30 percent, outdoor advertising signs from 35 to 20 percent, public utility property from 6 to 4

percent, buildings from 5 to 4 percent, and earth-moving equipment from 50 to 30 percent.

6. This pyramiding does, however, also broaden the base of the tax, causing items that are legally exempt to effectively bear some tax.

7. A CCA rate of 30 percent will be allowed to apply against other income.

8. This section, like the previous one, draws on material in Hamilton and Whalley (1989a) providing an evaluation of efficiency and distributional effects of Canadian tax reform, as well as more broadly, the papers contained in the Canadian Tax Foundation volume edited by Mintz and Whalley (1989).

9. Hamilton and Whalley express these efficiency gains as the change in aggregate welfare measured in dollar terms. Welfare gains are measured using Hicksian equivalent variations. An equivalent variation is the amount of additional income available to consumers beyond that which would enable consumers to reach their welfare level achieved under the original tax policy regime. For the dynamic model, these are expressed in terms of the present value of the welfare gains over time.

10. In fact, it is worse since clothing, as defined here, is actually a luxury (expenditures as a percentage of income rises with income).

References

Ballard, C. L., J. B. Shoven, and J. Whalley. 1985. "General Equilibrium Computations of the Marginal Welfare Costs of Taxes in the United States." *American Economic Review* (March).

Browning, E. K. 1978. "The Burden of Taxation." *Journal of Political Economy* (August).

Canada. Department of Finance. 1985a. *The Corporate Income Tax System: A Direction for Change.* Ottawa.

———. 1985b. "Theory and Empirical Methodology Underlying the Measure of Marginal Tax Rates." Ottawa. Mimeo.

———. 1987a. *Tax Reform 1987: The White Paper.* Ottawa: June 18.

———. 1987b. *Tax Reform 1987.* Ottawa.

———. 1987c. *Tax Reform 1987: Sales Tax Reform.* Ottawa.

———. 1987d. *Tax Reform 1987: Income Tax Reform.* Ottawa.

Canadian Tax Foundation. 1988. *National Finances, 1986–87.* Toronto.

Davies, J. B., F. St.-Hilaire, and J. Whalley. 1985. "Some Calculations of Lifetime Tax Incidence." *American Economic Review* (September).

Due, J. F. 1988. "The New Zealand Goods and Services (Value-Added) Tax: A Model for Other Countries." *Canadian Tax Journal* (January–February).

Gillis, M. 1985. "Federal Sales Taxation: A Survey of Six Decades of Experience, Critiques and Reform Proposals." *Canadian Tax Journal* (January–February).

Hamilton, R. W., and J. Whalley. 1989a. "Efficiency and Distributional Effects of the Tax Reform Package." In *The Economic Impacts of Tax Reform,* edited by J. Mintz and J. Whalley, 373–98. Canadian Tax Paper No. 84. Toronto: Canadian Tax Foundation.

———. 1989b. "Reforming Indirect Taxes in Canada: Some General Equilibrium Estimates." *Canadian Journal of Economics* 22, no. 3 (August) pp. 561–75.

Harberger, A. C. 1974. *Taxation and Welfare.* Boston: Little, Brown.

Japan. Ministry of Finance. 1988. "Outline of the Japanese Tax Reform Proposal." Tokyo.

King, M. A., and D. Fullerton. 1984. *The Taxation of Income from Capital: A Comparative Study of the United States, the United Kingdom, Sweden and West Germany.* Chicago: University of Chicago Press.

Kuo, C. Y., T. McGirr, and S. N. Poddar. 1985. "On Measuring the Effective Federal Sales Tax Rate in Canada," Department of Finance, Canada. Mimeo.

Mintz, J. M., and J. Whalley, eds. 1989. *The Economic Impacts of Tax Reform.* Canadian Tax Paper No. 84. Toronto: Canadian Tax Foundation.

Morgan, D. R. 1986. "The Government's Tax Reform Package: An Overview." *Australian Tax Forum* 3, no. 1.

Royal (Carter) Commission on Taxation. 1966. *Sales Taxes and General Tax Administration* 5. Ottawa: Queen's Printers.

Thirsk, W. R. 1980. "Giving Credit Where Credit Is Due: The Choice between Credits and Deductions under the Individual Income Tax in Canada." *Canadian Tax Journal* (January–February).

Chapter 6 Eytan Sheshinski, "The 1988 Tax Reform Proposal in Israel"

Notes

1. It should be noted, however, that the upper decile contributes about 70 percent of the total income tax revenue. Thus, an elimination of tax expenditures accompanied by a *proportional* reduction in tax rates would be somewhat regressive.

2. We shall not elaborate on these reforms, since corporate taxation was not in the terms of reference of the current reform proposals.

3. This rate reflects three months at 60 percent, nine months at 48 percent, and a 10 percent surtax throughout the year.

4. This rate includes the average rate of state taxes.

References

Center for Social Policy Studies in Israel. 1985. *Changing Social Policy: Israel 1985–86.* Jerusalem.

Israel. Ministry of Finance. 1988. *Report of the Committee of Experts on Individual Tax Reform.* Jerusalem.

Kondor, J. 1987. "Tax Evasion in Israel." Tel Aviv: Tel Aviv University, The Sappir Center for Economic Research.

Pechman, J. 1988. *World Tax Reform.* Washington, D.C.: Brookings Institution.

Chapter 7 Yukio Noguchi, "Tax Reform Debates in Japan"

Notes

1. Contributions to the employees' pension are determined in terms of their ratio to "regular earnings," which is wage earnings minus bonuses. In the case of the people's pension, contributions are set at fixed amounts.

2. An "automatic increase" is defined as the rise in tax revenues that can be expected if no revision is made to the tax laws. The increase is caused not only by bracket creep but also by growing numbers of taxpayers, as the number of those whose income exceeds the minimum taxable level rises. The number of salaried workers paying income taxes increased from 24 million in FY 1975 to 33 million in FY 1985.

3. Nonincorporated businesses are subject to personal income taxes on business income, while incorporated businesses are subject to the corporate income tax.

4. The following numerical example will help to clarify why this is a favorable treatment. Suppose that sales revenue is 100 and expenses (employee wages, interest payments, rent, depreciation, and so on) are 60. In the absence of the special treatment, taxable income is 40, which consists of the business profit and labor income of the business proprietor. Under the special treatment, the labor income portion (say 30) can be deducted in calculating the taxable business income. In addition, since this is regarded as the salary income of the proprietor, a certain proportion (about 30 percent) is deducted in calculating the taxable income. The tax base is thus reduced to $(100 - 60 - 30) + 30 \times 0.7 = 31$.

It is true that the same procedure is applied if the business is incorporated. In this case, however, the corporate income tax rate, which is higher than the individual income tax rates for relatively low income, is applied. Moreover, formal bookkeeping is required.

5. Although some of the income withheld is interest and dividend income, most of it is in the form of wages and salaries.

6. There are a number of related studies: Honma, Atoda, Hayashi, and Hatta (1984), Tajika and Yui (1988), and Takenaka (1984).

7. Estimates of future pension benefits are based on the assumption that the present formula for calculating benefits will remain unchanged. This assumption causes an overestimation bias, because the replacement ratio will rise from the present level due to the maturing of the system. The contribution rate is assumed to be the same as the present level as long as the reserve fund remains. After it vanishes around the year 2000, the rate is assumed to be determined on a strict pay-as-you-go basis.

8. This estimate was submitted to the Budget Committee of the House of Representatives on March 10, 1988.

9. A tax on income applies to both consumption and saving. Thus, if 1.0 unit of income tax is imposed and the propensity to consume is, say, 0.7, tax on consumption is 0.7 and tax on saving is 0.3. A consumption tax, however, applies only to consumption. It follows that if a revenue-neutral tax reform reduces the amount of income tax and replaces it with a consumption tax, taxation of consumption rises by 0.3, and consumption will decline over the short term.

10. Noguchi (1988) estimates that the effective property tax rate in the Tokyo metropolitan area has fallen by as much as 48 percent.

11. An important reason for the confusion is that most salaried workers are not very knowledgeable about the tax system. Because their taxes were withheld at the source and deduction of actual expenses are not admitted, they have no incentive to study the tax system.

Misunderstandings also arose because of a lack of detailed explanation by the government. Deliberations on a broadly based consumption tax began in earnest only after the LDP's landslide victory in the July 1986 election. The LDP Tax Council established the detailed structure of the new tax in late 1986 and failed to adequately explain to the public how the tax would work. If the details of the tax had been made clear before the submission of the reform bill, the attitudes of journalists, labor unions, and the general public might have been different.

References

Ando, Albert, and Alan J. Auerbach. 1988. "The Cost of Capital in the United States and Japan: A Comparison." *Journal of the Japanese and International Economies* 2, no. 2 (June): 134–58.

Economic Planning Agency. 1982. *2000 nen no Nihon* (Japan in the year 2000). Tokyo: Government Printing Bureau.

Fujita, Sei. 1986. "Ogata Shohizei Donyu ha Fukushi Mokutekizei de" (The new consumption tax should be earmarked for welfare). *Ekonomisuto* (Sept. 30).

Hatta, Tatsuo. 1988. "Shingata Kaisetsuzei ha Hontoni Hitsuyo ka" (Is the new indirect tax really necessary?). *Keizai Seminor*, no. 401 (June): 54–59.

Honma, Masaaki. 1986a. "Nenshu 500 Manen ika ha Zozei ni" (Burden is increased for annual income under 5 million yen). *Ekonomisuto* (Oct. 7).

———. 1986b. *Zeisei Kaikaku no Simulation* (A simulation of tax reform). Tokyo: Seisaku Koso Forum.

Honma, Masaaki, Toshihiro Ihori, Masumi Atoda, and Junki Murayama. 1984. "Shotokuzei Futan no Gyoshukan Kakusa" (Interoccupational inequality of income tax burden). *Kikan Gendai Keizai*, no. 59: 14–25.

Honma, Masaaki, Masumi Atoda, Fumio Hayashi, and Kuniaki Hata. 1984. "Setsubi Toshi to Kigyo Zeisei" (Business fixed investment and corporate taxation). *Keizai Bunseki*, no. 41.

Honma, Masaaki, and Masumi Atoda. 1987. "Genzeikan ni toboshii Seifu Zeisei Kaikakuan" (Insufficient reduction in burden in government tax reform). *Ekonomisuto* (Feb. 23).

Honma, Masaaki, and Sin Saito. 1987. "Zeisei Kaikaku no Shoten" (The focal point of tax reform). *Keizai Seminor*, no. 384.

Ishi, Hiromitsu. 1979. *Sozei Seisaku no Koka* (Effects of tax policies). Tokyo: Toyo Keizai Shinposha.

———. 1984. *Zaisei Kaikaku no Ronri* (The logics of fiscal reconstruction). Tokyo: Nihon Keizai Shinbunsha.

Itaba, Yasuo, and Toshiaki Tachibanaki. 1987. "Measurement of Tax Progressivity When the Forms of Both Income Distribution and Tax Function Are Given." *The Economic Studies Quarterly* 38, no. 2: 97–106.

Iwata, Kazumasa, Ikuo Suzuki, and Atsushi Yoshida. 1986. "Zeisei to Kokusai Kyocho" (Tax system and international harmony). *ESP*, no. 170.

———. 1987. "Setsubi Toshi no Shihonkosuto to Zeisei" (Cost of capital and the tax system). *Keizai Bunseki*, no. 107.

Japan. Ad Hoc Council on Administrative Reform. 1981. *The First Report on Administrative Reform*. Tokyo: July 10.

———. Maekawa Committee. 1986. *The Report of a Committee for Adjustment of Economic Structure for International Harmony* (in Japanese; English translation available). Tokyo: April 7.

———. Special Committee for Adjustment of Economic Structure. 1987. *The Report of a Special Committee for Adjustment of Economic Structure* (in Japanese; English translation available). Tokyo: April 23.

————. Tax Council. 1986a. *Zeisei no Bapponteki Minaoshi nitsuiteno Toshin* (A report on fundamental tax reform). Tokyo: October 28.

————. 1986b. *Zeisei no Bapponteki Minaoshi nitsuiteno Toshin, Hokoku, Shingishiryo Soran* (Reports, memorandum, and discussion materials on fundamental tax reform). Tokyo: October.

————. 1988a. *Zeisei Kaikaku nitsuiteno Soan* (A draft for tax reform). Tokyo: March 25.

————. 1988b. *Zeisei Kaikakuan nitsuiteno Chukan Toshin* (An interim report of tax reform). Tokyo: April 28.

————. 1988c. *Zeisei no Bapponteki Kaikaku Taiko* (An outline of fundamental tax reform). Tokyo: April 7.

Kaizuka, Keimei. 1987. "Zeisei Kaikakuron" (Tax reform debates). *Keizaigakuronshu* 53, no. 2 (July): 14–24.

Keidanren Jimukyoku. 1985. "Wagakuni Kigyo no Zeifutan o Megutte" (On the tax burden of Japanese corporations). *Keidanren Geppo* (November).

King, Mervyn A., and Don Fullerton. 1984. *The Taxation of Income from Capital.* Chicago: University of Chicago Press.

LDP Tax Council. 1986. *Zeisei Kaikaku no Kihonhoko* (The basic direction of tax reform). Tokyo: LDP Tax Council, Dec. 5.

Miyajima, Hiroshi. 1985. "Nanten Ooi Fukakachizei Donyu" (Many problems of VAT). *Ekonomisuto* (Nov. 12).

————. 1986. *Sozeiron no Tenkai to Nihon no Zeisei* (Tax theory and the Japanese tax system). Tokyo: Nihon Hyoronsha.

————. 1987. "Tax Reform Gone Awry." *Japan Echo* 14, no. 2.

Nagano, Atsushi. 1987. "Japan." In *World Tax Reform: A Progress Report*, edited by Joseph A. Pechman, 155–62. Washington, D.C.: The Brookings Institution.

Nakatani, Iwo. 1985. "Tax Summit no Teisho" (A proposal for a tax summit). *Toyo Keizai Kindai Keizaigaku* series no. 72 (May).

————. 1987. *Borderless Economy* (in Japanese). Tokyo: Nihon Keizai Shinbunsha.

Noguchi, Yukio. 1980. *Zaiseikiki no Kozo* (The structure of fiscal crisis). Tokyo: Toyo Keizai Shinposha.

————. 1982. "The Government-Business Relationship in Japan: The Changing Role of Fiscal Resources." In *Policy and Trade Issues of the Japanese Economy: American and Japanese Perspectives*, edited by K. Yamamura. Seattle: University of Washington Press.

————. 1983. "The Failure of Government to Perform Its Proper Task: A Case Study of Japan." *ORDO* Band 34: 59–70.

————. 1985a. "Failings of the Income Tax." *Japan Echo* 14, no. 1.

————. 1985b. "Japan's Warped Tax Structure." *Japan Echo* 14, no. 4.

————. 1985c. "Nihon Kigyo no Zeifutan" (Tax burden of Japanese firms). *Kikan Gendai Keizai*, 61 (Spring).

————. 1985d. "Tax Structure and Saving-Investment Balance." *Hitotsubashi Journal of Economics* 26, no. 1 (June).

————. 1986a. "Overcommitment in Pensions: The Japanese Experience." In *The Welfare State East and West*, edited by Richard Rose and Rei Shiratori. Oxford: Oxford University Press.

————. 1986b. *Zeiseikaikaku no Koso* (A plan for the tax reform). Tokyo: Toyo Keizai Shinposha.

————. 1987a. "In Defence of the Sales Tax." *Japan Echo* 14, no. 2 (Summer).

———. 1987b. "Koteki Nenkin no Shorai to Nihon Keizai no taigai performance" (Future of public pensions and external performance of the Japanese economy). *Financial Review*, no. 5 (June).

———. 1987c. "Public Finance." In *The Political Economy of Japan, Volume 1, The Domestic Transformation*, edited by Kozo Yamamura and Yasukichi Yasuba. Stanford: Stanford University Press.

———. 1987d. "Tax Reform: The Missing Rationale. " *Japan Echo* 14, no. 1 (Spring).

———. 1988. "Koteishisanzei Sozokuzei no Keigen ha Hokochigai da" (Property tax and inheritance tax should be strengthened). *Ekonomisuto* (Jan. 26).

Shoven, John B., and Toshiaki Tachibanaki. 1988. "The Taxation of Income from Capital in Japan." In *Government Policy Towards Industry in the U.S.A. and Japan*, edited by John B. Shoven. Cambridge: Cambridge University Press.

Tachibanaki, Toshiaki. 1981. "A Note on the Impact of Tax on Income Redistribution." *The Review of Income and Wealth*, series 27, no. 3: 327–32.

Tajika, Eiji, and Yuji Yui. 1988. "Shihon Kosuto to Hojin Jikko Zeiritsu" (Cost of capital and effective rate of corporate income tax). *Keizai Kenkyu* 39, no. 2: 118–28.

Takenaka, Heizo. 1984. *Kenkyu Kaihatsu to Setsubi Toshi no Keizaigaku* (Economics of R&D and business fixed investment). Tokyo: Toyo Keizai Shinposha.

Chapter 8   Ingemar Hansson and Charles Stuart, "Sweden: Tax Reform in a High-Tax Environment"

Notes

1. We noted above that spending on public goods amounts to about 10 percent of GDP and that redistributional spending amounts to about 50 percent of GDP, implying total spending of about 60 percent of GDP. This spending is financed mainly by taxes, amounting in 1989 to about 56 percent of GDP, and by nontax receipts including certain fees.

2. The reader may note than this 73.2 figure, which is reported in Hansson (1986: 88), differs from the marginal tax rate reported in Table 8.1 of 76.4 percent in 1978. The rates reported in Table 8.1 are somewhat cruder, being calculated from available comparable international statistics.

3. Further discussion of some of the problems that have arisen in Sweden due to high taxes is in Lindbeck (1988).

4. Interestingly, a large increase in the size of the underground economy does *not* seem to have occurred. Available evidence suggests that unreported taxable income has been essentially constant in recent decades in Sweden and may amount to 4.5–7 percent of GDP, which is on a par with levels in other developed countries.

5. Because business-cycle improvements have tended to raise aggregate labor since 1982, one should not conclude from Figure 8.2 that there are no lags between tax changes and the response of labor.

6. Academic criticism of the corporation income tax in Sweden and advocacy of a shift to a cash-flow tax for corporations appears in Södersten and Ysander (1984) and Calmfors et al. (1986).

7. During the period 1982–1987, profits have been relatively high, so many corporations have exhausted their options for postponing tax payments. Such corporations must report taxable profits in excess of what is required for dividend

payments, which weakens the tendency for the corporation tax to resemble a cash-flow tax. In any case, receipts from the corporation tax amount to less than 2 percent of GDP, which is low by international standards.

References

Blueprints for Basic Tax Reform. 1977. Washington, D.C.: U.S. Government Printing Office.

Calmfors, L., I. Hansson, L. Jonung, J. Myhrman, and H. Söderström. 1986. *Nya spelregler for tillväxt* (New rules of the game for growth). Stockholm: SNS Förlag.

Hansson, I. 1986. *Skatter och samhällsekonomi* (The economics of taxation). Stockholm: SNS Förlag.

Hansson, I., and C. Stuart. 1988. "Why Are Taxes So High in Sweden?" Mimeo.

Kanniainen, V. 1988. "Corporate Taxation and Investment Behavior: The Nordic View." Mimeo.

Lindbeck, A. 1988. "Individual Freedom and Welfare State Policy." *European Economic Review* 32: 295–318.

Meade, J. 1978. *The Structure and Reform of Direct Taxation.* London: George Allen & Unwin Ltd. for the Institute of Fiscal Studies.

Normann, G. 1983. *Skatter och inflation* (Taxes and inflation). Stockholm: Allmänna Förlaget.

Rivlin, A., ed. 1986. *Den svenska ekonomins framtidsutsikter* (The Swedish economy: Prospects for the future). Stockholm: SNS Förlag.

Södersten, J., and B. C. Ysander. 1984. "Bolagsskattens verkningar" (Effects of the corporation income tax). *Ekonomisk Debatt.* no. 8.

Sweden. 1976. *Progressiv utgiftsskatt* (Progressive expenditure tax). SOU (Public Report) 1976:62. Stockholm: Allmänna Förlaget.

———. 1986. *Utgiftsskatt* (Expenditure tax). SOU (Public Report) 1986:40. Stockholm: Allmänna Förlaget.

Chapter 9   Andrew W. Dilnot and J. A. Kay, "Tax Reform in the United Kingdom: The Recent Experience"

References

Blinder, A. S., and H. S. Rosen. 1985. "Notches." *American Economic Review* 75, no. 4: 736–47.

Devereux, M. P. 1988. "Corporation Tax: The Effect of the 1984 Reform on the Incentive to Invest." *Fiscal Studies* 9, no. 1: 62–79.

Dilnot, A. W., J. A. Kay, and C. N. Morris. 1983. "The U.K. Tax System, Structure and Progressivity, 1948–1982." *Scandinavian Journal of Economics* 86: 150–65.

Hills, J. 1984. *Savings and Fiscal Privilege.* Report series no. 9. London: Institute for Fiscal Studies.

Inland Revenue. Various years. *Inland Revenue Statistics.* London: Her Majesty's Stationery Office.

Lawson, Nigel. 1988. "Tax Reform: The Government Record." London: Conservative Party Research Department.

Sabine, B. E. V. 1966. *A History of Income Tax*. London: George Allen and Unwin.

Saunders, M. H., and S. J. Webb. 1988. "Fiscal Privilege and Financial Assets: Some Distributional Effects," *Fiscal Studies* 9, no. 4: 51–69.

Symons, E., and I. Walker. 1986. "The Reform of Personal Taxation: A Brief Analysis." *Fiscal Studies* 7, no. 2: 38–47.

United Kingdom. 1988. Financial Statement and Budget Report 1988–89. London: Her Majesty's Stationery Office.

———. Parliament. 1976. *Local Government Finance: Report of the Committee of Enquiry* Cmnd. 6453. London: Her Majesty's Stationery Office.

———. Parliament. 1980. *The Taxation of Husband and Wife*. Cmnd. 8093. London: Her Majesty's Stationery Office.

———. Parliament. 1981. *Alternatives to Domestic Rates*. Cmnd. 8449. London: Her Majesty's Stationery Office.

———. Parliament. 1982. *Corporation Tax Green Paper*. Cmnd. 8456. London: Her Majesty's Stationery Office.

———. Parliament. 1985a. *Reform of Social Security*. Cmnd. 9517. London: Her Majesty's Stationery Office.

———. Parliament. 1985b. *Reform of Social Security: Programme for Action*. Cmnd. 9691. London: Her Majesty's Stationery Office.

———. Parliament. 1986a. *Paying for Local Government*. Cmnd. 9714. London: Her Majesty's Stationery Office.

———. Parliament. 1986b. *The Reform of Personal Taxation*. Cmnd. 9756. London: Her Majesty's Stationery Office.

Chapter 10   John B. Shoven, "The U.S. Tax Reform of 1986: Is It Worth Copying?"

Notes

1. For those not familiar with the conventional American grading system, an A grade indicates outstanding work; B, good; C, fair; D, poor; and F, failing.

2. Treasury I refers to the Treasury Department's initial 1984 proposal to the president contained in the three volumes entitled *Tax Reform for Fairness, Simplicity, and Economic Growth: The Treasury Department Report to the President*. Treasury II refers to the president's proposal presented to Congress contained in *The President's Tax Proposals to the Congress for Fairness, Growth, and Simplicity*, May 1985.

3. It certainly is true that the social security surplus contributes to national saving. My point is that the burden of the foreseeable baby boom retirements should cause us to save more (an above normal amount). This seems best facilitated by having that saving accrue in a separate account.

4. These efficiency gain estimates are very sensitive to the openness of international capital markets and the tax rules that apply to foreign capital income.

References

Aaron, Henry J. 1987. "The Impossible Dream Comes True." in *Tax Reform and the U.S. Economy*, edited by Joseph Pechman, 10–30. Washington, D.C.: Brookings Institution.

Auerbach, Alan J. 1987. "The Tax Reform Act of 1986 and the Cost of Capital." *Journal of Economic Perspectives* 1, no. 1 (Summer): 73–86.

Auerbach, Alan J., and Laurence J. Kotlikoff. 1987. "Evaluating Fiscal Policy with a Dynamic Simulation Model." *The American Economic Review* 77, no. 2 (May): 49–55.

Ballard, Charles L., Don Fullerton, John B. Shoven, and John Whalley. 1985. *A General Equilibrium Model for Tax Policy Evaluation.* Chicago: University of Chicago Press.

Ballard, Charles L., John Karl Scholz, and John B. Shoven. 1987. "The Value-Added Tax: A General Equilibrium Look at Its Efficiency and Incidence." In *The Effects of Taxation on Capital Accumulation*, edited by Martin Feldstein, 445–80. Chicago: University of Chicago Press.

Bernheim, B. Douglas, and John B. Shoven. 1987. "Taxation and the Cost of Capital: An International Comparison." In *The Consumption Tax: A Better Alternative?* edited by Charles E. Walker and Mark A. Bloomfield. Cambridge, Mass.: Ballinger Publishing Co. for the American Council for Capital Formation.

Bradford, David F. 1986. *Untangling the Income Tax.* Cambridge, Mass.: Harvard University Press.

Bradford, David F., and the U.S. Treasury Tax Policy Staff. 1984. *Blueprints for Basic Tax Reform.* Arlington, Va.: Tax Analysts.

Deloitte, Haskins, and Sells. 1986. "The Tax Revolution: A New Era Begins." Washington, D.C.

Feldstein, Martin S., and Joel Slemrod, 1978. "How Inflation Distorts the Taxation of Capital Gains." *Harvard Business Review* (September/October): 20–22.

Fullerton, Don, Robert Gillette, and James Mackie. 1987. "Investment Incentives under the Tax Reform Act of 1986." *Compendium of Tax Research 1987.* Washington D.C.: Office of Tax Analysis, Department of the Treasury.

Fullerton, Don, Yolanda K. Henderson, and James Mackie. 1987. "Investment Allocation and Growth under the Tax Reform Act of 1986." *Compendium of Tax Research 1987.* Washington D.C.: Office of Tax Analysis, Department of the Treasury.

Gravelle, Jane G. 1987. "Efficiency Gains from Capital Reallocation in the Tax Reform Act of 1986." Paper presented to the American Economic Association annual meeting, Chicago, December 28–30.

Hendershott, Patric H. 1988. "The Tax Reform Act of 1986 and Economic Growth." National Bureau of Economic Research Working Paper no. 2553. Cambridge, Mass.

King, Mervyn. 1987. "The Japanese Tax Reform Proposals." London School of Economics. Mimeo.

McLure, Charles E., Jr. 1986. "Where Tax Reform Went Astray." *Villanova Law Review* 31, no. 6: 1619–63.

———. 1987. "US Tax Reform." *Australian Tax Forum* 4, no. 3: 293–312.

———. 1988. "The 1986 Act: Tax Reform's Finest Hour or Death Throes of the Income Tax?" *National Tax Journal* 41, no. 3 (September): 303–15.

Prentice-Hall. 1986. *A Complete Guide to the Tax Reform Act of 1986.* Paramus, N.J.: Prentice-Hall.

Shoven, John B., and Toshiaki Tachibanaki. 1988. "The Taxation of Income from Capital in Japan." In *Government Policy Towards Industry in the United States and Japan*, edited by John B. Shoven, 51–96. Cambridge: Cambridge University Press.

Steuerle, Eugene. 1987. "Effects on Financial Decisionmaking." *Tax Reform and the U.S. Economy*, edited by Joseph Pechman, 55–70. Washington, D.C.: Brookings Institution.

Summers, Lawrence H. 1987a. "Should Tax Reform Level the Playing Field?" NBER Working Paper no. 2132. Cambridge, Mass.: National Bureau of Economic Research.

———. 1987b. "Reforming Tax Reform for Growth and Competitiveness." Harvard University. Mimeo.

U.S. Department of the Treasury. 1984. *Tax Reform for Fairness, Simplicity, and Economic Growth: The Treasury Department Report to the President*, vol. 2. Washington, D.C.

U.S. Office of the President. 1985. *The President's Tax Proposals to the Congress for Fairness, Growth, and Simplicity*. Washington, D.C. (May).

Venti, Steven F., and David A. Wise. 1988. "The Determinants of IRA Contributions and the Effect of Limit Changes." In *Pensions in the U.S. Economy*, edited by Zvi Bodie, John B. Shoven, and David A. Wise, 9–52. Chicago: University of Chicago Press.

Chapter 11   Roger H. Gordon, "Economic Reform in the People's Republic of China, 1979–1988"

Notes

1. University students and faculty were one key group whose real income fell quickly.

2. A commonly heard statement is that China, at least until recently, did not even have taxes. Certainly, calling a transfer a tax indicates that the taxed individual or organization has a claim to the income being taxed, whereas the traditional view in China is that the government has the sole claim to resources, which it may then allocate to particular individuals or firms.

3. Definitions of both revenue and national income, as used in the Chinese accounting system, differ from the Western definitions. For example, reported revenue consists largely of transfers from state-owned enterprises, so is net of subsidies to cover losses. National income excludes what the Chinese refer to as "nonproductive" activities, principally services and government.

4. Several Chinese sources have given me unpublished figures for the deficit which are much larger than the published figures.

5. After the first few years, these crops could be purchased from other farmers, then resold to the government.

6. On occasion, the procurement price went above the market price, leading to substantial revenue costs to the government. Sicular (1988) argues that signing a contract to sell to the government has been attractive in part because the contract commits the government to a price at the beginning of the growing season, eliminating any risk to the farmer from price fluctuations.

7. The national tax rate varied between 0 percent and 25 percent by region, with a local surtax as high as 30 percent of the base tax. See People's Republic of China (1987b).

8. This limit on the sales price seems to restrict severely the turnover of land, however. This is particularly a problem since in 1979, to avoid inequities in the assignment of land, land of *each* quality and type in a given district was divided among the families living in the district, resulting in small dispersed holdings.

9. These transactions reduce urban consumption of grain, and are an efficiency gain since the cost of producing the grain exceeds the amount urban residents charge

to forgo consumption of the grain. This occurrence indicates that grain supplies are larger than would occur in a free market.

10. To help counterbalance these heavy tax rates, new community enterprises and new products produced by existing community enterprises were normally tax-exempt for two or three years, though this was reduced to one year in 1985. It has been fairly easy to close and reopen a firm and so qualify for a renewed exemption period. In practice, however, most firms do face very high tax rates.

11. Tax revenue is shared between various levels of government based on rules that vary by region. In general, the bulk of the revenue is retained by the level of government that set up the firm.

12. Of course, local governments may base their decisions on quite limited information, since local firms will generally wish to describe themselves in the way most likely to generate further financial support.

13. Other objectives for local governments that I have heard proposed include increasing employment, growth, or tax revenue. Attempting to increase any of these measures is not inconsistent per se with an objective of maximizing welfare of local residents. For example, firms normally have to pay workers more than their marginal product, implying that their desired employment level is inefficiently small. The local government would want to remedy this. Since local residents face a very low incentive to save, because of the regulated interest rate, the local government also has an incentive to intervene and increase the savings rate. Finally, since local governments have little flexibility in obtaining tax revenue, public expenditures can easily be too small, implying a desire to find additional sources of tax revenue.

14. For example, each division might be rewarded based on its accounting profits, with the division's accounting profits being reduced by some given opportunity cost of funds when it undertakes new investments. Note that the division may end up keeping only a small fraction of the profits it generates and financing most of its new investments with funds transferred from the central organization—the relationship between divisions and the central management within a Western firm are in principle very similar to the relationship between Chinese community enterprises and the local government.

15. After the military crackdown in June 1989, many private enterprises were closed.

16. Given the almost complete lack of capital flows between firms, this policy leads to new investments being concentrated in the most profitable firms rather than in the most profitable new projects.

17. Worker benefits include housing, medical care, education for children of workers, recreational facilities, and related goods. These goods are typically allocated more equally than wage payments.

18. Loans could in principle cover 70 percent to 90 percent of the cost of new investments.

19. In addition, half of the depreciation reserves had to be paid to the government.

20. If the return from new investments were not subject to tax, then in making investment decisions the firm would compare the present value of returns from a dollar of new investment, denoted by V, with the present value of the costs incurred from borrowing a dollar from the bank, denoted by D. (At market interest rates, the present value of these costs would equal a dollar, but the reduced interest rate lowers the net cost.) The firm would be willing to invest as long as $V \geq D$. Under the existing tax system, if the firm's tax rate is t, then the net after-tax value to the firm of the

returns to the project would equal $(1 - t)V$. Since *all* repayments on loans are deductible, the costs of the debt repayments would equal $(1 - t)D$. In addition, the firm can depreciate the new investment, saving taxes whose present value is denoted by tz, but half of the depreciation reserves must be paid to the government, costing the firm $.5z$. On net, the new project is attractive as long as $(1 - t)V \geq (1 - t)D - (t - .5)z$, or as long as $V \geq D - (t - .5)z/(1 - t)$. It follows that the tax system makes the new investment slightly more attractive since $t > .5$. The increased attractiveness arises from a net loss in tax revenue to the government from new marginal investments.

21. Auditing is made particularly difficult by the wide variety of prices that might plausibly have been paid for inputs or received on outputs.

22. Several other experimental systems have been tried on a much smaller scale.

23. Profits in the initial year of the contract were forecasted based primarily on actual profits earned during the previous three years. Profits were then expected to grow at a negotiated percentage rate each year.

24. These contracts are typically for five years. Although a variety of forms of contracts exist, I describe a particular example known as "two guarantees and one link." Some of the details come from the contract of a specific manufacturing firm in Beijing where I conducted lengthy interviews and are of unknown generality. Another common contract, known as "one guarantee and fixed sharing," does not have the guarantee on investment but is otherwise very similar. Since these contracts vary by firm, there is substantial pressure to use legal or illegal means to obtain a more favorable contract.

25. The procedure for calculating these rates is quite complicated; the numbers reported in the text are only illustrative. Technically, the tax rate on net profits in the first interval equals 45.4 percent, and 35.1 percent in the second interval. However, when profits increase, as measured using the original wage payments, deductible wage payments are also allowed to rise, lowering net profits. Formally, the allowed percentage increase in wage payments equals 0.75 times the percentage increase in the sum of net profits and sales tax payments. In the calculations reported in the text, I assumed that wage payments were one-third the size of net profits plus sales tax payments, and assumed that the hypothesized increase in profits arose from reduced costs with no change in sales. If sales also rose, the effective tax rates would be slightly lower.

26. Payroll is also tied to sales revenue.

27. For example, in the one contract examined closely, an extra yuan in pre-tax profits above the initial amount forecasted resulted in about .20 yuan in extra wage payments, .363 yuan in extra taxes, .27 yuan in extra investment, and .167 yuan in extra worker benefits.

28. New workers, however, are now generally hired on a five-year contract, at the firm's initiative, giving the firm much more flexibility.

29. A related outcome is observed in unionized compared with nonunionized firms in the United States.

30. This form of welfare system undoubtedly discourages the development of alternative jobs in the private or collective sector, because of the attractiveness of keeping or waiting to get a relatively highly paid job in the state sector. Given the nature of the government oversight, state-owned enterprises do not have the flexibility to expand into other areas of production to make better use of extra workers.

31. Often, however, these subsidies to inputs are tied to a cheap sales price for the output.

32. If the price were being set by that governmental unit supervising the demander rather than the supplier of the product, the price chosen would normally be lower. To what degree these prices are higher than would occur in a competitive market is unclear since most inputs are likewise not priced competitively; since accounting costs for capital do not appropriately reflect capital's opportunity cost, for essentially the same reasons as exist in the accounts for Western firms; and since a sizable component of payments to workers is not included in accounting costs.

33. As has been shown in studies of the Yugoslavian economy, maximizing worker welfare can lead to quite different behavior than occurs when share values are maximized. In particular, since the future return from previous investments cannot be sold by a worker at retirement, investment incentives can be much reduced. In addition, firms will be reluctant to take on new workers, since the return from previous investments must be shared with these workers. It is common in China, however, for firms to hire the children of existing workers, an observation that is also consistent with the idea that the firm's objective is the maximization of worker welfare.

34. The government has had little ability to enforce its restriction that at least a given fraction of retained earnings be used for new investment. As a result, the government initially enacted a very high tax on bonus payments in excess of a third of a year's wage payments, in order to limit this use of retained earnings. Later, it explicitly specified investment expenditures and wage and bonus payments under the contract.

35. With the drop in the marginal tax rate under the contract system, debt-financed investments are now slightly taxed on net.

36. This is the same incentive faced by firms in Yugoslavia.

37. Bribery also seems to have become common, though obviously there are no statistics on its importance.

38. Banks also face a soft budget constraint, dampening their incentives to cut off funding of firms nearing bankruptcy.

39. For the case of the firm described above, a yuan of extra profits results in an immediate tax increase of 0.363 yuan. In addition, forecasted profits increase by 0.33 yuan, implying extra taxes during the five years under the next contract of at least 0.695×0.33 yuan = 0.23 yuan each year, assuming no forecasted growth in profits. For reasonable discount rates, the total increase in the present value of taxes exceeds the dollar increase in profits. If future profits were forecasted instead based on actual profits during the previous five years, then the effective marginal tax rate would be virtually 100 percent throughout the five years of the existing contracts.

40. At the end of the current contracts, the government would face the temptation to further raise the tax rate on forecasted profits and lower the tax rate on extra profits, in order to create the incentive to undertake new investments. This temptation has been referred to in the U.S. economics literature as the "time inconsistency" of government policy.

41. Either a personal income tax or a destination-type sales tax or VAT could be used to tax consumption within the jurisdiction.

42. Given the low interest rate available on financial savings, however, and the heavy taxation of investments in collectives, investments in other areas, particularly in housing and consumer durables, have undoubtedly been inefficiently large.

43. Individuals can in principle use their savings to help finance a new private or collective business, though this has not been very common in urban areas due to the attractiveness of jobs in state-owned enterprises.

44. This has occasionally led students to drop out of university in order to have the right to seek their own job.

45. See Naughton (1988) for further discussion.

46. In both cases the lack of a market-clearing interest rate was probably an important cause of the difficulties.

References

China Statistics Bureau. 1987a. *China Employment and Wage Statistics, 1949–1985.* Beijing: China Statistics Press.

———. 1987b. *China Fixed Assets Investment Statistics, 1950–1985.* Beijing: China Statistics Press.

———. 1986 and 1988a. *China Rural Statistics, 1985–1987.* Beijing: China Statistics Press.

———. 1982, 1985, and 1988b. *China Statistics Yearbook, 1981, 1984,* and *1987.* Beijing: China Statistics Press.

International Monetary Fund. 1979–1988. *International Finance Statistics.* Washington, D.C.

Naughton, Barry. 1988. "Industrial Decision-Making in China." Mimeo.

People's Republic of China. Ministry of Finance. 1987a. *China Finance Statistics, 1950–1985.* Beijing: China Finance and Economics Press.

———. 1987b. *PRC Finance and Tax Laws.* Beijing: China Finance and Economics Press.

Sicular, Terry. 1988. "Plan and Market in China's Agricultural Commerce." *Journal of Political Economy* 96: 283–307.

Chapter 12   Charles E. McLure, Jr., "Tax Reform in an Inflationary Environment: The Case of Colombia"

Notes

1. For surveys of the history of such efforts, see Lent (1975, 1976), Tanzi (1976), and *Adjustments for Tax Purposes* (1984).

2. For a description of this process in several Latin American countries, see *Adjustments for Tax Purposes* (1984).

3. The historical material in this study draws heavily on Perry and Cárdenas (1986), McLure (1989a), and Thirsk (1988), which also discuss aspects of Colombian tax reform other than inflation adjustment.

4. For further discussion, see Aaron (1976b).

5. The choice of the proper price index to use for this purpose is beyond the scope of this paper; see, however, the papers in Aaron (1976a) and McLure, Mutti, Thuronyi, and Zodrow (1988: ch. 7).

6. The primary inconvenience would seem to be caused by the fact that inflation adjustment would generally produce numbers that are not multiples of tens, hundreds, or thousands of the local unit of currency; this can easily be avoided, with little loss of the benefits of indexation, through a statutory provision for rounding.

7. For further discussion, see McLure, Mutti, Thuronyi, and Zodrow (1988: ch. 7). The reader should note that the version of the 1988 report published by Duke

University Press in 1989 contains an eleventh chapter not found in the 1988 version published by the government of Colombia, a "postscript" written in early 1989 that describes and evaluates the 1988 reforms. References to the "1988" version in what follows are equally applicable to the 1989 Duke University Press version; references to the "1989" version apply only to that version.

8. *Adjustments for Tax Purposes* (1984) and Massone (1981a, 1981b) describe this evolutionary process in several Latin American countries.

9. On June 20, 1989, the net wealth tax was eliminated, effective on the date of introduction of the integrated system of inflation adjustment described below in the section entitled "The Government's Response to the 1988 Report." Little attempt has been made to reflect this important change in the present paper, which was completed several months earlier. Since Colombia continues to utilize a presumptive income tax based on net wealth, most of the discussion of the importance of the measurement of net wealth remains relevant.

10. A third study of the tax system of Colombia by an individual scholar, Bird (1970), has also been influential in affecting tax policy in Colombia. Bird (pp. 68–69 and 84–85) argued against inflation adjustment for both capital gains and depreciation allowances, despite having stated that, "Important as some of the reforms discussed in the remainder of this chapter are, none is more important than 'inflation-proofing' the income tax." Interestingly enough, what Bird had in mind was the need to avoid delays in collection of taxes, which caused considerable erosion of the real value of tax collections and thus fiscal difficulties any time there was an acceleration of inflation, as well as necessitating higher tax rates in a time of high but stable inflation. Of course, while the fiscal problems caused by collection lags are aggravated by inflation, they have nothing to do with inflation adjustment of the tax system, per se; they are not considered here.

11. It appears that 100 percent declining-balance depreciation was also an option; of course, it is less generous than straight-line depreciation.

12. Further discussion occurs in *Fiscal Survey of Colombia* (1965: 263–67). Note that no distinction is made between replacement cost depreciation and depreciation based on inflation-adjusted basis. For a discussion of this important distinction, see McLure, Mutti, Thuronyi, and Zodrow (1988: ch. 7).

13. The report continued, "This is especially true of making an adjustment for a devaluation, for any adjustment, in effect, serves to defeat the basic purpose of the devaluation."

14. In contrast to the blurred vision of the Taylor mission, the Musgrave report (Musgrave and Gillis 1971: 71) makes the distinction between indexing nominal amounts and inflation adjustment in the measurement of income quite clearly: "In comparing a nominal capital gain due to price rise with a nominal increase in other (say, wage) income due to price rise, we note that inclusion of the latter in the tax base results in an inequity only to the extent that the taxpayer is moved into a higher tax bracket. In the case of capital gains, failure to make an inflation adjustment impairs a taxpayer's net wealth." On the issue of indexing capital gains, see also White and Quale (1971: 364–70).

15. See also the brief discussion in the staff paper by Slitor (1971: 480–81). In contrast to the Taylor report, the Musgrave mission explicitly distinguished between replacement cost depreciation and general revaluation of assets.

16. For further description, see Perry and Cárdenas (1986), Gillis and McLure (1975, 1977), McLure (1989a), and Thirsk (1988).

17. Perry was director general of Internal Taxes at the time of the 1974 reforms.

18. This system is described in greater detail in McLure, Mutti, Thuronyi, and Zodrow (1988: chs. 3 and 7).

19. For a somewhat more complete discussion of these concerns, including quotations by Colombian observers and public officials, see McLure, Mutti, Thuronyi, and Zodrow (1988: ch. 7).

20. For a more complete discussion of the mechanics and rationale of this system, see McLure, Mutti, Thuronyi, and Zodrow (1988: Appendix to ch. 7). Harberger (1982, 1988) contains a more condensed description of the calculation of taxable income under this approach.

21. This judgment is echoed in the following assessment by Massone (1981b: 60):

> It is worthwhile to point out that some countries first used partial adjustment measures and then shifted to a global or intermediary system. . . . Those countries which introduced the global system earlier . . . underwent several years of experience with it and then introduced a complete adjustment system.

> This kind of experience, where simpler methods are first used and then more accurate methods are introduced, should be taken into account by those countries which are considering the introduction of adjustment methods. Under this approach, the tax administration, tax advisers and taxpayers gradually become acquainted with the adjustment techniques.

> . . . Although the complete method is not so excessively complex as to exclude its introduction, its widespread use by taxpayers demands a period of development, spreading and training because in most developing countries it is known to a few experts only.

> Even in those countries where the integral adjustment method is better known there are issues for which an agreement has not been reached or which are still being discussed. It is therefore inconvenient to introduce directly integral methods in countries where adjustment is just beginning to be used. In these countries the complete adjustment can be a final target to be reached gradually after going through partial and intermediary levels of adjustment.

22. Chile adopted the basic system of inflation adjustment still in effect in 1974, after "a gradual evolution extending over more than four decades" (Casanegra 1984: 25). After running at an annual rate of 17 to 35 percent during the period from 1965 to 1971, inclusive, Chile's inflation rate, as measured by the percentage change in the consumer price index (CPI), during the five-year period from 1972 to 1976 was 163.4, 508.1, 375.9, 340.7, and 174.3 (Casanegra 1984: 100). These figures are well above the rates of inflation experienced recently in Colombia, as reported in Table 12.1. Massone (1981a: 4) notes:

> It is not, therefore, surprising that Chile was . . . a leading country in introducing measures to adjust law and taxation for inflation and to shift from partial adjustment of income to more sophisticated methods, namely the global adjustment and the integral adjustment.

The following similar assessment has been given by Casanegra (1984: 28):

The new revaluation scheme . . . was enacted in late 1974 during a period of hyperinflation, when only a fully comprehensive system could be expected to correct grossly unrealistic income statements. Moreover, the lengthy previous experience with less comprehensive systems had shown that they gave rise to a host of administrative problems and inequities.

23. The SAT is patterned after the tax proposed in Hall and Rabushka (1983, 1985) and Bradford (1987). The 1988 report actually considers two alternative consumption-based taxes. The second, involving the more familiar cash-flow tax on individuals, is rejected in favor of the SAT for administrative reasons; see McLure, Mutti, Thuronyi, and Zodrow (1988: ch. 9), or Zodrow and McLure (1988).

24. See McLure, Mutti, Thuronyi, and Zodrow (1988). For a more complete discussion of these problems, see McLure (1988, 1989b).

25. For further development of this theme, see McLure (1989c).

26. For further discussion, see McLure, Mutti, Thuronyi, and Zodrow (1988), chapter 9, or Zodrow and McLure (1988).

27. The two laws dealing with inflation adjustment are Decrees 2686 and 2687 of December 26, 1988. In addition, decree 2633 of December 21, 1988, eliminates taxes on dividends received by Colombian branches of foreign corporations, and Law 84 of December 29, 1988, establishes a special tax regime for nonprofit organizations.

28. See McLure and Zodrow (1989) or McLure, Mutti, Thuronyi, and Zodrow (1989: ch. 11), for a more complete description of the 1988 changes in Colombian tax law, including provisions relating to adjustment of the value of shares in "open" (publicly held) corporations, capitalization of the inflationary component of income, temporary three-year freeze on the phase-in of disallowance of the deduction of the inflationary component of interest, application of inflation adjustment to leasing companies, repeal of the measure of presumptive income based on gross income, reduction of the net wealth tax rate, full valuation of cattle and land for purpose of the net wealth and presumptive income taxes, a 20 percent tax on income of nonprofit organizations not used for approved purposes, five-year carryforward of losses, and elimination of the distinction between ordinary and capital gains and losses for taxpayers subject to the integrated system.

29. The law states that all taxpayers will be required to use the integrated system, except (a) individuals qualifying to use the simplified system under the sales tax (even if they do not pay the tax) and (b) nonprofit organizations. Those not required to use the system have the option of doing so, provided they maintain registered books of account.

30. For a description of how and why this happens, see McLure, Mutti, Thuronyi, and Zodrow (1988: ch. 7). Under the new law, interest incurred before an asset is placed in service (for example, construction-period interest and interest expense connected with acquiring inventories) will be capitalized, with no disallowance of the inflationary component of interest; interest incurred after the asset is placed in service is eligible for deduction in the year incurred, but deduction of the inflationary component is disallowed (on a partial basis, during the phase-in period). This was proposed in McLure, Mutti, Thuronyi, and Zodrow (1988: ch. 5).

31. A technical difficulty in the 1988 law involves the decision to base inflation adjustments of the change in the consumer price index over the year ending in October of the year before the taxable year. See McLure and Zodrow (1989) or McLure, Mutti, Thuronyi, and Zodrow (1989: ch. 11) for a discussion of the difficulties this causes. In

addition, the use of the integrated system for some taxpayers and the ad hoc system for others inevitably creates opportunities for abuse; see McLure, Mutti, Thuronyi, and Zodrow (1989: ch. 11).

32. For a discussion of the lack of logic of such an offset, see McLure, Mutti, Thuronyi, and Zodrow (1988: ch. 7).

33. See McLure and Zodrow (1989) or McLure, Mutti, Thuronyi, and Zodrow (1989: ch. 11) for a similar but more extended discussion of the decision-making process in Colombia.

34. Many of the observations reported here are based on the author's personal conversations with Santiago Pardo, the director general of Internal Taxes from 1986 to 1988; they are, however, solely the responsibility of the author.

35. For more exhaustive discussions of lessons from Colombian experience in tax reform, going beyond the area of inflation adjustment, see Thirsk (1988) and McLure and Zodrow (1989).

36. Since this chapter was completed, the author, together with Santiago Pardo, has prepared a paper describing adminstrative reforms put in place since 1986 (McLure and Pardo 1990).

References

Aaron, Henry J., ed. 1976a. *Inflation and the Income Tax.* Washington, D.C.: Brookings Institution.

Aaron, Henry J. 1976b. "Inflation and the Income Tax: An Introduction." In *Inflation and the Income Tax,* edited by Henry J. Aaron, 1–31. Washington, D.C.: Brookings Institution.

Adjustments for Tax Purposes in Highly Inflationary Economies. 1984. Proceedings of a 1984 seminar of the International Fiscal Association held in Buenos Aires. Deventer, The Netherlands: Kluwer and Taxation Publishers.

Bird, Richard M. 1970. *Taxation and Development: Lessons from the Colombian Experience.* Cambridge, Mass.: Harvard University Press.

Bradford, David F. 1987. *Untangling the Income Tax.* Cambridge, Mass.: Harvard University Press.

Casanegra de Jantscher, Milka. 1984. "Chile." In *Adjustments for Tax Purposes in Highly Inflationary Economies,* 25–35. Proceedings of a 1984 seminar of the International Fiscal Association held in Buenos Aires. Deventer, The Netherlands: Kluwer and Taxation Publishers.

Carrizosa S., Mauricio. 1986. *Hacia la Recuperación del Mercado de Capitales en Colombia.* Bogota: Bolsa de Bogotá.

Chica A., Ricardo. 1984–85. "La Financiación de la Inversión en la Industria Manufacturera Colombiana: 1970–1980." *Desarrollo y Sociedad* (Centro de Estudios sobre Desarrollo Económico, Bogota) 15–16 (September 1984, March 1985): 220.

Fiscal Survey of Colombia. 1965. Baltimore: Johns Hopkins University Press.

Gillis, Malcolm, and Charles E. McLure, Jr. 1975. "The Colombian Tax Reform of 1974." Washington, D.C.: World Bank. Mimeo.

———. 1977. *La Reforma Tributaria Colombiana de 1974.* Bogota: Banco Popular.

Hall, Robert E., and Alvin Rabushka. 1983. *Low Tax, Simple Tax, Flat Tax.* New York: McGraw-Hill.

———. 1985. *The Flat Tax*. Stanford: Hoover Institution Press.

Harberger, Arnold C. 1982. "Notes on the Indexation of Income Taxes." Memorandum prepared for the Finance Ministry of Indonesia.

———. 1988. "Comments." In *Uneasy Compromise: Problems of a Hybrid Income-Consumption Tax*, edited by Henry J. Aaron, Harvey Galper, and Joseph A. Pechman, 380–83. Washington, D.C.: Brookings Institution.

Impuesto sobre la Renta en Colombia: Compilación Cronológica de Normas Vigentes del Impuesto sobre la Renta, Complementarios, y Procedimiento. 1984. Bogota: Ministerio de Hacienda y Credito Publico.

Lent, George E. 1975. "Adjustment of Taxable Profits for Inflation." International Monetary Fund, *Staff Papers*, vol. 22 (November): 641–79. Washington, D.C.

———. 1976. "Adjusting Taxable Profits for Inflation: The Foreign Experience." In *Inflation and the Income Tax*, edited by Henry J. Aaron, 195–213. Washington, D.C.: Brookings Institution.

Low M., Enrique, and Jorge Gomez R. 1986. *Politica Fiscal*. Bogota: Universidad Externado de Colombia.

Massone P., Pedro. 1981a. "Adjustment of Profits for Inflation: Part I." *Bulletin of the International Bureau for Fiscal Documentation* 35 (January): 3–15.

———. 1981b. "Adjustment of Profits for Inflation: Part II." *Bulletin of the International Bureau for Fiscal Documentation* 35 (February): 51–61.

McLure, Charles E., Jr. 1982. "Income and Complementary Taxes." Washington, D.C.: World Bank. Mimeo.

———. 1988. "The 1986 Act: Tax Reform's Finest Hour or Death Throes of the Income Tax?" *National Tax Journal* 41, no. 3 (September): 303–15.

———. 1989a. "Analysis and Reform of the Colombian Tax System." In *Lessons from Fundamental Tax Reform in Developing Countries*, edited by Malcolm Gillis, 44–78. Durham, N.C.: Duke University Press.

———. 1989b. "Lessons for LDCs of U.S. Income Tax Reform." *Lessons from Fundamental Tax Reform in Developing Countries*, edited by Malcolm Gillis, 347–90. Durham, N.C.: Duke University Press.

———. 1989c. "U. S. Tax Laws and Capital Flight from Latin America," *InterAmerican Law Review* 20, no. 2 (Spring): 321–57.

McLure, Charles E., Jr., and Santiago Pardo R. 1990. "Improving the Administration of the Colombian Income Tax, 1986–88." Stanford: Hoover Institution. Mimeo.

McLure, Charles E., Jr., Jack Mutti, Victor Thuronyi, and George Zodrow. 1988. *The Taxation of Income from Business and Capital in Colombia*. Bogota: Dirección de Impuestos Nacionales (also Durham, N.C.: Duke University Press, 1989).

McLure, Charles E., Jr., and George R. Zodrow. 1989. "Tax Reform in Colombia: Process and Results." Washington, D.C.: World Bank. Mimeo.

Musgrave, Richard A., and Malcolm Gillis. 1971. *Fiscal Reform for Colombia: The Final Report and Staff Papers of the Colombian Commission on Tax Reform*. Cambridge, Mass.: Harvard University International Tax Program.

Nueva Reforma Tributaria. 1987. 2d ed. Bogota: Cámara de Comercio de Bogotá.

Pardo R., Santiago. 1987. "Fundamentos, Objectivos e Instrumentos de la Reforma: Alcance de las Facultades Extraordinarios Otorgadas al Ejecutivo." In *Nueva Reforma Tributaria*, 21–31. 2d ed. Bogota: Cámara de Comercio de Bogotá.

Perry R., Guillermo, and Mauricio Cárdenas S. 1986. *Diez Años de Reformas Tributarios en Colombia*. Bogota: Fedesarrollo.

Slitor, Richard. 1971. "Reform of the Business Tax Structure: Analysis of Problems and Alternative Remedial Proposals." In *Fiscal Reform for Colombia: The Final Report and Staff Papers of the Colombian Commission on Tax Reform*, edited by Richard A. Musgrave and Malcolm Gillis, 463–529. Cambridge, Mass.: Harvard University International Tax Program.

Tanzi, Vito. 1976. "Adjusting Personal Income Taxes for Inflation: The Foreign Experience." In *Inflation and the Income Tax*, edited by Henry J. Aaron, 215–31. Washington, D.C.: Brookings Institution.

Thirsk, Wayne. 1988. "Some Lessons from the Colombian Experience." Provisional Papers in Public Economics. World Bank, Washington, D.C.

U.S. Department of the Treasury. 1984. *Tax Reform for Fairness, Simplicity, and Economic Growth*. Washington, D.C.: U.S. Government Printing Office.

White, Melvin, and Andrew C. Quale, Jr. 1971. "The Colombian Individual Income Tax: Rates, Exemptions, Deductions, and Administrative Aspects." In *Fiscal Reform for Colombia: The Final Report and Staff Papers of the Colombian Commission on Tax Reform*, edited by Richard A. Musgrave and Malcolm Gillis, 301–30. Cambridge, Mass.: Harvard University International Tax Program.

Zodrow, George R., and Charles E. McLure, Jr. 1988. "Implementing Direct Consumption Taxes in Developing Countries." World Bank Discussion Paper no. 131. Washington, D.C.

Chapter 13   Malcolm Gillis, "Tax Reform and the Value-Added Tax: Indonesia"

Notes

1. The tax-credit method of collection allows firms to subtract taxes paid on their purchases against taxes due on their sales, remitting the remainder to the treasury each period. With this method, firms need not directly calculate value added each period and then apply the applicable tax rate to determine tax liability.

2. By 1992, EC countries will have made a fundamental alteration in the treatment of traded goods under the VAT: all member nations will adopt the origin principle. Definitions of these technical terms are found in Shoup (1989), for instance. The consumption-type VAT taxes only consumption goods. Capital goods are excluded by allowing taxes paid on their purchases to be credited against taxes due on sales. An alternative to the consumptive VAT is the income-type VAT which has for its base all types of income, including capital income. Among LDCs, only Argentina, Peru, and to some extent Turkey, have chosen the income-type VAT over the consumption type, although the early Colombian VAT (1966–1984) was of the income type. The destination-principle VAT taxes value added, at home or abroad, of goods that have as their final destination the consumers of that country. In this case exports are zero-rated (see note 3), but imports are taxed. In contrast to this is the origin principle, wherein exports are taxable, but imports are exempt. The origin principle is compatible with the income-type VAT but not the consumption type. The destination principle is compatible with the consumption-type VAT but not the income type.

3. Under zero-rating systems for exports, a zero tax rate is applied to the sales of exports. Upon presentation by the exporter of proof of VAT paid on purchases, VAT is refunded on all export transactions.

4. The architects of the Indonesian tax reform believed that, in the Indonesian context, a shift toward more uniform taxation was tantamount to a shift toward more "efficient" taxation. But "uniformity" was never confused with "optimality."

5. The reform went to great lengths to avoid disturbing the status quo in oil taxation, in order to avoid a repeat of the acrimonious exchanges between the companies and the government in 1976, when the latter undertook the renegotiation of production-sharing contract arrangements in oil, to increase taxes due to Indonesia (Gillis 1980: 6). In response, most of the companies undertook sharp cutbacks in exploration in 1977, 1978, and 1979. The government did not wish another such confrontation. Accordingly, it was decided that oil companies with production-sharing contracts signed *before* the effective date of the reform would be entitled to retain the tax treatment specified in those contracts. For contracts signed after the effective date of the tax reform, the new tax law would apply, but companies were to be assured that *total* tax obligations to Indonesia (given prices and production volumes) would not be materially changed by tax reform. Thus, any increase in income tax obligations arising from reform would be compensated by reduction in royalties or other levies; any decrease in income tax rates on oil companies would be made up by other levies upon them.

6. These modifications were all adopted in 1986. As in the Benelux countries in the EC, VAT liability may be deferred for machinery imported for projects with long gestation periods. The Indonesian system allows deferral for one to five years, or until the project begins commercial operation. In addition, raw materials and equipment imported for use in export manufacture may qualify for suspension of VAT, which for all practical purposes amounts to exemption. The government pays the VAT on such goods as imported components for low-cost housing, imports by the armed forces, and water. All departures from universal application of the VAT to products are summarized in "Special Provisions Regarding Value-Added Tax" (Indonesia 1987).

7. Cattle feed and poultry feed produced by domestic firms are not subject to VAT but, strictly speaking, are not exempt as such. While there are no exemptions by product category, VAT is not collected on the sales of small enterprises (firms with an annual turnover of less than US$5,000 or total capital level less than US$8,000).

8. Where agricultural firms do make significant use of inputs and machinery taxable under the VAT, they may actually seek to register for VAT, in order to enable them to credit taxes paid on their purchases against taxes due on sales.

9. The decision to include refined petroleum products in the VAT base was made at some political cost, as gasoline, kerosene, and similar products were never subject to the old turnover tax. Once that decision was made, however, it was apparent that with a uniform rate, and virtually no exemptions, the VAT would be among the simplest and most collectible of any tax ever implemented anywhere.

10. In the early stages of VAT registration in 1984/85, district offices ignored central directives on registration procedures and failed to forward applications to become a VAT taxpayer to the computer sections of district tax offices, thereby reducing the utility of the master file system for the 90 percent of VAT taxpayers who registered prior to correction of this problem. In addition, government regulation number 31 of July 1986 limits audit powers of the director-general of taxes to narrowly

defined particular cases. Unless this regulation is materially changed, taxpayers will be able to largely circumvent many key audit requirements.

11. For example, loudspeakers and stereo systems are subject both to the VAT and to the special luxury tax. When these items are sold to traders or consumers, they are taxed only once. But when they are sold to electronic companies to be incorporated in their stereo systems, they are taxed twice, and the electronic companies cannot credit the luxury tax against VAT due on sales. On the other hand, automobile air conditioners are subject only to the VAT, not to the luxury sales tax. But sedans are subject to a 20 percent rate of luxury tax. If the sedan is sold with air conditioning, the unit is taxed at 20 percent, as part of the value of the car. But if the buyer takes the car without an air conditioner, purchases one, and has it installed at a garage, the unit escapes luxury tax.

12. Data provided by the Directorate General of Taxes for fiscal year 1987/88.

13. One careful estimate by Jenkins et al. (1988) suggests that if the state electricity enterprise pays tax on as much as half of its capital purchases and on all fuels utilized, extension of the VAT to electricity would result in a revenue loss of Rp 25 billion, or about 1 percent of 1987 VAT collections. If, for political and income distribution reasons, the 16 percent of residential users of electricity who use least electricity were exempt from the VAT, overall revenue losses from extending the tax to electricity would be as much as Rp 63 billion, or about 2 percent of 1987 collections.

14. Larger roles in expanding manufactured exports have undoubtedly been played by two devaluations, one in 1983, the other in 1986. Further, the rupiah, geared to the dollar, has been "riding the dollar down" (that is, depreciating along with the dollar as the dollar has fallen in value relative to the yen, the mark, and the Swiss franc) since February 1985.

References

Ahmad, Ehtisham, and Nicholas Stern. 1987. "Report on Tax Reform in Pakistan." Warwick University, Warwick, England. Unpublished, November.

———. 1989. "Taxation for Developing Countries." In *Handbook of Development Economics*, edited by Hollis B. Chenery and T. N. Srinivasan.

Casanegra de Jantscher, Milka. 1989. "Problems of Administering a Value-Added Tax in Developing Countries: An Overview." In *The Value-Added Tax in Developing Countries*, edited by Malcolm Gillis, Carl Shoup, and Gerardo Sicat. Washington, D.C.: World Bank.

Cnossen, Sijbren. 1975. "What Kind of Sales Tax?" *Canadian Tax Journal*, vol. 23 no. 3: 514.

———. 1985. "Review of the Value-Added Tax." Jakarta: Unpublished memo for Ministry of Finance, Republic of Indonesia, December.

Due, John. 1957. *Sales Taxation*. Urbana: University of Illinois Press.

———. 1963. *State Sales Tax Administration*. Chicago: Public Administration Service.

Gillis, Malcolm. 1980. "Energy Demand in Indonesia." Development Discussion Paper no. 96. Cambridge, Mass.: Harvard Institute for International Development.

———. 1984. "Episodes in Indonesian Economic Growth." In *World Economic Growth*, edited by Arnold C. Harberger. San Francisco: ICS Press.

———. 1985a. "Micro and Macroeconomics of Tax Reform: Indonesia." *Journal of Development Economics* 19, no. 2: 221.

———. 1985b. "Federal Sales Taxation: A Survey of Six Decades of Experience." *Canadian Tax Journal* 33, no. 1: 68–80.

———. 1986. "Worldwide Experience in Sales Taxation." *Policy Sciences* 19, no. 1: 125.

———, ed. 1989a. *Lessons from Fundamental Tax Reform in Developing Countries.* Durham: Duke University Press.

———. 1989b. "Tax Reform: Lessons from Post-War Experience in Developing Nations." In *Lessons from Fundamental Tax Reform in Developing Countries,* edited by Malcolm Gillis. Durham: Duke University Press.

———. 1989c. "Comprehensive Tax Reform: The Indonesian Experience 1981–1988." In *Lessons from Fundamental Tax Reform in Developing Countries,* edited by Malcolm Gillis. Durham: Duke University Press.

Gillis, Malcolm, and Robert Conrad. 1984. "The Indonesian Tax Reform of 1983." Development Discussion Paper no. 162. Cambridge, Mass.: Harvard Institute for International Development.

Gillis, Malcolm, Carl Shoup, and Gerardo Sicat, eds. 1989. *The Value-Added Tax in Developing Countries.* World Bank Symposium Paper. Washington, D.C.: World Bank.

Hutabarat, Homomongan, and Malcolm Lane, 1989. "The Computerization of VAT in Indonesia." In *The Value-Added Tax in Developing Countries,* edited by Malcolm Gillis, Carl Shoup, and Gerardo Sicat. Washington, D.C.: World Bank.

Indonesia. Ministry of Finance. Directorate of Indirect Taxes. 1987. "Special Provisions Regarding VAT." Jakarta, unpublished, May 19.

Jenkins, Glenn, Jeffrey Lewis, and Sharif Lofti. 1988. "Memorandum on Extending the VAT to Electricity." Harvard Institute for International Development, Jakarta. Unpublished memo.

Shoup, Carl S. 1969. *Public Finance.* New York: Aldine.

———. 1989. "Criteria for Choice among Types of Value-Added Tax." In *The Value-Added Tax in Developing Countries,* edited by Malcolm Gillis, Carl Shoup, and Gerardo Sicat. Washington, D.C.: World Bank.

Stern, Nicholas. 1987. "Uniformity vs. Selectivity in Tax Structure." Discussion Paper no. 9. The Development Economics Research Program, London School of Economics.

Stockfish, James A. 1985. "Value-Added Tax and the Size of Government: Some Evidence." *National Tax Journal,* vol. 38, no. 3: 547.

Tait, Alan. 1989. "The Value-Added Tax: Revenue, Inflation, and the Foreign Trade Balance." In *The Value-Added Tax in Developing Countries,* edited by Malcolm Gillis, Carl Shoup, and Gerardo Sicat. Washington, D.C.: World Bank.

Tait, Alan, Wilfred Gratz, and Barry Eichengreen. 1987. "International Comparisons of Taxation for Selected Developing Countries." *International Monetary Fund Staff Papers* 26 (March): 123–56.

World Bank. 1981. *Indonesia: Development Prospects and Policy Options.* Washington, D.C.: World Bank.

———. 1988a. *Indonesia: Adjustment, Growth, and Sustainable Development.* Washington, D.C.: World Bank.

———. 1988b. *World Development Report 1988.* New York: Oxford University Press. Appendix Table 1.

Chapter 14   Francisco Gil Díaz, "Tax Reform Issues in Mexico"

Notes

1. Mexico's personal income tax was perhaps preceded by only a few years by the United Kingdom's (1798). Saxony introduced the tax in 1834; France, in 1830 (although it had had rudimentary direct taxation since the French Revolution); Italy, in the 1860s; and the United States, in 1913. See Tanzi and Casanegra (1987).

2. The reform was effective December 15, 1813, and signed by Viceroy Felix Maria Calleja.

3. An updated discussion of the virtues of consumption taxation appears in a paper by McLure (1988). It discusses the limitations imposed on income taxation by international capital movements, as well as some of the practical aspects of consumption taxation.

4. If the net yield of financial assets is competitive even though the tax on interest income is higher, the financial system may yet suffer, since the lending rate will be forced upward, allowing inroads from informal lenders and borrowers.

5. There were rumors and even an article published in the treasury's tax magazine *Numerica* (1974) about a proposal to tax wealth. This publication provoked a press uproar and an angry denial from the treasury.

6. The firm raises capital through a bank loan that is backed by a deposit of an equal amount by the firm's owner. There is a tax gain here since financial interest is taxed at a lower rate than corporate profits.

7. Net of shares in other firms.

References

Col, Lorenzo. 1975. Thesis, Universidad Nacional Autónoma de Mexico.

Creel, Santiago. N.d. "Una Prueba Empírica al Orden Jurídico: La Celebración y Cumplimiento de los Contratos de Arrendamiento para Casa Habitación en el D. F." In Francisco Gil Díaz and Arturo Fernández, forthcoming.

Gil Díaz, Francisco. 1984a. Mexico's Path from Stability to Inflation." In *World Economic Growth*, edited by Arnold C. Harberger. San Francisco: ICS Press.

———. 1984b. "The Incidence of Taxes in Mexico: A Before and After Comparison." In *The Political Economy of Income Distribution in Mexico*, edited by Pedro Aspe and Paul E. Sigmund. New York: Holmes & Meier Publishers.

———. 1987. "Some Lessons from Mexico's Tax Reform." In *The Theory of Taxation for Developing Countries*, edited by Nicholas Stern and David Newbery. Washington, D.C.: Oxford University Press for the World Bank.

McLure, Charles E., Jr. 1988. "Saving, Investment and Fiscal Harmonization." Paper prepared for the conference on Dynamics of North American Trade and Economic Relations, University of Toronto, June 12–14.

Mexico. Secretaria de Hacienda y Crédito Público (Department of the Treasury). 1974. *Numerica*, no. 3 (November).

———. Dirección General de Política de Ingresos (Office of Revenue Policy). 1988. "Evolución de la Carga Fiscal del Impuesto Sobre la Renta a Personas Físicas 1978–1988." Internal document.

Ortíz-Mena, Antonio. 1969. "Una Década de Estrategia Económica en México." *El Mercado de Valores* (Nacional Financiera, Mexico), no. 44: 721–37.

Simons, Hency C. 1938. *Personal Income Taxation*. Chicago: University of Chicago Press.

Tanzi, V., and Milka Casanegra. 1987. "Presumptive Income Taxation: Administrative, Efficiency, and Equity Aspects." IMF Working Paper WP/87/54. Washington, D.C.: International Monetary Fund (August).

Tenenbaum, Barbara A. 1985. *Mexico en la Epoca de los Agiotistas, 1821–1857*. Mexico City: Fondo de Cultura Económica.

Chapter 15   Charles E. McLure, Jr., "Appraising Tax Reform"

References

McLure, Charles E., Jr. 1989. "International Considerations in U.S. Tax Reform." Paper presented at the VIII Munich Symposium on International Taxation, July 3.

McLure, Charles E., Jr., Jack Mutti, Victor Thuronyi, and George R. Zodrow. 1989. *The Taxation of Business and Capital in Colombia*. Durham, N.C.: Duke University Press.

Pechman, Joseph A. 1988. *World Tax Reform: A Progress Report*. Washington D.C.: Brookings Institution.

Tanzi, Vito. 1987. "The Response of Other Industrial Countries to the U.S. Tax Reform Act." *National Tax Journal* 40, no. 3 (September): 339–55.

U.S. Department of the Treasury. 1977. *Blueprints for Basic Tax Reform*. Washington, D.C.: Government Printing Office. Also available as Bradford, D. F., and the U.S. Treasury Tax Policy Staff. 1984. *Blueprints for Basic Tax Reform*. Arlington, Va.: Tax Analysts.

———. 1984. *Tax Reform for Fairness, Simplicity, and Economic Growth*. Washington, D.C.: Government Printing Office (November).

U.S. Office of the President. 1985. *The President's Tax Proposals to the Congress for Fairness, Growth, and Simplicity*. Washington, D.C.: Government Printing Office.

Whalley, John. 1989. "Foreign Responses to U.S. Tax Reform." Paper presented at a conference on the Economic Impact of the Tax Reform Act of 1986, Ann Arbor, Michigan, November 9–11.

Witte, John F. 1985. *The Politics and Development of the Federal Income Tax*. Madison: University of Wisconsin Press.

Zodrow, George R., and McLure, Charles E., Jr. 1988. *Implementing Direct Consumption Taxes in Developing Countries*. Policy Planning and Research Working Paper no. WPS 131. Washington, D.C.: World Bank (December).

About the Contributors

Michael J. Boskin is chairman of the President's Council of Economic Advisers. He is on leave from his position as the Burnet C. and Mildred Finley Wohlford Professor of Economics at Stanford University. Boskin is the author of *Reagan and the Economy*, as well as other books and numerous journal articles.

Charles E. McLure, Jr., is a senior fellow at the Hoover Institution at Stanford University. From 1983 to 1985 he served as deputy assistant secretary for tax analysis of the U.S. Treasury; in that capacity he had primary responsibility for development of the Treasury Department proposals to President Reagan that became the basis for the Tax Reform Act of 1986. He recently directed a study entitled *The Taxation of Income from Business and Capital in Colombia* for the government of Colombia.

Andrew W. Dilnot is program director of the Personal Sector of the Institute for Fiscal Studies, London. In the policy area, Dilnot served as a specialist adviser to the House of Lords Select Committee on European Communities in 1987 and was a member of the Gammie Committee on Capital Taxation in 1988. He wrote *The Reform of Social Security* (with J. A. Kay and C. N. Morris) and edited *The Economics of Social Security* (with I. Walker).

Francisco Gil Díaz is undersecretary of revenue of the Ministry of Finance, Mexico. He was formerly director of the School of Economics at the Instituto Tecnológico Autónomo de México. Gil Díaz is a consultant to the World Bank and the International Monetary Fund and has published numerous articles on foreign debt, taxation, and the Mexican economy.

Malcolm Gillis has been a policy adviser to a number of developing countries. He is currently dean of the graduate school and vice provost for academic affairs at Duke University. He has written widely on economic development, public finance, and natural resource policy. Among his many books are *Tax and Investment Policies for Hard Minerals: Public and Multinational Enterprises in Indonesia* and *Economics of Development* (with Dwight Perkins, Michael Roemer, and Donald E. Snodgrass).

Roger Gordon is a professor of economics at the University of Michigan and associate editor of *Econometrica* and the *Journal of Public Economics*. In 1986 he was a visiting professor at the People's University, Beijing. Gordon is the author of *Essays on the Cause and Equitable Treatment of Differences in Earnings and Ability*.

Ingemar Hansson, on leave from his position as docent at the University of Lund, Sweden, is currently serving as secretary in the Parliamentary Commission on Income Tax Reform, Ministry of Finance, Sweden.

Arnold C. Harberger is Gustavus F. and Anna M. Swift Distinguished Service Professor at the University of Chicago and professor of economics at the University of California, Los Angeles. He has been a consultant to many developing countries, as well as the World Bank, International Monetary Fund, and the foreign aid agencies of the United States and Canada. His many publications include *World Economic Growth*, *Taxation and Welfare*, and *Project Evaluation*.

J. A. Kay is professor of industrial policy, director of the Centre for Business Strategy, and research dean at the London Business School. From 1981 to 1986 he was director of the Institute for Fiscal Studies, London. Kay was also a member of the Meade Committee on the Structure and Reform of Direct Taxation. He has written *The British Tax System* (with M. A. King) and *The Reform of Social Security* (with A. W. Dilnot and C. N. Morris) and edited *Mergers and Merger Policy* (with J. A. Fairburn).

Yukio Noguchi is a professor of economics at Hitotsubashi University, Japan. He also served ten years in Japan's Ministry of Finance. Noguchi has written many articles in both Japanese and English on issues of public finance.

Michael Porter is director of the Centre of Policy Studies at Monash University, Australia. He has been a visiting scholar at the Hoover Institution, Stanford University, a visiting professor at Yale University, and a consultant to the Board of Governors of the U.S. Federal Reserve System. Porter is editor of *Spending and Taxing: Australian Reform Options* (with J. W. Freebairn and C. Walsh) and *The Role of Minerals and Energy in the Australian Economy* (with L. H. Cook).

Eytan Sheshinski is Sir Isaac Wolfson Professor of Public Finance, The Hebrew University, Jerusalem. He has served as a consultant to Israel's Knesset and prime minister's office and to the government of Mexico. He also chaired Israel's Committee on Tax Reform in 1987.

John B. Shoven is chairman of the Department of Economics at Stanford University and codirector of the West Coast office of the National Bureau of Economic Research. In addition to writing many articles, he has written and edited a number of books, including *Government Policy Towards Industry in the USA and Japan*, *Pensions in the U.S. Economy*, and *Computation of General Equilibrium for Tax Policy Analysis*.

Joel Slemrod is associate professor of economics and business economics at the University of Michigan, where he is also director of the Office of Tax Policy Research. He is also a research associate of the National Bureau of Economic Research. Slemrod has been a consultant to the U.S. Internal Revenue Service, the World Bank, and the Canadian Department of Finance.

Charles Stuart, professor of economics at the University of California, Santa Barbara, was a senior staff economist for the President's Council of Economic Advisers in 1985–1986. He has also been a research economist at the University of Lund, Sweden, where he received his Ph.D. His articles on public finance have appeared in journals both in the United States and in Sweden.

Christopher Trengove is a research fellow at the Centre of Policy Studies, Monash University, Australia. In 1985–1986 he served as a research associate at the Institute for Fiscal Studies, London. Trengove has written on the economics of public enterprises, telecommunications, energy and resources, and aviation.

John Whalley is William G. Davis Professor of International Trade and director of the Centre for the Study of International Economic Relations at the University of Western Ontario, Canada. He is also a research associate of the National Bureau of Economic Research. Whalley has written extensively on trade policy, taxation, and general equilibrium. His books include *Applying General Equilibrium* (with John Shoven), *Perspectives on a U.S.-Canadian*

Free Trade Agreement (coedited with Bob Stern and Philip Tresize), and *General Equilibrium Trade Policy Modeling* (coedited with T. N. Srinivasan).

Index